The N

The Man

The Man Behind The Man

Looking from the Inside-Out

Demetrius Smith Sr.

Library of Congress Control Number:		2011902523
ISBN:	Hardcover	978-1-4568-7052-2
	Softcover	978-1-4568-7051-5
	Ebook	978-1-4568-7053-9

To order additional copies of this book, contact:
Xlibris Corporation
1-888-795-4274
www.Xlibris.com
Orders@Xlibris.com
82213

CONTENTS

DEDICATION:

I dedicate this book to the Holy Spirit, my Lord and Savior Jesus Christ; to God be the Glory; to my mother, Willia Mae Williams for the faith and strong will she had raising 9 of us as a single parent; to my 4 children, Demetrius Jr., Ashley, Deontae and DeAndre Smith—I love you and I am sorry for the pain you suffered in my absence during your teenage years; to my grandchildren, Demetrius Ja'Mare Smith, Lauren Smith and Amir Jinan Malik, you are the next generation and I hope to have made a better way for all of you. To my entire family, I love you more than words can describe. Family should always come first. Let us all make better decisions for the well-being of our loved ones and be willing to sacrifice for one another. Doing anything foolish is not worth the sacrifice of your presence. The sense of duty and honor should always be upheld with family. We cannot raise our children by ourselves. We need each other! What you do in your life effects the lives of others. It is not about you; it is about us as a whole and as a family!

Mathew 6:26— "Look at the birds of the air, for they neither sow nor reap nor gather into barns: yet your heavenly Father feeds them. Are you not of more value than they?"

In Loving Memory of, Mr. Vincent Evans, The Soto Brothers, Fred Hampton and Mark Clark, Aaliyah, Al Cover, Bernie Mac, Robert (Bobby) Hardaway, Gerald Levert, Torrey Diggs and Troy (Trouble T Roy) Dixon.

Your life was a blessing to many
Your efforts never went unnoticed
Your talent and drive made an impact on the world
May your memory live on forever?
Rest in Peace.

By: Demetrius Smith

ACKNOWLEDGMENTS

I AM FIRST AND foremost indebted to God because He knew what I needed to go through in order to be the man I am today. *"Thank you Father God for not sparing the rod."* I also cannot go without thanking special people that are instrumental in the promising new chapter of my life. Thank you: John Jevial Smothers, an awesome writer I worked with at Solano State prison, for listening to my story and having me to write it down. You helped me to see something in my writing I didn't know existed; Cheri Woodard Ramseur your support was my inspiration; Lisa Metoyer, My friend & personal assistant, thank you for having faith in my writing and for working countless hours with me to complete this book. You have made all the difference; James Johnson, your support kept me grounded. It was the lift I needed to keep my focus on what was the right thing to do in spite of the adversities. My daughter-in-law, Africa Baxter, for helping me to get the ball rolling by typing my manuscript from handwritten pages. You are a true blessing; Kenneth Styles and Mark Reed, The bible say's, "There is a friend who sticks closer then a brother", you two brothers fit that description; To my aunt Delores Kitchen, thank you for your love and support. You have been a way out of no way for me, I thank God for you; To Denise Landa-Witcher, you come through like a sister with tough love and all, seeing the strength in you strengthens me. The world should know you; To Ms. Sherri Washington, I truly thank you for your time and for keeping it real with me with the comments in your edit that helped me to organize my work; To All my friends and family I thank God for each and every one of you. I love you all.

A NOTE FROM THE AUTHOR

"THE MAN BEHIND the Man/Looking from the Inside Out", should not be disregarded as yet another tell all about what you see and hear of the fabulous life of society's high regarded celebrities. It is also not an attempt to play victim or take others in as casualty; this is not my intention. I consider this my closure and my rebirth!

This book is a notification of my story as I remember it. All of the events and experiences detailed are true and have been written as I remember them. Some of the names in this book are of actual people, and for the sake of those who are dear to my heart some are fictional. For the truth in me, I am not interested in protecting the integrity or confidentiality of any of the various individuals involved who have shown no consideration for me.

This writing is not written to represent word-for-word documentation. However, I have retold this story in a way that expresses the real feeling and meaning of what was said, in keeping with the true essence of the mood and to bring to life the spirit of the event. I spent half of my twenties and most of my thirties grooming one of my former best friends, Robert Kelly, for stardom. Resentment was very much present, and this writing helped me to release that pain. For years I have had a personal battle within myself for all of the bad decisions I made. Those left offended should consider this one question, "Have you thought of me?"

The Man behind the Man is a pivotal testimony. I welcome you to follow me on my pursuit of restoration. It is said; "The truth will set you free."

Luke 12:2—*"For there is nothing covered that shall not be revealed; neither hid, that shall not be known."*

CHAPTER 1

The Sacrifice

LIFE IN THE music business, the glamour, the fame and the hype of it wasn't all that it claimed to be, at least not for me it wasn't. It all started off with us believing we were on a mission or a spiritual calling. I have always thought everybody should be helping somebody, allowing that somebody to help somebody else. In doing so, everybody would be looking out for one another. It would be a great big beautiful world. But with the lumps and detours along the way, I didn't see what was to come.

We were young singers with a strong desire to become successful entertainers in the music industry. We made it all the way to Milwaukee, Wisconsin, in my broken-down 1973 burnt-orange Chevy Station Wagon. The notion that we would ever achieve success seemed far fetched, but I had a vision. I put my heart into the journey and I was taking the steps to bring my dream into reality.

It was 1985 and we were sitting in the home of one of the NBA's star point guards for the Milwaukee Bucks, Craig Hodges. He was my brother-in-law, married to my younger sister Ce-Ce. I felt as if Craig was the connection needed to open a door for me into the music industry in order to get this young, multitalented artist that I was working with heard.

With Craig being a professional basketball player, he got to meet many influential people, and everybody that was somebody was at the NBA games. This was during the time when Kareem Abdul Jabar was at the height of his career, and then there was Julius Erving (Dr. J), Earvin "Magic" Johnson and Larry Bird. This was at the beginning of the Michael Jordan era. All the top names were at the games to see these greats perform. Yes, the entertainment industry, lights, cameras and action—it was where I wanted to be.

I knew early on things were in place for this to happen in my life. The first door for me now was Craig! I had no doubt in my mind he'd like young Robert because I was crazy about him. Besides, Craig had always told me he would invest in my musical career. I was just starting up as a singer but my young protégé, Robert Kelly, was ready!

As I saw it, for me to put my career on hold to get this kid started was well worth the sacrifice. However, when I asked Craig for his assistance to promote somebody else, who he didn't know, he was hesitant at wanting to talk to me about it. I knew it would take some extreme convincing, so I told Ce-Ce about Robert first. She had a good ear and could even hum a few tones herself. I felt that she would be receptive and she'd help me in getting through to Craig.

When I found out that she was coming up to Chicago to visit our mother, I told young Robert that I was going to take him to meet her. He was modest in saying, *"Yea right, man I don't believe you!"* but at the same time he was asking when was she coming and shyly, the boy was blushing as he sat at his keyboard, fumbling around and humming to a new melody.

I made all of the necessary provisions to be at my mom's home when Ce-Ce arrived. After introducing her to young Robert Kelly later in the afternoon, she whispered in my ear, *"That little boy got some big ears."* At that point, I knew that she wanted to see and hear all that I had been telling her about my young artist. It was time to let her hear this little boy with the big ears sing. As Robert performed for her, he touched her with his voice. He was smooth. He sung as if he went into the debts of his heart so you could feel his soul.

I watched Ce-Ce melt as she was enchanted into amazement. This little boy, as she called him, brought a sparkle into her eyes and made her gasp for breath. He displayed elegance along with grace as he sang and played the piano. I think what amazed Ce-Ce most were the songs he sang. They were songs she had never heard, but yet, the passion he released while singing touched her. Looking at her, I could see she felt the waves and fell into the bliss of the boy's sound. I knew after Ce-Ce heard Robert sing that she would go back to tell Craig about him. I felt she wasn't going to be able to get this "little *boy*" off of her mind. Little Robert Kelly had gone Donnie Hathaway on her and serenaded her with "A Song for you."

After his performance, she was all in my ear asking questions: *"How old is he?" "What are you going to do with him?"*, and *"What is it you want me to do to help?"*—Those were welcome words to my ears. As the afternoon went into the evening, we were all feeling good. We sat around talking and laughing right into the night. Before Ce-Ce left, she told me she would indeed tell Craig of my young artist and how she thought Robert was someone she could see her and Craig investing in.

As I was driving Robert home that night, I remember word for word telling him, *"Boy, you fixna be a star dude. The door is opening for us."* I was excited and feeling real good about the direction this would take my life. To me, Craig was the link to help me on this journey to the next level.

"Man, this is unreal. I was singing in front of Craig Hodges' wife, Johnny-man. Awl man," Robert said as if he was in awe.

He kept asking me, *"Was that for real, Johnny? I was singing for Craig's wife, man, Johnny,"* he said, sounding as if he was lost in wonderland,

"Yeah, Rob, you were awesome, dude. She was crazy about you. We'll be going to see Craig next," I told him. We both seemed to let our thoughts drift away as we rode to his house in silence.

It was less than a week later when Craig called and offered to help me. He said Ce-Ce spoke very highly of young Robert and had been talking about him all week. He told me he looked forward to meeting and hearing him soon. The door was opening! I knew Craig had the finances that would help get things started for us. Rob and I felt it was a blessing for us to have met each other. I was feeling real confident about this journey!

Success seemed inevitable now. It was within our grasp. I figured my decision to put my own singing career on hold while I worked with this young cat, Robert Kelly would be well worth the sacrifice. Plus, I thought I could learn from him! However, as life moved on, time unfolded a reality of deceit, broken promises, shattered dreams, endless debts and now with me, serving time in California's Solano State Prison.

I thought I had a focus on things in the direction my life was going when I was released from prison in May of 1983, after serving two and a half years of a six-year sentence for armed robbery and released early on good behavior. I thought I had my future all planned out. I was never a professional criminal, but I guess you could say I was a bad boy. I got into mischief just like any other young kid, except for me I never got away with doing wrong. I don't care what it was; if it had something to do with doing something wrong, I got caught. I just wasn't cut out for the horrid life.

When I went to prison in 1980, it was the first time I had ever been arrested in my life. I was just one of the unfortunate ones cursed with bad luck and it seemed I had to endure the worst of everything. I was a victim of Murphy's Law for sure. For me, anything that could go wrong did! The crime I committed and went to jail for was a crime of passion and of anger.

I was distraught over something that was taken from me. I felt robbed of all my hard work and earnings. I felt robbed of a piece of me.

I was working for Canfield's Beverage Company at the time. I had worked long hours each day and I saved my hard earned money to be able to afford my own place to live. I found a nice one bedroom back house, basement apartment. It was the source of my peace of mind, my own space and accomplishment. I went right to work making the place my home.

I bought a nice Roland piano and hooked it up with the microphone to my speakers which were connected to my stereo receiver. I had my own little private studio. My plan was to make singing my career. I worked countless hours in my little apartment, comfortably recording and trying to teach myself how to play the piano as well as sing. The only company I had was my Doberman pinscher, Neva. I would smack kiss at her and call her. *"Nene girl come here girl,"* and she'd come running to me wagging her no tailed butt. It was me, Neva (man's best friend) and my music.

One night I came home after work and discovered my apartment had been broken into. After I pushed the door open, the first thing I noticed was the fact that my piano was gone. Everything was gone as I looked around-my piano, my stereo, I peeped into the bedroom, the closet was opened and most of my clothes were gone too. Everything, gone! It was as if I had moved out. I walked in and looked around more and I saw blood. Immediately, I yelled for Neva: *"Neva!* I overlooked the fact that she had not met me at the door! *"Nene girl where are you?"* I was shouting as I hurried towards the kitchen and there she was lying next to the stove with her head split open. Somebody had beat Neva in the head with a pipe, bat or something big and deadly. I broke down and cried! I kneeled down and began rubbing my dog, rocking back and forth. I was so hurt. Neva was a beautiful dog. She was Obedient, Joyful and Vicious. She was a true gift and a kind dog. I sat there on the kitchen floor, so hurt. *"Why? Why did they have to kill my dog?"* I asked myself as the tears ran down my face.

I knew the only one that could do something like this, had to be somebody I knew. It was obvious that they timed my workday. I was so mad. I had to know exactly who did this? Who killed my dog and my best friend? I didn't call the police, nor did I confide in anyone. I just sat with Neva: crying out of anger and wanting vengeance. After about forty-five minutes, it was over. I began picking things up and cleaning up Neva's blood. At moments I felt like I wanted to hurt someone. Anger filled my veins even more, and as the minutes passed, I figured I had cried and felt sorry for myself long enough. I needed to know who did this.

I rolled Neva into a blanket and took her to a field a few blocks down from my apartment and buried her. After saying a prayer, I figured that whoever did this was out trying to sell my things. I knew everybody in Harvey, Illinois, or they knew me. Everyone called me Johnny Cool. I had a little reputation out there, so getting to the executioner wouldn't be impossible.

When I finished burying Neva, I set out in search of an answer. I went to hang out on 147th and Winchester Street where I ran into my homeboy, Bobby. I told him what happened. It seemed he didn't know anything. Wallowing in my sorrow, I took a hit from the joint he was smoking. Then we decided to go get some Richard's Wild Irish Rose wine. I ended up getting pretty drunk. Bobby then started talking about going to get some money, some fast cash as he put it. *"Cool we'll go get you another piano tomorrow,"* he said. The getting the piano part was the only thing I heard him saying. I was dazed, I just saw him moving his lips. Everything looked as if it was all going fast and around, like a merry-go-round.

I wasn't in my right mind. Blinded and consumed with a foolish thought of wanting to replace that which was taken from me. I was drunk with interest, dizzy having thoughts without thinking. In this drunken state I was in, I was feeling the trait of the Indian blood of my grandfather's heritage in me. Woo-woo, I didn't give a fuck! I was ready to go on a war path. The spirits of anger and revenge were running through my veins. To make a long story short, I went with Bob and we ended up doing some dumb shit. I allowed anger to overshadow my thoughts and I allowed myself to be talked into robbing a gas station.

During the getaway, I looked out of my rear-view mirror and saw a police car that had passed us, make a U-Turn. I assumed he had got the call and was now coming after us.

At the first corner I got to, I made a quick right and Bob jumped out of the car. My mind was racing faster than the car was going. My chances of losing the police coming up fast behind me, was zero to none. After a mile of eluding the cops, I finally stopped and was arrested. I gave them a story. *"I was so glad when I saw yawl turn around I didn't know what was gone happen to me. Thank you!"* I pleaded to the policemen as if they had rescued me.

"That guy jumped in my car at the light, put a gun on me and made me rob a gas station. He had another gun in my back," I told them. I kept talking. *"I thought he was going to kill me. Thank you, thank you officers so much."* I kept pleading for their sympathy. The amazing part of it was that

they were listening to me enough to investigate my story. In doing so, the gas station attendant told the police that I did look like I was a bit scared and he said the other guy just stood behind me with his hand in his pocket, without saying a word. Things were looking good. I was thinking they were thinking of letting me go. My story was good all the way up until I saw them bring Bobby in. They had chased him and lost him but later after bringing out the dogs they found Bobby hiding out up in a tree. After that there was no need to fight, I was charged with armed robbery and sentenced to six years in the Illinois State Penitentiary.

Granted, it was my first time ever being arrested. I called it bad luck to have to go to prison for my first offense. I felt that the theories of breaking mirrors and black cats running across your path were all true. Those things had all happened to me and now it had all caught up with me. But in reality, "stupid is what stupid does." And I had did something really stupid. I guess I got what I had coming.

I was twenty-four years old when I went to Statesville Penitentiary, a maximum-security prison. I was devastated. Six years seemed so far away; I felt as if it were a lifetime. I was put in a cell and told, *"This is your new home, buddy. Make yourself comfortable,"* the officer said as he slammed the steel cell bars shut, sealing me in. I was shouting inside my body through my mind because I couldn't let my sorrow be heard. *"Help, Lord, God, Ahaaaaaa,"* I cried. I had to hold my breath as I trembled, wishing I could call my mother and she could come and pick me up. I kid you not, at twenty-four years old going into prison—I was scared out of my mind!

For seven days, I was confined to a cell and only let out for ten minutes to take a shower. This was a traumatizing experience for me. When I was brought out of the orientation process into prison, I was taken into the general population, to C house. This was a roundhouse unit where they shot a scene for the movie Bad Boy starring Sean Penn. I was actually there at the time the movie was filmed. The only difference was this was real life. For now this was where I lived. I had been placed into a cell with eight other convicts, none of whom I knew.

My first day into the general population, behind the wall as it was called, brought me a rude awakening as to where I was. After settling into my newly assigned cell, I decided to step out onto the gallery and get familiar with my surroundings. Whatever I had to deal with, I wanted to be aware of what was out there. The Cook County Jail in Chicago was no play pen. There was no calling Mama to come pick me up. I had to handle this situation on my own. It was my own self-inflicted burden to bear.

I decided to go down to the weight room. I thought, what better time than now to start getting my body in tip-top shape. I was 165 lbs., 5'11", slim, trim in the waist and real handsome in the face. A little body toning would do me well, get me fit, and put an edge to my "pretty boy swag." I walked down and around the ramp into the basement area where the weights were. It seemed somewhat strange to me that there were no guards posted anywhere. As I walked into the weight room, even in there, there were no guards.

The reality of where I would be residing for the next few years was starting to sink in. The guards were all posted in the tower looking down on us. In all actuality, I was left to the mercy of the hardened criminals, but I saw them as being regular people. On the outside I appeared composed, but on the inside I was crumbling. Subconsciously, my ghetto instincts rose up. I had been raised on the West Side of Chicago, K. Town, and brought up in the two worst housing projects in the country, Cabrini Green and The Henry Horner projects—In a lot of ways, those were the real prisons.

As a kid, I hid and watched as the national guards jumped out of a helicopter onto the top of the 16 story, 2245 building across from the one I lived in, in the Henry Horner projects. Gunfire was the sound that filled the air. The police were shooting into an apartment and at the same time gunfire was coming from the windows of the people that lived in the building firing at the police. *"Piggy wiggy, you gotta go now! Oink, oink! Bang, bang! Dead pig!"* That was our marching song. Vietnam had been brought to the streets for me coming up in 1968.

That day the police killed one of the Soto brothers, who had just come home from a funeral, burying his own brother. It was war growing up in the projects. One's mind had to be trained to defend and be on guard at all times. And not long after that, I heard the gunfire from the police and the F.B.I. the morning they raided and gunned down Fred Hampton and Mark Clark, strong brothers from the Black Panther Party who lived down the street. Where I grew up, there was always something going on, so I reminded myself when I walked out of my cell, that there was no fear in me. I recited Psalms 23 over and over in my head. *"Yea though I walk through the valley of the shadow of death, I will fear no evil: for thou art with me."*

I didn't know these people, but in some ways I did know them; I reminded myself that these were the same people I grew up around. I felt that there was no one tougher than the guys I grew up with—Harold, Collie Mitchell, Anthony Brittmon, Jeffrey Burns, Charles, Richard Story and Lenny, just to name a few; these were my running buddies. We weren't hardened criminals, but we held our own and were respected because we didn't run from a fight—we went to it, if you brought it! For those reasons I didn't stay in my cell. Everybody was out hanging out, so I went out to hang out too.

As I was walking deeper into the back of the weight room, an animal instinct to survive awakened in me. Like a deer feasting on the leaf of a bush, suddenly hearing the breaking of a branch, and without hesitation makes a dash to get away from the sound—I made a slow U-turn as my eyes wandered towards the back of the room. What I saw was so unreal and frightening. It was some movie shit and it was happening so fast. I saw more than four, and I didn't look long enough to see if it was less than eight, Hispanic men sticking and stabbing another Hispanic man with metal objects. To me it looked like they stabbed him twenty or thirty times in the few seconds I saw. I didn't need to see no more. I removed myself from the situation, hopefully unnoticed.

It was most definitely survival of the fittest in this camp. It was at this moment I was awakened to the reality of where I really was. I went back up the ramp at a cool pace and calmly walked to the front desk where the inmate clerk was sitting. On the inside I was nervous, but I didn't panic. I didn't want anyone to know that I was frightened. Even though I didn't see who was who, seeing a man being stabbed was enough for me. I wanted to be away and somewhere safe. I had never witnessed anyone being stabbed or being hurt really bad for that matter.

I sat in an empty chair next to the clerk's desk. The clerk was a young light-skinned brother. He looked at me like I was trespassing in his space. *"What's up with you, man?"* he asked as if he was trying to portray that he was tough. I sat paralyzed. He seemed to sense something was wrong with me, so he changed his tone, *"You all right, you're new, huh?"* he asked, seeming somewhat concerned.

"Yeah," I nodded my head, looking at him. And before we said anything else to each other, we looked up and noticed the guy that had been stabbed walking towards us from around the ramp; his whole body was bloody. His skin was hanging off his body as much as his ripped shirt. He was holding onto the rails, struggling to hold himself up to make the next step towards his survival.

The clerk looked at me because he knew that just moments before, I had just come from around the ramp myself. As the guy got closer, he looked as if he was about to fall. The man was so close to me, that without thinking, unconsciously I got up to give him a hand. The clerk reached to grab me— *"Don't touch that guy, man. You don't want to be involved in that,"* he said. I took his advice and sat back down while looking away tortured inside. Seconds later the man fell, and then an alarm went off sending everybody, including myself, scrambling to our cells. We stayed locked down for ten days while they investigated the stabbing. I had witnessed a man's bloody demise. Internal affairs came to everyone's cell and questioned everyone. It seemed no one knew anything and no one saw me going to or coming up from the basement that day, nor did I mention it to anyone.

When the lockdown was finally over, I got a visit from some of the Latin Kings. Immediately, I knew exactly who they were. They wanted to know what I saw in the basement. *"Y'all got a basement here"*, I asked? They laughed. I went on to tell them that I had just got there and had not been out yet. I told them that I didn't know what they were talking about, and that they had me mixed up with someone else. They were satisfied with my answers. For a week or so, the Latin Kings befriended me. They always sent someone asking if I was okay or if I needed anything. I never once, after that day, took for granted where I was.

I was amongst the celebrities of the underworld. I saw the Chairman, Larry Hoover, leader of the Gangster Disciples, and his crime partner, Lil-Dee-Dee, make their rounds throughout the prison on a daily bases. There was also the Vice Lord leader, Willie Lloyd; Hell, Richard Speck, who had killed seven nurses, worked as a painter and walked around daily painting the walls of the prison. There was no doubt in my mind that I had to stay sharp in order to survive the hellhole I had found my way in. This was no place like home and nowhere I had ever been before.

When the Lockdown was over, everything went back to a normal program. At least, for what normal was in there. To my surprise it was as if nothing ever happened. I found out that the name of the brother that I sat with at the front desk was Tripp. He and I became friends. We had a common interest—music. He played the guitar for one of the prison bands. I, along with him and another brother, Lucky, who also played the guitar, got involved in the music program. I started off singing in the band. This was still all a learning experience for me and I was learning a lot, but I wanted to play an instrument.

When I learned it was possible to get an instrument brought into the institution I called my mother. She who in turn spoke to my grandmother, and being the sweet woman she was, knew of my desire to play music, so she volunteered to help. She bought me a portable Wurlitzer piano. I was too happy when Lucky spoke to the director of the music program, and I was allowed to have my family bring my own piano inside the prison. I thanked God, because I knew it was Him, making a way out of no way for me.

I don't know what I would have done if I weren't able to participate in the music program. Being in the band kept me out of the way of all the viciousness that took place behind the wall. During my stay there, I traveled through the tunnels of the prison, pulling my piano on a cart from my housing unit to the gym where we practiced twice a week.

Because of my inexperience as a musician, my desire to learn and the fact that the piano was mine, Lucky and Tripp took special time out and taught me how to play cords on the piano. When we did shows they would shout out the chords to the songs; "G-major7, F-Sharp, F-major7, C-minor," and I would fumble my way connecting the cords with a facial expression as if I was jamming on stage with Earth, Wind, and Fire—feeling the music. I loved it. It made my time in prison meaningful. Even though I didn't know a lot about what I was doing, being able to do this with Lucky and Tripp was an experience that I will never forget.

As a child, there were only two things that seemed to show a door of opportunity for me—that was boxing and singing. As a youngster, I decided early on that boxing wasn't something I wanted to do. I didn't like to take punches. If you hit me, it wasn't a fair fight anymore. I was a laid back kind of guy until the beast was awakened. If I felt threatened to a point of being hurt, I was monstrous. I didn't mess with people and I didn't start fights.

It was in Statesville Penitentiary I made the decision that I wanted music to be my career. As it got closer to my release date, I felt I had a better sense of direction. Singing and learning to play the piano was something better for me to do with my life. I developed a passion and found myself singing every day, wanting to be better. It seemed music was the direction ordered for my life. The more I participated, the more it felt a part of me. I had found my gift. I had a direction to go in my life and I had a strong will that told me I could achieve my goal. With the belief I had in myself I told myself, I would never again belittle myself or subject myself to being locked up behind steel bars again.

It was May of 1983 when I was released, and within three weeks I hooked up with a band on the streets. When I met Donald "Donnie" Evans, a Keyboard player at a club, we became instant friends. He invited me to one of his rehearsals and introduced me to his band. The scriptures I read and prayed while in prison were manifesting the direction for my life. Psalm 37:23 says, *"The steps of a good man are ordered by the Lord."* My steps had to be ordered, I thought.

My next meeting with Donnie was at his house in Markham, Illinois; when I arrived he was practicing, so I jumped in and started singing along with him. He was impressed that I could sing. It wasn't long before he quit the band he was with and formed another band, and he asked me to be the lead vocalist.

Life could not have been better for me. I didn't want for anything. I had my music and was making a little money. I was doing exactly what I felt happy doing. We had a booking agent, this cool white cat named Clifford Rubin, who got us shows performing in the college circuit, prisons, and local juke joints in and around Illinois and Indiana. Clifford, reminded me of Charlie Sheen, the character from the series Two and a Half Men. I met him through one of the other band members. Right away Cliff and I became friends. In his eyes, I was a young Marvin Gaye, waiting to be discovered. He would always say I had a voice that women would fall in love with and the men would support to get to the women. I liked Cliff. He was every bit of cool, for a white boy, that is!

This was the beginning for me. It was fortunate for me to have this connection and love for music at a very young age. Singing brought me peace and filled a void inside of me that otherwise would have had me wandering. With this new position on life, I felt, I had arrived!

On the road, I made anywhere from $100 to $150 a night for myself, while the band members got paid anywhere from $75 to a $100 a gig. Clifford got 20 percent of whatever the gig paid off the top. All payments were sent directly to his office. He would then Western Union the band's share to me, in which I would distribute accordingly. By the time I got home off of the road, I'd have a couple of thousand dollars or more in my pocket, with more gigs ahead to do. This was the business for me. It was exactly where I wanted to be.

We were all living out of the back of a U-Haul truck, heated by a portable kerosene heater, keeping busy and traveling from city to city in the dead of the harsh winter colds! I was on cloud nine, making money and having fun at the same time. The group only had one issue—alcohol! It was each man's weakness. Every night I had to fight with the band members about staying sober until after the show. It was a task rounding them up to ensure we didn't miss a show! My nights were spent monitoring everybody. These gigs meant everything to me.

It was a good thing our shows at the prison and the colleges were during the day because these cats were totally different characters when they were drunk. There wouldn't have been any standing ovations if those drunken egos would've hit the stage. Don't get it wrong, we had a tight sound. A sound that made the crowd move and scream for an encore. Everybody in the band was good and had perfected their gift. Donald Evans played the keyboards, Thomas Goodlow played the lead guitar, Norman Douglas played the drums, and his brother, Clifford Douglas, played the bass guitar. I loved these dudes. If only there wasn't so much stress dealing with them on the road.

The constant confrontations were starting to take a toll on me so I talked to Cliff about the situation. I was at my wits end. I decided I did not want to deal with the business aspect of the music industry. I wanted to entertain, not manage irresponsible adults. After four three week tours the band and I took our last trip together. After the last tour Cliff and I talked about other ways to make money until we could piece together a better, more disciplined band. Cliff was most definitely a go-getter. He had his hand into all types of things on the North Side of Chicago.

Cliff and I got acquainted mostly by phone, but as soon as I came off the road, I went to work for him in his office. To my surprise, Mr. Clifford Rubin had it going on! He had a storefront that he used as a modeling agency. Paparazzi Pretty had girls coming in from near and far! I answered the phones, made out going phone calls and set appointments for Cliff, recruiting beautiful ladies. They paid a $25 registration fee, brought a headshot and filled out a questionnaire before going in the back to meet with Cliff for an informal interview.

It was a good hustle. I recruited anywhere from eight to twelve females a day, receiving the registration fee from at least 45 percent of them. We were averaging anywhere from $200 to $400 a day. Clifford was impressed with my gift of gab! I had a mean mouthpiece. *Conversation rules the nation,"* He would always say I could talk my way into anything. Cliff called me *"spit-'ems."*

When the girls went in the back office to see Cliff, he would interview them in front of a camera with a background setup. He never wanted me to hang out in the back with him while he was taking shots of the girls. He said he was going to help the girls that did not have a portfolio build up their resume and refer them to different agencies for jobs. Little did I know, he was doing a bit more than building portfolios! Did I mention that Cliff resided in a small loft in back of a business front?

Demetrius Smith Sr.

He set up cubicles to make the loft appear to have a set up like an office space and always demanded that I use the intercom before entering the backroom. One particular day, a young girl came in with her mother. After thoroughly filling out the questionnaire, the mother was very curious about the agency. She asked questions that I didn't have the answers to. *"What type of connections does the agency have? How many models from your agency have been discovered? And where are the models working?"* Normally Clifford would be right in position to meet the clients right after they finished the application process.

Several times I told the impatient mother that Mr. Rubin would be able to answer all her questions during the interview. She was growing impatient waiting to be seen. I buzzed the intercom a few times, whispering into the intercom, *"Cliff, a client and her guardian are here to see you. Come out here man"*, I would mumble into the phone. There was no answer.

After many failed attempts, I decided to go back there myself and inform Cliff we had a pit bull in a skirt waiting to see him! I headed for the room I never fully entered before. I walked in on Cliff with his face buried deep between two sexy brown thighs. She was a gorgeous 5'8",coco honey dip that I had just sent in no more than thirty minutes earlier. Cliff was surprised to see me standing in the doorway; I had caught him in the act. I kept a straight face and got back to business. *"Hey, man, there's a parent out here, and she's got a few questions that I think you need to deal with"* I told him. Cliff broke out in a hardy laugh and said he would be out shortly.

When he got there and took the mom on her interview, I don't know what he did but whatever Cliff told that mom, she was convinced because she paid the registration fee and left with a mile-wide smile on her face. It was at that time I discovered I was running the front office of a porno ring. I thought we were truly running a modeling agency when all the time in the backroom Cliff was screening girls for his movies. After the little walk-in, Cliff and I grew even closer. I learned not to walk in during brunch time. He started schooling me on all kinds of ways to make money. I wasn't interested in getting into the porn industry. However, I did have my way with a few of the girls that came into the office. Working for Cliff was some of the greatest times in my fifty years on this green earth.

For months things were running smoothly. But, like all good things, this too had come to an end. It was September 1984 when we were busted. The police came in with warrants, requesting paperwork and a license for operating an agency. Of course, Cliff did not have any type of permits or license, so Cliff's operation was shut down. A week later I got a call from

Cliff. He was excited over another legal idea for us to start working. "*Come on man suit up, I got lie's to tell and people to fool,*" he would say. Immediately we reconnected and turned our focus back to the music business. Cliff told me about a record label he had already established called Grandville Records. He felt it was time to use it. His focus was finding some original music material for me to sing.

Keep in mind, Cliff was the hustle man. He was all about making moves. His next idea was ingenious. Cliff had all kinds of gadgets somewhere stored away—He was into some of everything. He had this huge TV reporter camcorder, so he trained me to be his reporter. At this time the VHS was in high demand. I got a three-piece ensemble and suited up; I was now an entertainment reporter. Daily we would go to city hall to get a listings of activities going on in the Chicago park districts; Talent shows, plays, musicals, anything that was in the entertainment field—we wanted to be where the people were.

We would watch and record the talent and after their performance I would interview them, asking a series of questions. We appeared to be so important and so serious that people were walking up asking for a card so that they could contact us. Cliff's camera was huge, identical to the equipment real news reporters used. This is what I think attracted the people the most. We were in the mix. We gave out business cards and invited the artist to come to our office location to watch the tape that we recorded of their act. I talked to them about where their future in music was headed. Our goal was to sell them a copy of their performance, in which we had converted over to a VHS tape for $15 a copy. Come to think of it, we could have started the *American Idol* phenomenon back in the late '80s if we would have been thinking in that direction.

It was January 1985. We were in Hyde Park at the Kenwood Academy Annual Talent Show. This kid graced the stage with a presence so strong that Cliff and I gave each other the same unspoken approval. This skinny kid with big ears sat at his piano and serenaded the audience with an original song called "Strong Enough to Be." Clifford and I knew we had to talk to this kid after his amazing performance. His sound was of pure emotion.

The kid came across as really shy and soft spoken. Cliff no doubt recorded his show and after the performance I got to talk to the kid. I was interested in his song "*Strong enough to be*" That was a man song. I had become a fan; but the kid didn't know. I was nonchalant when I complimented him on his performance. I told him we recorded his performance and were interested in the song he sang. He mentioned that we would need to speak with his manager, so I gave him a business card and hoped his manager would give us a call.

Later that week, I got a call from a guy named Chuck, who introduced himself as Robert Kelly's Manager. We spoke a great deal over the phone. We discussed the performance we recorded of the kid, and I expressed interest in getting that song he sang during his performance. We set up an appointment for the two of them to come to our office to discuss the possibilities of working together.

The next day, Robert and his manager Chuck came into the office. Chuck was a cool guy; he was a 5'7", 165 lbs., brown skin, George Jefferson look-alike, minus the bald head. Robert performed his repertoire of songs for us. I have to give credit where credit is due; Robert had hits even at sixteen years old. Many looked at him as this skinny pimple-faced kid with big ears and a squeaky voice, but I saw a vision of super stardom in the boy.

Cliff, on the other hand, didn't care too much about Robert. He thought that his voice was too squeaky Cliff was more interested in using Robert's songs. He favored my vocals and liked my rich voice. He said it had more feeling to it. Cliff wanted to obtain a deal with Chuck and Robert to allow me to record Robert's songs on the Granville Record Label. Truthfully, my mind was entirely somewhere else. Although I did see Cliff 's perception and his angle, this kid, Robert Kelly's greatness was more promising. With a little bit of a makeover and a little polishing, this kid was born to be a star.

Chuck was no amateur manager. He knew the business, and he was not impressed or interested in being offered a contract, especially with no advance payments being offered upfront. Since we didn't have any cash to give out, it didn't look promising for us to obtain songs from Robert. Although that deal fell through, I was still interested in the kid's raw talent. He reminded me a lot of myself, a talented diamond in the rough. Before they left the office that day, I told Chuck he should keep in touch with me because I had some people I wanted to introduce him and Robert to. However, I didn't know that this would be the beginning to a long drawn-out dilemma—a dilemma that would eventually leave a lot of people hurt and separated over mere greed, notoriety, and material issues.

CHAPTER 2

He Would Be a Star

ONLY A FEW days went by, and Robert called the office to speak with me anxiously wanting to know who I wanted to introduce him to. The kid really wanted to be busy at working at his gift and he was very enthusiastic. After work one day, I went by his house on 107th and Parnell street. I told him all about my famous NBA relative. Robert was ecstatic that I knew Craig. He was a huge fan. The fact that I wanted to introduce him to Craig was reason enough for him to feel comfortable with me. Robert, Chuck and I formed a verbal business bonded friendship from that day forward. We were all feeling good in acquaintance with one another. I made sure not to make Chuck feel in any way that I was trying to step on his toes as manager or steal his talented artist away. I wanted to be an addition to this growing corporation and not a liability.

Chuck and I were both serious about the music business. He respected me for my experience and knowledge of the business. That made it easy for me to want to work with him and to be a part in helping to develop Robert's career. I shared stories with them about my old touring days and how we could start booking Robert to do some of the same tours. We all agreed that this could help Robert get more exposure, experience on the stage and in the long run he will master working the crowd.

Chuck and I worked the business during the day and I hung out with Robert at night, taking him everywhere with me. He was like my kid brother, but at the same time, my best friend. He would sing everywhere we went. I wanted the world to hear him sing. When he performed, you didn't see that bashful, shy, funny-looking, big-eared kid. When he performed you were entertained. Robert and I would ride around looking for girls to pick up. He loved to sing to them. He could create a song for a girl on the spot. Robert was quiet but not as shy as he portrayed. He got anything he wanted. All he had to do is sing. He knew how and exactly when to go into his shy boy routine. He could put anybody under his spell.

One day we were rolling through Harvey, Illinois, where we spotted these three honeys walking up the street. I pulled over to the crib and told Robert to sing something to them. He was use to being put on the spot to sing, so he was always ready to belt out a tune. He picked one of the three girls watching and sang off the top of his head. *"Girl, I was wondering if you would like to come with me, to a place where our love would flow, a place where only you and I could go."*

The nineteen-year-old girl Robert was singing to was named Yolanda. She was a red bone, about 5'5" with big pretty round eyes. She wore a fitted buttoned-up shirt with a few buttons left undone. Where she tied it into a knot to expose her belly button. She asked where we were going, so I told her Burger King and then back to my house to practice some music with my cousin. He's (talking about Robert) working on a record deal. This is what I would always tell the ladies.

You could tell Yolanda was digging Robert. She asked if they could go with us. I nodded to Robert to open the car door and let the girls in. Yolanda was not shy at all. She made it obvious she was feeling Robert. The other two girls eventually introduced themselves as De-De and Tonya. Yolanda started rubbing up and down the side of Robert's face, touching his lips. He played the timid role and the girls just giggled from the back seat. We rode right past Burger King. I didn't have enough money to offer to feed them all, so I drove us straight to my house.

De-De had the prettiest green eyes. She was so gorgeous I couldn't stop looking at her through my rear-view mirror. She kept her eyes on me as well. Her brown tanned skin was perfect with her eyes and full pink lips. She was Halle Berry gorgeous! Tonya wasn't bad-looking herself. She had the hottest body of the three. Her jeans showed her back side to be her best asset. Tonya was the playful one. She thought everything was funny. She kept giggling the entire ride back to my moms' house.

As soon as we got there, we went to my room in the basement. We had the house all to ourselves. We sat around getting acquainted and listening to Rob sing and play the piano. Just like I knew they would, the girls went into a trance. Yolanda and Tonya stood around Robert like star struck fans while De-De and I sat back on my bed watching. He sang a few original songs as he always did. Watching him was so amazing. You could hear the passion he had for singing in his voice.

He was singing and looking into Yolanda's eyes. *"You are so beautiful to me,"* It was a song Ray Charles had sang. Yolanda started to freak on Robert then. She started kissing him on his neck, his ears, rubbing her hands all over him and then she slid her tongue in and out of Robert's mouth. I was in awe when I saw Tonya began to unzip his pants. All I could say was *"Wow!"* and thought to myself, *I'd better get my butt back to singing too. The perks were amazing!*

De-De took my mind off them and what they were doing when I looked over towards her and her eyes were sparkling at me. I walked over to her, looking into her tiger brown beautiful eyes. I leaned in to kiss her. When she showed no resistance, I took her hand and led her off into a dividing room. When I peeked back at Robert I saw Tonya and Yolanda down on their knees. All that was heard after that were moans from both sides. By the way he was acting I could tell this was probably Robert's first time getting his dick sucked as well as a threesome.

After that rendezvous, Robert was a completely different person. He had come out of his shell. Now breaking out in a song and dance routine at any given time was second nature to him. I watched in wonder as this young man found himself. It was clear to me I had my work cut out. I was determined to do everything I could to get this kid where he needed to be so the world could see what I saw in him. In my eyes, he would be a star.

The more I hung out with Robert, the less I worked with Cliff. I had another plan. I wanted to take Robert and Chuck to Milwaukee, Wisconsin, to meet Craig. We had one pit fall, it was basketball season and Craig was working on a tight schedule. He was getting ready for the playoffs and clearly did not have time to meet with us.

Times were hard. Robert started complaining about always being broke, and I couldn't afford to keep giving him the little money I was having. We started going down to the subway with the portable piano to hustle for chump change. We would work from 8:00 a.m. until 6:00 p.m. This had become a full-time job for us. As people waited on the train, Robert would put on his dark sunglasses like Stevie Wonder, and play the piano while he sang.

We had a tip-hat sitting out. People would gather around and listen, leaving change as well as dollar bills in the hat. Robert even made up his own McDonald's jingle for the younger children who gathered around. *"McDonald's is a place for you when your day is through. You can go to McDonald's get yourself a Big Mac, a Big Mac, an order of fries, an ice cold Coke and an apple pie. No one does it like McDonald's doo-Ohoooo McDonald's and you!"* He was a hit in the subway just like he would be a hit to the world in just a matter of time.

People started looking forward to seeing and hearing him sing on their way to work. At times some people would miss their train trying to watch Robert perform. I took him down to the subway every day. This helped him grow confident and secure with me. We had some great times in those subways. They provided some of the most genuine moments of our friendship. I missed those days. Those days were the best of Robert Kelly to me.

At the end of our long working day, we would go up to the Water Tower Plaza to eat at McDonald's. Even till this day, I bet Mickey D's is still one of Robert's favorite places to eat. Once at McDonald's we would count the earnings for the day. Robert used to bring in $200 to $300 daily; in a twelve hour day. He would give me $20 or $25.00, depending on how much he made. I didn't mind. I was there for support and to keep him motivated. My interest in the day was to collect names and numbers of the people that stood around enjoying being entertained by him.

Chuck and I had already worked out a 5 percent cut for me out of his percentage he had with Robert. We both believed this kid was destined to be a success. There was no doubt that money would not be an issue. I wanted to be right there with him because I really believed in this kid. My mind was set, patience was to be my virtue. Robert had often talked to me about how other people came and made false promises but never delivered. He told me he felt a connection meeting me, and he had a feeling we would be good friends a long time. I felt the same way; there was a reason for us to have met. I felt we were all spiritually connected. And for true success to come, I felt, we all needed each other.

During this period, I had a chance to meet Robert's mother, Ms. Joann Kelly, who was motherly and hospitable to me. She sat me down and wanted to know me as a person. Over time, as we associated with each other, she grew to be dear to me. Thoughts of her now bring a smile to my face. She was so kindhearted and blunt. She told it like it was in the sweetest way. She was like a second mother to me. Like my mother, she was also a true believer of the Bible. *"I believe you were put in Robert's life to look out for him because Robert needs you Demetrius,"* she told me one day. *"You are one of the genuine ones in his corner,"* she told me on another occasion.

Talk about a singer holding a note—in my opinion, Mrs. Kelly could've sold a million records herself! Until I heard Mrs. Kelly sing my favorite female singer of all time was Ms. Gladys Knight. It was no doubt Robert had gotten his gift of singing from his mama. Mrs. Kelly and Robert would sometimes sing together. It was touching to say the least Ma Kelly had the voice of a true angel; her tone would touch your spirit. The only reason she didn't make it in the music industry, in my opinion is because she didn't pursue it.

Time was moving and it was time to put my plan in motion. Now I had to connect with Craig. It was a priority for me to get to him. It was March 1985, the NBA regular season ended and the playoffs were starting. This meant Craig had a couple of weeks where he would be at home. I had spoken to Ce-Ce—she was already on board. Robert was fascinated over my sister. He would tell me how he felt himself shake and tremble with nervousness whenever she would come around. At first I didn't pay attention to what he was saying. He was a youngster, and Ce-Ce was a beautiful married and mature woman. I understood his infatuation and thought it was appropriate. But little did I know Delilah was Ce-Ce's alter ego.

Ce-Ce invited us to attend one of the Milwaukee Buck's home games. Chuck decided not to go because he didn't feel it was a business trip. He was right—it wasn't a business trip, but it was an opportunity to plant seeds. Robert on the other hand, was star struck and was eager to go. The fact that we were attending a professional basketball game and having seats on the floor level was exciting to Him.

Robert and I rolled out in my burnt-orange 1973 Chevy station wagon. The paint blended with all the rust from the dents that were on the car. The oil was leaking, there was a hole in the muffler and it had no hubcaps. The car was truly a trap car. Nonetheless, we made it to Craig's house; loud, smoke and all. We drove happy as if we were in a Lincoln Town Car.

It was an hour-and-a-half drive. On the way, all I talked about with Robert was how big he was going to be. I was always inspiring Rob's ego with regards to how awesome of a singer and songwriter he was. He knew he had a gift, but he was shy and I wanted him to believe in himself more than he did; I wanted him to have the confidence that he was a great entertainer. After all, we shared the same dreams, and I wanted him to be and to know, in the entire world, that he was one of the best at what he did.

When we got to Craig's house, Robert was like a little kid on Christmas day, as if he was going to meet Santa Claus. He was both excited and scared at the same time. Craig wasn't at the house when we arrived. Ce-Ce said he had gone to practice and would be returning shortly. In the meantime, Robert was going through his shy kid act. He began pulling on my shirt to indicate to me he was extremely nervous looking at Ce-Ce's beautiful almond-shaped eyes and honey-smooth skin. I could imagine, being as young as Robert was that it was like having a crush on your teacher. Ce-Ce was a very beautiful woman; She had done a little modeling and singing in her past.

To break the ice of Robert's jitters, I took him out back where the basketball court was so he could relax and get a grip of himself. Robert prided himself at basketball. He felt if not for music, he would pursue a career as a basketball player. I admit, he had a little game, but it was no comparison to the gift he had in music. After we shot some hoops I took him to his favorite eating place, McDonald's, and afterwards he seemed to be himself again.

When we got back to the house, Craig was home. He walked past us. *"What's up, Johnny"* he said to me as he headed to his room, acting as if he didn't want to seem like he was really interested in meeting Robert. I didn't say anything to get his attention in respect to introducing him to Robert. I knew how to loosen Craig up. You see back in the day, Craig liked to smoke bud; *"Ganja,"* as he would call it. It just so happened I brought a sack with me because I liked to smoke me some bud too. Robert, didn't smoke weed or drink so I kept it from him. Even though he said he liked the smell of weed, I never enticed him towards indulging.

Robert was kind of uneasy because Craig didn't say hi or acknowledge him. I felt I had to make up an excuse for Craig by making Robert laugh telling him Craig was probably stinking and didn't want us to smell the funk of practice. After giving Craig a few minutes I went to his room and knocked on the door. When he told me to come in I stepped in the room and when Craig looked over at me, I was holding a fat joint. *"Can I light this up,"* I asked.

"Come on in," he said with a welcoming smile on his face. After he took a hit, he zoomed right into his fantasy world, taking on the personality of being a black militant, brothers gone work it out, power to the people frame of mind. Craig was crazy like that. He stayed on some Black righteous stuff. He was still a Black Panther and had never gone to a meeting. While he was talking brotherly love, I was pumping him up about how talented my young artist was and if he helped me with him, I would be in the studio next.

After we finished smoking, Craig was ready to meet and listen to Robert. When we returned to the living room, Robert and Ce-Ce were sitting on the couch playing Pac-man. He didn't look nervous at all now. He was totally relaxed. Ce-Ce did the introductions and afterwards, Robert obliged my request and played a number of original songs.

While Robert was singing, Craig looked over at me like Cliff and I looked at each other the very first time we heard Robert sing. You know the look, like on the cartoons when a character's eyes turn into dollar signs—$$$—that's how Craig looked. After Robert was done, Craig asked, *"What do y'all need?"* It was at that moment that I thought the hardest part was over. It should be smooth sailing from here on out, I told myself.

I mentioned to Craig that I wanted to put a band together for Robert and to get him in the studio. I let him know that I didn't want him to totally support us. I wanted to put the band together so we could be self-sufficient and at the same time build a fan base that would follow us as we would rise. It all sounded good to Craig until I told him Robert had a manager and he was contracted. It seemed then he had a change of heart. Craig wanted to know the extent of Robert's contract. I told Craig how cool Chuck was and how I didn't think Chuck would have a problem with anything and that he was truly a man who, I felt, had Robert's best interest at heart.

As far as I was concerned Chuck was cool and the contract thing, I figured we were going to all have to sit down to renegotiate that anyway. I needed Craig's financial backing to get me started so I could put a band together, find a place to rehearse, get some equipment and get us busy to start generating us some funds and becoming a self-sufficient independent organization.

Craig was on that 'brother love' frame of mind which had nothing to do with the business. *"Brothers need to form a stronger unity with one another. Look at it brother man, a Black man with no money, got this young brother under a contract."* Craig was in la-la land the way he was talking I thought. Craig didn't know anything about all the work Chuck had put in with Robert. He knew nothing about the fact that Robert was illiterate and that Chuck was helping Robert in that area of his life too. Yeah, that's right. Robert Kelly couldn't read or write well at all. So what, no one was taking advantage of him. He was fortunate to have good people around him; that loved him. When I found out I didn't look at Robert differently; I was eager to help him.

I am not speaking of his illiteracy to make him look bad because over the thirteen years I spent working with Robert, he learned to read, and because of the way we used to practice signing autographs and writing memos, he learned to write too. So saying this is not to discredit Robert in any way, like my old friend Bernie Mac used to say, *"I'm telling it like it T.I. is."* Anyway, Craig and I concluded to schedule a meeting with Chuck. I gave Craig his phone number and told him to give Chuck a call. I knew Chuck would have no problem doing what was needed to get Robert's career off the ground.

Demetrius Smith Sr.

Robert and I were invited to stay over for the weekend. For the rest of the evening Robert serenaded Craig and his wife. He took advantage of the opportunity to show them his gift as a writer. He wrote songs for them right off the top of his head. He really got Craig's full attention then. Craig told me I had in my hands, *"a goose that could lay golden eggs."* And he was right; all what was left to do now was get this goose situated so we could hatch those eggs. The next morning, Craig returned the favor to Robert by inviting him to watch him perform. He took us to practice with him and after practice Robert and I shot hoops with Craig and his teammates. It was a fun filled day mingling with the pros.

After the shoot around of Craig's practice, Robert sang a few songs for the players, amazing them with his talent. A few of the players joked around asking Robert for his autograph. After we left the practice facility, Craig took us to the golf course; to play a sport we knew nothing about. It was a funny sight. Robert and I could not hit that little bitty ball. We had a really great time hanging out with Craig and Ce-Ce that weekend, a moment neither of us could ever forget.

Once Robert and I returned to Chicago, we met with Chuck. Robert told him about our weekend with Craig in detail. Chuck informed us that he did get a call from Craig and scheduled a date for them to meet. We all felt good about what had transpired over the weekend. We believed things were about to start getting better. The three of us talked about forming a band. Robert told me his older brother Bruce played the bass guitar, and he wanted his brother to play for him. Over the next few days, I traveled around the city with Robert putting his band together. Things were looking up.

CHAPTER 3

Humbled Beginnings

ROBERT'S OLDER BROTHER Bruce was a funny dude and he should have been a comedian. He use to have us all laughing out of control every single time he came around. And not only was he funny but the boy had talent. He could really play that bass guitar. Bruce was the first member of the three piece band we put together behind Robert. Then there was Poochie who played the drums; He was a real serious brother who didn't want to waste time playing in a band that wasn't going anywhere. As a student, he would much rather spend his time at home studying. However, he believed in Rob and was willing to make a sacrifice and join the band. Finally there was my boy, Donald (Donnie) Evans. He was the keyboard player who traveled the road with me and my band. Regretfully, Donnie's stay with us was short because he had a bad drinking problem. His skills on the keyboard were of the greatest quality, but his vice and inclination towards alcoholism overshadowed his gift to play music. We had to let Donnie go his own way, and I had to call on other musicians I knew to fill in.

We were a three piece band, with Robert playing keyboards as well. Chuck arranged for us to practice three times a week in the banquet hall at the Chatham Bowl on 79th street. Our sound was developing, but we needed better equipment. I even started to put together a mailing list of fans who wanted to be notified of our first show. Robert Kelly impressed people everywhere we went. His humble beginnings towards stardom were coming to life, and we were there as witnesses to see how it all began.

Robert and I continued to perform in the subways and in the streets. It was just something about being down in the subway's and bringing home money daily that made sense. So I would always encourage Robert to go—letting him know I was with him and willing to go with him any time. The money helped, but more important was the list of names and addresses that I was gathering from the spectators as they watched Robert sing. I figured if I could build a fan base for the shows we were putting together, and if a third of the people who signed our mailing list would show up, at $10 a head we would make out good. In addition, I figured our fan base could become so large that we would have the support of the people, and they would spread our name throughout the city of Chicago and the surrounding communities.

We all worked hard in the early days and we were all working for free. We all shared the same belief that with Craig's assistance, we were headed to the next level. However, because no money was coming in, everyone's attitude was changing. To be more specific, the disgruntlement began to take over, and it showed. People were beginning to become distrustful of the whole process. Receiving fruit for our labor, that was foreign language to us—we had a hard time interpreting how this plan would work out.

In the meantime, Chuck was talking to Craig giving him an update on our overall progress and he let him know of our financial situation. We needed to set a date to display our act and we needed to form that date around Craig's schedule. A date where he would be free to attend the show so he could see the polished act we put together. Although we were putting in the time and working hard there was only so much a person could sacrifice. Now, it was on Craig to meet us halfway. We needed that equipment because we needed to work to generate funds for us to continue. We needed to be able to feel things were headed upward. Time was moving but yet things seemed to be standing still. We were stuck waiting on Craig at that point.

Finally, Craig invited us to his house again. He said before he would release any funds, he needed to review the contract Robert was obligated to, which was only fair and right. Chuck, Robert, and I drove up to Craig's house for a scheduled two o'clock meeting. During the hour and forty five minute drive, I talked to Robert and Chuck about the kind of person I felt Craig was. I wanted them to be prepared for the meeting so they would not be passive with Craig because he had money. Chuck assured me he was in no way intimidated.

To our dismay, when we arrived Craig wasn't home. Ce-Ce greeted us cheerfully, informing us Craig was out playing golf. Wow, what a way to start a relationship. My grandpa told me, *"First impressions always count."* We were disappointed that Craig wasn't there. We had driven there with the sole purpose of discussing business. While we were waiting we chit-chatted with Ce-Ce while she cooked dinner. Ce-Ce can be very opinionated at times. Over the course of her going back and forth from the living room to the kitchen, she voiced her opinion about Robert. She felt that Robert should not be singing in a band nor performing in the subways. This was not a conversation Chuck and I wanted to entertain with her. Therefore, we kept the conversation short with short responses to her comments like *"It's only temporary."*

We were there for over two hours before Craig showed up. When he came in, he went straight to his room to shower, nodding his head at us, his way of saying hello. This gesture gave an impression of arrogance as if he looked down on us. I didn't try to go talk with him. I was there for the business.

When Craig came out of the room dinner was ready, and the aroma from the meal Ce-Ce prepared had all of us ready to dig in and feast. She made a huge pot roast, macaroni and cheese, green beans, sweet potatoes and dinner rolls. She topped it off with some good old-fashioned grape Kool-Aid. For dessert we had chocolate cake. The meeting was put on hold for a moment because, to say it in simple terms, dinner was all that.

After dinner, Ce-Ce cleared the dining room table while Craig slipped away back into his bedroom for another ten to fifteen minutes. Once Ce-Ce was done cleaning, we gathered back at the dining room table for the grand meeting. We were waiting on Craig for what seemed like forever. I already knew what he was up to—he had to have a tote of the ganja. He had to smoke a joint in order to relax before handling business. When he returned, I suggested we start our meeting off with a prayer, which I felt was important. The saying (a family that prays together stays together) was relevant to me. I wanted us to stay together. I wanted this thing to work.

After prayer, to start the meeting off, we discussed what we had been doing with the band and how hard it was to develop our sound without equipment. I showed Craig the mailing list I formulated. We also presented an itemized accounting of what equipment we needed along with the approximate cost. We discussed what everyone's position would be in detail. He was pleased that everything was good, but Craig wanted to look over the contract. Chuck gave him the contract, and after going over it, we found that Chuck was getting 30percent of Robert's earnings. We were all very surprised by that because Chuck previously informed us that the contract was for 20 percent and we believed it.

Chuck then went on to explain why his percentage was so high. He said that when other investors like me and Craig came to the organization, he would be responsible to pay their portion out of his percentage. He explained that this way, Robert would have 70 percent to himself. Chuck felt like he was acting in Robert's best interest.

Chuck broke the percentages down with Robert still getting 70 percent, Chuck would get 15 percent, Craig would get 10 percent as an executive producer and investor, and I would get 5 percent. Chuck also suggested that we all consult with our own entertainment lawyers to have a contract drawn up. He even reiterated the fact that he would not have a problem at all with redoing his management contract with Robert. Whatever was right for Robert was okay for Chuck.

I thought it was fair, and I believed that Chuck meant every word he said. But all of a sudden, Craig went into some revolutionary shit, some dumb shit if you ask me. *"Brothers, brothers, that's what's wrong with our people today. We wanna hold each other to some binding contract when we need to embrace one another and believe in one another. What we need to do with this, young brothers, is build a trust with each other and then we can go from there."* Chuck and I looked at each other like "Where is this dude coming from? What planet is he from?" It was like Craig was not present while Chuck was breaking everything down about the contract.

I was thrown into a tizzy listening to Craig. Really though, I wondered where was his head at, but I knew all along it was the weed talking. *"Craig, in business, people sign contracts. That's business! Contracts show love, trust, and gives security. That is why the NBA has you under a contract; you're secure knowing your team has your back,"* I told him.

Craig stated the NBA gave him something up front. He asked Chuck, *"How much are you giving this young brother?"* Chuck explained his position as a manager and my position as Robert's personal assistant and future tour manager. He informed Craig we were sacrificing our time and money for Robert's future development. Chuck told Craig we were aids in a corporation, each with an important job. To me, he was right because at this level, we all needed each other.

Chuck further expressed why we weren't supposed to pay Robert money up front. He felt that Robert should be paying us a weekly check for the work we were doing, but because he wasn't able to pay us, he felt that it was only right that we are paid a percentage because of our sacrifice. Chuck told Craig, *"There are no guarantees that we will be reimbursed for our services, the time we invest, and the money we spend daily. And furthermore, because we all share the same dream and we are working together to bring that dream to reality. We've become a corporation together, shareholders, and this is a sacrificial investment we are all a part of and that is where the percentages come in."*

We talked a little more about contract issues. Craig was not receptive to Chuck's resolve to being open to change and what was needed to be able to move forward. Craig continued trying to get us to see his point of view. I couldn't understand it. Craig couldn't get off the subject of getting Robert out from under a contract with Chuck. Chuck had already said he would do whatever was needed in Robert's best interest, but Craig refused to hear that part of the conversation. It seemed he had something else on his mind or his brain was being clouded by the weed.

There was nothing we could say or do to make him agree. The conversation started to go in a different direction so I changed the subject. I started talking about our need for equipment. *"Craig, you said you'd give us a check for some equipment. Will we be able to get that today?"* I asked. He looked at me with a disgusted, surprised look as if I should not have asked him that question. I went on to let him know how disgruntled we were all becoming because we weren't able to work. I told how important it was for us to do shows.

I knew Craig wanted to procrastinate. He suggested that we have another meeting before handing out any funds. Chuck told Craig that he could not afford to continue to ask the people that were working with us to sacrifice while we went month to month, back and forth having meetings. I interrupted the conversation and said to Craig, *"Our whole thing is for us to be able to be self-sufficient. We don't want to lean on you financially when we can market our product and fend for ourselves. We should have meetings on a weekly or monthly basis if that is what we agree on, but we're working now and trying to get things rolling."* Everybody sat with different looks on their faces as if they were surprised at my sudden outburst. We had been talking and getting nowhere for over an hour! My interceding had caught them all off guard.

I looked over at Craig and saw that I had his attention. I took advantage of the moment. *"I mean, hey, Craig, I thought we were all on the same page wanting the same things. We have the ball rolling already. Every day, we're rehearsing, making phone calls to set up dates, and telling people of the engagements we have coming up. We're doing our part, and now we need to know where you're at with us. Either you're with us or you're not, Craig,"* I said, frustrated with the whole thing. Craig looked over at Ce-Ce with a look as if I put him on the spot. The room fell silent. Everyone present looked at one another and then back to Craig. I was eager to hear my brother-in-law's response. I was tired of the bullshit.

Demetrius Smith Sr.

Craig was hesitant for a moment. My statement caught him off guard. He looked at Robert and then said to me, *"Johnny man, I want this to move forward too. And if I wasn't with you, we wouldn't be having this meeting. I just want to make sure that the brother understands his contractual obligations."*

I responded, *"But we can have more meetings on that Craig. I'm just speaking on the production part of the group. The check would get us going, and entertaining is what Robert does. I wanna get him busy"* was my plea to Craig. *"I can understand that. So how much will y'all need,"* Craig asked?

I was relieved when he asked that. I then directed the conversation over to Chuck, asking him for the budget. As he was going through his bag, I asked to be excused. I needed some air. It had taken a lot for me to stay cool at that table. I didn't feel that Craig and my sister were thinking about me at all. I was thinking to myself their questions should have been in support of me, and following my lead, but they weren't. Craig, being the man with the money, was tripping thinking he was Donald trump. He must have smoked a different brand of weed before coming to the table.

I was a bit angry at how the meeting had gone. As I got up from the table Robert got up after me and went to the den, where he began playing his piano and I stood outside the door just taking in some fresh air; leaving Craig, Ce-Ce and Chuck at the table to go over the budget issues. When Robert and I returned Chuck explained to us that he had went over everything. As a result of my outburst, Craig gave us a check for $3,500.00. It was a start and it was what we needed. I felt we had accomplished something. Talking about working hard for the money, I could only shake my head thinking with the goose that we had in our hands we should have been having a party and counting our blessings.

On our way home, Robert said that he was glad I spoke up for the check. Robert and Chuck said they didn't think we were going to get anything because Craig kept talking about us having another meeting. Chuck also told me that I showed real loyalty speaking up in that meeting, and as far as he was concerned, I already earned my right to the 5 percent I requested. This made me feel good. I told them, *"Just like Craig works for the NBA and has to at times make sacrifices for his family that they might not always agree on; I'm the same way. I work for Robert Kelly. I was just doing my job."* We all laughed. On the way home, we were all in a positive state of mind and had faith that everything was going to work out with Craig.

While at rehearsal the next night, Chuck came through the door carrying new microphones and asked us to go with him outside to carry in the rest of the equipment. We had a sound system, microphones, cords, drum, heads, two big speakers, and three monitor speakers. Even though Chuck got all the equipment from a pawnshop, we were excited just as if it was new. Our sound changed immediately from a transistor sound to a Hi-Fi stereo sound. The sound took us all to another level. We felt we made a step forward towards professionalism.

After rehearsal that night, Chuck called Robert and I to the backroom, gave us an envelope and said it was a little something. He believed everybody deserved a little something for the work we put in. I opened the envelope and there was $175 in it. I was so happy; it was my payment of 5 percent, and I sure needed it. I don't know how much Robert had, but when he came out of the office, he didn't seem too happy. He was acting like something serious was on his mind. Since he didn't say anything to me about it, I didn't give it a second thought. All I could think about was how Chuck was on the up and up with us. He showed me that he cared about us all.

That same night, as we were all leaving, I was waiting on Chuck. I was about to thank Robert for the money and see what was wrong with him earlier, but Chuck came out, looked at me, and shook his head side to side as if he was disgusted with something.

I asked him, *"Is everything all right?"*

Chuck replied, *"It'll work itself out."* I thanked him for the money, and then he said, *"You earned it."*

Then he shook his head again, so I asked him again, *"What's wrong, Chuck?"*

He replied slowly, *"I don't want this to get back to, Robert."* I nodded, assuring him that I understood. *"I can't believe it Demetrius. Robert got mad at me because I gave everybody some money. I can't believe Robert is that selfish of a person to think that the people who work with him and sacrifice for him are not worthy to eat what he eats. That really upsets me. It makes me wonder what type of a person I'm working for."*

I couldn't believe it either, so I asked him, *"Was he mad because you gave me some money too?"*

Chuck replied, *"Everybody! Robert didn't think anybody should have received any money. He wanted all the money from the balance of the equipment."* Chuck went on to tell me that Robert felt that he should have gotten the equipment and given the remainder of the cash to him. Robert did not feel like Chuck should concern himself with the needs of all the people helping him. Robert felt everyone should be paid once we started doing a gig.

This was one of the first signs of Robert's selfishness. I was pretty upset after hearing that and wanted to approach Robert about it, but Chuck had already asked me not to say anything so I kept quiet. As time went on, I started to regret the fact that I did not confront Robert about his selfishness because it grew to be a big negative part of his character. It irked me to know this about this young man. Little did I know then that this was the beginning of a long line of lies and deceit.

We continued to rehearse at the Chatham Bowl three days a week. We scheduled our first concert to take place in April 1985. Everything was working out. The band was tight, and everybody was feeling good about our upcoming show. I sent flyers out to everyone on our guest list. Now all that was left was for the band to put on a great show for the people. On the night of the show, we had tables set up for our VIPs. The hall was filled with so many people. It was standing room only and the beautiful thing about it, everybody was sociable and seemed to be having a good time. There were smiles all over the place, and everybody was excited and supportive of Robert.

The first act was a comedian friend of ours, Jeff Arnold. He performed a lot in the Cotton Club with Bernie Mac back in those days. Jeff got down and got the crowd relaxed and buying drinks. After he finished his segment of the show, Mrs. Kelly, Robert's mother, honored us with her soulful voice singing Gladys Knight's song "You're the Best Thing That Ever Happened to Me." After Mrs. Kelly performed, I went up and did two songs, "Too Hot" by Kool and the Gang and "Don't You Know That" by Luther Vandross.

The ultimate moment arrived when Robert came on. The band played an original intro song for him, and he came out dancing. Robert Kelly was truly a showman. The songs he performed that night were a rendition of Donny Hathaway's song "A Song for You," Luther Vandross' "A House Is Not a Home," and then he did about three of his original songs: "Hard Times," "Say It," and "Strong Enough to Be." Those are songs many are not familiar with, but Robert had a library full of songs inside of him. The show was hot. We made a very nice profit off the door that night. We had 300 people at $10 a head and I know the facility made a lot of money off the bar. The show was a true success.

After the show, we were on a cloud. We felt like we were on our way to the big times. The show was a complete success and gave us an opportunity to show people our great talent. If only I would've known then what I know now; we would have had cassette tapes for sale at the show that night.

The way Robert writes songs, we will never hear them all. His song writing ability is truly a gift; A gift that he loves to give unselfishly. The sad thing is that, he couldn't give people their due in all things—like money!

Craig and my sister felt like Robert was ready. Craig even complimented me on my performance and said, *"We have to get you in the studio next."* I really didn't think about my performance until I kept getting compliments from the people we greeted after the show. I was feeling very good about everything.

Afterwards, we all went out to eat on Seventy-ninth and Jeffrey. We talked about the show and the other shows that we had coming up. Craig talked about putting Robert into the studio, and said that he had a friend that he wanted us to go see in the next couple of days. He wanted Robert to start recording his songs and go to the next level. I thought things were moving right along smoothly until Craig said, *"The show was nice guys, but I feel that we shouldn't be doing shows right now, nor do I think that Robert should be performing in the subways. We see that the people love you, so let's put the music on tape, get the deal, and then the public will be waiting for you."* I shook my head and thought to myself, *He must have had a smoke in the car on his way over here from the show.*

Chuck looked at me too. We laughed, and then Chuck said, *"I agree, just not right now. Craig, we don't want to lean on you totally for financial support. There are six mouths to feed here Craig. I am sure you don't want to put all of us on your budget. So it is only temporary; let us build a fan base. It's gone blow up for us man, watch,"* Chuck said, nodding at Craig while biting off the big burger he had ordered. Listening to Craig, I just couldn't understand him; I couldn't see his vision. I was glad Chuck said what he did. We did well financially from the show. Not only were we all paid, but there was money left over to use for the growth of the business. We made $3,200 that night. Everybody seemed happy but Craig and Ce-Ce. They were looking at us as if they were our parents and we were brought out to have a good time, but they were there to keep us in line. They should have been having fun and laughing with us but all Craig kept saying was, *"y'all don't see the big picture bro!"* I knew it was the weed.

We were all feeling good, and I was sure we were seeing the bigger picture. It was obvious we all wanted to grow. Robert was ready to get it cranked up, and so were we. I decided to agree with Craig, so I said, *"Yeah, Craig, you're right. Let's get our boy in the studio."* I figured we would all work everything out, but as we were sitting in the round booth at the restaurant, I took one more quick glance at Craig, I thought to myself, *I better keep my eye on him.* I felt like the man wasn't keeping it real. We were supposed to be a team. With Craig being a point guard on a professional basketball team, you would think he would have the basic concept down, but he didn't. He wanted to control things and people. This among other things would drive a wedge between Craig and the rest of us. I sat back and just watched him.

A few days later, Chuck called and asked me to have Robert at an address where he wanted us to meet up with him and Craig. The address was located on 148th and Winchester in Harvey, Illinois, which is my hometown. I had no idea a studio existed there even though I used to hang out down the street. Craig introduced us to the sound engineer that he hired to record Robert's songs. Craig and Chuck left, leaving Robert and I there to work. Bruce, the engineer, had a small studio, and I do mean small. The studio was so small that we had to stand on our tiptoes to let one another get by.

Once we started, Robert began to lay down some drum tracks. I thought we were going to start with the songs we had been rehearsing since those were the songs we knew, but Robert was feeling the quality of the sound coming out of Bruce's speakers, so he created a new song according to the richness of the music. That's how Robert was; he wrote songs in the moment, which never ceased to amaze me. This kid was bad! He appeared to be so relaxed in the small space we were working in. Bruce operated on one side of the forty-eight-track mixing board where he would change reels and switch wires around. Robert stood on the opposite side where he worked the keyboard, mixing his beats and creating sounds. I stood up on the chairs out of the way while the two artists worked their magic.

The sound that came out of Bruce's tiny basement was pure quality. The bass sound was so deep coming out of the speakers, you could feel the vibrations like there were hands on you swaying you and pulling you from side to side. We stayed there the first day three to four hours. In that short length of time, Robert laid down drum and keyboard tracks for two completely new songs. We would have stayed longer, but Bruce tended to take a while to change over tracks.

It seemed that every time we looked at Bruce, he had a newly rolled joint in his mouth. He would light it and go right back to talking to himself, *"And then I'll take this one and stick it here an ahhh, sweeeet,"* taking pulls from the joint he had lit. Robert and I would just laugh. Bruce was like that dude in the movie *Half Baked* that Dave Chappell starred in. Everything the dude did in the movie, he did it smoking weed. That was Bruce, a straight weed head, but the man knew how to build and develop a sound in that basement studio of his.

Craig gave us the green light to produce an entire album. He was financing the whole studio session. Once Robert knew that he could be in the studio every day, he didn't want to go to practice. On the days we were in the studio and needed to end the session early to go to rehearsal, Robert would have me call Chuck to cancel. From time to time, Chuck would call Robert and ask him if he wanted to do certain shows that were available and Robert would cancel those too. Out of the three days a week we scheduled for rehearsing, Robert would attend one and drop through for an hour on the other days.

Ce-Ce began to show up at our studio sessions and was in Chicago a lot more than usual. It seemed she was always in Robert's ear. I didn't pay too much attention to it, but I did notice that she and Robert were becoming very chummy with each other. He was a lot more comfortable around her now. I thought it was a good thing. I enjoyed the fact that my sister was a part of something that I believed in. I felt like this was something that was bringing Ce-Ce and I closer together.

When Ce-Ce was young, I wasn't there at all and there is a five-year gap in our age so we didn't grow up together. When she was eleven, I was sixteen running the streets with my young friends. I did not have time for Ce-Ce. And when she was in high school, I was in jail. Even though I got caught up in a life of crime at a young age, she respected me and looked up to me as her older brother. As a matter of fact, all of my family looked up to me despite my shortcomings.

In fact, Ce-Ce honored me by coming to visit me at Statesville Correctional Center in 1982. She brought Craig with her because she said she wanted Craig to meet her big brother before they got married. I thought so much of that moment and felt so proud. My sister touched my heart when she came to visit me that day. She was seeking my approval of her marriage and that felt so good to me. So as Ce-Ce and Robert were becoming friends, I felt it was harmless. I thought it could only bring all of us closer together as one big happy family.

We spent so much time in the studio that the band began to complain, especially after Robert had Chuck cancel a couple of the shows. I told Robert about the band member's complaints and asked him if he wanted to continue with the band or if he wanted to let them go. Robert said he would start attending rehearsals and asked me to call the guys and have them at rehearsal the next day. He also mentioned that he wanted me to come get him the next morning so that we could go to the subway to perform because his funds were getting low.

The next morning, I was at his house at 7:00 a.m. We went on with our normal routine in the subway, concluding our day at the same time. Except that on this particular day, instead of going to the Water Tower Plaza to eat as we normally did, Robert wanted to go home. He said he wanted to work on a new song that he had in his head. I dropped him off, and reminded him of our 4:00 p.m. rehearsal with the guys. He told me he'd meet me there, and I was cool with that and didn't give it a second thought.

When I arrived at rehearsal that evening, the guys were all there and glad to see me. Bruce asked in a joking manner, *"Is your majesty with you?"* he was speaking of Robert. *"He should be on his way, I told them, I had not spoken to him since I dropped him off earlier*. Poochie was beating the drums, and a new guy was there, whom they wanted Robert to hear in hopes he would consider allowing him to join the band.

As I watched, they started having a jam session. I saw an expression of freedom on them as they played. Music was a joy to them; A language in itself that made it easy for them to communicate their feelings with one another. The music could easily bring them closer, and if not, it would pull them apart. As they warmed up, I noticed it was four-forty-five and Robert was already forty-five minutes late.

I stepped out of the room and went to the pay phone to call him at his mother's house. Mrs. Kelly answered, *"Robert's gone honey. He left over an hour ago. Practice is where he told me he was going."* According to my calculations, he should have been hereby now. At five-thirty, he was still a no show. The guys kept asking about his whereabouts. I could only answer, *"I don't know where he is."* At six o'clock, we ended rehearsal with everyone feeling disappointed.

Something was not flowing smoothly. Poochie and Bruce had said they had talked to him and he said he would be here; this was not like him, especially him not calling me. We talked about everything and I hadn't heard from him since dropping him off. I didn't know what to think. I just wondered where he could be.

After we all said our goodbyes for the evening, I decided to walk down the street to McDonald's to grab a bite to eat and clear my head. As I approached the building, I noticed a silver Toyota 4Runner truck with Wisconsin license plates; coming out of the parking lot. It looked just like Ce-Ce's truck. I sped up my pace. The truck stopped at the stop light. I then chased it down to get a closer look at the driver. Sure enough, it was

Ce-Ce and comfortably slouching in the passenger seat was none other than Robert Kelly. As I approached the vehicle, I asked myself, *What is going on?*

When I knocked on the door, they looked at me surprised. Ce-Ce opened the door with the automatic button and I jumped in the truck because the light had changed to green. The entire way Ce-Ce kept her focus on driving. *"What happened to you, Rob? Did you forget about rehearsal?"* I asked him. He nodded his head towards Ce-Ce, indicating to me she was to blame for his absence. I told him how disappointed the band members were and how I wouldn't be surprised if we didn't have a band tomorrow. He simply said that he would talk to the guys.

Turning my attention to Ce-Ce, I asked her what she was doing up there in Chicago. *"I had some things to talk over with Robert,"* she told me. *"That's messed up girl. You could have at least brought him to practice and talked to him there. You should be talking with Chuck anyway if it's something that pulled you from home to come up here,"* I told her. She kept her eyes on the road and didn't respond. I left it alone as well. I didn't want to start an argument. However, I was truly disappointed with Ce-Ce. I felt right then something was going on with them, hoping at the same time my premonition was not a reality. I could not conjure up in my mind a reason why she had Robert with her, or what she could have to talk with him about that she hadn't told me about. I thought it had to be some shady business going on.

I asked her to drop me off at my car and as we drove back to the Chatham Bowl, there was total silence in the car. Ce-Ce, Robert and I had always had an open communication. We would always laugh and joke with one another. There was always something to talk about that was relevant to our being together. I felt this was not the place Ce-Ce wanted me to be with them. This time together was different; silence was all there was. This looked to me like one of those instances that bring truth to the saying *"What's in the dark will come to the light."* Something was going on. I could just feel the tension in the air. Things were definitely changing, and it didn't feel like it was a change headed in the right direction.

I felt frustrated with Ce-Ce. At this point, I didn't feel she was helping me; at that moment, she was in the way. When she dropped me off at my car, we didn't say a word. The only person that said something was Robert. He told me Ce-Ce was taking him home. The vibe felt so awkward. It seemed as if Ce-Ce was purposely bent on ignoring and avoiding direct contact with me. I didn't know what to think of her or what she was going through. I wondered where her head was.

CHAPTER 4

Forces of Negativity

AFTER THEY DROPPED me off I drove to my mom's house. When I got there my mom was sitting in the kitchen. I don't know how my mother suspected something was wrong with me, but as soon as she looked up at me, she said, *"Johnny boy, what's wrong babe? You look like something's bothering you."* She was looking through the smile I had on my face. It was strange to me how Mama could always see something in us even if we made it our business to go into the house in a happy mood. It was evident she saw through my facade. What's that saying? *"Mothers know best?"*

I sat down at the table with her, placed my hands on my head, and let the fake smile fade. I told her what was bothering me. My mother agreed with me, saying Ce-Ce had no business picking Robert up, at least without speaking with me first to let me know the business she had to discuss with Robert. *"Put it in God's hands, Johnny boy. What God got for you can't nobody interfere with it babe. But you got to be able to let it go and let God do it"* was the advice Mama gave me as she looked up from reading her Bible. She got up, came over, stood behind me, and rubbed my head. *"Whatever it is babe, it'll happen but it's gonna be in God's time, not yours. You've got to be able to talk to Ce-Ce and not be angry when you're doing it,"* she said with sincerity in her voice. *"Pray for me Mama!"* I asked her smiling while looking up at her. *"That goes without asking boy,"* she said as she leaned down smiling to kiss me on my forehead.

Moments later, Ce-Ce walked in the front door. I did not want to see her. I just looked at her as she walked into the kitchen. *"Hey Mama,"* she said, looking right past me. I couldn't contain myself. I figured it was a good time to ask her something while in front of my mother. *"Ce-Ce, why are you up here in Chicago picking Robert up and keeping him from rehearsals?"* She looked at me like a snake ready to strike with her poisonous venom. Then she looked at my mama, which made her contain herself from whatever harsh words she wanted to say to me. *"I think I should be Robert's manager. I was talking to him about that today,"* she calmly said.

"Are you serious? I asked. I gave her a cold 'you did something wrong,' stare! I stood there looking at her shaking my head. *"So the whole thing is for y'all to get Chuck out of the picture right?"* I asked? *"Boy, looks like y'all got some plans of your own,"* I told her. I felt as if Craig knew and had to be a part of this too.

I felt like everything she and Craig were doing with and for Robert was behind my back. Like Mama said, she should have been communicating with me. After all, this was my project. Why were they trying to take over? Or why didn't they at least have enough consideration of me to share some of their thoughts with me instead of going around me and behind my back, as if I weren't important. It was bad enough they had no respect for Chuck's position as Robert's manager, but I was family. I had come to them for their help. The treacheries had begun; That much I could see. It hurt deeply to have my family act this way towards me.

"What you should be doing is helping me with this project by talking to Chuck about things concerning Robert and not up here chasing Robert down and disrupting everybody else's life Ce-Ce," I said angrily without thinking. And when I told her, *"You should be at home taking care of your kids."* Oh, that pissed her off.

Ce-Ce had a bad habit of snapping at people and not having any restraint on the words she would use, but I wasn't ready for the response she gave me. *"Fuck you motherfucker. Who the hell do you think you are?"* Before she could say anything else, I jumped up.

"Johnny," my mother yelled as I stood up over my sister. Looking to my mother and back again at my sister. *"Girl you'd better get yourself in order. You see my mama here, don't you ever disrespect her again like that."* I told her. I don't know what I was gone do but she was not going to have a freedom of speech being disrespectful in front of our mother.

Ce-Ce looked in my eyes and knew her little nasty mouth would get her in trouble that day. Angrily she stood up and pushed past me; quickly walking to the back room. My mother knew my anger and she knew it's rage was because of the disrespect. My mother knew I would jump through a window or off the top of a building on top of a motherfucker for her; demanding her respect.

After Ce-Ce had pushed past me I walked over to my mother, and I apologized to her for my outburst. I kissed her on the cheek and went down the stairs to my room. I heard Ce-Ce and my mother talking, but when I came back upstairs, a half hour or so later, Ce-Ce was gone. Nothing was the same with her and I after that day, for a while. This was the beginning of the wedges that had formed, and now I saw a whole other side to the people around me, including Robert.

The next day at the studio I got a chance to talk to Robert about the confrontation I had with my sister. He told me he knew about it and said Ce-Ce had called him and talked to him about it already. I asked him what was going on with them. I also asked him about the conversation they had regarding her becoming his manager. Bruce was at the sound board eavesdropping. *"Let's go outside,"* Robert suggested. He had a look on his face as if he was about to do a man thing for the first time. Life was growing into something new for Robert. He was having growing pains I believe. I liked when we would have serious talks. These were bonding times for us. I believed.

We sat on the steps of the front porch. *"What's going on Rob?"* I asked.

"Nothing Johnny man, really. Ce-Ce wants a position in this with us, but I told her that Chuck was my manager. I can't stop her from calling me. And most of the time, when she calls, she be up here and we hang out. But ain't nothing going on," he said, hunching his shoulder. He then asked, *"What am I supposed to do, tell her not to call me or come around me?"* I told him that he is supposed to keep things business, just plain and simple.

He sat with his head hanging down, rubbing and squeezing his head as if he was confused about something. *"Rob, Craig is sponsoring your project, not his wife. We can't allow her to interfere with us moving forward. You can't let the little head overrule the big head in this Robert,"* I told him. *"You can't be hanging out with a man's wife Robert. Ain't that much fun in the world? That's my sister and I love her dearly. She's married and that's the bottom line to that Robert."* I said.

"I want us to keep this business. I don't know what you and my sister got going on, all I know is this secretive shit you and her doing, it don't look right man and shit can't turn out right if it ain't right. I'm just saying, we need to keep our focus Rob." I was trying to nip this in the bud.

My sister and I were supposed to be a team. I felt this was really a great time and opportunity for us to make big, do something together and together take care of our family. She was truly frustrating me.

Robert just sat there, attentively listening. I was glad he wasn't trying to be in denial of their actions that had a look of deceit. I wanted him to understand clearly how things were looking and that it wasn't right. I went on to ask him, *"As my friend and out of respect for Craig, put some distance between y'all Robert. That's all I'm asking?"* I knew this was easy for me to ask of him more so then the task itself of him not talking to Ce-Ce, but I also knew what Ce-Ce wants, Ce-Ce gets.

Craig was on the road with the team during the confrontation I had with Ce-Ce. I wondered if he knew his wife was driving back and forth from Milwaukee to Chicago, spending her time, secretly, with Robert. If he did, what were they up to? I just couldn't understand why they were not communicating with me. These were the kinds of things that got under my skin and irked me the most. I hated betrayal. My heart told me that they were up to something foul in nature, something that threatened to destroy the whole thing.

I decided to ask Robert if he thought Craig knew that Ce-Ce was traveling back and forth. He said he didn't know. He said, whenever he talked to Craig, he never mentioned anything about Ce-Ce. Robert seemed stressed so he stood up. *"Man, I just want to focus on this album. Ce-Ce is a cool person, and she's fun, but I just want to finish this album Johnny man."* I didn't want to pressure him anymore; I just hoped that he got the message. I just hoped he was being truthful and that there was nothing going on between him and Ce-Ce.

I stood up and put my arm on his shoulder and then told him, *"Let's go do that then. Let's go finish this album."* When we went back inside the studio, he went straight to the drum machine and began to lay down a beat to a new song. Robert didn't talk while he worked. His focus took him into another zone. It was amazing to watch him and to be there when his songs materialized. He wrote what he was living, and when it was a finished product, you saw a glimpse of his heart. That night, he wrote a song called "I Can't Wait."

As Robert stood in the recording booth singing the lyrics to that song, I thought about Ce-Ce. I thought about how much I loved her and about how much I really wanted us to get along. As I looked at Robert and thought about her, I got sad. I was caught between a rock and a hard place. I didn't want to push Ce-Ce away because family was important to me, and she was family. I always felt, if a person has nothing worth dying for, then he has nothing worth living for. Family to me is all that. My life is dedicated to the prosperity of my family. I watched Robert in that booth, and I thought to myself, I would make a determined effort to get to the heart of my sister; we needed to be on the same accord.

As the days and weeks went on, Robert and I stayed in the studio. Working with the band and performing shows were no longer on our schedule. We attended one, maybe two rehearsals after Robert's last no show. There was no money coming in for any of us, but I felt Craig and Ce-Ce were seeing to it that Robert had money in his pocket even though they thought that no one knew. Ce-Ce even started getting close to Robert's family and spending time at his house with his mother. Ce-Ce was like a Delilah, you know, the woman who seduced and fooled Samson. She and her cunning ways were moving in.

It became more and more visible that Ce-Ce and Robert were spending a lot of quality time together. People were starting to talk and rumors of them having an affair were going around throughout his and my family. Whenever Ce-Ce and I were together, I had to really humble myself to prevent an argument. We weren't functioning as a team growing together. We were shutting down. The forces of negativity were coming from all directions like termites tearing our house down. Things were ugly!

The band was totally frustrated and after a few more weeks of cancellations, the band decided to break up. They were upset and disappointed in how things turned out. They regretted the fact that they gave their time and did not feel that they were included in any of the plans being made. None of them felt that Robert looked at them as a part of his group. They felt that he was on a personal mission and not considerate of what anyone else was going through. They all wished him well but did not feel that there was a place for them in his vision.

Chuck, at the same time, was upset with the way Craig and Ce-Ce were going all around him to get to Robert. He also felt that Robert was no longer communicating with him as they had in the past and began to regret the decision to get involved with Craig. Things were going in an entirely different direction than I wanted.

Both Chuck and I were upset over the band breaking up. What should have been the building of a great corporation—the Dow Jones was collapsing. Disrespect was an understatement for the way Craig and Ce-Ce were making moves with Rob without consulting Chuck. He asked one day, *"Demetrius, what are they trying to do, or what is it that I am not doing?"* I sympathized with Chuck and simply told him I didn't know and that I felt just like he did. I didn't know which direction we were going in anymore.

"Demetrius, I'm trying to do things the right way, but it's not working out. Craig and Ce-Ce don't show me any respect as Rob's manager. And Robert, I don't even know him anymore." Chuck said while we were sitting at the bar in the Chatham Bowl. The two of us were meeting this particular day.

Chuck was not his usual up-spirited-self. He had a disappointing look of frustration on his face. I think Chuck was hoping Robert had his back. He looked like he was feeling that he was alone.

Before leaving Chuck told me that he was going to call Craig to schedule a meeting. He said he couldn't tolerate the way things were going any longer. Hearing this made me excited all over again. Things hadn't been going as smoothly as I thought they would, but hearing Chuck talk about having a meeting just somehow sounded right to me. We were about to stir up a fight! Two days later, Chuck called me on a conference call with Craig on the other line. Craig asked me if I would ask my mother if we could meet at her house Sunday while she was at church.

He said that he would be in Chicago already and that he would be staying with his mother and would drive to our house from there. The meeting was scheduled for that upcoming Sunday at 9:30a.m. The timing was especially good for me because things had been going wacky. It was time to organize and put things back on course.

Sunday came and everybody showed up on time. I picked Robert up at 8:00 a.m. When we arrived at my mother's house, Craig and Ce-Ce pulled up behind us. They brought coffee and donuts. Chuck pulled up a few minutes later. He brought some orange juice and some donuts too. We all gathered at the table in the kitchen. The first order of business, according to Craig, was to continue conversations with Chuck regarding his contract with Robert. After Chuck heard Craig out, he, being the cool collected guy he was, told him *"I'm not here for that Craig. It was already established that we were to get with our attorneys to draw up a new contract that would be satisfactory for all of us. Now if you have a contract for me to look over, then yes, I'd like to read it. Other than that, I would like to focus on the things that have been happening since you and your wife came into this with us Craig."*

Rob and I looked at each other. Rob had a silly grin on his face, but we both knew that Chuck was there for business. Chuck had a look on his face that said he was in a no-nonsense frame of mind. He went on to say, *"Every time I call Robert now, he's never available. He's always somewhere with you guys doing something for either you or your wife. I have had to cancel shows in which I think Robert should've done. Whenever I had the chance to talk to him about them, he would tell me that you and your wife don't feel that he should be doing shows; and that's a decision I should be discussing with him. Or you guy's should be discussing with me."*

Craig spoke up, interrupting Chuck's flow. *"That's right, Chuck. We don't feel the young brother should be doing shows. He should be recording."*

Craig was about to continue to say more, but Chuck replied aggressively, *"And that's my point Craig! He can do that. He can record, and he can entertain. But you guys don't talk to me. And that is something you guys should be doing; You should be talking to me about Robert. I am his manager. You guys aren't showing me any respect. It has been four or five months since we first met and not once have you or your wife called me to talk to me about anything concerning Robert. You two have been doing whatever you have wanted to do. It's time now that you and your wife, Craig, collaborate with me concerning anything with Robert. I am his manager, and I will be respected as his manager. Or we will stop our association with you as of today. I will not be disrespected by you or your wife any longer."* Chuck said with his brown skinned face turning a shiny bronze color showing he was frustrated and serious. This was strong language coming from Chuck.

Craig wasn't hearing Chuck at all it seemed, because Craig went on into something else designed to arouse confrontation. *"That's what I'm talking about. The brother shouldn't have to be in a situation like this where people who want to assist him have to go through somebody else to get to him. This is exactly why this young brother doesn't need to be in no contract,"* Craig said. Craig was looking at me as if I agreed with him. I didn't!

Chuck shook his head and asked Craig, *"Can Jerry Krause just come and pick you up Craig? Wine and dine you, tell you what you should or should not be doing for your team? No he can't,"* Chuck said, answering his own question. *"Why, because it's disrespect, a violation of NBA rules,"* Chuck said, again answering his own question.

"This brother is not on an NBA level," Craig said, with a bit of confidence as if he had made a point of something.

Chuck jumped in again, taking the conversation back, to our first meeting. He assumed after our first meeting we were going to be working together as a team and forming a partnership. *"All I am detecting now from you, Craig, is malice. The only communication going on has been between you and your wife, and you have brought chaos into our circle from the very beginning."* Chuck kept his business like attitude while holding nothing back. He was expressing exactly how he felt. His tone was not of anger but of disappointment. He made an appeal to Craig to bring understanding and order within our organization. In my opinion he was right in his observation of how disgruntled things had gotten the more involved Craig and Ce-Ce was with Robert.

Chuck was in rare form, adding, *"Robert should be working right now, entertaining people, enjoying his youth, getting to know how to deal with people and preparing himself for a celebrity life. Everybody that has made sacrifices should be working right now, building as we go."* I nodded my head in agreement. I didn't know what was wrong with Craig. He was just objecting to everything and didn't seem to have a clue that he needed to come aboard to work with us and not against us.

Craig was acting as if he was a prosecuting attorney; he was playing the devil's advocate. Everything he was speaking about regarding Robert was directed in the opposite direction of where we were trying to go. Then he proceeded to let some more dumb shit come out his mouth. *"We should be backing Robert up by making sure he is comfortable enough to create his music and not focus on how we can make money off of him. Everybody that considers themselves working for this brother should get a job and not be looking at him as a meal ticket."* When he said that, it had to have struck a nerve in Chuck because he got angry.

Robert and I just looked at each other. I had never seen Chuck angry. He was always smooth and in control, but the look on his face turned sinister. The old South Side Gangster Disciple looked as if he wanted to make his presence felt. You could see the frustration in Chuck begin to boil over as he stood up. He looked Craig up and down with a look of disgust. Craig looked a little worried. *"How dare you! Who do you think you are?"* Chuck asked. Things were getting heated.

Chuck looked at the rest of us at the table and then calmed down. He leaned over on the table to regain his composure. He shook his head and continued in a calm tone. *"You know what Craig? I don't need you to tell me I need a job. I have a job. Managing Robert is another job—A very stressful job since you became a part of it. I don't need you, and I don't need your money. How dare you insult me indicating I see Robert as a meal ticket! If Robert has doubts about my loyalty to him, then we don't have the relationship I thought we had."*

It was obvious Craig was not going to reconcile and be on the same page with us. *"If you had love for the brother, you wouldn't be trying to hold him back with this contract you have him in. That ain't love,"* Craig said. I thought to myself, *"What the hell was he trying to prove?"* The intensity of the meeting was flowing in another direction than where it should have been going. The whole time Robert sat still, saying nothing at all even though the topic was all about him.

Chuck was right. We should have been at this meeting reading over a new contract or signing a new deal. Most certainly we should have been meeting over something that was joining us together, not separating us. We should have been turning the page of progress. Yet here we were; instead of progressing, we were regressing. I decided to step in at that point. I stood up. *"Hold on y'all; we need to gather ourselves and focus on getting this thing right. Chuck is the manager. Maybe we need to work more closely with him,"* I suggested. While I was talking, Chuck settled himself down and began taking papers out of his briefcase as well as writing something on a blank sheet of paper.

Chuck interrupted me as I was speaking and turned to Robert. *"Robert, I would never do anything to hurt you or hold you back, but as of today I won't work with Craig or his wife, and if you insist on doing so, then I resign as your manager. I'm leaving now, are you coming with me?"* he asked Robert. *"Man, Chuck we don't need to do this,"* Robert said. Chuck then handed Robert a piece of paper. *"This is a release freeing you of any contractual obligations you have with me. I cannot and will not work with them,"* Chuck said.

When Robert didn't respond Chuck began putting his papers back into his briefcase. It was a sad moment. Robert asked Chuck to hold on, and told him he was just upset, suggesting to Chuck that we should work it out, but Chuck was serious. We just sat there and watched him while he finished stuffing all those papers back into his black briefcase.

Once he was done he walked over to me, reached out to shake my hand, and cautioned me to take care of Robert. He said he knew my heart was with Robert. *"Hold on Chuck, we can work this out,"* I said. But he waved me off. *"I don't want to do this anymore. I thought this was going to be a better situation for us Johnny and I know you meant well but I can't do this with them".* Chuck said, pointing and waving at Craig and Ce-Ce. *"Chuck, this ain't the way to do this man"* I said.

I wanted to make sure that I was showing compassion, but I didn't want Chuck to do what he was doing. At this point he was compromising of what we were trying to do. I knew what he was feeling and I was on his side, but Chuck was not paying any attention to me. He was hurt, but he stood strong. He had laid his cards on the table, and I felt he needed to know where Robert's loyalty lied. Robert didn't have any loyalty for him; he didn't even respond at all.

When Chuck was done putting his papers into his briefcase, he closed it and made his way to the front door. As he was walking Robert motioned and whispered to me, *"Johnny go talk to him!"* Chuck was already out the front door. When I got outside his car was pulling off. *"Chuck,"* I yelled to him, but he didn't stop. I stood there for a moment before going back into the house. I didn't feel good about this at all. At one point we were all in a perfect situation feeling that we were all put together to be a blessing to one another. Now within a matter of months, the dream was beginning to turn into a nightmare. This was not supposed to be happening. I was saddened.

When I went back in the house everyone was still sitting at the table. I glanced around at the faces and knew I was alone now that Chuck was gone. I believed that Chuck was good for Robert and he was good for the team, but as Robert said-he made his decision, and we just sat there and accepted it.

Craig was sitting at the table looking over the release Chuck signed. After reviewing it, he stood up and walked away from the table. *"Well, black man, you're free,"* he said smiling at Robert. Surprisingly Ce-Ce sat through the whole meeting and didn't say a word, but after Craig told Robert he was free, she told Craig that he should have an attorney look at the release and make sure it was binding. I felt that they had this planned from the beginning. It was obvious that their plan worked.

"Where do we go from here y'all?" I asked. *"We continue in the studio,"* Craig said. *"When Robert's done we'll shop the demo"* he said sarcastically, as if *"oh well it's done. Next!"* Nobody said anything about Chuck after he left or about him leaving. It was as if he was never there. It was obvious Chuck's quitting was cool with everyone.

On the way to take Robert home I asked him what he thought about Chuck resigning. He said Chuck made a decision for himself and all he wanted to do was finish his album. He didn't want to talk about what had transpired. We rode the rest of the way to his house listening to his songs. That's how Robert dealt with things he didn't want to face. He would hide behind his music. He didn't seem to have any compassion regarding Chuck's departure. Where was his loyalty to Chuck?

Since the band broke up and Chuck resigned, we spent more time in the studio. The tracks Robert laid down were good, and we were confident that if his music were put in the right hands, a deal would be on the table. Being in the studio was all there was to do. We worked from six in the evening until three or four in the morning.

After leaving the studio, we would go to White Castle's Restaurant on Seventy-ninth and Stony Island and order a bunch of gas burgers. We would sit in the parking lot, eat and listen to the songs he did. It would be six-thirty in the morning by the time I would get home.

I didn't know what direction we were headed now. Robert was in Craig and Ce-Ce's hands, and they were in power since they had the money. I was broke and I felt with Craig and Ce-Ce helping Robert out with his financial situation he would be ok. Well the truth of the matter was that Chuck was gone due to foolishness and selfishness, the band was broken up due to the same reason. Robert and I were still together and at my position I needed to stay tight with him in order for this to work for me.

CHAPTER 5

Deception

HE 1984-85 NBA Playoffs were about to begin, and Craig arranged for Robert to sing the National Anthem at one of the Buck's home games televised on national television. This was big for Robert. I knew how good he was. For him to sing in front of a crowd of forty-five thousand people or more, I knew that his name was going to be remembered in the State of Wisconsin and buzzed around the country from that day forward. I knew that Robert was going to sing the National Anthem unlike anyone else's version of the song. The way he would sing that song would be a part of the games conversation not only by the fans, but by the players and the commentators as well.

We arrived in Milwaukee Friday afternoon. We wanted to get there early so that we could go to the practice facility and shoot around with the players. Once we left the gym, Craig took us to eat. At that time he informed us of how the team was looking forward to Robert performing at the game. But, but I don't think any of them were more excited about him performing than I was.

Later that evening Ce-Ce decided to take Robert to the mall to buy him something to wear for the event. Craig had a team meeting he had to attend, so I stayed at the house and watched my nephews. When she returned I had to go out to the car to help them with all of the bags they had. She took Robert on a makeover shopping spree; she bought him a suit, shirt, tie, shoes, the works. Not only was he going to impress everyone with his singing, he was going to make a fashion statement as well. Robert said that he had never worn a suit before. He was going to be GQ material for this event, that's for sure. This was his Christmas. We were especially surprised when Craig came home carrying a new keyboard. Right away Robert got on it and began to get familiar with it. While doing so, he came up with a new song.

Later that evening Robert became ill; he came down with a fever, a touch of the flu we had all assumed. Ce-Ce made him some tea and gave him Tylenol, and then he went to bed. He coughed in his sleep all through the night. When he woke up the next morning, he wasn't feeling any better. Ce-Ce wanted to take him to the doctor, but Robert didn't want to go. He said all he needed was some rest. His day started off with breakfast in bed, more Tylenol, and plenty of juice throughout the day. It was questionable if he would be well enough to perform.

On the evening of the event Robert gathered enough strength to get up and to get dressed. He was looking sharp, but he also looked sick. When asked how he felt, he told us that he had chills and his body was shaking, but he would be able to sing. We left for the arena about 5:30 that evening.

We made it to the arena, but Robert was shaking all the way there. The heat in the car was on full blast because he kept complaining that he was cold. Once we were seated Ce-Ce asked me to sit with my nephews while she took Robert to the hospitality room to meet the coordinator so that they could show him which location on the court he would perform. When Ce-Ce came back to the seats she told me that once Robert got to the room he got very dizzy. She said they had to call the team doctor and the doctor recommended he cancel his performance and be taken back home. He was sitting in the back waiting for her to take him to the house. Now we were all worried. I had never seen him that sick before. It was decided that Ce-Ce would take Robert back to her house, and I didn't want to leave so I volunteered to stay at the games with my nephews; afterwards, we road back to the house with Craig.

Robert stayed in the bed the whole weekend, and all Ce-Ce and Craig talked about was how Robert didn't need to be obligated in any kind of a contract. I asked Craig how he was going to be reimbursed for his investment for the equipment and all of Robert's studio time. He told me that once the brother got a deal, he was confident that Robert would pay him back. He said we had to be able to trust each other before we could work together.

After the All-Star Weekend Robert and I drove back to Chicago. He was feeling a little better. However, he was a little down in spirit because he wasn't able to sing at the game. He said he had never been that sick before. I made small jokes about him having the cooties from the private nurse he had, Ce-Ce. He said they were friends and admitted that at first he was very nervous whenever he was around her, but now he was a bit more relaxed in her presence and did enjoy her company. When we got back, I dropped him off at his mother's house and from there I went home.

That same evening, Robert called me, said he was feeling better, and asked if I could pick him up the following morning to work the subways with him. The next morning Robert and I resumed back to our normal program in the subway and then to the studio. I didn't mind working with Robert in the subway; the only problem was that things were tight for me financially and I was only making enough for gas money.

Over the next few weeks we spent less time in the studio and more time hanging out with the crew: Larry, Torrey, Mouse, Jim, and Dewayne. We would meet up with them on the basketball court on Thirty-Third Street in Hyde Park. We would play a few games and then end up at McDonald's. All of us were believing in Robert for the potential of talent he had, and we all felt fortunate to be in the position we were in to be on board when that big deal came along. We believed that the album Rob produced was just as good, if not better, than the tunes we were listening to every day on the radio.

We spent a lot of our free time hanging out at the Hyde Park movie theater. On the weekends we would go to different parks and I would arrange for Robert to sing, or we would have people play his demo. Mostly everywhere we went people wanted copies, but we weren't in the market to sell. We wanted to be on the radio first and then sell tapes. We wanted to build the anticipation of his upcoming album so we promoted his demo every time he had a live performance.

We were grooming ourselves for the jobs we were assigned to do. I believe those positions fit the character of our lives. Larry acted as Robert's personal security, Torrey would dress him and always made sure he had extra clothes for Robert, he would even have us take off our own clothes at times if he needed Robert to have a certain look, Dewayne was Robert's personal barber, and me, I was his personal assistant and acting manager. I made sure that everyone was on point and at the same time, we all were looking at the same picture of success. I was making all of the arrangements for any event that came up. I was the one that was making things happen, keeping Robert busy and in the spotlight. I created a job for everyone working with Robert. I wanted to make that dream come true.

We were all making a sacrifice because we all believed in what we were doing and that it was going to pay off for us in the near future. I think we all felt it was natural for it to all work out for us. Besides, we called ourselves family, and that's what family does for each other; they take care of one another. We were a personable crew of people geared towards getting the job done. Everybody liked us all and complimented us individually for a job well done.

Everything seemed to be heading in the right direction. The only problem that we had was the fact that Ce-Ce would always find her way to Chicago, showing up wherever we were. She had no problem with making an appearance and getting in the mix of the guys hanging out. I tried very hard to conceal the fact that I was uncomfortable with her presence. Only because whatever her business was, it never seemed to have anything to do with what we had going on. She was never in agreement with anything we were doing, and all we were doing was working to see to it that what we were building was not jeopardized or destroyed in any way, but Ce-Ce was definitely a liability when it came to that.

I felt like her appearances around us should have been to check and see how she could assist me with Robert. But no, Ce-Ce had one agenda on her mind, and that was having things her way. Everywhere Ce-Ce and I went, the crew could see and feel the negativity that existed between us. It was weird. We had different opinions about everything, and I felt she was against everything I wanted to do and objected to anything I had to say. All I wanted to do was keep busy, have fun, and make some honest money at the same time. Where was I going wrong?

Her anger with me seemed to intensify. We didn't see eye to eye on anything. This experience gave life to the saying *"Cum is thicker than blood."* Whatever Ce-Ce and Robert had going on, it was driving a rift between us.

Robert already made it clear to her that he was not ready to sign any type of binding contract with anyone. Nonetheless, it didn't stop Ce-Ce from coming around, picking Robert up and taking him places. Apparently, they had some unfinished business that had nothing to do with anyone but them. I wondered if whatever her business was with Robert, Craig knew of it as well. When the guys and I were together waiting on Robert and he was nowhere to be found, we knew they would be together. I always felt that Ce-Ce should have communicated with me and maybe we could have made things turnout better than they did. I needed her, but her actions made it was apparent that she didn't need me. Plain and simple, her goal was to gain access to Robert, and that is what she did.

Once we were finished mixing the songs, our time in the studio with Bruce ended. Craig called me a week or so later and asked me to ride with him to go and pay Bruce. I was at my mother's house, so I had him pick me up there. As we rode, we listened to Robert's music, and we both agreed that we had some quality material to work with. Craig liked Robert a lot, but there was something on his mind that day. I could tell something was bothering him. I had this feeling that this something had everything to do with his wife.

At some point during the ride, he turned the volume down on the stereo. *"Johnny, what is going on with you and your sister? Every time y'all around each other, it's an uncomfortable place to be. How we gone work together if you two can't get along?"* he asked me. Craig continued to share his thoughts and he wouldn't give me a chance to speak; he just kept talking. *"I mean, I'm hearing some way out things man about Ce-Ce and Robert, but what I do not understand is the two of y'all not getting along. What's happening with that?"* he asked, finally giving me a chance to speak.

Craig had a real puzzled look on his face, the kind that said he was sincere. I knew right then that he had no idea his wife had been traveling back and forth from Milwaukee to Chicago spending time with Robert, and I was not going to be the one to make it known to him. So in answering his questions, I told him, *"Ce-Ce is always calling me asking questions about what I am doing with Robert. She thinks he shouldn't be in the subway and that I shouldn't have him in the streets singing to everybody. I don't want to answer her questions, so she gets mad at me. And you know Ce-Ce Craig, she gets to cursing at me and then when I tell her to find her some business she'll hang up and then when we see each other, she holds a grudge."* I was lying with a straight face. Yes, I was lying to this man, but how else do you avoid telling a man that you think his wife is having an affair. I couldn't, so I continued my assault of words that turned into one big lie.

Craig started to laugh because he knew I was describing his wife and her ways to a tee. Ce-Ce was a real firecracker. He knew he had married a little feisty one. I went on to tell him how everything had changed from the vision we had in the beginning. *"With the way you and Ce-Ce are in Robert's ear about not doing shows broke up the band, and Chuck is no longer a part of it. Now Robert is not obligated to anybody or anything. The only money I make is the handouts I get from you. Craig we need to get this thing rolling, man. I can't make it like this."* Craig told me I needed to get me a job.

I smiled and shook my head and wondered what Craig had learned in college. He was a wise man, but couldn't read signs right in front of his face. His wife was too involved with this thing, but Craig couldn't see it. Maybe it was his career or his trust in her. He kept her on a pedestal. She could do no wrong in his eyes. Whatever it was, he had his blinders on and I actually felt sorry for the man.

When Robert was in the studio and needed something, I was the one who got it done. When there were places Craig wanted Robert to be, I was the one everyone would call on to make sure that Robert would be there. When he wanted him in Milwaukee to sing for his friends, I was the one that he would call to get Robert up there. When we worked in the subways, Craig was the one who told me to make sure that I was with him to look out for him. So I told Craig, *"Working with Robert is a job."* It was the truth, but how many people paid attention to that truth?

We finally made it to Bruce's house. When we went in, Bruce was doing his normal thing, smoking a fat joint, so Craig and I joined him. We talked a little about how good we thought Robert's music was. Craig gave Bruce a check, and we were on our way back to my house. We were a little bit buzzed, so as we rode we just listened to the music. When we got to my house Craig handed me two one hundred dollar bills, and as I was getting out of the car, I thanked him. He said, *"Don't worry bro, we gone get blood's music on the radio."* He was bobbing his head to Robert's music that played as I closed the door of his car. I stood there for a moment and watched the car pull away from the curb. I was happy for Robert's emerging success, but where was my own life heading? I seriously didn't know anymore.

As the months went on, Robert and I began to go back to the old school way to make money. We didn't have a choice because Craig was getting ready for the NBA Playoffs. Nothing was going to go on with shopping the tape until the season was over, according to Craig. We were back to hanging out singing wherever I could get him a gig. We would ride through parks, and as people were having picnics or there was a big gathering going on, I would set Robert up with his portable piano, and he would do his standard routine and entertain people for whatever they would put into our bag.

Regardless of what Ce-Ce or anyone else would say, we were having fun hanging out making money like that. Sometimes the crew would hang out with us, which was really a blast, but most of the time it was just the two of us. We went all over, and it kept us busy. I learned a lot about dealing with people one on one, when representing Robert. He sang at parks, hotels, subways, and all over the city of Chicago.

The playoffs were over for the Milwaukee Bucks. Finally, Robert and I figured Craig would be free to shop the demo. We had fourteen songs on the tape, and we felt that every one of them were hits. I wanted Craig to put copies in the hands of the influential people that he was in contact with. I felt confident that if he could put me in front of any of the top executives in the business, I could get Robert a deal. I just needed Craig to get me in. The moment was right, and the time was now.

There was still one area I wanted to familiarize myself with before we really got things rolling; I wanted Craig to put Robert under a contract. It was business, and it was time to start thinking that way. I knew that once we met with someone and they decided to deal with Robert, the first thing they were going to want to do is put Robert under a contract. Again, that was business, and it was time for us to start thinking that way. When I brought this to Craig's attention again, he didn't want to do it. He said he couldn't see the brother being tied down. I won't say he was stupid, but I will say he was a man with no business sense.

I couldn't understand that part about Craig at all. As I saw it, we would have been tied in with Robert, and to be tied to a goose who laid golden eggs to me was a no brainer! At this point I was even open to the idea of Ce-Ce managing him. Unfortunately, I knew Robert was not with that. Craig and Ce-Ce messed Robert's head up when it came to a contract; with them at least. Robert was not an altogether stupid person. "Why pay for something when you can get it for free?" That is how I felt his relationship was with Craig and Ce-Ce.

I wanted us to sign him and have it all in the family. I saw our team as big business that could open doors and opportunities for our entire family, as well as for other people, but I couldn't get Craig and Ce-Ce to work with me to see things my way. They had their own agenda, and though I was viewed in Robert's eyes as his main man, I don't think they knew how I was going to fit into their plan.

Two weeks had passed since the last time I had spoken to Craig or Robert; The last time Craig and I talked he told me he was going on vacation. Ce-Ce and I weren't talking at all. She told me on one occasion, *"Die motherfucker."* She hated me, and it really hurt because she was my sister and I loved her more than anything in the world. I was seeing a part of Ce-Ce I never could have imagined. I loved her, but she was pushing me away from her. My other family members were concerned about Ce-Ce's actions as well.

To make matters worse, my youngest sister told me that on several occasions Craig was making trips to Chicago to pick Robert up and take him back to Milwaukee to hang out there with him. I could only guess their motive was to build a stronger relationship with him before they went on vacation. It hurt when I heard that they were going behind my back and not keeping me in the loop when it came to Robert. I would wonder why I was being left out. I was upfront and honest with people. I couldn't understand why things weren't going smoothly and why they weren't supporting me to make things happen for Robert. Wasn't I the one that brought Robert to them for their support? I didn't bring him to them for them to make all the decisions for me.

My association with Robert was solely because we were in the same business, and I knew what I was doing. I wondered, shouldn't I have been the one being motivated and pushed to take my business to the next level since financial support was what I went to my family for? Shouldn't I have been the one being supported? Why do people feel like they could take from you and disregard you as if you're not important? Why are people not considerate of your feelings? I was angry and totally disappointed with Craig. They were taking advantage of me because I was family. Because of that, I felt that they overlooked the thug in me. Little did they know, they were knocking on the thug's door?

I was tired. I was tired of being broke, tired of feuding with Ce-Ce, and tired of them treating me as if I didn't matter at all. I knew that Craig was going on vacation, so I figured that while they were gone, it would be a good time for me to get with Robert and see where his head was regarding my position. I was ready to call it quits at this point and I knew it was time for me to start looking out for myself and stop being a nice guy. I made up my mind that once Craig and my sister were gone, I was going to contact Robert. To my surprise—on the day they left, I got a call from Craig while he and Ce-Ce were at the airport waiting for their flight to depart.

I thought it was strange to hear from him, but nonetheless, I was glad. Craig was beating around the bush with what he wanted to tell me. *"Johnny, we're about to leave. We wanna straighten out everything when we get back. You, me, Robert, and Ce-Ce, we're going to all sit down when we get back and get this thing in order. Is that cool?"* he asked. I was like *"Cool man, I'm going to get with Robert while y'all gone and see where his head's at."* Again, there I was being loyal my whole objective was for the one purpose of making it happen for the whole crew. Then he said, *"Robert's at the house. You can go up there with him."* I replied "What house?" *"He's in Milwaukee. I wanted to talk to him before I left and decided to let y'all keep the place and give y'all some getaway time too,"* he said. *"Can you go up there with him for me? I know things don't look right, but can you go up there with him for me?"* he kept asking. I told him that I would and wished them a safe flight.

After I hung up the phone with him I was mad. My feelings were hurt. I even felt betrayed by Robert. He shouldn't have wanted to go to Milwaukee without me. Where did his loyalty lie? He was supposed to be my boy. What kind of scheme did he have on his mind? It was clear something was up, but what? Ever since I brought Robert to these people, my so-called family, they were keeping things from me. I didn't know who to trust.

Nobody seemed to be playing fair with me. I was giving my heart and my time but wasn't making any money. I felt alone and unappreciated. Robert was playing both sides and only looking out for himself. Even at this early stage in the game, he was being manipulative. As I thought about it, this wasn't the first time I felt he was not true to the game when it came to showing where his loyalty lied. All kinds of things were going through my head. I felt I was being used as a pawn. Then I thought, *"Maybe I'm just being paranoid. After all, Robert was just eighteen years old. This was all new to him too. This was my boy, my protégé, and right now he needed me. Let me get on up there to Milwaukee,"* I concluded. Soft ass me; believing in things as though they were, was a belief I had all my life. I wanted to be positive and believe things would work out. There was just too much to win to give up without a fight. My heart's desire was to pull all this together. True enough, I was a bit overboard with my devotion, but in my heart I believed in loyalty. Robert was that brother I bonded with that I never had.

After contemplating things over in my head, I decided to call Robert. He answered.

"What's up, Robert?" I asked. *"Johnny,"* he said, *"I was just about to call you."*

I didn't beat around the bush or pretend as if I didn't know anything. *"What's happening with you man? Y'all got me messed up in the head dude. I'm wondering why you up there without me and why I didn't even know you was up there. This shit's crazy man,"* I said to him. *"I know man. Craig came and got me last night. I didn't even know he was coming. I didn't know until we hit the highway that he wasn't coming to get you,"* Robert said. He then told me that when he asked Craig about me, he said he was going to call me and get me to come up there after they left because he didn't want me and Ce-Ce to get into it before they left for their vacation.

It made sense because it was obvious for all to see that Ce-Ce and I were not getting along. Nonetheless, I still felt that Craig should have made it known to me instead of just coming to Chicago, picking Robert up, and riding right past me without saying a word. He didn't show me any consideration at all. And because of that, ill feelings began stirring up inside of me. I didn't know who to trust and I didn't know who was keeping it real. I felt as if they were trying to cut me out of the equation. Robert was not just a cash cow to me as he was to others; he was my friend.

In the back of my mind, I also knew that Robert needed me in Milwaukee with him. He was in Northridge, Wisconsin, which is the suburbs of Milwaukee; twenty-five minutes northwest of the city. The Northridge Mall was about a mile away from the house where Robert was staying. The buses were on a schedule and probably didn't run on the weekends, so Robert was pretty much stuck in the house. He didn't know anyone and he wasn't a person to wander around a foreign place alone.

Yeah, my boy needed me, and I was going to have his back. Besides, there was always an adventure when Robert and I hung out together. I went to Milwaukee on the Greyhound bus and when I got there I caught a cab that took me straight to the house. Craig wired me $200 to make the trip. When I got to the house, it felt strange going into my sister's house and being welcomed by my friend as if I was visiting him at his relative's house. Nonetheless, it felt good to be in that big beautiful house knowing in my mind that for the time being, I had the freedom to come and go as if it was mine. My plan was to make the best of this uncomfortable situation.

Robert was glad to see me when I got there. The first thing I did was go into the garage to retrieve the keys to one of the cars; Craig had a Volvo and a 4Runner truck. I was ready to start my vacation the moment I got out of the cab. To our surprise, the keys were nowhere to be found. We were totally disappointed realizing that we didn't have any transportation, but Robert and I were used to making a way out of no way traveling all over the city of Chicago. We weren't going to let not having a car spoil what we could make happen as a team.

The next morning, we set out on a mission to make the best of what we had. We packed up the Casio piano that Robert brought with him and we went out and caught the bus to downtown Milwaukee. We didn't know there was no subway in Milwaukee, so we went to the mall and sat in a certain location and casually played as if we were just playing around on the keyboard. We didn't have a peddler's license to perform in the mall.

We had to play it cool; I would have Robert play when certain people would walk past. We attracted lots of attention in the mall, but we had to do what we did while moving around to different locations. We could not stay in one place because once a crowd would start to gather, the mall security was sure to follow. To avoid them, we had to keep it moving; we were just there to connect with some girls any way!

The batteries in the piano were low, and we needed some new ones. I didn't have much money, so I suggested to Robert to get the generic batteries for the time being, but he didn't want them. I told him that I was short on cash, but he told me that we could go half on the batteries. When we went to the counter to pay for the batteries, Robert tried to hide the wad of cash he pulled out of his pocket. I purposely looked at what he was doing when he went into his pocket. I said, *"Wow, boy, you loaded!"* He separated a few hundred-dollar bills to get to the ten-dollar bill he gave me for the batteries. When I looked at him, he looked as if he made a mistake in pulling out all of his money allowing me to see it. I didn't say anything else about it. I knew that Craig left him with some money.

Robert was being bought. It was obvious and sad at the same time. I was sad because I could see that I was being used. Craig was investing in Robert by making sure he had money in his pocket, yet Robert, knowing my financial situation, continued to allow me to invest the few dollars I had whenever he needed or wanted anything.

I started to think about the money I had already spent on the way to the mall; we stopped at McDonald's for breakfast and I paid for both of us. He did not say anything about having money. Deceiving me was becoming the thing to do, and it appeared like it was something that everyone I was involved with was doing. My thoughts changed when I noticed two white girls that had been following us around the mall.

Robert sang at three different locations, and they were at all three places. Now they were at Walgreen's just waiting up front at the entrance. I told Robert that they were there and that I was going to check them out while he paid for the batteries. I approached the two young ladies and found out that their names were Robin and Kelsey. After Robert finished paying for the batteries, we all walked around the mall together. I bought them ice cream as we sat and got acquainted.

Robert and I walked them to their car, and I gave Robin the phone number to Craig's house. She said she knew where Northridge was. Before leaving, Robert sang another song for them. After that Robin assured me that she would give me a call and said that she would try to come and see us. When they left, Robert and I went to the Waterfront which was on the lake, east of downtown Milwaukee. After Robert sang a few more songs it was time to make it back to the house because the buses didn't run all night.

Once we got back to the house, Robert kept getting on my case because I didn't get Robin and Kelsey's phone number. I told him that I believed that they would call us. Besides, I got numbers from several other girls, and I was confident that I would be able to talk one of them into coming over with a friend. It wasn't long after we got into the house when Robin called, said they were close by, and asked for directions to where we were staying.

I gave her directions on how to get to the house. I didn't say anything to Robert about the girls being on the way so when they arrived, Robert was surprised. When I let them in the door Robert whispered *"That's why you gone be with me boy, 'cause you the best."* He was just too happy. I just laughed. We went up to the den where Craig had his big-screen television and his stereo. We let them listen to the demo tape, and then Robert got on the piano and played them some songs. The girls thought that hearing him sing live was better. I did too because you could see that the people listening were feeling him.

As Robert was singing, Robin asked me to show her the rest of the house. I grabbed her by the hand, which she gave me so freely, and walked her around the balcony of the upstairs that overlooked the living room downstairs. We leaned on the rail as we listened to Robert play and sing in the other room. Robin's hair was as red as cooper, shiny and beautiful. I was totally attracted to her, so I began to run my fingers through her hair and telling her how much I liked her hair. She didn't stop me. In fact, she pulled a pin out of it that was holding her hair up, and her hair fell free. It was so long it fell down to the middle of her ass at its full length.

I then pulled her hair back and kissed her on the neck. She tilted her head to the side and moaned. Her white skin and the feel of her soft hair turned me on, and I had an immediate hard-on. I rubbed my hands down her body and squeezed her ass to see if she would reject me; she didn't. I then turned her around and kissed her softly on her pretty pink lips. I took her by the hand and led her down the stairs to the room where I was sleeping. Her willingness made me want her that much more.

I didn't know what Robert and Kelsey were doing. It was about 2:00a.m when they came knocking on the room door. The four of us spent the week together, going to the movies and hanging out. During that week, I thought that Robert and I had gotten closer. However, it was back to life, back to reality, the vacation was over. Craig and Ce-Ce returned.

When they walked through the door, old feelings resurfaced. It was obvious that Ce-Ce's feelings for me had not changed as well. When she walked past me she would look at me and roll her eyes. The only person she spoke to was Robert. Craig noticed it too and just shook his head. That whole night we had very little to say to each other. It was a very uncomfortable feeling to be there. I thought about going out to sleep in their car. I was in a hurry for the morning to come. Craig told me that he rented a car for us to drive back to Chicago, and the car would be delivered to me the next morning.

Other than me having a moment to talk to Craig, I stayed to myself that night. When I talked to Craig, I told him I would not be able to work with Robert as I had in the past because I couldn't afford it. I told him I was taking his advice and getting a job. It was impossible for me to survive living the way I was living. After we talked, I went back into the room I had been sleeping in for the week and my mind drifted back to Chicago and my living situation. *"How was I going to eat every day and pull myself out of the rut I was in?"* I drifted off to sleep. It hurt to think about tomorrow.

When the guy brought the rental car I was all packed and ready to go. Craig had gotten up early to go and play golf. When we left he wasn't there. My sister told us to drive safely and asked Robert to call her once he'd gotten home. It felt good to be behind the wheel of a new car. Being a dreamer, I felt this was where I should be in my life. I should be able to afford a car like this. Yet I was going back to Chicago broke with $60 in my pocket that Craig had given to me.

As Robert and I rode back, Robert just came out and told me that he did not like the way my sister treats me. He told me that he thought that she and Craig were wrong for the way they treat me. I was surprised to hear him say that. It made me feel like I was not alone. He then said, *"In a minute they gone be coming to your office cuz they gone have to go through you to get to me."*

"That's how I would like it to be," I told him. I looked at Robert. He had grown. He had come into his own. I could tell that he was beginning to experience a new degree of power within himself, recognizing a power that he could have over people.

"Robert you're growing up man. Listen to you, sounding like a wise man, foreseeing the future", I said to him.

As he bobbed his head to the sound of his music coming out of the car stereo, he said *"Don't worry about it, you gone be right there with me. But still, try to get along with your sister,"* I told him that I would.

As we drove my mind still would not let me escape the reality of my present living situation. I was thirty years old and didn't have a pot to piss in or a window to throw it out of. I felt that I should be somewhat better off in my life. I should have more to show for my hard work and loyalty. I was fair to people, loyal and dependable to say the least. Yet here I was, always the one that wasn't paid even though I put in the most work. It seemed like every time an opportunity came my way, someone else always seemed to come along and steal the good that I had coming in my direction. In the end, I felt like I would be the one suffering with the prospect of having to start all over again. I constantly reminded myself that GOD would not forsake me.

A lot was said on the ride home that day. Robert confirmed that he and I were a team and that we were joined together with the same goal. He said that he wholeheartedly needed me with him as his personal assistant as well as his closest friend. I was happy to hear him say that. With all that said, I became more relaxed in my position.

I started thinking; I have to do something for me once I got back to Chicago. I had to make some money for myself. I was tired of asking people for money. I was tired of the people who came into my life that had the means to help me, but didn't. I was tired of having people step in on my projects and change my ideas, but then try to take over because they couldn't humble themselves to let go and let me do things the way I saw fit. I felt that my life was going around in a circle and I was continually ending up in the same predicament—broke and starting all over again.

I had to do something fast, and the first thing that came to mind was going back to the West Side of Chicago where the streets were always beneficial to me. As we were driving and listening to Robert's demo tape, I turned the volume down on the stereo so Robert and I could talk business. I had to let him know that I now needed to do something for myself. I was riding with high hopes being on the team with him and I believed in the vision we shared. At that point in my life, I was hurting on the inside, and on the outside, I wasn't profiting from a damn thing.

I wasn't able to have a relationship with a woman because I wasn't able to offer her anything or take her anywhere. As I reflected on all of this I realized that I was thirty years old, for crying out loud, and still living with my momma. I made up my mind right then; I promised myself that I wasn't going to live like that anymore. I expressed this to Robert, and I told him that I would not be able to be with him in the subway every day because of my financial situation. I told him that I had to go and get a job. *"I need to break away for a minute Robert, so I can come up,"* I told him.

Robert told me that he needed me to hang with him and to give Craig a little more time. He believed that we would start having money. He made it sound good too, putting emphasis on the word "money." But by then, my mind was made up. I was no longer going to go along with what someone else said. From then on, I was going to focus on what they did. Action speaks louder than words and it seemed like no one was doing anything. When we had things happening, I made them happen. I was always making moves. While Robert was talking, I suddenly realized that he was naturally good with words, so I blocked what he was saying right out of my mind and began conceiving my own master plan.

I let him know that he could handle going in the subways alone if he had to, but if not, Larry was available. Larry was six feet and two inches, a smaller glasses wearing version of Suge Knight. His name was Larry Hood, but he carried himself like Larry Smooth, a levelheaded, laid-back, smooth brother. He was to be Robert's personal security. They had been friends since childhood. I was letting Robert know that it was time for the other friends to put in some voluntary time. He had too many hands waiting on him to be discovered. I told him to tell them it was time for them to lay some bricks. In other words, put in some work!

Besides Larry there was Torrey, Mouse, Dewayne, Jim Pratt's, Holland and Terrance Davis. These were his boys, and these cats loved Robert. I told him we needed to find out who was truly down with us anyway. In the end, I still knew I had to start looking out for me. No one else seemed to be concerned about how I was living. I took my foot off the accelerator and held it up to him and pointed to my shoes. He looked at them and laughed. We both laughed. My shoes were worn down with a big hole on the bottom where you could see my socks.

Robert looked at me with a serious, compassionate look and said he understood and that we'd make it through this rough period. *"Johnny! We gone look back on this day and laugh about it again,"* he said. And then he shouted, *"'Cause we gone be rich!"* I laughed along with him.

For me, the statement itself touched my feelings of hope. I think after our laugh, we both felt better. Tomorrow was going to be a whole new day. An ironic moment occurred as we rode and listened to Robert's music. The song Robert recorded called "Brighter Days" started to play. As that song played, I could do nothing but envision brighter days ahead. At this point in my life, I was going through a real storm.

CHAPTER 6

Tables of Judgment

WE GOT BACK to Chicago about 3:30 p.m., right ahead of the rush-hour traffic. We zoomed straight through the city to Robert's house. After I dropped him off, I went straight back to the Westside where it all started for me. The Westside of Chicago was my birth place and my old stomping grounds. There I learned most of what I knew. All that I grabbed hold of had sprang from that circle of influence-the Westside.

To some, the West Side was seen as a place of terror, mayhem, and murder. It was the home and the beginning of the gang world for black America. After all, the Vice Lord Nation received its birth from this place, but to others, it was just home. Along with all the bad and good, it was my home.

I grew up at 1322 S. Tripp Street. That's where I learned to ride my first bike, I met my first girlfriend, and where I got my first piece of cherry. I was the second oldest and my mother's firstborn son. My mother, Willie Mae (nicknamed Betty or Bet Jane, as my Uncle Bubble would call her) had a total of nine children, and she was a single parent, I might add. I lived on Tripp Street from birth until I was 13 years old.

Mama was overly protective when it came to her children. We hardly ever went outside. Franklin Park was a block up from where we lived right up on 14thStreet. That's where the West Side gangs crossed paths. There were four gangs: The 4 Corner Hustlers, The Egyptian Cobras, The Vice Lords and The Mad Black Souls (MBS). For that reason, Mama didn't want me going anywhere alone. The only time I got to go out really was when I went to spend the weekends at Uncle Bubba's house with my cousins, June-Bug and Nate.

June and Nate lived over on Thirteenth and Kolin Street, five blocks west of where we lived, but still right up the street from the park. They didn't have a problem going outside to hang out and would always come over to pick me up to get me out the house. We went all over, walked in every neighborhood. June-Bug was pretty well-known for fighting amongst us youngsters in the area where we lived. We called it "humbugging" back in the day. June-Bug was like a little Joe Frazier and was built like him too. We used to call June "Gorilla Man" because he resembled a little ape and would go ape shit crazy on your ass. His younger brother, Nate, was a bigger version of his brother, taller with a wider body. Nate was cool and big, and not anyone you would want to just pick on. My cousins were the brothers I didn't have as a child growing up and they were everything to me.

We were young and wild, but we had fun. We hustled many of the gang members. *"You got a quarter, Lil Ronnie?" "Byrd, can I get a quarter?"* All day we'd ask the older guys for quarters. Throughout the day, we had money for our sodas and popsicles. When they saw us coming, they would call us the quarter babies, and they'd give us our quarters. They liked us because we didn't back down and we were always willing to fight other little dudes that hung out as we did, if they asked us to.

Boxing was a natural thing for me. I was always eager to get down because my cousins and I wouldn't go outside unless we slapped each other around first. June and Nate taught me that if you could box, people wouldn't mess with you once you proved yourself. And if you could sing, *"then the girls gone be all over you,"* June would say. Singing and boxing were my second nature. I never started fights, and other than you offering me some money, it would take a lot to make me fight.

When it came to boxing, I was always considered fast. The thought of someone hitting me in my face kept me moving and sticking. I had gotten really good with my hands when I met AJ, everybody call him Ne-Nee. We met at the Albany skating rink on Roosevelt and Albany. That area was MBS territory. My cousins and I went skating every week. One night, after we left the rink, we went to a corner restaurant to get something to eat. I ordered a polish sausage, some fries and a Coke.

As we were leaving, one of the guys who were waiting in line behind us, picked me out and said that he wanted my polish sausage. *"What you want a dollar?"* I asked him? *"I could buy you one"* I told him.

I could look at the dude and tell he wanted to start something and I didn't want any trouble. I just wanted to enjoy my polish and go home with my cousins. I was only 12 years old going on 13. My cousin June was the same age as me except I was a few months older, and Nate he was 11. They were both bigger than me, but nonetheless, we were kids.

Demetrius Smith Sr.

I remember my cousins use to pick on me because I was what they called easy. They use to tell me, *"Don't you ever go to jail, cause they gone get you,"* and they would ball their fist with their elbows bent pumping their thighs in and out as if they were screwing; all the while laughing at me. It was at those times I would get mad at them and chase them trying to hit em for making fun of me.

Nonetheless, it didn't stop me from giving. They would tease me and say I gave people things because I was scared of them. That was not how I saw myself. I was just a nice guy and making friends I thought. The people I hung out with, if they needed something and I had it, I didn't have a problem with helping them out.

However, when it came to taking something from me, it was a matter of pride and character. My cousins strengthened me when it came to standing up for myself. After going a few rounds with June Bug I felt that I had the courage to fight anyone and the belief that I could beat anybody whom I fought.

When the older boy asked for my polish and I offered to buy him one, I wasn't punking out. I felt as if it were easier to buy him one and make a friend at the same time. I thought he would appreciate that, but he rejected my offer. *"I want the one you got,"* he said!

"Cuz, you ain't gotta buy him shit!" My cousin June Bug said, stepping in to defend me.

Then he and his friends grouped together as if they were going to make a move on my cousin. I could see Nate picking up a Coke bottle out of the corner of my eye. There was no doubt in my mind that he was going to straight go upside one of the boy's head if I had not extended my arm at him telling him to hold on. I asked June to hold my polish. I then pointed to the door and told the dude that wanted my polish, *"Let's step outside, cause the only way you gone get this, you gone have to take it!"* I told him.

The guy and his two friends looked at me and laughed; backing out of the door at the same time. The guy was a little taller than me, but for some reason, he didn't scare me. I went into my boxing stance. The dance was on. I began to bounce around on him like Muhammad Ali did his opponents. It was serious once it started. This kid was gone beat me up if he could. I began to call him out. *"Where you at boy, come on with it; cause I'm gone dog your ass",* I told him!

When the polish bandit threw his first punch, I ducked and like spring action I jack-knifed right up into him with a left jab that immediately closed his right eye. After I connected with the first punch I lit into his ass so fast he didn't get a chance to see me again. I kept dancing around him, punching him in his face.

There was a guy inside the restaurant watching the fight the entire time. He stepped in and grabbed me by one hand and held the other out towards Nate to keep him back while his partner stepped in and grabbed June. The guy that grabbed me yelled, *"Hold on, hold on, young demon!"* When he said that, Nate also stopped his pursuit of lighting his ass up with a soda bottle. The man who had grabbed me, reached into his pocket and handed me a ten-dollar bill and told me that I was too much for the older boy and asked me if I would let him go for $10.

I looked at my opponent. I had already hit him seven or eight time's in the face. His nose was bleeding and his eyes were closed. His boys didn't even get a chance to get into that fight because it was over so fast. I took the $10 from the guy. He told me that I had skills. Come to find out, his name was Ne-Nee, a nineteen-year-old amateur boxer. He took a liking to me after that fight and invited me to Archie Moore's gym on Pulaski where he trained.

When I got home after the weekend with my cousins, I told my mother about it. I was excited and asked her if I could go to the boxing gym and train with Ne-Ne, but she was totally against it. She didn't want me boxing. Once she said no I never asked her again. My cousins would come to get me out of the house. We would tell my mother we were going to the park. Twice a week I would meet Ne-Ne at Archie Moore's gym on 15th & Pulaski Road; walking distance from the house.

Shortly after I started boxing I quit. I had three fights. Of course I didn't tell my mother about any of them because that would have been a fight I had no chance of winning. My main concentration I kept in my mind when I put on those big boxing gloves was not to let anyone hit me in my face. I won the first two fights because I hit the other guys in my class with too many punches and they were ruled as knock outs.

The boy's I fought their mothers would be shooting out, *"That's enough hitting my baby,"* and the refs would stop the fight. But in the third fight I was hitting this young Mexican with a bunch of punches, and he just would not stop coming at me. I kept hearing his family shout, *"Go get him Ramon, Get him Ramon."* All the while his nose was bloody and I was thinking, why won't they stop the fight because I was beating him up, and I was getting tired of running around ducking the left roundhouse he kept throwing at me. He just kept coming at me, and they wouldn't stop the fight.

Demetrius Smith Sr.

Finally he hit me and I got dizzy. He kept hitting me. I started seeing people watching the fight moving around me in a circular motion. I saw Ramon, who I was fighting, coming back at me. He had broken away from the referee. I got scared. I don't know what happened. I looked around and all I saw was the corner stool. I grabbed it and held it up to club Ramon with it. He was not going to hit me again. Ne-Nee jumped into the ring yelling. *"Johnny boy, what are you doing?"* Ramon began to back up as Ne-Nee rushed in and grabbed me. He was laughing at me; I told him I didn't want to fight anymore, I was dizzy.

Everybody in the audience laughed. I didn't care. I wasn't getting ready to let that dude hit me again. I didn't feel it in me to just get beat up. It wasn't fair fighting when it came to hurting me or just trying to take something from me. After that fight, I didn't get back into the ring anymore. I was cool with that. Fighting wasn't for me. As I remember the only times I did fight were when someone tried to take something from me. It was at those times I didn't give a second thought to defending myself.

I was thirteen years old when we moved from our home on Tripp Street into the Cabrini Green projects at 1340 N Larrabee, on the fourth floor. It was there that I got stabbed on the left side of my face. My sister Dee-Dee and I were victims of robbery when my mom had sent us to the grocery store to get bread and milk.

On the way back home, this guy tried to rob us. I was carrying the bag and my sister had the money. She didn't have much; maybe $5 or$6 dollars at the most. The guy approached my sister; I guess he had watched us at the store to know she was the one who had the money. The guy was bigger and older than us. He had a piece of metal in his hand, not a knife or anything, just a little long piece of chrome metal. Like a piece off the door of a car.

When he attempted to put his hands on my sister I dropped the bag and began yelling at the dude *"Get your hands off my sister, man we ain't got no money!"* I was pushing him at the same time as I was yelling at him. He raised the piece of metal he had in his hand and swung it hard at me. I raised my arm to block it, but the metal piece bent when it hit my arm and the force of his swing caused the metal to cut me across the face. When he saw he had cut me, he ran.

I didn't really feel a thing, all I know was that there was a lot of blood coming out of my face and my sister was yelling and screaming. I didn't know how bad my face was messed up and I don't remember crying, but I do remember feeling sad. All I remember was my face had been split open.

I received eleven stitches. This incident left me with a lifelong scar under my eye on the left side of my face. I felt ugly for so many years and the image of the face of that guy is still stained in my mind.

After that incident, it wasn't long before we moved again. This time, we moved to the Henry Horner Projects at 2245 W Lake Street. Living in the projects was a different lifestyle. We stayed on the eleventh floor, which often times we had to walk up the stairs to get there.

The elevators were always broken and there was always drama in the projects. Each floor you traveled up or down, there were obstacles to overcome. You had to fight the boys on the ninth and tenth floors. Most of the time, I would take off running until I reached the first floor. It was really bad every month when we had to carry the groceries all the way upstairs. There was a group of guys I ran with in the projects and we had fun together. I learned a lot, especially how to steal. I learned that from Jeffrey, Harold, and Anthony. Jeffrey use to sew all kinds of pockets onto his coat, go into the store and when he would come out, he would have cartons of cigarettes, steaks, and whatever else wasn't nailed down.

Stealing was an adventure for us and hanging out with them was fun for me. I never got into any real trouble living in the Horner Projects, but Mom always wanted better for us, so once again we moved. This time we moved all the way out to the south suburbs, to Dixmoor, Illinois. I was seventeen when we moved out there. She had finally received her Section 8 government grant to move into her own first home. We were all excited. We moved out to where white people lived, and I went to Thornton Township High School in Harvey, Illinois.

I had never lived around white folks before, let alone sat next to them. I wanted to do well in this new environment. I even had thoughts of becoming a lawyer. However, things didn't work out for me in high school. I ended up being expelled for fighting this white kid for calling me a nigger. My mother sent me away to the Job Corps in Indianapolis, Indiana, where I completed Job Corps in seven months, receiving my GED in the process. Upon completion I returned to Harvey Illinois and got a job at Wyman Gordon Steel. After a year, I was told by my white foreman to get my black ass over to the heat treat department. I told him to fuck himself, and that was the end of that job.

I never felt that working in a factory was for me anyway. After I left Wyman & Gordon, I joined the Army and after a month, I got kicked out of there for fighting. I know I should have stayed in the boxing ring; maybe that was my true calling. When I got back home from there I began to hang out on the corner of 147th and Winchester Street, with my friend Carlos Landa. We stood on the corner during the day selling weed and at night we would be in the alley in back of his house selling weed and harmonizing. On the weekend we would go from house party to house party selling weed. It wasn't until I met Donnie Evans that my life began to show some purpose. He was playing with his band at Southern Lounge Night Club on 159th Street in Harvey.

It was my association with Donnie that drew me back to the West Side too. I hadn't been over and seen them for a while. Donnie's family, the Evans owned a liquor store at 2922 W Roosevelt Road and several buildings all over the West Side of Chicago. It was his family I went to work for after I dropped Robert off once we got back from Milwaukee.

The Evans was like family to me. They made me feel welcomed; for that reason, I will always have love for them. When I arrived on the West Side this particular day, Donnie and his brother Cranston were working on one of the buildings in the back of the store. Mrs. Evans didn't have a problem putting me right to work when I told her that I was going through hard times. That night I stayed at Donnie's apartment on Eleventh and Fillmore Street. He had a three bedroom apartment on the 3rd floor in one of their buildings. The next morning, I was working gutting out apartments and laying drywall.

Mr. Vincent Evans, Donnie's dad, (R.I.P), I respected, loved and looked up to him as the dad I never had. He taught me everything I know today about renovating apartments and homes, and he taught me to not limit myself in music. He was one of the coolest cat's you could ever meet. He would remind you of Chuck Berry, his love for music was just as deep. He would have us doing shows with him, and he would have me singing country & Western music. I was singing Bob Seger songs, *"Shame on the Moon"*. I would work in the daytime with the Evans and in the evenings I would head south in my heavy Chevy Wagon and check on Robert. He was still working in the subways. He told me sometimes Larry would go with him, but most of the time he said he went alone.

Robert was doing what he had to do to make money and I was doing the same. Craig was straight when it came to money. He had a nice contract with the N.B.A. So, to keep hope alive, we had to do what we had to do to generate funds for ourselves. I could not see letting Craig's lack of experience, knowledge and focus stop us from moving forward.

I felt I had to make plans to get us to the next level so I decided that New York would be a good place to start. Getting Robert to perform in the streets of "The Big Apple" right outside the record companies would definitely boost his career. People would surely recognize true talent and want to hear more of his great music. Craig did have the networking connections I thought he had. Debbie Allen use to attend some of the sport events at that time. Her TV show, *Fame,* was airing back then, and I thought Robert would have been perfect for her show. All Craig had to do was introduce me to Debbie Allen and I would have taken care of the rest, but, he didn't want to do it. He didn't seem supportive of my ideas at all. Since I did not have the money to get us to New York, I had to do things I did not want to do to get us there.

In between working and visiting Robert, I took the little money I made at work and bought eight balls of cocaine to sell on the streets outside the store on the corner of Richmond. I sold bags of cocaine for $10. An eight ball would last me an hour at the most. Business was so good that after a few weeks, I was buying half ounces.

I was doing so well I bought me a 1983 Chevy Camaro; It was fully loaded with a cassette tape pioneer sound system and a nice set of rims. I came up in a matter of months and it felt good to be able to buy things for myself. I even paid my mom's bills. I was *"The Man."* I did not have to ask anybody for anything. I was getting full on the taste of money! All that cash was making me lose focus. Along with the money came the girls and the late night parties.

I started to spend more time in front of the store and less time with Robert. I went from selling the drugs while standing on the streets in front of the store to selling from inside the store. Mr. and Mrs. Evans would leave for the day and Cranston worked with me to make it happen. Working from inside of the store made it safe for us. It offered security from the stickup man and the police.

V&W Liquors had security glass all around the front of the store as well as a steel security door which secured the entrance into the back of the store. The store was built secure like a currency exchange or a check-cashing business. You had to be buzzed in to get behind the counter. This was not a self-serve business. Whatever you wanted to buy, the person behind the counter had to get it for you. When Cranston came in with me, the money really started coming in. Business picked up for the store too. People were coming from all over the West Side to purchase our product.

We would work the buildings in the daytime and the store in the evenings. We would close the store at midnight and meet up in the back of my apartment to smoke whatever we didn't sell that day. I became one of my own best customers; I had become a crack head and didn't even know it. I was out of touch with everyone and lost track of the days. Thuggin' and smoking cocaine began to take over my life. I had lost my focus on Robert and everything else for that matter. Now I was waking up chasing a hit. We began smoking on the job while we worked on the buildings.

One day Craig called me. His call brought me back to reality. Hearing Craig's voice was like a breath of fresh air; I was very surprised to hear from him. He told me he'd spoken to Frankie Beverly's tour manager, Joe Douglas, at a concert he attended and wanted me to take Joe a copy of Robert's demo. Later that evening Jonathan, one of Donnie's younger brothers, and I went to the Hilton and took Joe the tape. I wanted to go a step further than just delivering the tape. I tried to talk my way into Joe's room to give him a bigger presentation of Robert, but Joe said he was too busy at the time. Joe gave me his number and told me to call him in a week giving Frankie time to listen to the demo and let me know what he thought.

After I dropped the tape off I drove out to meet with Robert because he was eager to know details of what happened when I delivered the tape to Joe. We met at the McDonalds in Hyde Park. The whole crew was there—Larry, Torrey, Mouse and a few others. Being there with the guys made me feel somewhat out of touch. I needed them, but they didn't know it. I wanted so much for us to work and do shows as we should have been doing. We were all optimistic because we all believed in Robert, but in the meantime, my mind and life was clouded with dope. I needed help, but I didn't know how to ask for it. These guys didn't even smoke weed. How would they relate to my drug addiction? How would they respond to my sense of powerlessness and need for help? My biggest fear was that they wouldn't understand or rather than treat me like a man, I would be treated like a dope fiend. It was a dilemma, and I knew I had to do something. How and when was my question? I was confused.

Robert asked me why I wasn't coming around anymore. I told him that I was working and trying to save some money so that he and I could go to New York. I let him know that by the end of the basketball season, if Craig had not made anything happen, we would go to New York and push the demo ourselves. Larry and the guys all thought that it was a good idea and agreed to assist in any way they could. They also told me that they were sure that Craig's wife would help me as well. This kind of let me know that they were still dealing with Ce-Ce.

They all knew of Ce-Ce, and they were excited about her association with Robert. I didn't make any comments during the conversations when they mentioned her. I just wondered why she wouldn't communicate with me. In my opinion, she and Craig's lack of communication with me resulted in this thing not running as smoothly as it should have been running. Neither Craig nor Ce-Ce was using any of the influential power they had. They wanted to run everything, but had no idea what it was they needed to do and were really in the way. They both were on two different pages and weren't even communicating with each other as they should. As time went on, it became evident that even the two of them were not seeing eye to eye.

When I was with Robert and the crew that day I felt as if I belonged there with them, but once I got back on the West Side, it was back to being submissive to the power of the white girl that I had fallen victim to. Cocaine was her name, and I was seeing her faithfully every night. I would bust crack pipes up out of frustration, saying I would stop but I couldn't. Right after I would break one pipe, I would go and buy another one. Sex, drugs, late-night parties, and alcohol were my routine. I was making money during the day and smoking it all up at night. We would go on four and five day runs smoking without eating or sleeping. I was crazy! I was strung out!

It was a Saturday morning when I got up and decided to ride out to my younger sister Dosheall's house in Harvey, Illinois. I needed to get away and clear my head. My sister Dosheall, "Doddie" is a realist. She would look at you and tell you exactly what she thought of you. If she didn't like you, she would tell you. She considered herself a psychic. She felt she had the gift to read people. I don't know if I believed in that kind of stuff, but I was desperate. I needed her to read me. I just needed to be around her, and to be honest, I needed my ass whipped for losing control of myself. As soon as I walked in her house I saw her sitting in the kitchen smoking a joint. That was her drug of choice, and to my knowledge, weed was all she used.

When I walked in she did not say a thing, not even hello. She looked at me and said, *"Johnny boy, you need to go get yourself some rest. You look like you got everybody's worries on you. I don't know why you're letting Ce-Ce and Craig hanging out with that boy get to you."* She freaked me out when she said that. She had not seen me in months, yet as soon as I walked into her presence, she saw right through me. I felt like a little baby in front of her. I wanted to cuddle right up on her lap like a baby needing his mothers' loving arms around him. Instead, I gave her a hug, kissed her on the jaw and said, *"I was just working hard girl".* *"Yeah right,"* she said, taking a tote from her joint!

We sat and talked for a while. Doddie agreed with me; she didn't think Ce-Ce had any business hanging out with Robert. With Robert being a man Doddie felt that *"Robert was only gonna use her to get what he want for himself anyway in the long run."* Everything she said was on point. She told me again to go get some rest. I took her advice the second time and went downstairs to her basement to stretch out on the bed. I needed some rest before driving back to the West Side. As I laid in the bed and drifted off to sleep, I thought about how twisted my life had become.

Doddie came downstairs and woke me up to tell me that she had just gotten off the phone with my mother. Mom said that Craig had been trying to get in touch with me. I told her that I would call him later and turned back over and went back to sleep.

Johnny, Johnny, Brother Man!" I heard a voice shouting. Thinking that I was dreaming, I didn't respond right away, but then I looked up, and it was Craig standing over me. He called while I was sleep and told my sister not to wake me. This was odd for Craig to just show up looking for me. We were cool and everything, but Craig just never showed up unannounced like that.

He appeared anxious to talk to me. For him to just show up like that made me sit up and get focused. I had to make sure I was seeing this clearly.

"What's up Craig?" I asked.

"Brother, man! Have you seen Ce-Ce?" he asked?

"No I ain't seen her," I answered. Craig had a serious look on his face as if he had something deep on his mind. *"What's happening with you Craig?"* I asked.

"Brother, man, shit just ain't going right. My wife disappearing on me, and I'm hearing things about her when I'm on the road making a living for her to live a comfortable life. I'm hearing that she's up here hanging around yo boy. What's up with that Johnny?"

I had just come out of a deep sleep. Craig had somewhat caught me off guard. I looked up at him and he had a hurt look on his face. Right then I was wishing that I was his blood brother, then I could be totally honest with him; and say what I thought, but being that I wasn't, I had to divert the conversation. Ce-Ce was my sister. I believed in marriage but at the same time I didn't want to be the cause of them breaking up. Also, I had never seen her and Robert together, other than the time I caught up with them at McDonald's.

Lie, I kept telling myself. This was a defense mechanism towards what I really felt in my gut. Ce-Ce and Robert were fucking, but I didn't have any real proof. Even though I was hearing the same rumors regarding them having an affair, there wasn't anything concrete I could give him. I definitely was not about to reveal my assumptions to him. I wanted him and his wife to make it. He was providing a good life for her, and I respected him a lot for that. I also felt that he deserved her loyalty and Robert's respect.

I was just as hurt as he was. *"I don't know anything about Ce-Ce and Robert hanging out man. I know that Robert looks at her like a big sister. That boy too nervous around Ce-Ce, that's crazy!"* I explained.

"I'm helping y'all. When I'm on the road I'm telling people about Robert and letting them listen to his demo. I don't need this man. The brother should have morals to draw a line with the people that are in his corner. How you gonna bite the hand that's feeding you Johnny?" Craig said.

"Craig quit jumping to conclusions." I told him.

"Then why you and Ce-Ce don't get along?" He asked me.

He gave me no time to answer. He went on to tell me *"I have been trying to figure that out ever since before we went on vacation. Y'all can't stand each other, and I can't understand it. Tell me what's going on with that. You know it for a fact it's because you don't like what she's doing!"* He said as if he had gained some ground and touched on something relevant.

I responded telling him, *"My problem with Ce-Ce is that she wants to be Robert's manager. That's crazy! She don't know nothing about the business. Y'all supposed to be backing me. I came to you for your assistance, not so you can take over like y'all have. Now look at us unorganized in every way. The only one coming out of this with something is Robert. No contract no nothing. Robert's a free agent waiting for the next person to come along and sign him."* I said to Craig. I was frustrated.

I wanted to divert away from talking about Ce-Ce and Robert messing around. I had his attention, and he was actually listening to me. I went on to say,

"Now everything we started seems to be breaking down. When you came on board Craig, we were ready to start performing. But nooooo, you and your wife didn't feel Robert should be doing shows. I bet if we would have been working we would not be here talking about some hear say, he say she say shit!" I felt I was gaining ground when I told Craig that.

But Craig flipped the script, he told me that he hired a private detective and had his home phone bugged. He said that the whole thing is crazy and that he didn't want anything else to do with Robert. He caught me off guard again. I was speechless. He told me that he heard conversations between Ce-Ce and her girlfriend talking about her meeting up with Robert. I told him if she was meeting with Robert, it was to talk about her being his manager.

Demetrius Smith Sr.

"*Ce-Ce ain't into Robert for any other reason man,*" I told him.

Craig wasn't listening to me. He was fixed on his belief. He wanted me to understand him and his pain.

"*Man my whole point is that the money she spends with him, it's my money. If I was to cut her off, she couldn't do anything for him. Don't she know that?*" he asked me. Craig was hurting over the things he was hearing; I could see it in his face.

"*Craig, Ce-Ce doesn't need to be all in the business man. That's all I'm saying. Now I don't believe her and Robert is messing around. All of that is speculation, assumptions, and hearsay. Ce-Ce ain't stupid!*" I was trying to put some emotions behind what I was saying hoping Craig would bite. Craig wasn't hearing me though. I guess he had done his investigative work and his mind was set.

"*Brother man, you're on your own with Blood. I'm done! He can keep what he's gotten out of me. I don't need it or him. My focus now is to try to keep my family together. That's what's important to me,*" he said, slowly walking towards the stairs.

I told him it wasn't as bad as he was making it and that it would all work itself out. He raised his hands up as he began to walk up the stairs.

"*This is the thanks I get? Your boy showing no respect or appreciation. The brother coming in between my family got me messed up in the head. That's why you and my wife don't get along, and I appreciate you for that. I know now that you were trying to really keep things in order. I'll holler bro. Call me if you need anything. You need to get back into your own singing career, find your way, and do you.*"

Those were his last words he said to me before leaving the room. Once he was gone I sat back and thought about how crazy life was. Now the tables of judgment had turned on Craig. In the beginning it was both him and his wife working hard to steal Robert, a protégé I brought to them, away from me. Now it was Craig who was having something stolen from him, his wife. She was his main accomplice at first, but in the end, without a second thought, he was thinking she had betrayed him.

I shook my head for a moment, thinking the same puzzling thought over and over again. Life sure was crazy. I laid back down and closed my eyes. It was nothing I could do about it. Ce-Ce's assumed infidelities and Robert's lack of understanding and youth, really caused something serious to happen. I had enough on my mind dealing with my own life, so I laid back down and went back to sleep.

CHAPTER 7

Despair

THINGS WEREN'T GOING well back on the Westside either. Jonathan, Cranston's younger brother, was working in the store. One day he was getting high in the store, left the entrance door unlocked and fell asleep at the front counter. Out of nowhere the police raided the store and had easy access behind the counter. The cops found the drugs we were selling, as well as Jonathan's pipe. Jonathan was arrested, and to make a long story short, his arrest shut down our little drug-trafficking operation.

Jonathan's arrest caused the store to be closed temporarily. The courts had to rule on whether or not the owners had any knowledge of wrongdoing taking place in their place of business. It was not as easy to sell our drugs on the streets as it was out of the store. Standing out on the corners all day long was not something that any of us had the patience to do. We had protection working from inside the store. Everybody that came into the store made a purchase, and we had the security from the steel doors to stop the police and the stick up man. Being out on the streets forced us into competition with the other dealers as well as the Vice Lords that had drug houses set up in the area.

It was a whole different ball game dealing from the streets. For one, our location was hot and because of that we couldn't stand out in front of the store. Two, the store was our security. Now we didn't have any set place to deal from. The corners and the sounding areas belonged to the other dealers. So, we were down and out of business.

Since none of us were willing to stand out on the corners at night selling drugs, we would put our money together and smoke. Now that I wasn't able to make the money I made selling cocaine, things really began to go downhill for me. I started selling personal items from my house—my TVs, VCRs, and anything else that would sell quickly to supply my habit. Once I ran out of things to sell, I started committing burglaries. My whole life was going in a different direction and I was not feeling comfortable with being me. At the same time, I had no will power to rebel. I was cocaine's disciple and her loyal servant.

I became the Robin Hood of the ghetto. Every day at 4:00 pm I went out to do burglaries like it was a regular job, and every night after 8:00 pm., whatever I had stolen I was selling. Every night I had something for sale. People were leaving messages on my pager, placing orders for TVs, VCRs, jewelry, coats, microwave ovens, you name it and I went and got it.

Every night, I would get a quarter of an ounce to a half an ounce of coke and hang out around the store on the corner. We still had loyal customers who wanted our product. Whatever money I had spent to buy the product, I made it back by working the streets. After I sold what I needed, I would meet with a girlfriend of the day to be my smoke buddy, and some other friends and then we would get our smoke party on. They had their stuff and I had mine.

We would smoke the whole night away. The more I smoked, the faster I smoked. It was getting really bad because I was taking hit after hit. I was caught up. I started putting an entire quarter bag and sometimes more into the pipe and would hit it. *"Man, dude crazy than a motherfucker,"* people would say. One of my female friends even started to get frightened for me. She kept warning me that I was putting too much coke into the pipe and smoking it all too fast. She would beg me not to take so much at one time. *"Babe slow down please,"* she would say, kissing me on the jaw or on my lips to let me know she was truly concerned about me. Sometimes she would try doing sexual things to me to take my mind off smoking, but I would just push her away or grab the pipe and take a hit while she was doing whatever she did to arouse me.

Daily, my quantity consumption increased. I had it so bad that people didn't want to smoke with me anymore. Everyone I smoked with felt the same way about me. They all felt I was doing too much at one time and doing it too fast. I was smoking an eight-ball within an hour. At the rate I was going, I was on a self-inflicted mission to kill myself. I would wake up in the mornings and the first thing I would do I would grab the pipe from the night before and hit it before I got out of the bed. I was so bad the woman after watching me smoke they didn't want to stay with me, out of the fear I was going to kill myself. It didn't matter to me though, more for me. *"Get the fuck out,"* I'd tell them; and I would smoke on.

After a while my body began to have a reaction to cocaine. Right after I would take the first hit, my body would tense up. I would just sit motionless and hold my chest as if I was having a heart attack. I was paranoid that eventually my heart was going to stop. I would hold my chest with my eyes bucked wide as if my heart was slowly stopping. It was an unconscious reaction to the pain I was putting my body through. Some nights, when there wasn't any more to smoke, I would scan the floor on my hands and knees searching for dropped rocks. I would get so frustrated at myself that I would break my pipes.

I felt like Pookie, Chris Rock's character in the movie *New Jack City*. *"She just keeps calling me man, and I keep answering,"* I would cry, lying to myself and telling myself that I would not smoke anymore. Then I would go out and buy a new pipe. In my agony I would pray, begging God to please help me. Where was he? Why wasn't he answering when I would cry out? He promised to never forsake me. I was out of control. What began as a recreational pastime intensified into an excessively costly, idiotic habit. I was summoning my own death.

I remember one particular time when it really got bad. I was out smoking with a friend of mine, and this guy named Eric offered me a really great deal on some crystal cocaine. This was supposed to be cocaine of a higher grade and quality. I met Eric at his apartment and tested the potency of the product by sticking my finger into the powder and spreading it around my gums. Instantly, my gums and the top of my lip became numb. This numbness indicated to me that the product was real good quality. My body ached for a hit. I wanted to cook some of it right then and there, but I knew that I would have lost my cool and didn't want to expose my weakness to this stranger. I purchased half of an ounce, and as soon as the purchase was complete, I was ready to leave. I wanted to hurry home so that I could cook it up, rock it up and smoke it.

I thought about Cranston. He lived in Riverdale, Illinois, which was ten minutes north from where I was in Calumet City; I had to go past his house, so I decided to drop in on him. Lucky for me, he was home, and to top it off, his wife wasn't there with him. He told me she was at her mother's for the weekend. I told him where I had come from and what I had. He was just as excited as I was. He welcomed me into his house leading me to his kitchen. I got relaxed and took out my stash of cocaine snorting a few lines while he went upstairs to his room to get his cooking tools and pipes. When he returned, I didn't waste any time cooking the first gram out of the ounce.

I was shaking nervously as I pulled the rock out of the tube and spread it over the mirror. The first hit felt real good. Cranston then took his. After the first hit I took, I began to take hit after hit. Cranston kept telling me to slow down and to take a break in between smokes. He warned me to at least let the pipe cool down. After we smoked the first gram, I couldn't hold myself still enough to cook up the next batch. I let Cranston do it. While he cooked, I watched intently as the gooey gummy substance began to formulate inside of the tube. As Cranston was stirring it around, connecting it all together and pulling the stem out of the tube with cocaine on it, I had my pipe ready and told him to let it drop down into the pipe instead of spreading it onto the mirror.

A big lump of the gooey substance dropped into the pipe. *"Man that's more than half a gram Johnny. Come on man, that's too much to put in there at one time. You need to slow down,"* Cranston warned. But I was shaking too much, wanting it too much to hear him. I put the pipe in my mouth, put the fire to the crystal coke and hit it. The pipe clouded up. The smoke was pure white like a cloud in the sky. It was a hit that was like no other I had ever had. I instantly began to hear bells ringing in my head. My whole body became numb and I couldn't feel a thing. I felt so relaxed it was scary. I was floating on that cloud I had just inhaled. *"Ah man, this feels so good,"* I lazily said to Cranston as I slowly sat down giving him the pipe. I felt so light, like a piece of paper when you release it in the air—it floats down. I was floating

Cranston, without putting any more cocaine into the pipe, took a hit, and it clouded right up again—a pure white, perfect cloud of smoke. From the amount I had put into the pipe it could have been hit ten more times before having to add any more to it. I didn't know if I was going to pass out or what. I thought, *If I was going to die right now, I wanted to hit it one more time.* When Cranston finished taking his hit, I quickly grabbed the pipe out of his hand with one hand and used the other hand to scoop another gram of rocks up and put them in the pipe. *"Johnny! Man what are you doing?"* Cranston asked. *"You don't need to put no more in there man. That's too much Johnny. Come on man! You gone mess around and bust your heart open! Fuck what are you trying to do?"*

Again, I wasn't listening to him. What he said went in one ear and out the other. I was lost in the thought that I was about to die and I wanted to get one more hit. While he was moving his lips, I was putting the torch to the pipe. I took a big pull of the pipe and choked. As I was choking, I was still pulling, sucking in that white cloud. I was trying to suck it all in. I was out of my mind. When I couldn't suck in anymore, I held the smoke in for as long as I could. When I blew it out, I became stiff. I felt the weight of my whole body lift off me; I felt light and free. I spread my arms wide apart as if I was about to float in midair.

I felt a waving orgasmic sensation roam through my body, which felt so good. *Oh my God!* I thought. *"Oh shit, umm, man, shit!"* I kept saying. I felt so lightheaded, and all of a sudden, an eruption began to rise within my body as if an earthquake had suddenly erupted. I couldn't sit or stand still.

"Cranston something's about to happen," I said with fear.

"Man you can't put that much in there and hit it like that," Cranston said, as he was about to take a hit himself. I began to shake and my arms began to twitch; I couldn't keep still and I started pacing back and forth from the front door to the kitchen.

I felt like I had to keep moving. I walked to the front door, back to the kitchen, to the front door, and back to the kitchen. After the third or fourth time I opened the front door and I ran into the streets. It was about three or maybe four o'clock in the morning. I felt like I needed to go to the hospital and I was really scared. I thought this was the end and it seemed like my insides were going to explode.

My heart was pounding so fast that I looked down inside of my shirt, and I could see the impression of my heart pushing hard as if it was trying to come through my skin. I couldn't keep still, so I ran and started knocking on the doors of Cranston's neighbors. I didn't know where Cranston was. He was probably paranoid and scared to death like always when he was getting high. Like the time me, Cranston and a few friends were smoking and decided to drive over to the projects to get more coke. As we were driving, Cranston started talking crazy, asking us why we wanted to kill him and wanted to know where we were taking him.

"Cranston sit your crazy ass down man! We going over in the jets to get some of that powder. What's wrong with you fool?" I said as we all laughed.

As we were approaching the expressway about to get on, Cranston eased towards the back of the van and said, *"I ain't never done nothing to y'all man. Why y'all wanna kill me man?"* We didn't pay any attention to him. Our mind was on getting where we were going and getting our drugs. All of a sudden, the back door of the van popped open, and Cranston jumped out. We were going at least twenty to twenty-five miles an hour. He really thought we were driving him somewhere to kill him.

As I knocked on his neighbors' doors, I didn't stop long enough to wait for anyone to respond. I kept moving from door to door. I was freaking out, and I was scared. I glanced at the street and saw a police patrol car

Demetrius Smith Sr.

pull up. I quickly started walking fast in the direction of the police, and as I got closer to them I started breathing and talking fast. *"I need to go to the hospital. I need to go to the hospital,"* I kept saying to them as they sat in their car looking at me. I couldn't catch my breath. I was breathing as hard as a dog after running a quick distance.

The police got out of the car, immediately put handcuffs on me, and put me in the back of the patrol car. Irately I shouted, *"What are you doing? I need to go to the hospital. I need to go to the hospital!"*

After they put me in the car, we just sat there parked for what seemed like hours.

"Look at him, he's drugged out of his mind," I heard one of the officers say.

"Yeah he's a goner," the other officer said to his partner, looking back at me.

"Yawl just want me to die. Take me to the hospital!" I ordered them. *"I'm not gonna die,"* I kept repeating out loud, inhaling long deep breaths and exhaling air out slowly in hopes of controlling and slowing down the beating of my heart.

My heart was starting to hurt and I felt as if it was straining to keep its beat; Inhale, exhale, inhale, exhale; I kept taking long suctions of air. I was relying on my mind to overpower my body to pull me through this. The police pissed me off, and I didn't want them to have the satisfaction of seeing me die right there in front of them. Mind over matter was my thoughts. The next thing I remember, I woke up handcuffed to a bed at Ingalls Memorial Hospital in Harvey, Illinois. How I got there, I don't know, but I was alive. A doctor was standing above me, patting me on my wrist. *"Just relax, that's all you have to do. Just relax",* the doctor said. *"The drugs you took will wear down. Just relax. "What saved you is that you have a strong heart young man,"* he said, smiling.

I was tied down, but my body and mind were still speeding. I was moving my head from side to side and flinching my shoulders. I did not want to be tied down. The doctor told me that I was tied down because it was necessary that I remain still in order for my heart to slow down.

"You put your heart through a lot of strain over the night Mr. Smith. It was working overtime to keep you alive. Now how long will it continue to take abuse like that? It's no telling. You're a very lucky man."

I was still moving trying to free myself. *"Relax, just relax, you'll be okay now. You were given some medication that will help slow your heart rate, so just relax."* After that, he walked away.

I began to relax as I lay in the bed telling my mind to tell my body to slow down. I was alive, and I was glad. *"Thank you Lord,"* I said aloud.

I must have fallen back to sleep because I woke up to the sound of my mother's voice on the telephone. I was in a different room, and I was no longer tied down. I wondered how my mother knew I was there.

"Hey Mama," I said, turning to her, feeling weak and drowsy.

"He woke now De-Dee, so let me call you back. I will, baby. Okay, I won't. I'll call you back okay. Bye bye!" she said to my older sister. My mother looked at me with pain and love in her eyes. I felt bad and embarrassed at that moment. I hate that my mother was seeing me like this. She now knew that I was a dope fiend.

I felt stupid and ashamed of myself. I let my mother down. My mother was my pride, and my every desire was to do well and make my mother proud of me. She's my heart, and I have always wanted to make a better way for her for all the hard work and sacrifices she made for me and my brothers and sisters. I had let my mama down.

"I'm sorry Mama," I said to her as she looked at me with her red tear-stained eyes.

"Baby why are doing drugs?" She said as a tear began to fall down her cheek.

All I could say to her at the moment was "I don't know." I lied and told her that I was trying it out and that I really didn't mess with the stuff, but once I tried it, I did too much of it. She told me that the doctors and nurses were standing over me in the emergency room with the defibrillator, thinking that my heart was going to stop at any moment. She said the doctors kept saying that I had a strong heart and kept repeating how lucky I was.

"Do you believe it was luck? It wasn't. What it was is God ain't done with you yet. He's got something for you to do. So you can count your blessings, that's for sure." Mama was talking to me with sincerity and worry at the same time. I was definitely counting my blessings, but at the same time, I was wondering if I should try to get into a drug rehab center. Naw, I thought, I'll get through it. I didn't know it then, but I was in total denial.

I stayed in Ingalls Memorial Hospital for four days recovering from the strain I had put on my body. When I was released I felt rejuvenated and strong. I headed back to my apartment. One would have thought from the experience I went through coming close to death that I would have learned a lesson. On the way home, all I could think about was money and the fact that I needed to start saving some so that I could get Robert signed.

As I was driving north on the I-57 expressway, circling around the junction into the Eisenhower, my thoughts started to drift to my cocaine

Demetrius Smith Sr.

addiction. I was feeling weak by the power it had over me. A sudden fear was overpowered by an urge that gave me a craving for a hit of that white powder. I was sick and knew it. I had been conquered. The closer I got to the house, the stronger my craving became. I began to feel sexually aroused anticipating the feeling of the first hit. I wanted to feel that waving sensation go throughout my body, and at the same time, I wanted to have some control of the sickness that had me so weak and out of control.

As I drove, I prayed and asked the Lord God Almighty to help me. I asked Him to allow me to conquer the demon that was choking the life out of me. The sad thing was, while I was praying for deliverance, I was in a hurry to get home to surrender myself to that white powdered demon. Even though I was praying, I knew as soon as I got home I was going to take a hit, but I still prayed. I was lost and wanted help. I felt if God was real, He would be the only one that could save me from the destructive road I was traveling down with my addiction. As for Robert, I barely thought about him. I just wanted to feel what I wanted to feel and do what I wanted to do. I wanted that white girl, Crack Cocaine.

As soon as I got home I noticed that the store was open. I thought that was good, maybe we could get the business back up and running. Maybe I could start over and save some money this time. When I went into the store Cranston was working.

He was surprised to see me and he had a big smile on his face. *"Man you are crazy. I thought you were gone die man, you okay?"* He asked.

"I'm cool. I was pretty out of it though huh?" I asked him smiling back at him.

"Man, I was scared for you. I thought the police was gone come in on me so I put everything up and hid under my bed. Shit man, I ended up falling to sleep under there. I didn't smoke it all up though" he said.

I was taken off guard with that statement, so I listened intently as he went on. *"But I have been pinching off it some though."* He said.

I was disappointed and overwhelmed at the same time hearing that he still had some of the crystal cocaine left. I thought for sure it had all been smoked by now. I thought to myself, *I have to be crazy to even think about wanting some more after what I just went through.* But then I thought, *It was only because I put too much in the pipe.* I wanted it, whatever he had left, I wanted it.

I didn't want to seem like I was anxious to get right back into it, even thought my mind was telling me go get it now. I changed the subject. *"So man, when the store open back up,"* I asked?

The Man Behind The Man

"Oh that's right you didn't know—two days ago. The lawyer ma-ma got made it happen," he said.

A customer came into the store so I moved out of the way so he could be served. Cranston yelled out to me, "I'll bring that back there to you soon as Donnie get back and I'll tell you what's happening then." he said.

"Ok", I said as I left out of the store and went around to the back to my apartment.

My apartment was just as it was when I left it. There were beer cans and cigarette filled ash trays laying on every table. I started picking things up as I walked through the house. Fifteen minutes later Cranston knocked on the door. When I let him in, he handed me a plastic bag with about a quarter of an ounce of cocaine. "Man you ain't gone fuck with that shit again like that are you?" he asked. I told him I was cool, but he evidently had doubts because he went on to say, "Man Johnny, don't be putting that much in the pipe man. I thought you was gone kill yourself man."

When Cranston left, I sat the package down on my dresser. It was hard to continue cleaning without going back in the room and looking at it. After going back several times, I decided to snort a line. I kept going back and getting yet another snort. After a few more snorts, I pulled out the tools and quickly cooked up a small piece. I took a hit, and I was cool. All I needed was some company. All I could think about was my friend Judy. She was a brown-skinned twenty-seven-year-old woman. She was 5'6" with nice size breasts, thick hips, and big pretty full lips. She was just what I liked—a gorgeous black woman.

We hadn't talked since we all use to get high together. I saw her phone number lying on the table right in front of me. The fact that she also liked to get high was a plus and she was just the company I needed. Swiftly I reached for her number and rushed towards the phone. When I called her, I had my pipe ready to take a hit because I wanted her to know that as I was talking to her and I was getting high at the same time. I was hoping that would entice her and make her want to stop whatever she was doing to get to me. I dialed the number.

"Hello," someone said answering the phone.

"Hi, it's Demetrius. May I speak to Judy please?"

"Judy, telephone, it's Demetrius," the person shouted out. A few moments later Judy came to the phone. I began taking a pull from the pipe.

"Hey Judy, what's up babe?" I asked in a coarse voice, trying to hold in the smoke I just inhaled.

"Hey Demetrius, what are you doing?" she asked.

"Getting high, thinking about you," I told her, blowing the smoke out as I answered her question.

"Oh really," she said as she laughed. I asked her to come over. Forty-five minutes later, she arrived.

When she walked into the apartment, I was already buzzed. As soon as she got into my bedroom, the drugs were waiting for us. I gave her the pipe that I'd already prepared for her. As she was taking her hit, I began to undress her. She didn't put up any resistance. She willingly allowed me to take off her clothes piece by piece. She was feeling the drugs, and she was feeling me. She kept biting her bottom lip which made her so sensuous. All the time, my mind wasn't really on sexing her. I just wanted to get high and look at her beautiful brown-skinned body, butt the fuck naked. But as I began kissing and sucking her nipples and her breast popped out of her bra, I couldn't help myself from helping myself. Her nipples were as thick as milk duds and tasty as caramel. I ended up sexing her and falling asleep with her in my arms.

A knock at the door woke us up. It was Cranston and Donnie. They had just closed the store and came by with some female friends to get high. They didn't know that Judy was with me. It didn't make a difference though because I wasn't about to turn them away. I was wide awake and ready to get a party started. I invited them in and told them to make themselves feel at home. While Cranston and his guest did their thing, Judy made sure I didn't venture off to be entertained by other females. She stayed close under me all night. Whatever I needed, she was right there to get it for me. I felt comfortable with her around.

I decided that night that I wanted to keep Judy around. I wanted Judy by my side. I didn't want to smoke without her. We smoked all the drugs we didn't sell earlier that night. When we ran out, we went out to the streets and bought more, spending most of the money we made from the drug sales that day. That was the first of many nights staying up all night long doing drugs, drinking alcohol, and having sex. As time went on, I got more and more out of control. I was slowly heading for a fall. It was just a matter of time. I was lost. I felt I totally belonged to the devil.

The old serpent had done it again. He devised a plan to make me his by working through my addiction for cocaine. Every night after the store closed, we would all meet in my apartment. It pretty much had become a smoke gallery. Every night there seemed to be a new face joining us. For months we did the same thing every single night. It wasn't long before I started smoking throughout the day again and going without sleep for days. As we used to say right before we would take a hit, *"Beam me up Scottie."*

It seemed as if I could not escape the hold this drug had on me. To say I was powerless was an understatement. I would get paranoid and hear my mother's voice. *"Pray baby, just keep praying. In all things pray. God hears you."* I started remembering scriptures that she would tell me to read:

Romans 8:26-27 says, *"The spirit makes intersession for us and prays for us because we don't know what to pray for."* I was just hoping the spirit was hearing me cry out. The more I smoked, the more I prayed. I wanted God to know that I needed him. I kept praying even though it seemed useless. I didn't think God was listening. There was no doubt about the fact that I had been conquered beyond measure. The devil was winning over me with my addiction. *"The Lord works in mysterious ways,"* Mama used to say. I couldn't tell. At this point Satan was my shepherd.

One day, as I was returning from Judy's house, I was pulling into a parking space in front of the store where a police car pulled up behind me. When the police approached and asked for my driver's license, I didn't have one. I hadn't had one for years. My license was suspended for a year for having three moving violations. It seemed every time I came close to getting my license back I would get yet another ticket, and that one would be for driving with a suspended license. Here I was, a few months before being able to get my license again, I get another driving while suspended license ticket. I just couldn't win, it seemed, when it came to me getting valid driver's license.

After the cops ran my name, they came back with a warrant for my arrest. I was arrested and for four days I had to sit in the county jail on Twenty-six and California. It was weird but, jail time seemed to always come on time because at those times I was at the brink of losing my life every single time I went to jail. I needed a break. I needed time to clear my mind and body of the poison I was putting in me.

I was walking through the jail on the way to my unit, returning from a visit, when a jail house preacher came to me and handed me a Bible. We were just crossing paths and hadn't said anything to each other. He just unexpectedly gave me a brand-new leather Bible. *"God's got a word for you,"* he said as he casually walked past me. I looked at him as he walked down the hall, and then I looked at the Bible. I began to read as I walked. When I got to my unit and into my cell, I found myself reading it intently. I would just open the book up to any page, and read what was in front of me. I felt it was the Lord talking to me.

Joshua 1:9 said, *"Be strong and not afraid."* It told me that God would be with me wherever I would go. I felt like I was hearing the Lord's voice as I was reading the words. I felt cradled. I began to feel like crying, and I felt God was right there with me. I couldn't see Him, but I felt His presence. I felt a chill all over my body. I got down on my knees once I got to my cell and I started praying. Somehow, I just knew He could hear me and He was listening to me. I cried, and when I was done crying and praying, I continued to read the Bible. It was all so strange. As I read, I began to feel empowered. I began to read and memorize the verses that appeared as I flipped the pages.

Psalm 23 says, *"The Lord is my Shepherd I shall not want."* As I read, I began to feel that God was saving me. Strange as it was, being locked up and all, I felt at peace being in the cell and off the streets. The days I spent seemed to go by fast. When my name was called to be released, I felt I had gotten in touch with God. I didn't feel like I was over my addiction, but I felt I had a stronger degree of faith inside of me. I felt like I had hope. I didn't know what tomorrow would bring, but for today, I had hope.

I knew that I had to go out there and deal with my problem. The difference was now I felt a spiritual connection and was confident that whatever I was going to go through, I wasn't alone. When I was released, I only had $2 on my books. I was hungry, and Popeye's chicken was right on the corner of Twenty-sixth and California Street. I had to make a decision whether to buy myself a piece of chicken or get on the bus with that $2. If I got the chicken, I would have to walk for at least two and a half miles to get home. That meant walking through the Latin Kings territory. Now that was dangerous. But with my new found faith, I couldn't resist treating myself to a piece of the crispy fried chicken.

As I walked north away from the jail into the Kings' hood, I walked without fear. I was thinking about all that I read in the Bible while I was locked in the cell. Joshua 1:9 says, "Be strong and not afraid. Wherever you go, I will be with you." I believed in what I read, and I was feeling the words from the good book. When I would walk up on a group of young Latinos gathered together, I walked past them feeling joy. I had no fear. Right before I would get right up on them, I would recite Psalms 23: *"The Lord is my Shepherd; I shall not want. Yea though I walk through the valley of the shadow of death, I will fear no evil, for though art with me."* I was really feeling covered.

On my way home, I stopped in on a few church revivals that were going on. I just wanted God to be miraculous in my life right then. I felt if nobody else knew he should of known how hurt and afraid I was. I sat for a few moments listening as people were singing and giving praise to the Lord. I wasn't in a hurry to get back home. I was searching for someone to notice me and see how much I needed help. I wanted somebody to say, hey come in, the Lord's been waiting on you. I wanted somebody to see my pain and to reach out to help me.

I didn't want to go back to my life doing drugs and drinking, but for the time being, I had to. Nobody was paying any attention to me, a stranger just showing up at his or her church. Nobody even cared and all I needed was a caring soul to talk to me.

When I got home it was back to the same thing. As I got high, I prayed. I was depending on God to rescue me. He was my only hope. I hadn't slacked off with the way I was getting high. I decided not to fight my addiction anymore. I made up my mind to totally surrender to my addiction. *"If I'm gone die, then I'm gone die, fuck it. Beam me up Scottie!"* These were my thoughts as I puffed nonstop. What I didn't understand then was that I had to have a covering over me. I smoked so much and for so many hours in a day I should have been dead. My ma-ma would always tell me to pray in all things, and this is what I was doing. All the time I was relying on God, but I wasn't making much of an effort to help myself, other than pray. I learned quickly that in this life, one can only serve one master, and I was trying to serve two.

The real harsh truth of the matter is that a hard addiction to drugs or any sinful lifestyle will not coexist with God's unbreakable instructions to his children. *"Thy will be done on earth as it is in Heaven."* I couldn't hear God's voice or see the covering he had over me. One thing was for sure, I was still here to write about it. And because of that I am also sure he was listening to me.

CHAPTER 8

Web of Destruction

SOMETHING INSIDE MY gut was telling me it was time to separate myself from the drug world I was finding it so easy to get lost in. I needed a break from the West Side. At the time, I didn't want to go around Robert. I didn't want for him to see me in the down-and-out shape I was in. I was a cocaine addict and I was ashamed of myself. I had to get myself together. I had to start thinking differently. I had to find a way to come up somehow and to find my way back into the limelight of society.

I was losing it and I didn't want to be like that. I had to overcome the demon that was sucking the life out of me. It was like my life was programmed for dumb shit to happen. It was as if all the good in me was overcome. It was like I was two people three or four people as a matter of fact. And the person that I was and the good man who I wanted to be was lost inside of the evil that was consuming me. I was there sitting back waving out to myself, *"hey, hey, no, no, I can't, hey!"* But I could not hear myself. There I was leaving me behind. Talking about being Schizophrenic! I was on the inside looking out and no one knew how much I needed for someone to look at me and care.

My intentions and my heart were always in the right place, but what I was going through I had no will power to gather any strength to fight. God are you real, I would ask myself? Although I was smoking as if I didn't care, but I did. I didn't know what to do. All I knew was I didn't want to die. Somehow I had to find a way to prevail. I got in my car, and I just started driving. I was an alien, lost in another world. I didn't know where to go, I didn't have any friends who I wanted to be around. I found myself on the Dan Ryan Expressway heading south, toward Harvey, Illinois. The only other place I knew as home. I wanted to be around loved ones. As I drove I thought about an old running buddy of mine, Robert Hardaway, we called him Bobby. The same Bobby I was with the first time I went to prison. Somehow I overlooked that time in our life.

Bobby was my Ace boon Koon, my dog and my friend. As I drove I was thinking about him wondering how he was. I know the last time I saw him he was into church and getting on my case about how devoted I was to Robert. he'd say, *"Cool you always working to get that young boy's career off the ground. Man fuck that dude Cool, you got flavor man!"*

He would always tell me I should have that young boy write songs for me. Bobby brought a smile to my face when I was with him. So I popped up on him at his apartment on 146th and Halsted. When I arrived at Bobby's apartment, he greeted me at the door with a smile as if I were a welcomed surprise.

As he led me to his living room, to my dismay, surprise and craving, I noticed a pipe and a mirror full of white powder. *"Yeah, Cool man, I was just relaxing a little bit, checking out some of this new product I just got hold of. You wanna hit this?"* he asked, holding the pipe toward me, offering me a hit. *Wow,* I thought, *what did I come over here for?* I asked myself, reaching at the same time, accepting the pipe.

As he began to scoop powder off the mirror and place it into the pipe, my thoughts of sobriety had vanished. *"What we working with man"* my alter ego stepped in asking as I walked over and sat down next to him; eagerly, grabbing the pipe. It seemed there was no escape from this evil white demon. As we sat there and smoked for hours, Bobby told me that a lot of our friends were smoking cocaine as well. It was truly an epidemic during the '80s. That day we smoked for hours.

It was early evening when the powder ran out. Bob suggested we go out to one of the spots to get more. I was in full agreement with him. That's what cocaine does to you. It will keep you chasing a feeling. That feeling from the first hit, the one that will keep you never satisfied. We went to a drug spot not far from his house. As we were returning, we noticed a family leaving their home. *"Cool look at that dog, they leaving. We got to get that,"* Bobby said, dancing joyfully to the music playing in the car.

Bobby taught me the burglary game. He could get into your house in thirty seconds. Bobby was a real good guy and a good friend to me. In spite of us having drugs in common, we supported and looked out for each other as brothers. However, committing a burglary was the farthest thing from my mind.

While Bobby was talking about burglarizing the people's home he had seen leaving, my body was craving another hit of the cocaine I was holding in my hands. The little dime bags were talking to me. I was thinking to myself as he was talking, *"Yeah, we are going to need some more after we finish this, so yeah. Why not? Ok! Let's get that money."* I thought! But first things first! For the moment, I wanted only to get to Bobby's house to take another hit. That drug demon had a strong hold on me.

Taking that hit was exactly what we did. I was so high and wanting more when Bobby jumped up, *"Let's go Cool, let's go do this. It ain't gone take us long. We gone just go for the gold and snatch a few VCRs to put in the air after we're done,"* Bobby said. The thought of being able to go and buy some more powder had me ready to get the job over with. It only took us ten minutes to get to the house we saw the people leave from earlier.

It took Bobby no longer than five seconds to get into the house. Slowly, I went in behind him. The house was big. The white family had pictures all along the wall of the house leading all the way up the stairs. As Bobby ran to the upstairs, I went searching the rooms on the first floor. I was high and running out of breath in every few steps I took. I just wanted to sit down. I didn't want to be where I was, nor doing what I was doing, but I was caught up and I felt I had no control of who I was. I was lost inside of me!

When I got to the kitchen, I sat down in one of the chairs feeling guilty and stupid. I just closed my mind to where I was, and I took the pipe out of my pocket I had taken from Bobby's house. I had plans to take a hit on the way back to his house. Without giving in to a second thought, I got up from the chair, went to the stove and got a light. As I put the pipe to the fire it clouded up with white smoke as if I had just put a fresh hit in it. The rush I got from the hit was a head banger. I began to hear bells and shit ringing, and I became instantly paranoid holding my chest. I thought I was going to have a heart attack right there at the crime scene. I felt that something was not circulating through my body. My chest felt clogged up, and the smoke was not passing through my body. I held my chest and sat back down.

I was so high. My mind wasn't where I was or on what I was doing. I didn't wanna feel anything, and I didn't care. I was numb as I sat in the kitchen I thought I was gonna die. I was scared, but there was nothing I could do. I had done it! I had taken a hit at the wrong time, and I was out of my mind with fear and guilt. I was lost. I was a danger to myself, so I just sat there. I exhaled what I thought was my last breath, and I let go saying, *"God, I'm in your hands."*

In my state of mind I didn't wanna move. Things were not going right, and nothing I could do was ever the right way. I felt like I had the whole world on my shoulders. Then there was calmness, and I just let go. I talked to God for a minute. *"God works in mysterious ways baby, and it is all in his time,"* I could hear my mama say. I know you think that it's crazy, how I always go back to thinking about God, but the Bible says acknowledge him in all things. Why was I feeling like I was on the way to see Him? But thank God, I was awakened out of my mystic mind to the reality of where I was. Sluggishly, I looked in response to hearing Bobby's voice yelling and a sound of him running down stairs *"Cool, Cool, let's go, let's get outta here. What the fuck!"* Bob said, shocked as he looked at me high as if I had just shot up some dope. *"I'm outta here! You done lost yo mind Cool,"* Bobby yelled on his way out the door.

My boy left me. Slowly, I got up, tried to follow behind him, but I didn't know which direction he went in, and I didn't know where I was. All I knew was I was not about to run. I just was not in any shape to be running. I was dizzy with just the thought of having to run. When I stepped out the back door, I didn't see anybody. I began to walk, but I was bent over, hung over and drained. The powder had dried out my insides, so I was dehydrated. Anybody riding by would have noticed that I was going through something. The worst thing about it was I didn't care. I felt out of my onw hands; I was a man with no control.

Nothing mattered to me. Even though I tried to make up some logical, lame, and rational reason to make myself try to feel good about robbing people, I didn't feel good about my lifestyle at all. I thought of Robin Hood. I felt like I was taking from the rich and giving to the poor. For real though, we didn't have shit in the hood. A new color TV, man please. I told myself that I was looking out for the hood; I knew what I was doing wasn't right.

In my mind, I was giving up. *"God, help me,"* I prayed. It seemed as if I could not do anything positive without something negative happening in response. All of my good intentions were being devoured by evilness. There was no way to fight this evil demon. *"Okay God, I give up. I give up because I can't win without you. I'm yours. Whatever happens to me, it's where you want me to be. I surrender"*. At that moment I wanted help. I really didn't want to do what I was doing. Using drugs and stealing out of people's homes really wasn't me. This is not the way my mamma raised me.

I was at the end of the block when a police car pulled up on the side of me, with a lady in the back seat. She looked out of the window and nodded her head to the officer. Another squad car pulled up on me and two officers jumped out. *"Turn around, put your hands on your head,"* the one officer said while the other stood with his pistol drawn and pointed at me.

Doing as I was told, I asked, *"What's the problem officer?"* The one officer came up behind me, grabbed my hands, and handcuffed me. *"You're under arrest for burglarizing that house you just came from,"* the officer said. I was at a loss for words; I didn't even try to talk my way out of the situation. I didn't want to do what I was doing. *"You have a right to remain silent,"* the officer began reading me my rights. I knew that I was once again on my way to jail. The strange thing was that I didn't care. In fact, I felt somewhat relieved. I knew I was not going to be getting high that night, and I felt good about that.

Once I was put into the squad car, my thoughts were numb. I had no strength for sadness. Even when going through the county jail's processing, wherever I was placed, I was safe with my mind resting—not thinking about a thing. Exhaling never felt so good. I knew what I had gotten myself into; I was caught up again. In spite of wanting to do the right thing, I had given into doing the devils deeds.

Things were now going in another direction. I knew the consequences of what I had done. As I sat in my cell, I did not have a worry on my mind. I felt in some way like I was being cradled and God was involved in my direction. Being processed through the jail system has always been an uncomfortable process, but this time I didn't stress it at all. Three days passed before I called Bobby to check on my car. When I got in touch with him, he told me he spoke to my mother and took my car to her.

I knew my mother was worrying about me, crying and praying for me. It bothered me deeply that I was hurting my mother, so I called her and had her laughing with me over the phone. I told her how comfortable I was and how I needed to be there. I was honest with her, telling her that my drug addiction had gotten out of hand. She felt better when I told her I felt it was God answering my prayers, when asking him to save me from my drug addiction. She felt better.

I stayed in the county jail for about two weeks. I hadn't called anyone. One day out of nowhere, I was sitting in the dayroom playing cards, and over the intercom, the officer called out, *"Smith, G28, pack it up!"* I was shocked; I didn't know what was happening.

I couldn't understand why I was being transferred. So I went to the desk and asked the officer. When he told me my bond had been posted, I was happy and scared all at the same time. I wanted to leave, but inside I didn't feel that I had a grip on my cocaine addiction at all. Nonetheless, I had no choice. I had to leave. I had no idea who was there to bail me out.

While they were processing me out, I wondered what I was going to do when they let me out and where I was going to go. To some extent I was grateful, but at the same time I was scared. Once I finished processing out, I stepped through the gates, and to my surprise Craig was waiting for me. *"What's up brother man?"* he asked while extending his hand out for me to shake it. Humbly, I shook his hand. *"Hey Craig, what's happening man? Thanks for bailing me out."*

"Well your mom was worried about you, and I didn't want you staying in there. We got to get you back straight," he told me. I looked at him, and I felt his sincerity. He told me that he had been thinking about me and that he wanted to help me get myself together.

When we walked out of Cook County Jail, I became scared. I didn't want to go back to the West Side, and I didn't want to go to my mama. I wanted to go back inside the jail! As we were walking to the car, Craig told me that he was taking me out to Milwaukee with him until I got myself together. I felt relieved, but at the same time, I thought about my sister and how we didn't get along.

I shared my feelings with Craig, but he told me not to worry about it. He said that he and Ce-Ce were working at putting their marriage back together. He said that she agreed to me coming to stay with them. It was good to know that I was welcomed at my sister's house because GOD knows, I love my sister!

As we were riding my thoughts were about getting myself right. I wanted to be in tune with my heart. I didn't want to do wrong or live a life of crime, and I wanted to be in touch with the good inside of me. In doing that, I knew that I had to have a relationship with God.

I found myself quietly praying as we were riding to Milwaukee, Wisconsin. I knew prison was ahead waiting for me. I thought about it, and I thought about Malcolm X because I felt it needed to be *"By Any Means Necessary"* to get that drug demon out of my life. So prison wasn't worrying me. I wanted to be right with myself starting right then. I stayed with Craig and my sister Ce-Ce for over two weeks.

Craig and I went to play golf every morning. This was Craig's way to relax in preparation for the NBA Playoffs. Now that I was spending time with my family, I felt the time I would have to spend in jail would be hard for me. I didn't want to go back to jail, but here I was again, caught up in my own web of destruction.

I thought about the past months, what I had taken myself through and how I had gotten here. A question still pondered my thoughts—Why couldn't everybody have followed my lead? I was again thinking about the possibilities I had when I brought Robert to Ce-Ce and Craig. Why couldn't they just have supported me in that venture? I sat there sad with my head hung down. There was a beautiful picture in my mind of how things could have been. I smiled at the thought. I was supposed to be out in some city working, doing what I love, mingling with people and presenting them their Superstar, Robert Kelly.

The O'Jay's performed and said it better than anybody with the song, "I Love Music." In my opinion that says it all. Show business for me was where I wanted to be. I was not interested in becoming a star in the prison system, but somehow I signed my life away to the State for a few seasons. Even though this wasn't the ideal, I was grateful. I was grateful that God had interceded to slow me down. All of my hopes and dreams for now were going to be put on hold. It hurt now that I was about to be taken out of the equation and away from my loved ones.

I felt that I had blown everything, and at the same time, I wanted to blame someone for the way things had turned out, when in reality it was my own fault. I had just about given up on me. If not for God's grace to stop me in my web of destruction; tomorrow might not be. But for today, I feel better about their being a tomorrow. I thought about Robert. I was gonna miss him too. I hadn't talked to him because I never wanted him to know how weak I was when it came to drugs. I was really grateful to my sister. During the two weeks that I spent with them, we got a little closer to each other. Her actions towards me showed me she was concerned about me. As the saying goes, *"Blood is thicker than water."* and that's the truth. The truth of the matter was, she was my sister, and that never changes. I could see my mother in her ways. I think sometimes if man sees the true value of a woman, we would let them be themselves and love them for who they are. All women to me are special. In my eyes they are God's crown of creation.

When it was time for me to go back to Chicago for court, Craig wanted to take me so that he could bring me back. I wanted to be able to come back to his house, but I knew that I was going to take a deal from the DA. I wanted to start my sentence as soon as possible so that I could get it over with that much sooner. Craig ended up agreeing with me and allowed me to travel back to Chicago on the Greyhound. When I got to court things turned out a little better than I anticipated. The judge offered me a deal to enter into a drug rehabilitation program. This would require me to live in a halfway house for eight months. If I completed the program successfully, I would be released and my charge would be expunged. It was a deal I could not refuse, and it was what I needed to help me overcome my addiction. I accepted the deal and requested that I begin serving my sentence that day.

My request was granted. Right after my case was heard I was taken into custody. After being processed through the county jail, I was transferred to Statesville Prison. My path always seemed be hardcore. I couldn't go to a medium-security prison; I had to go straight to the big house, a maximum security prison with the killers, rapist and the thugs. I was so sorry. Trust me, anybody who's got to do time in prison, they're going to be sorry.

At Statesville I went through the lockdown orientation week. And then, to my surprise, I was transferred to a medium-security section, also located on Statesville grounds.

My daytime job in the joint was picking watermelons. I was on the farm at Statesville for four months before the Human Resource and Development (HRD) Drug Rehabilitation Department was given custody of me. I had been drug free for some months and was eager to get involved in the program. The whole battle for me was going to be mental. I wanted to be successful in overcoming my drug addiction. Even though I was in a drug rehab unit, I didn't lose sight for one minute that I had a drug problem. I reminded myself that if I was terminated from this program, I'd be back in Statesville Prison serving an eight-year sentence. That in itself was all the motivation I needed to force me to work extra hard towards getting my life back on track.

CHAPTER 9

Rehab

$\mathcal{I}$ ARRIVED AT A treatment center on Eighteenth Street, east of Ashland Avenue. I was greeted by the staff, which wasted no time explaining the rules and regulations of the house. I was impressed by the fact that the father of child star Malcolm Jamal Warner, *of The Cosby Show,* Mr. Robert Warner, was the director of the program. There I was, I had been out of touch with Robert for more than six months and I still had him on my mind. If I could meet Malcolm, I thought maybe I could persuade him to listen to Robert and off we would be.

Mr. Warner's introduction speech let me know that he meant business in respect to our recovery. If we worked the twelve-step program, he was there to give us help, but those that took the program for granted, he dismissed them without regret.

The first week I was gung-ho in being an active member in the entire group meeting. I wanted to know all there was to helping me overcome my drug addiction. The facility I lived in was a big sixteen-room boarding house with two big meeting rooms, a game room with pool tables, a TV room, and in the basement, a big kitchen that took up the whole bottom floor.

There was a wall built around the outside where there were weights and benches for us to use when we had free time. There were six meetings a day which lasted all day. There were people there that were serious and then there were people that were not.

One day after a meeting, I walked into the room of one of the older residents to talk with him about the program. When I walked in on him, he was about to take a hit off the pipe! I was surprised, and so was he when he looked up and saw me. *"Ain't no need to panic now, fool, what you doing?"* I asked. I was smiling like everything was cool. Instead of me running out of there, I told him it was cool and inquired on how I could get some. Since I caught him in the act, he offered me some and I accepted.

When I took that hit, I was so angry at myself, I felt sick. I felt beyond stupid. I knew I had a serious problem. I was really sick. I felt so sick over what I had done I made up my mind right then and there that I would not accept another hit—I got real mad at myself. Just like when I used to get disgusted with myself and break a pipe after I smoked all my money. I had thrown away my sobriety and everything I thought I had learned. The word "strength" didn't even come to mind when I saw my senior about to hit that pipe. I felt weak and didn't like myself. I wasn't there for that, to get high, that is.

I came to my senses, and I told the older guy that I didn't appreciate him being the senior in the program and not being a better example. The fact that he was influencing those of us that had a desire to do better was not cool! I told him that I was there to rehabilitate myself in order to recover from my addiction. I also told him that I needed his help and that I was also there to help him.

After we had that conversation he separated himself from me. At one of our confrontation group meetings, I called him out. Mr. Warner was not present at these meetings. It was our house and he left it to us to straighten it and keep it in order. It was when we couldn't do it he would step in. In this meeting, the two people with a problem would sit in the middle of the group and talk about their problem. To solve the problem, it was up to the comments of the rest of the group to help bring a solution. I didn't come straight out and tell on him, but I let it be known I was there for help to change my life I was emotional in letting them know I needed there help and that if I couldn't get it I wasn't going to sit back and turn my head ignoring the fact that people were still getting high while living in the house.

I earned a lot of respect in that house for my straightforwardness because most of us there were there for help. As time went on, no one would get high in that house any more. The ones that did got caught and nobody had to tell on them! Their actions did it for them. What's that saying? "What's done in the dark will come to the light." That's what would happen to them.

I remembered reading in Joel 2:12, the Lord says, *"Turn to him with all your heart, with fasting, with weeping and mourning and he would restore all the years that were taken away,"* I had prayed and cried and fasted a lot during this period in my life. I was looking at how I was beginning to grasp some control of my actions and I was feeling good about me in making a better decision. In the group meetings I shared all I had taken myself through. I was beginning to see some things that were reflections

Demetrius Smith Sr.

of the words I had read in the bible. For instance, 2 Corinthians 12:9-10. *"For My strength is made perfect in weakness"*. I was feeling myself getting strong after being so weak and in my weakness I was feeling strong. When I would experience a discovery such as that I would just feel God's presence and thank Him.

After the house was cleansed of all the darkness, the light began to shine more on the whole program. I looked forward to participating in the group sessions. I was very vocal in our sessions, which made everybody else feel comfortable when it came time for them to share their drug experiences. By listening to others testimonies, I knew that I was given another chance with my life. Thanks to GOD, by directing my path to the program. The fight was still on for me, my prayer for guidance had delivered me there, and I wanted to make the best of the situation.

After being in the program for four months, Mr. Warner started to notice how involved I was in all of the group sessions. He would facilitate the meetings once a week and everybody in the house would have to show up. I was impressed with how Mr. Warner ran his house. He was a no-nonsense, potent man; a Malcolm X type of a person. He was serious about giving the right guidance to the people in the house. He showed no favoritism. He was about the business of recovery.

When he spoke, he spoke with wisdom. If you were there to better yourself, he was there to help you. And if you were there to escape doing jail time, Warner knew all of the tricks of the trade, so back to the big house you would go. I didn't ever want to take that bus ride again, so I got involved. It was a win-win place for me to be. More importantly, I did not ever want to hit that pipe or associate myself with any kind of drugs or the people that indulged in drugs ever again.

In the group sessions, I was called on to answer more questions than everybody else. Somehow, I felt Mr. Warner knew that I was unpretentious with regards to prevailing over my addiction. He was the positive mentor I needed in my life. Often he would call and invite me into his office just to ask me how I was doing and what thoughts I was having towards helping me to stay clean and sober.

The one-on-one sessions I had with Mr. Warner were significant to me. His positive influence and dedication to the struggle for intellectual awareness of the black man strengthened my desire to want to do better with my life. He helped me stay focused to contain the monster inside of me that was trying to destroy me. The group meetings, the one-on-one sessions, and working the twelve-step program were all added objectives equipping me with the ammunition I needed to fight the diabolical spirit trying to possess my life.

When Mr. Warner saw how everyone participated in his group meetings, he said it was because of me. He said I had a competitive spirit that gave the ones who were laid back, shy and fearful, confidence. He said I was inspirational. Warner made me feel good about myself often. My confidence in myself was building and I was beginning to feel like the man my mama had raised me to be.

The holidays were approaching and there was a big Christmas party planned for the HRD Center. This was a combined party that would include the female facilities. We were all excited about that. I know for me it had been close to a year since I had been around a woman. There was also going to be a talent show competition, with a first-place prize of $100 to the best talent act. I felt the old rhythm in my spirit come alive as I read the poster that hung on the bulletin board.

It had been a while since I had done any singing. Nonetheless, I entered into the competition. To get away for some private rehearsal time, I would slip away to the top floor of the building where there was an old recreation room that was no longer in use. I would go up there to be alone. Before anyone really paid attention or begin to wonder where the music was coming from, I would have already had an hour to myself. It felt good preparing for the talent show.

The night of the party, those that were eligible to go boarded the vans. We were taken to a community center out on 108th in the Roseland Community. Eighteen of us were granted permission to participate in the holiday festivities. We were all excited about getting out of the house, having some fun and be around some women. I was even teased by one of my house brothers, Shun: *"The way Smithy singing, we just gotta stay around him because that's where all the ladies gone be."* We'd all laugh.

Reality set in on us when we entered the recreation center. The lights were down low and we were ready to mix and mingle with the ladies. The women that were there were from one of HRDC's women facilities.

The staff watched closely as we danced and mingled. There was said to be strict consequences if we got caught indulging in any sexual acts. Me, even though the ladies looked exquisite I did not have a problem with obeying the rules. I danced with a few of the ladies, but my mind was on the talent show. I was so nervous that I continued to watch the time. With every minute that passed I realized I was that much closer to them calling my name.

Even though I had been practicing for over two weeks, the jitters were bouncing away inside my stomach. Those minutes had finally boiled down to that moment. It was Showtime. The competition had gathered together. It was like *The Gong Show*; there were some talented people, and there were some not-so-talented people. When it was my turn to go on stage, the guys from my house cheered for me hella loud. I was super nervous, and I thought I was going to have to go to the bathroom. My stomach was jumping.

But just like old times, when the music started to play, I went into my act, closed everybody out, and became Bobby Brown, feeling myself. After all, it was my prerogative. The nervousness left me as soon as I blew out the first note. I went into a zone when the ladies started to scream. I was live at the Apollo Theater, in my mind that is. I was pointing, posing for the ladies and spreading my arms out like I was the shit.

When the song was ending, I didn't want it to end, nor did I stop singing. When the music went off, I continued to sing, *"It's mine, it's mine. It's mine, it's mine."* The crowd was right along with me, together we shouted, *"It's mine, mine!"* I sang as I walked off the stage and in the back when I got behind the curtain, I sang, *"The $100 is mine."* All I heard from the crowd was clapping and men shouting, *"Woo, woo, woo."* It was a whole lot of fun. I won second place, which was $75. They judged us like they do on the Apollo; by applauses. The lady of the house won first prize. I was cool with the $75.

Once back at the center, it was business as usual; group meetings and anger management classes. I was down to my last couple of months and would be allowed to go out for eight hours a day, job searching Monday through Friday. This was a good thing. I felt I was ready to take on the world again and all the responsibilities that came along with it. I was hoping to be able to find a job fast. I didn't want to go back home to my mother's, nor did I want to go back to the West Side. I wanted to find an apartment and start over. After the show, I was singing more often than I had in previous years. I even thought about getting a band together.

I began getting passes every morning to go out looking for a job. I put in applications everywhere, but nobody wanted to hire an ex-con and are covering drug addict. Things weren't looking too good as far as getting a job and having my own apartment before being released. I used my mother's address for parole purposes. It was all good. I made up my mind to put a band together once I got settled in at my mother's house. I was not going to be sitting idle.

Mama was excited when I told her I was going to start back singing. She was my biggest fan. *"That's my son,"* she would stand shouting out in the audience. Some mornings, instead of going to look for work, I would spend my days with her. I owed her for all the pain I had caused her from the bad decisions I made embarking in a career of drugs and crime. It wasn't the way she had raised me. I wanted to do good for her, as well as for myself. Throughout my life, she's been the only person that has always been there for me.

Her faith in me strengthened my faith in myself. She would always tell me that I'd get through the rough times. She would always associate a Bible verse with whatever it was we were going through. *"Keep your head up, babe."* 1 Corinthians 10:12 said, *"God is faithful, who will not allow you to be tempted beyond that which you are able to bear it."* Psalms 30:5 said, *"Weeping may endure for a night, but joy comes in the morning."* Mama would recite those scriptures to me, overwhelmed with joy. *"What don't kill you will only make you stronger,"* she would say.

The closer I got to graduating from the program, the better I felt. I was two weeks shy of completing the program. One day I was on the Dan Ryan Train heading back to the center, the train stopped on Roosevelt and State Street and I looked out the window. There sitting playing the piano and singing, with dark glasses—looking like a young Stevie Wonder was Robert Kelly. I couldn't believe it. Still working in the subway and playing the same piano my sister had bought some years before. I immediately got up to get off the train before the doors would close.

As soon as I hopped off, he saw me. He stopped in the middle of his song, swiftly sat his keyboard on the side of the bench and came up and hugged me. *"Man, I can't believe this. Where you been, man? I missed you"* were his first words to me. We were happy to see each other. I took the few minutes I had letting him know what I had been through and the fact that I had to get back to the center.

We exchanged phone numbers and he made me promise that I would call him. He told me he had some things going on and again how he was so happy to see me. It was a beautiful moment for me. I don't think he knew how glad I was to see him. I felt spiritually touched when we departed from each other that day. It was meant for us to work together, I thought. When I got back on the next train, I sat relaxed, smiling within myself, thinking things were going to work out after all. I could hear my mother's voice in my head: *"Nobody can stop what God's got for you, baby."* I felt it was truly fate that brought me back to Robert Kelly. The reception I received from him made it that much more believable.

I was anxious to hook back up with Robert. It was hard to believe that he was still performing in the subways. I would have thought with all the talent this young man had and the I thought someone would have signed him by now with all the work we put in to secure him a fully produced demo tape and the master tapes of his recordings. I thought that window to work with him as his personal assistant was closed. But nonetheless, the door of opportunity was there for me.

The next day when I got up, I left the center leaving them under the impression I was going on job interviews, and in a way I was. Going to see Robert was definitely a job interview. When I got to Robert's house that day, I was greeted by his mom, his sister Teresa and his brother Bruce as if I was truly missed. Mama Kelly would say, *"Babe, if you need anything come talk to me. You're always there for me with my son, and I don't want you to leave Robert again. You're supposed to be with him,"* she told me. I would just listen to her. She would make me feel as if working with Robert was where I was supposed to be.

CHAPTER 10

The Big Break

WHILE ROBERT AND I were at his mothers' house, Larry Hood, another one of Robert's close friends had come by. When Larry saw me, he got excited. *"Johnny,"* he yell out looking surprised *"Oh man!"* he said as he walked over to give me a big bear hug, like homeboys do when their reunited with former friends. We talked for what seemed like hours. The joy we felt and expressed about being in each other's presence was overwhelming. As much as I hated to, I had to cut my visit short. I had to be back at the center within the next forty minutes. I had come too far to fall back now. Especially, with the prospect of joining back up with Robert Kelly.

This was a happy time for me. I still had faith in myself that I could beat my drug addiction and find my way to the top with Robert. In my eyes he was the superstar the world was waiting on. I was ready to complete this program and get back to promoting my artist. I thought about the things Robert and I talked about. *"Man, I need you with me, Johnny,"* he'd say.

"Man, ain't no more going away." His words were like music to my ears.

Larry was a kind hearted 220 pound, 6'1" bundle of smoothness. Robert mentioned that he still wanted Larry as his personal security. Everyone that surrounded Robert stepped in place to ensure that Robert had what he needed to become a mega star. It was the relationship we shared that got us to this point. We had bonded together, broke bread together, and shared our monies to help further develop Robert in his career. We partied and stood toe to toe with each other when confrontations came about.

We were all loyal, die-hard friends to each other. We all had the same high hopes. After Larry and I talked for a while, it was time for me to head back to the center. The next day Robert suggested that we pick up another member of the crew. Torrey! He was another person I met through Robert. A friend I had come to know and love. I hadn't seen him. I smiled at the thought of going to get him. The Pillsbury dough boy is what I called Torrey. He was short, light skinned and one of the sharpest, coolest cats I knew. The girls loved Torrey. He was cuddly and charming to the ladies.

His position in the crew was to be Robert's stylist. Torrey knew his style so the title fit him perfectly. In addition to being up on the latest in fashion he was also an innovator when it came to creating a style to fit Robert. We pulled up in the alley behind the building where Torrey lived,. I got out of the car to let him get into the back seat. *"Johnny B, boy what's happening man,"* he asked looking me up and down. He extended his hand out for a shake and pulling me into him when I grabbed his hand.

"Boy you still straight ain't you", he asked, as he got into the back seat of the car?

"What are you talking about" I asked? I didn't have a clue to what he was asking me, what I was straight in.

"You know, they ain't tap it back there did they," he asked, being funny; insinuating some homosexual stuff because I had been locked up?

"Man get your little humpty dumpty looking ass in the car'" I told him. We all laughed as we rode off.

I felt that I was back home and back with the family I wanted to be with. I loved these guys. After we picked Torrey up, we went to Forty-seventh and Cornell, right off the lake, to play basketball. While Torrey and Larry played ball, Robert and I waited on the next game.

While on the sideline we talked about what had transpired over the period of time I had been away. He told me he had been to LA and had worked on a project with Bennie Medina and that things hadn't worked out for him. He even tried to shop the demo Craig financed for him but he really didn't know how to get people to listen to him and back him without signing a contract.

Since his trip to LA, Robert was working with a guy named Eric Payton. He wanted me to work closely with Eric. He said Eric wanted him to be a part of a singing group. Robert wanted me to be a part of that and said he was glad I was back. He knew that I had his best interest at heart. It felt good to be close to him and still in a position to work as his personal assistant. I asked him if my 5 percent was still part of the deal. He told me yes so I took the job and was anxious to get started.

After the game, Larry dropped Robert and me off at Eric's house on Seventy-fifth and Yates. Robert introduced me to Eric, and we talked about the position Robert wanted me to have being with him. Robert let him know right then I was the one responsible for the demo tape Robert had.

Eric was cool about everything. Eric talked about his singing group, MGM (Mentally Gifted Men), a three guy group. He wanted Robert to join the group and Robert agreed. In the meeting Robert mentioned that he wanted me to be responsible for the production and development of the group. We ended our meeting feeling good about what was to come. I was invited back the next day to meet MGM. Timing could not have been better for me; I was in the beginning of something new with Robert, and I was in the same position as before—His Right-Hand Man.

The next day, we met with MGM—Mark, Shaun, and Vince—at Eric's house around 1:00 p.m. We didn't have a band, so we performed off the recorded tracks from the demo Craig had executively produced for Robert. Rehearsals were strenuous and Robert's work ethic was unbelievable. He was a workaholic when it came to his music. Robert put together a dynamic show making R. Kelly and MGM a new force. In my opinion, they were untouchable. They were sharp, good looking and talented. They worked to achieve perfection. Their new jack style of dancing was as perfect as Michael Jackson's. Every move was precise. With the four of them performing together neither Bobby Brown, New Edition or any other group out there couldn't stand next to these guys.

I was in charge of the rehearsals, and I worked them hard. I gave them style and taught them how to capture their audience. My biggest asset was my ability to bringing out personality on stage. That's what I do. I let them all know how they were projecting to the audience. I taught them how to kneel down and how to reach out to the women and when to reach out to them. I gave them words to say. Basically, I put the "Cool" in them. Those were my boy's! R. Kelly & MGM were a true force to be reckoned with when I finished with them.

Eric's duties were to search for a record deal with the demo and he had the final say on the shows I booked. We performed in talent shows all over the City of Chicago becoming regulars at the Cotton Club on Michigan Avenue, the same club where Bernie Mac got his stat. Back in the late '80s we were all close. I remember back in the day when Bernie Mac was performing at the club and anybody that came in or exited the club would have to go past the stage to get in or out. If you knew how open-mic was at the Cotton Club, you didn't want to walk out when Bernie Mac was on the stage because he would surely roast you.

I remember one evening I had to leave while he was on stage. Even though we were cool, The Mac Man waited until I had committed myself to rush past the stage to get to the exit door. Knowing I needed to leave, he stopped me in my tracks and called me out. *"Demetrius! Where you going? Come on, man, go on by, go on by man, I ain't gone get you. I know you gotta go. I'm just glad you didn't try to slide your almost fat ass by here thinking nobody was gone see you."* The crowd busted out laughing and I did too as I made my way out the door as fast as I could. You could only laugh when he talked about you and try not to show the embarrassment at the same time. Bernie Mac knew how to get you and when to let up on you. He kept it all fun. I miss that brother, him just being here. The thought of him is of a smile!

Bernie Mac would have you laughing coming and going. Every Monday night people came to see Bernie Mac at the Cotton Club to watch him take on the competition, and have the club rolling with laughter as he held his title of top comedian at the Cotton Club. He was indeed one of the funniest men who could talk about you and you'd love him the same. He was not scared. *"Who you with?"* was his saying. He was truly an entertainer with style, charm, and a heart for others.

As I remember him, Bernie Mac, he was always on his business to open his door to be recognized for the greatness of the gift he had, to make people laugh. At one time, he asked me to help him write a bio to present himself to the market. He had read the bio I had put together for Robert Kelly. Bernie and I associated with each other when we saw each other at the Cotton Club. We weren't close running buddy friends, but we knew and had a mutual respect for each other.

Bernie had approached me to help him because he had heard about Russell Simmons' production of Def Comedy Jam, and he wanted to step his game up to the business of representing himself professionally. He told me *"D, it's time to get real with this."* I helped him to format an outline for his bio, and next thing I knew I looked around and Bernie Mac had a TV show. He had reached his dream. Bernie Mac was one of the true kings of comedy. R.I.P my brother, I love you Bernie Mac.

We had a lot of fun back in those days. We were club hopping all over the city R. Kelly and MGM were becoming a household name in the clubs of Chicago. We heard of a talent show audition at the New Regal Theater on 79th and Stoney Island.

The first place winners would receive a trip to LA to appear on Natalie Cole's *Big Break* show and compete against other contestants for a chance to win $100,000 in cash and prizes, plus a recording contract. R. Kelly and MGM were so hot; we were invited to the audition. We were on a mission to win that competition.

We needed to win that $100,000 cash. But more than that, the winner also had an opportunity to be an opening act for Heavy D and the Boyz, and we wanted that spot too. We rehearsed daily, at the Regal Theater from 1:00 p.m.3:30 p.m. We had the whole stage. We had access to all the equipment and the soundboard. It was a total professional environment for us. There was no doubt in our minds we were going to win this talent show. On the night of the show, we lit the stage up with our perfectly timed dance steps and smooth sex appeal that had the ladies screaming. We won that competition with the crowd screaming for an encore. We knew then that Heavy D was going to have a job to do following our act.

After winning the competition, we were excited. Winning that night was motivation for us. The following morning, we were up rehearsing, getting ready for the show with Heavy D; which was only a few weeks away. Showtime came, and we were on cloud nine. Although Heavy D was big, we knew that our show was on a professional level. We arrived at the Regal Theater where we were treated like celebrities. We stayed in the dressing room until Showtime. We prayed, and when it was time to go on, we lit it up again. Heavy D and the Boyz came out of their dressing rooms from stage left and stage right, to watch our show. *"Who are them cats?"* Heavy D would ask.

Performing that night was big fun for us. The ladies went crazy when Shaun knelt down at the front of the stage, pointed to a young lady, and smoothly said, *"Say, baby, can I talk to you for a minute? There's something on my mind."* As the music was playing, R. Kelly and MGM were doing some slow, sexy dance moves to Teddy Reilly's song *"Let's Chill."*

It was time for the Natalie Cole *Big Break* show. We never stopped working towards the goal to win $100,000 and be on TV. There wasn't a doubt in our minds about us winning the competition. We were confident in that. And because of the confidence everything should have gone smoothly; but it didn't. Money always seemed to find a way to change things. Everybody was trying to be a part of our click. The drug dealers wanted Robert to produce them in the rap game. Eric was taking money on the side, from small investors to keep money in Robert's pocket. And there was other confusions flaring up in the camp; egos were beginning to sprout up like weed.

One day when we didn't have a scheduled rehearsal, I was just hanging out and decided to drive to Eric's house. I didn't pay attention to the cars that were outside, I just parked and went up to the door and rang the bell. Eric answered, and as I stepped in there, to my surprise, there was my sister.

Everyone gave me a strange look when I stepped into the house, like I walked in on something I should not have. Ce-Ce was back in the mix. She was who Eric had gotten to finance the video Robert was about to shoot. *"Why you wanna play me!"* Robert was about to shoot.

Yeah, we needed the money for uniforms and for the video. But I was disappointed to learn that my sister was involved with us again. I felt as if she was playing herself. She gave Eric $15,000 to shoot the video. They were playing my sister just like when we first got together with her and Craig. They were spending money with no paperwork being signed. They were going on the belief that when he's straight, he'll look out for them. That's not how business is done. I could feel deceit in the air.

I wanted to talk to my sister. I needed to somehow get through to her that she and I should be working together but I knew she wouldn't listen to me. I went on pretending I was not bothered by her presence so I let it go. They had all kept me out of the loop with the production of the video anyway. This was all going on behind my back. Apparently, they didn't want me to know about it. My thoughts were, *"Here we go again"!* *I wondered w*hen the deceit would stop. What my being here did do was put me on point. Robert and I were going to talk about getting me signed to my five percent. And with that thought I kept my focus. I didn't let my sister's presence alter my emotions.

There was nothing more important to me than the tryouts for the talent show. Of course we won and the Grand Prize which was 5 round trip tickets to Los Angeles to be on the *Big Break Show* for a chance to win $100,000.Inorder for me to go, Eric was going to have to pay my way, and he claimed the group didn't have money for my trip. I was hurt over that, but what could I do other than wish them well. Ce-Ce went along with the crew.

R. Kelly and MGM won first place in Natalie Cole's *Big Break* competition. I was happy for them and I was over any ill feelings for not being able to go. They deserved it. They worked hard. We all worked hard. But little did I know of the confrontations that had taken place while they were in LA. When they returned from LA, everybody was mad over the money. Eric got 20 percent of $100,000 off the top. The whole debate was about how much everybody else would get. Eric was confused with the situation and wanted to do the right thing by everybody. Mark felt they should all receive an equal share of $10,000 apiece. Robert didn't agree with that and neither did I for the following reasons: 1.Robert wrote and produced all the songs. 2. Robert did the background vocals on the tracks that were used town in the competition. 3.Robert choreographed the dance routines. 4. Robert had to pay for the studio time needed to produce the tracks they danced to.

So in all fairness, I thought Robert should have given them a nice paycheck and they should have been happy. At the time as far as the group was concerned, MGM were just dancers and should have been paid as such. I told Robert and Eric, they were worthy of a nice paycheck but not an equal share. Eric should have established that in the beginning and Robert should have listened when I told him to get that establish with Eric making sure they all understood MGM's position with Robert as background dancers because that's what they were.

When the check came to Eric, he gave each member of MGM $5,000. That was cool, but because of the whole misunderstanding, that was the end of R. Kelly and MGM. I was paid $300, which was way short of 5percent, but I stayed optimistic. I believed things were going to work out.

After the big break up with MGM and Eric Payton, It was me, Robert, Larry and Torrey again. We were the ride-or-die crew with R. Kelly. again. I was back to booking shows for him at hotels, nightclubs, and any place that we could get in where there would be a crowd of people. I would go inside a joint, a party, or a hotel that had a piano in it and negotiate for Robert to perform for tips. Robert would always tell me, *"Man, you make things happen. Trust me; you are going to get paid when we get this deal. Just hang with me."*

For the next six or seven months, Robert and I worked the club circuits as well as on occasions, we'd go back down into the subway. I'd work in the daytime. At that time, I was still living with my mom in Dixmoor, Illinois. To make ends meet, I had gotten a little job at a sheet metal factory, Sanders Metals. My life was consumed with doing things for Robert Kelly. After MGM, it was me, Robert, Larry, and Torrey. We were the ride-or-die crew with Robert Kelly. As time went on, the crew worked diligently to prepare ourselves for the success we all believed was inevitable. We took our jobs seriously and we made it our business to perform so well at the clubs, leaving the impression that we were traveling with the next high-profile celebrity. The Bible says, *"Believe in things as though they were,"* and that's how we lived and believed daily. We were having fun.

During this time, I was pretty much working in a manager's shoes. Everything was coming through me. When people wanted to talk to Robert about something, he'd send them to me. If someone wanted him to sing somewhere, they'd call me. We took Robert's piano with us wherever. We were still street performers we just weren't in the subways anymore. We went through the city and surrounding suburbs working anywhere we could. We would enter any talent show and win. We were doing well for an inexperienced crew.

Robert had a girlfriend, Lonneice, who was a jewel and a special lady. Light-skinned, petite a Tia Mowry, from the show "The Game" type of beauty. Lonneice was a beautiful woman and she was down for Robert, but she was not a little girl. She didn't stay put up like Robert would tell her. Lonneice was not going to be treated like a child. Robert was crazy about Lonneice, but he didn't want to give her any freedom. He always had to know where she was, and most of the time, he wanted her to be confined to the house. They were together for awhile—she was with him through the Eric Payton and MGM era.

Lonneice was pretty much taking care of Robert. He stayed with her and her grandmother on Fifty-fourth and Daman. He even drove her car. I remember one night Robert called me in the middle of the night. Lonneice hadn't come home from work. I was way out in Dixmoor, Illinois, twenty-five minutes away, but my boy said he needed me because Lonneice was missing. I jumped up out of bed and drove over to Lonneice's house.

Robert was outside in the car waiting. When I pulled up, he had me drive around to where he thought she was. Come to find out, while we were riding around stalking and looking for her, she was at home. She was late because she had dropped one of her co-workers who had car trouble off at home. Robert was so jealous and controlling. He didn't want her to talk to anyone, not even us, his friends. This was my boy though; I was sticking with him through it all.

It was around November 1990 when we heard about a gospel play that was coming to town. They were holding auditions for singing parts, and I got Robert interested in auditioning. The only thing was neither Larry nor I were able to make it on the day of the audition because we both had to work. So instead of letting Robert go by himself, I called Al Cover (RIP), who was Eric Payton's uncle. Al was an older cat. He was actually around sixty, maybe seventy years old, but he hung around us like one of the crew, supporting us 100 percent. Al Cover was the man for us. He was cool, dependable, and loyal. Al believed in Robert as we did. He had all of us, catering to his needs.

Al Cover accompanied Robert to the Regal Theater for the audition, and I arrived later that day. By the time I arrived Robert had already performed.

We were invited back for a reading the next day. Robert wanted to sing, because he knew as I did, that he wasn't going to be able to read a script. Only Larry and I knew that Robert could not read or write well at all. He was offered a part in the play at a salary of $1,200 a week plus per Diem. We were there waiting for the play script, and at the same time, trying to figure out how we were going to get through to the producer of the play and convince him to allow Robert to sing without reading. I was going to have to workday and night with Robert because what he was going to have to do was memorize his parts, which in itself was a rough job.

The next day, when we arrived for the reading, Robert and I had already decided that I was going to talk to whoever was in charge. I learned through cast members that the guy to talk to was Mr. Barry Hankerson, the producer of the play. We found him sitting in the back of the theatre watching the rest of the entertainers.

I approached Mr. Hankerson and introduced myself to him as Robert's personal assistant. *"Mr. Hankerson, My name is Demetrius Smith, I'm Robert Kelly's personal assistant. Mr. Hankerson, Robert has so much more to offer you than just singing in this play,"* I said. Mr. Hankerson looked at me puzzled, like who are you. He was looking around as if he wondered if he might need some security.

I didn't stop talking until he said, *"Hold on hold on man! Who is Robert and what are you talking about"* He said.

"That's Robert He auditioned for you yesterday". I said pointing over to Robert who was sitting further in the back of the theater to the right of us.

"Oh yea, the kids got a nice voice, he's already hired", Mr. Hankerson said.

"Yea I know Mr. Hankerson, I know, and we thank you but *Robert got so much more talent than what you saw. He is a genius when it comes to writing songs, Mr. Hankerson,"* I told him. *"He can write a song for anybody. I'm telling you right now if you can just listen to him for one song. This kid can write, sing play the piano and dance. He got it all. If you can listen to him sing one of his songs I guarantee you you'll see what I'm talking about."* I was pleading with Mr. Hankerson. I was talking so fast I was just hoping to get through to him. I knew that if he would listen to Robert sing one song, Robert would win him over.

Mr. Hankerson asked me if I had a tape that he could listen to with some of Robert's songs. I told him, *"I don't have a tape, but I have a keyboard in my car. I can go and get it, and Robert will perform right here if you got a minute, just one minute and I'll go get it"*, I said. As I began to get up out of my seat, I put up one finger up to Mr. Hankerson, indicating one minute. *"One minute Mr. Hankerson, I'm a go get the keyboard, I'll be right back. Just give me one minute Mr. Hankerson,"* I pleaded as I began to walk away. And just like that, Robert Kelly's career started to unfold.

Mr. Hankerson agreed to let Robert perform. As I went to get the keyboard, Robert got up and came along with me. I told him what we were about to do, and we did it. Robert performed for Mr. Hankerson and won him over. It was on that very same day Mr. Hankerson no longer wanted Robert for the play. He was interested in getting Robert a recording contract.

We had no idea that Mr. Hankerson was already in the music business as the manager for the gospel singing group, The Winnans. He also managed David Peaston, Gavin Christopher, to name a few. He also was an executive producer for a few movies. Plus, he used to be married to Gladys Knight. Mr. Hankerson was the real deal.

Once Barry Hankerson became interested in Robert, he didn't waste any time getting things started. Within two weeks, Robert was moved into a two-bedroom high-rise apartment in downtown Chicago, and he gave Robert cash to cover the expenses he had accumulated under Eric Payton's management. Robert was in touch with Barry Hankerson on a consistent basis now. They were on the phone with each other all the time, and they became real close real fast. Barry came right in and went to work being Robert's manager.

When the money started circulating, it was pretty much Robert and Barry together all the time. Barry flew Robert up to LA and started Robert off producing. His first project was David Peaston, another artist Barry managed. We really started believing that we were on our way to the big times when Robert told me he was writing a song for Gladys Knight.

Even though things were moving in a positive direction, I felt kind of left out. I felt Robert should have had me with him. He should have told Barry to bring me up. I was the one that talked Barry into listening to Robert's music. Barry probably didn't even remember me after he heard Robert. Robert was not supposed to forget about me. After where we had been and what we had been through together, when Barry gave Robert some cash, Robert should have given me some. Robert always threw me kibble sand bits, but I was hooked in, and I couldn't let go. I just had to hold on and believe that I was going to be rewarded for the loyalty and hard work I had been putting in with him and for him. We had come a long ways together!

CHAPTER 11

Man behind the Man

WHEN ROBERT GOT back from LA, he called me and asked me to meet him at his new apartment. He had moved again. This time, he moved to a real deluxe apartment in the sky. He moved to the Lake Point Towers. This is where some big-time celebrities live, right on the lake in downtown Chicago, overlooking Lake Michigan and the Coastline of Lake Shore Drive. In this building there was a workout facility, cleaners, store, pool, sauna and a dance studio. You had to be buzzed in by the doorman to get to his apartment as well. Yep, it was indeed the next level.

When Robert and I met, he gave me a couple hundred dollars. At that time, anything was helpful because I was in need. It was only because of my belief that I would go on the payroll soon that made it easy for me to make myself available to Robert twenty-four hours a day. Since MGM was out of the picture, Robert decided he wanted some new dancers. I made some flyers and I passed them out at different clubs. We were searching for male dancers with vocals. On the day of the auditions we had a great turnout. We held the auditions at the dance studio in Robert's building. At that audition is where we met Earl, Rick, and DeAndre. Robert and I took a liking to these three cats immediately.

Earl, Rick, and DeAndre were already a group. They had been dancing together for a couple of years. Choosing them made the audition process short and easy. Robert and I came up with the name Public Announcement. I thought the name fit because we were making a statement to the public with our presentation. Barry decided for Robert to call himself R. That formed the group, R. Kelly and Public Announcement.

Once again I was assigned to the group to make sure they rehearsed and learned how to put on a good show. Robert would come through and choreograph the dance steps and then go into the studio with Barry. I drilled them to bring out the best in them. They could dance, but what they did really well was work hard. They knew the position they were in, and they wanted it.

While I was working with PA (Public Announcement), Barry was paying me $150 a week to keep me active and able to help my family and myself. Barry took Robert back to LA to work in the studio with David Peaston. Barry didn't meet with me again after the Regal Theatre. It was always him and Robert. I figured if I was going to get close to Barry, it was going to have to be with Robert pulling me in. And that's exactly what he did.

It was late spring of 1991; Robert left LA and went to New York. He called me from New York and said, *"Johnny, you gotta get down here. I'm in New York with Barry, and Jive Records wants to sign me. I need you down here with me. I told Barry you're my main man and to get you here."* I told Robert to hook it up and I'm on my way. I thought they were going to fly me up, but instead, a ticket was prepaid for me on the Greyhound bus. Nonetheless, I was going to New York City.

This would be my first visit to the Big Apple, and I was excited. Barry was making things happen. Things had come full circle. When I arrived in New York, I was met at the bus station by a limo driver, holding a sign with my name on it. I gave him a hand wave to acknowledge to him that I was the person he was waiting to pick up. I was taken to the Empire Hotel. Once I settled inside my tiny room, I called Robert at the studio to inform him that I had arrived. I was told to take a cab to Jive Studios where he and Barry were.

When I got to the studio, Robert and Barry were sitting in this big studio room. You know how it looks in the studio—a big console mixing board, about eighty tracks. It was the first time I had been in a studio this large or, should I say, a real studio. Robert looked like he was at home spinning around in the swivel chair. Barry had a serious look on his face. They both stood up to give me a welcome greeting by hugging me.

"You're a hell of a talker. That was a good job getting me to listen to this young genius; you were right. Are you ready to work man?" Barry asked?

"No doubt B" I said; with a big smile on my face shaking my head, yes.

We all started laughing. I know I was happy to be there. And Robert had made himself at home there in the studio. He looked as if he had been at it there for years. He was comfortable and looked happy. He was laying down some tracks for one of Jive records other artist. Barry told me to come with him into another studio room so we could talk. There, he told me that Robert spoke very highly of me and that he wanted me to stay as his personal assistant. Barry went on to tell me about the duties of a personal assistant, which was pretty much what I was already doing—taking care of Robert.

Now here we were, in a major studio. Barry was having meetings daily to discuss a major deal for Robert. I was never at any of those meetings, but Robert told me pretty much what was going on in respect to the album coming out and that we would be touring as soon as the album was done. My job was to take care of Robert; and that's what I was going to do. We stayed in New York for about a month. Robert was working on the album as well as working with and producing some of Jive Records' other artist.

I was at Robert and Barry's beck and call running errands for them. I would go out to find places for Robert to play basketball, I'd go get his food, and when he was feeling bad or having a toothache, I was the one who got up in the middle of the night to go get him medicine.

Barry had put me on a $350 a week salary. I was cool with that. It looked as if things were really about to start happening for us in a major way.

Every morning, when we would leave the studio, Robert and I would sit down at the hotel and talk about the events of that day. We talked about how when we got back home, we were going to work even harder. Robert would work at crafting his art and I would make sure Robert had everything he needed.

One particular night, I had a discussion with Robert about Barry putting me on a $350 a week salary. Robert told me he knew it because he had okayed it. He said that in the long run, it was coming out of his money anyway. I then asked him about the 5 percent he and I had talked about me getting once we got a deal. That was the one thing I needed for my security. Robert told me it was not going to be a problem. *"As soon as I finish with my deal, we can make that happen,"* he told me.

My mind was on cloud nine. I was making $350, but I had a vision of making a lot more money. I could see it right in front of me. Wow! We were about to get busy and be paid. Once back in Chicago, we all met at the Knickerbocker Hotel where Barry stayed. It was me, Robert, Barry, Public Announcement, Al Clover and Larry. This was a big meeting for us all. We all knew Robert was about to sign a major deal with Jive Records. Robert had already told me on our flight back that the papers to the contract were all being drawn up and we were scheduled to go back to New York the following week.

At that meeting, Barry gave us all our assigned duties. He said that our purpose for being with Robert was not to just hang out. He let us know we were in show business and that it was truly a business. It turned serious to me when he informed everyone that I would be the person in charge of all R. Kelly functions and, in doing so, let everybody know that I was the man in charge. He let us know he worked out of LA and New York and that he would communicate all activities through me and I was the one who would inform them of what's needed of them. Barry even mentioned that he wanted everyone on payroll and would wire money to me to distribute.

It was all about business from that point on and we were all ready to take on the challenge. My job was to keep everybody informed of rehearsals, photo shoots, radio interviews, personal appearances and anything else that was scheduled. Everything would come through me. I had become, *"The Man behind the Man."* This was happening just how we had all talked about. We were destined to make it to the big time amongst the celebrities. We had long-term goals to reach and the backing to make it happen. We were on our way.

That next day, we started working with more determination. Robert was a workaholic. He didn't slack off at anything, and he didn't allow anyone else to slack either. We were scheduled to go back to New York to close the deal. So Robert wanted to make sure to get his work in with Public Announcement. He had a routine he wanted them to perfect while we were gone.

The night before it was time to leave and go to New York, I was told by Barry I wouldn't be going. He told me it was a short business trip and there was nothing there I was going to be doing. I was confused. I thought traveling with Robert was a part of my job? Barry tried to pump me up by saying I was needed to oversee the rehearsals anyway. I was totally disappointed, but couldn't let him know. It was okay; I was still on a $350a week salary. Thus far, that three fifty was coming weekly and on time. I was beginning to save a little of it. I was on assignment, and I was cool with it. It inspired me to dwell deeper and do the best work I could do for the kid. To be paid was what it was all about anyway. *"Let them be gone,"* I said to myself, now more disappointed than mad at them for leaving me behind.

While they were gone, I worked with PA every day on the routine Robert had taught them before he left. The guys were workaholics and attentive executioners. They didn't stop until they had their routine in sync. They listened to me attentively; they wanted to perfect the vision of what being suave was, along with keeping it cool. They were as hardworking as the MGM group. Public Announcement wanted to be everything Robert envisioned as his background dancers because they believed in him. They felt lucky to be in their position.

Robert called me from New York to tell me how things were going. He told me that the deal was signed and that he would be returning in the next day or so. He was really interested in the progress of his new dancers. He wanted to know if they could be as good as MGM. I told him, yeah, it was no doubt in my mind they were ready and willing. I informed him we were rehearsing daily, they listened to instruction well, and they were hard workers. I told him all they talked about was how much they wanted to work with him. Robert told me that when he came home, he wanted to get right to work. He said he'd call me to give me his flight information.

Robert stressed the fact he wanted me and the group to meet him in Hyde Park at a rehearsal spot we had outside in a big parking lot on Forty-seventh and Cornell. It was an open field with a lot of rehearsal space. Right across the street was the park were we played basketball. Robert liked the attention we would get from the people who hung out there. They would come over from the park to watch us. We hadn't rehearsed there since the days with MGM. Back then, we would pull all our cars up, open the trunks and pump the music as loud as we could get it. The people would come from the park and gather around and cheer us on.

Robert called me early in the day to inform me that he was on the way home and to make sure we were in the park rehearsing when he got there. I made sure the orders were followed. We arrived at the park around 3:30p.m., and around 4:30 p.m., Robert pulled up in a black Mercedes Benz. When we saw the car pull up, we didn't know who it was, so we continued with our rehearsals. Once we realized it was Robert, we stopped what we were doing to show our joy. We knew the deal was signed and all our hard work was about to start paying off. In my mind, I couldn't wait to get alone with Robert. I felt he should have some word for me about my money. But for now, congratulations was in order.

We examined the car inside and out; on the outside I was excited but on the inside I could not get my mind off of my 5%. I had waited a long time for this payday to come. After all the hype was over, I thought we were going to pack up to go celebrate. No Sir! Robert was strictly about business. He didn't want to do anything else but rehearse. For another hour and a half, we focused on the dance routines. We went over the routines several times, critiquing every movement. You could see that R. Kelly and Public Announcement were going to be dynamic and entertain the world.

Demetrius Smith Sr.

We were rehearsing for the future, believing in things as though they were. Nothing was scheduled as of yet, but I knew with this signed deal I was about to become really busy. The first week Robert returned from New York, the groupie thing began to become unveiled. Girls were always at our rehearsals. Robert, for the most part, kept his focus on rehearsing and perfecting the show we were putting together. He knew that he was an entertainer but something was different about Robert.

After the Regal Theater competitions, the clubs, and all the talent shows we won in the past, Robert Kelly became well known and won the hearts of the people in Chicago. Radio personalities were talking about us on the radio. When we went out on the town, we had an entourage with us. Our crew was expanding. Robert would perform and after that it was all about the girls. The added crew members were there to assist Robert with recruiting girls to his apartment, and it seemed that the younger girls were the ones who always showed up at his apartment and a tour rehearsals.

I was in total disagreement with Robert entertaining young girls in his apartment, and for that reason, Robert began to distance himself from me. When I would go over to his crib, the doorman would call him and tell him I was there and he would tell him to have me wait for him in the lobby. I wasn't hanging out with Robert like I use to because we didn't see eye to eye on anything when the girls were around. I guess it was because I was always complaining about him spending so much time with young girls. I mean, I let him know that I was afraid for him and that I was only trying to protect him. He would always tell me he was working with the girls on a professional level. He said he was producing them. I began to talk to the crew about them picking young girls up for Robert, but they were only interested in trying to make a lasting impression on Robert and staying close to him. They were living in the limelight and the women were coming to them easy. They didn't want to try to understand my reasons for wanting to protect Robert.

The time away from my job was spent with my two girlfriends Lawanda and Tamekia who were both expecting. Yep, I was going to be a father. I had two women pregnant. It's nothing that I was proud of. In fact, I wish I had been smarter. However, there are no regrets. I wouldn't give my children up for anything in the world. I just wish they were all by one woman, but it is what it is.

I met my first child's mother, Lawanda, at the Cotton Club. I had just walked into the club with Robert. We were in the middle section of the club where they were taking photos when Lawanda approached me. "Hey, I don't normally approach men. I'm sitting over there. Would you come have a drink with me?" she said, pointing in the direction of her table." Sure, I could do that. Give me a minute, okay?" I said to her as I turned back around talking to Robert. Robert was like, "Who is that?" I said, "You know how I do it, man. I get chosen all the time. I'll get back with her later, man. Let's go back here and get the DJ to play this tune." As we were walking, Robert complimented me on how thick and gorgeous Lawanda was.

Later, I went over and sat with Lawanda and bought her a drink. I wasn't much of a rapper, but since she'd chosen me I wanted to spend a little time with her. Our conversation was short and then we exchanged numbers. Later, we hooked up, and from there little Demetrius was born.

I met my other children's mother, Tamekia, when I was on my way to rehearsal. I was walking down 75th Street and I noticed a young lady standing at a phone booth crying. When I got closer to her, I asked her, "Hey, young lady, are you all right?" She was a pretty young lady. Light skin, reddish hair, with nice pink juicy lips. To be honest with you, I wasn't looking at her in a sexual way; I was really concerned about her. She looked as if she was going through something.

She pointed across the street where three guys were standing and told me that they tried to grab her. She said she broke away and ran to the phone. She was on the phone with her mother and said she was crying because her mother wouldn't come get her and she was scared. I asked her where she lived. She told me she lived on Seventy-fourth and Exchange. I told her, I was going on 75th & Yates and asked if she would like to walk with me. Exchange was about six blocks farther east. I told her she could trust me. I would make sure she got home safely. From there, I ended up walking her all the way home. When we got there, she thanked me and asked me for my phone number. Two days later, she called. I asked her out, took her to the movies. Well, to make a long story short, Tamekia became the mother of my daughter, Ashley, and later my twin sons Deontae and DeAndre.

When Lawanda first told me she was pregnant, I must admit I was happy and overjoyed. I was thirty-three years old and I wanted a child. I didn't think I could have children with all the unprotected sex I had in my past. I blamed that on all the drugs I had consumed over the years. Two months after Lawanda told me she was pregnant; Tamekia told me she was also. I was so confused because I wanted so much to be with my child and raise him or her, but now here I was with two women, having my babies. I didn't know what to do. So I ran from one house to the other, doing the best I could in satisfying them both.

Both Lawanda and Tamekia always found things to argue with me about instead of being by my side. When I told them both about each other and that they were both having my child—that was really sad. Lawanda burst out crying, *"I wanted to be the only one to have your babies."* Tamekia was so angry she tried to abort my daughter but she was too far into the pregnancy, so instead she tried by taking pills which resulted in her having to have her stomach pumped and a psychiatric evaluation for her. I did not feel good at all about breaking the hearts of the two women who had enough love for me to bear my children.

My life was just like a ball of confusion. Things just could not go straight for me. Once again I messed everything up and in the midst of it, there were children that I was going to be responsible for. I felt the same as Lawanda. I wanted children with one woman, but what was done was done.

On December 8, 1990, I was on my way to do what I did when my beeper went off. It was Dorothy, Lawanda's mother. I gave her a call. She told me they were on their way to the Bernard Mitchell Hospital on Cottage Grove. She said the baby was ready to come.

Work was postponed that evening. I rushed to the hospital to witness the birth of a little me. I was so happy. I was about to really become a father. I made it to the hospital on time. I was able to walk to the delivery room with Lawanda, holding her hand. I was right there looking as the doctor cut Lawanda open and peeled her skin back layer after layer. She had to have what they called a C-section. My son came out stretching like ET (in the movie), being pulled from out of her belly. Standing there, watching my son stretching out into the world at his first moment was amazing. He had his mother's eyes. This was a part of her I use to tell her I wanted him to have of her, and he had them. That was a blessed moment for me. I loved him before he got here. Now it was all so real.

Reality set right in on me. I couldn't do what I was doing anymore. All the stealing, the robbing and taking changes with my life, it all ended that night. At that very moment when my son was born I knew I had to be there for him. Nothing was more important than for me to get a job. The thought of being caught for any type of crime, and be taken away from my son was a thought I could not conceive, right at that very moment I knew I didn't want to do anything wrong anymore. This was the proudest moment of my life.

Lawanda, wanted to name our son Dominique. I didn't want to debate. She knew I wanted to name our son Demetrius. I babe booed her. I was being real sweet. I wanted to the moment to last forever. My family, I looked at Lawanda, I wanted her too. I wanted to love her. I told Lawanda I wanted my first son to be my Jr. Jokingly, I suggested we asked the baby. We walked up to the incubator, were the baby was. As we stood in front of the incubator, I asked my son what he wanted to be named. I said, *"Hey little man,"* I was grinning ear to ear. I said *"Hey Demetrius,"* He would look at me with his eyes wide open. *"Demetrius, do you want to be called Dominique?"* I asked and he'd close his eyes as if he was not answering to the name. I said Lawanda look at him, and I'd say *"Demetrius,"* and he would open his eyes. I would say, *"Dominique,"* and his eyes would close.

Lawanda couldn't believe it either. We kept doing it. I began to say it in a rhythm. *"Demetrius, Dominique. Demetrius Dominique."* Each time he would open and close his eyes. He opened his eyes to the name Demetrius. The baby made the choice. He was named Demetrius Smith Jr. I was there daily and all day sitting with my son. I day dreamed being with him how I wanted to give him so much more than I had had. I had done a couple of more burglaries and I was really frightened as I thought of being caught. I thought about how my luck was. On the day I picked Lawanda up I made up my mind I was through. I was through taking changes with my life. I realized as I was carrying my son my life was no longer just mine. I had a family now and I wanted to be there for them.

Three months later, March 20th, 1991, my daughter, Ashley Tierra Smith, was born. I was at home when she was born too. Except on that particular day, I was at a Chicago Bulls game. I was a Chicago Bull fanatic. With Craig being a Chicago Bull now I was able to get tickets to all the home games and I was at every one of them. The day Ashley was born they were playing the Atlanta Hawks. And Dominique Wilkins was in the house. It was to be a show down between Michael Jordan and Dominique.

The Bulls were the hottest thing on the planet. Tamekia told me she felt the baby was going to come that day. But of course, I didn't want to miss that game. I guaranteed her as soon as they would call I would leave. And I did. Right after the first quarter I got the page from Tamika's mother. It was time to go. It was a bigger moment for me ahead. It was time for my baby girl to come into the world. I went in a hurry.

Unfortunately though, by the time I had gotten to the hospital the baby had already been born. She came out in the ambulance her mother had told me. *"She just swoop, and slid right on out"* Tamekia said of my baby girls delivery. Tamekia was laughing about it. She was up and looked like she could be given a choice to stay at the hospital or to go home if she wanted. She wasn't at all out of it. She didn't look as if the baby had caused her any pain. When the nurse brought the baby to me Tamekia told me then she had named my baby girl Ashley. *"Hi Ashley",* I said kissing her. She was a pretty balled head baby. She was screaming, crying but she was on key as she screamed.

All I thought was that she had a set of strong vocal cords on her. Wow! She was amazing as well. I had a son and a daughter now. Looking at my baby girl, I stood there thanking God and wanting to cry because I wanted to give her everything too. I wanted my children to know each other and to grow up together.

My life was so off balance. I was having it real hard with Lawanda about Tamekia. I guess it was because I was living with Lawanda that she would be so jealous. It was too late for jealousy I thought. It was about the babies in my world. I wanted Lawanda and Tamekia to be on the same page I was on. I wanted them to really love me.

Wishfully thinking, I wanted us all to live together. I was wondering if I could perhaps persuade them to try liking each other for the sake of our children and maybe we could all live in the same house. I wanted to figure out a way for my children to grow up together under the same roof. I did not want to hurt either one of them.

Robert was a handful and he wanted me with him all the time, except for the times when girls came around. I used to ask Robert how old the girls were. He'd tell me that they were in his age bracket. I knew better, but I had to take it slow dealing with Robert. I couldn't get him to see the danger he was putting himself in being in the company of young girls. From that point on, I began to keep my association with Robert strictly about work.

A few weeks after Robert was signed, Barry told me that he could no longer pay me $350 a week. My salary would be $150 a week for weekly rehearsals at home and would increase to $350 a week on the road. I was messed up in the head when he told me that.

I went to Robert about it and he told me Barry was the manager and that I was being paid by him. I said, *"Robert, man, I been doing this with you for some years now, man."* I asked him, *"Don't you think it's time I start being paid?"*

"Johnny man," he said, *"that's going to happen, but you have to wait until we get started."*

"Get started! Robert, come on, man, we been started."

I asked him when we were going to get together with Barry to get the 5 percent taken care of. He told me Barry was coming into town the following week.

"Johnny man, just be a little more patience. Barry's making things happen, and it won't be too much longer before we get you straight. Hang in there with me, man. It's gone be all right real soon, I promise." I wasn't going to win in this conversation, and I knew it. Robert always knew what to say, how to say it and when to say it.

I was pissed. I felt like I already waited long enough. I wanted to quit but couldn't because now I had a son and a daughter to care for. I had to stick it out. I felt I had to make this work. Looking ahead in life for me then, I thought I had nothing else better going on for myself. As time kept moving, I kept telling myself, *"It's all gonna work out."*

I wasn't really feeling good about my relationship with Robert. This wasn't how you're supposed to treat your boy, I thought. I felt like when he was paid I should have been paid no matter where the money came from.

Robert was changing. He was becoming a dictator and this was the first phase of having to deal with his acting arrogant toward me and dealing with his friends, who were persistent with keeping young girls around him. I couldn't understand it. Things started off like everything was going to be fine, but here it was, every day it was some kind of drama going on. In regards to the girls, if they were a little older, I probably could have gotten along better with Robert. But with me being thirty-three years old, I just could not put myself in the frame of mind to entertain their company. So when I was with Robert, I kept it strictly professional; I took care of business and left. It was sad he couldn't see what was forming with the company he was keeping. I felt separated from him. He wasn't hearing me anymore.

Demetrius Smith Sr.

CHAPTER 12

Backed against the Wall

I ATTENDED THE REHEARSALS, but I missed a few of them too. A lot of times, I would make myself unavailable to Robert when he would call. I was beginning to feel used, especially when they cut my pay. I made up my mind that I wasn't going to be anybody's flunky anymore. Anger was setting inside me. So I spent a lot of my time with my girlfriend Lawanda. Nobody knew where she lived, so I was out of contact unless I called. I wanted to make a stand.

I wasn't getting money, but yet I was working. I had put in too much time already to not be paid. So I started to play hardball to see if I was valued. I knew the tour was coming up, and I was uneasy about staying away, but I just didn't want to do it for nothing. The only person I stayed in contact with was my mother. I gave her my phone number and the address where I was because I was hoping Robert would call there to find out where I was. I told my mom that if Robert called to give him my number but not to let him know that I said to give it to him.

I wasn't going to call Robert. I had proved that I was loyal to him. If I was not of value enough for him to come seek me out, then I never had a position with him anyway. If he didn't appreciate me for all that I had been through with him thus far, than to hell with him were my sentiments. I felt that I was being taken advantage of and I needed to stay away to contain the monster that wanted to come out of me. I was having it hard and I did not understand how a person could close off ones sense of compassion for another whom you would consider a loved one.

I was chilling at home when Robert called. *"What's happening with you, man? You ain't been around. What's going on,"* he asked? *"Robert, y'all keep building me up, to knock me back down, man. I don't know what I'm working for because I'm not getting ahead,"* I told him. He asked me where I was. He said we needed to talk and to let him come pick me up. I agreed and gave him my address.

He pulled up in the Benz and blew the horn. He was cleaner than I had ever seen him before. He had his hair cut and he was wearing black pants, a turquoise shirt, and a colorful tie with colors matching the shirt and suspenders. He looked RICH. I didn't give any compliments; I just got in the car. We sat in the car for a moment. Robert asked me if I felt he owed me. I told him we agreed that I would get 5% from the beginning and when he got paid, I should have been paid. When he got a big check, he should've written me a nice check. I let him know that I was in the same financial situation I was in back in the beginning when we were going back and forth to Milwaukee.

He told me he spoke to Barry about the 5 percent and Barry had told him that that's not how the business goes. Robert said he was going back to New York in the next couple of weeks and he wanted me to go with him. He assured me that we would sit down with Barry and talk it all out. He assured me that taking care of me once we got to New York was a priority.

It all sounded good to me, but I told him I couldn't go to New York and leave my woman here without money. I told him I had responsibilities and it wasn't just about me anymore. Robert then went into his pocket and counted out five one-hundred-dollar bills. He handed them to me and asked me if that would hold her until we get back. I took the money and told him it would help. He then told me that he needed me to go to rehearsal with him and he wanted me to stay on top of PA.

I was feeling a little better with the $500 in my hand. *"Give me a minute, man."* I went back up to the house and gave Lawanda the money. As we rode, we laughed and talked about old times. When we arrived at rehearsal, all the guys were really glad to see me and I felt really good being there at rehearsal with them. We were back at it; I was instructing and directing, and we were all just having a ball. You could really see the development coming again. We were going to be a force to be reckoned with.

Our rehearsals were open to the public, which consisted of young girls. If they were eighteen years old that was a good thing. However, from my knowledge, they were still at Kenwood Academy, which was a junior high school, the same school Robert had gone to. After rehearsals we would all gather around and talk and then we'd go our separate ways. Robert, the girls, Torrey, Mouse, and Dre of Public Announcement would all go up to Robert's apartment. I could see early that Dre was sucking up to Robert. It didn't matter what it was Robert needed, Dre was willing to go do it for the sake of kissing his ass. Rick and Earl, the other two members of Public Announcement, and I would always leave.

Demetrius Smith Sr.

We were on the same page when it came to entertaining the young ladies. We just couldn't do it. They just weren't on our level of maturity and we just simply had nothing in common. They were silly, young, and immature. I was simply not into hanging around kids. Whenever I would say something to the girls, I would say things like *"It's too late for you all to be out, you should be home."* It was getting very uncomfortable having these girls around.

It was a good thing Barry Hankerson arranged for us to go on a one week tour as an opening act for Heavy D and the Boyz. This gig came about from the Regal Theater Competition Showcase we had won along with MGM. When Barry came into the picture he took over everything that had anything to do with Robert. He resumed the negotiations and agreed that it would be a good thing for us to do the week tour with Heavy D. He wanted us to, as Barry said it, *"Get our feet wet"*. This would be a test run for us he said. We performed the same songs we had when R. Kelly & MGM won the Regal Talent Show Competition.

We were excited about going out and getting away for a few days. For me, in helping me to gain some control over Robert's free spirited associations with his new friends, the timing could not have been better

We traveled to four cities with Heavy D & the Boyz. The one week we were out there was plenty time for us to see what was to come. It allowed me to get a preview at how tough my job was going to be. When we returned home we went right back to work rehearsing to perfect our show. Being out with Heavy D & the Boyz that week we got to know them on a personal level.

We were at rehearsal just a few days later when we heard that Heavy D's dancer Troy (Trouble T Roy) Dixon had lost his balance and fell from a balcony, hit his head and died. (R.I.P. Trouble T. Roy.) We had just left them in Indianapolis, Indiana. Wow, was all we could say. It was hard to believe that happened. We had all joked around and played with them ourselves, and just like that, Trouble T Roy was gone. We were all saddened by the tragedy. The incident made me aware that I had to be conscious in monitoring how we carried ourselves once we really started touring. There was a lot of playing and joking around; a little too much playing, I would say. While we were out there with Heavy D. the entire crew was excited and just having a good time. The incident taught me right then that the road was not going to be a play place. We all gathered around—Rob, PA and I prayed for Trouble T, his family, Heavy D and his crew. The incident made us all grow up a little bit more that day.

However, it did not ease the clamorous daily activities with school girls coming around. I was so glad when I received a fax from Jomo out of Barry's office for Robert and I to go to New York again. It was official that it was my job to get us to New York. I called Barry when I received the itinerary so that he could go over it with me.

Barry was adamant in pointing out to me that it was a must that I saw to it that Robert was where he was supposed to be when he needed to be there. I was his security and everything at this point because no one else was scheduled to go along with us. I was looking forward to this time away. I figured I would start to get paid now. Shit, the work I had been doing thus far Robert was giving me money out of his pocket; I'd call it kibbles and bit's. He was handing me out money just to keep me active. As he had said we would work out my pay situation when we would meet with Barry.

Once Robert and I arrived at the airport, it was he and I again. We were so close and had a bond that made me feel like we were brothers when we were together. He would always talk about how large I was going to be; being his assistant. It all sounded good and it was the life I wanted. I felt confident at this time that those things were going to manifest themselves. It had become a norm for Robert and I too have long conversations while we fly. Robert had a fear of flying. And to keep his mind off of the flight; he would be very talkative. At that point he'd be open to talk just about anything. Before the conversations were over we were at our destination.

Once we arrived in New York, a driver was waiting for us. We checked into the Empire Hotel, which was the hotel spot where the record company always put us. We were scheduled to be at the studio at 8:00 p.m. After freshening up, we were summoned by yet another driver who was waiting for us in the lobby to take us to the studio.

When we arrived at the studio, a representative of Jive Records met us and took us to meet a new group called High Five. Robert was scheduled to write two songs for their album. He also had to write songs for Billy Ocean and work on a new album for himself, so we stayed in New York for a month.

Once inside the studio, Robert was amazing. The way he just came up with a song, was just simple—like talking. We completed the High Five and Billy Ocean tunes, and Robert laid down tracks for his *Debate* album. We had to go back yet another time to complete the album. This trip showed me what life was going to be like on that next level. Even though I didn't have any money, I felt like it was coming. I was eating steak, shrimp and making phone calls here and there. We were going shopping. Robert was buying video cameras, clothes, whatever else he wanted. It seemed like the sky was the limit. But for me, I wasn't making a nickel so I definitely wasn't buying anything.

I was running here and there making sure Robert did his phone interviews. Time seemed to be moving slowly because in spite of everything, I was waiting for Barry to get there. I wanted to hold Robert to his word. My mind-set was to jump right back on that plane if we didn't sit down and talk about me receiving the 5 percent I was promised. Even though I didn't show it, every time Robert bought a porno video, a camera or something he didn't really need, I was upset because he was spending money so freely and I wasn't getting any. It was like nobody was considering the fact that I had needs.

Barry finally arrived. However, his time spent was in meetings, and at night, Robert and I were locked in the studio. I definitely was not a priority. The next day after Barry arrived; I asked Robert if he would schedule a meeting for us. That's when he told me, Barry left early that morning for a meeting in California. I didn't show it, but I was totally disappointed. It was hard times for me and my loved ones. I wasn't trying to come off like I was all about the money, but the reality was, I had to share in the financial responsibility to help support and feed my family. I told Robert I couldn't do this anymore. I let it be known that once we got back to Chicago, we were going to have to have this meeting. I just wasn't into accepting handouts from him anymore.

I was done asking for money. My homeboy didn't have any consideration for me. I felt like I was being pushed into a corner. I felt like I would look like a fool to my family and friends. Here I was pushing a size 12 when the guy I started out with rides around in a Mercedes Benz. I'm out of town being a personal assistant to a guy who just signed a major recording contract, and I wasn't able to send money home. This was not a pretty picture at all. I had to ask for any and everything I wanted.

I called home and Lawanda told me that she was having it a little rough, so I told her I'd send her something. I was going to have to break down and ask Robert for some money. I went back into the studio and told Robert I needed some money to send home. I felt it should not have been a problem, but when Robert said to me, *"Right now, Johnny man, I don't have it. This money they gave me, man, I have to use for me, here, while I'm in New York. I'll call Barry and have him get on them to get you some per diem dough,"* he said as he swirled around in his chair to the console and turned up the volume to the music pumping to his tracks.

He was working on the mixes for the *Born into the '90s* album. Before Rob could get into the music, I tapped him on his shoulder. He turned the volume down and swirled around. *"When are you going to call Barry?"* I asked. He shook his head, still adjusting the volume as if to say, *"Let's make this quick, Johnny man."* As he looked to proceed to his music, I cut into him. *"Man, Rob, I gotta get some money to my girl man. You need to call Barry for me for real man."*

I wasn't going to count the man's money, but I was deserving of a pay day, just as he had received one. I paid my dues and did my part. Robert shook his head as I was pleading to him, as if I was disturbing him. *"I got you, Johnny man, Imma call Barry in a minute. You the first thing we gone talk about,"* he said, swiveling around in his chair and again turning the volume up. I yelled out to him, *"I need you to call him now, Robert. I'm serious, man."* He turned the music down and swirled around in the chair again with a bothered look on his face. *"I can't reach Barry right now, Johnny. Imma call him, man, in a minute,"* he said and, just like that, swiveled back around in his chair, turned the music up loud to totally block me out.

I just stood there for a moment, looking at him like *"You little punk dude."* He wasn't like that when my family was feeding his little hungry but. I was angry. He never saw the side in me I was feeling and he just didn't know how close he was to feeling me. Share the wealth, man—that's all he had to do and it just wasn't happening. He sat there focused on his music, not giving me a second thought. The fact I had a situation at home didn't even concern him. I turned to leave out the studio. I was totally disappointed. The struggle was supposed to be over for all of us, but I wasn't moving up the pay scale at all. I was being treated like an immigrant.

Always leaving me in a position in life where I am starting all over again. I felt betrayed, I was mad. I felt like a lion, I wanted to tear something up. My ace, Mr. R. Kelly, wasn't seeing me as having a part in the big picture we had graphed together.

I was distressed at this point. I felt I was being backed against the wall; backed into a corner. I didn't know what to do. I didn't want to call Lawanda, but I knew I had to tell her I couldn't help her. I wondered into the lounge to make a few phone calls to see if I could get hold of some money from somebody. As I sat there making calls, I thought about Robert again, and at that moment, I didn't like him anymore. He was supposed to be my boy and my friend, yet he was playing me. I couldn't believe Robert said no to me, especially after telling him my family was in need. On top of that, this was business.

Demetrius Smith Sr.

I thought about an incident that happened when we initially arrived at the studio. A Jive rep brought Robert an envelope, of which after signing for it, Robert quickly pocketed the fat envelope. *"What was that you signed?"* I asked.

"They said it was per diem, that's it, right? pa diem, money for me to eat, par diem, I said it right, didn't I?" was the way he put it. He was really asking—trying to make sure he signed the right papers. Prior to that day, I was the one that read everything to Robert. He had me review contracts, riders and banking correspondence. Robert would even look at pictures in magazines and if he saw something he was interested in, he would ask, *"What this say here, Johnny?"* It was without question, I'd take the time needed for him to help him to understand. So it was natural when I would ask, what it was he signed. By this time he was really feeling himself. He wasn't seeing me. He was comfortable with himself. He kept himself occupied, to avoid allowing himself to get into whatever it was I was going through. I kept humble, in spite of how I felt I was being left out.

Robert received per diem and I didn't have any money in my pocket. He was getting per diem for the week plus an allowance. Shit, where was mine? I needed to eat too. I was there working. I was looking for him to hand me an envelope to get my signature. Even though the business was new to me, I wasn't a fool. The work was put in and I was ready to start seeing some of this money Robert was spending so freely.

Robert must have forgotten I was with him when he received the envelope that morning. It hurt me when I realized that my needs weren't of importance. We were a driving force together and I had brought him there. Robert had no thought toward all the years we had worked together building to be in the moment we were in. I had been with him now for going on five years and not counting the time I spent away in rehab.

My assistance to his production was a great part of him being in the place he was in. Yeah, I thought we were creating a monster in him, but damn, this dude was fucking with the monster in me. I was confused and angry. Robert wasn't seeing shit right at all. This muthafucka had it twisted. If I didn't have so much time invested in this, I would have done something terrible to him. I was trying so hard to hold on and be patient because working in the music business was what I loved and wanted to do.

It was crazy for us to be having a financial disagreement. He had assured me several times that I would be taken care of. I thought of Robert with so much anger inside of me. *"Man, don't you know that I have nothing,"* I had said to him? He didn't care. I have had nothing. I had been putting all of me, my time and my money as well to get us to the moment we were in. Where was my share now? Hello, can you hear me, can you see me? Hello! But I stood alone. I was the only one seeing and hearing me. I did not know what to do?

While Robert was recording, I wandered into the lounge area of the studio. I noticed Robert's wallet sitting on the table. The stupid jerk had left his wallet out in the open. Normally, I would have grabbed it and taken it to him but here it was, I was hurting and felt I was backed up against into a corner. I thought about it, taking the money. I was hurting inside from the thought that I felt that I had to do it. I looked in side of his wallet and saw that he had a bunch of one hundred dollar bills. I got angry all over again. I took $200 out of his wallet and put his wallet back where I had found it. The thought comforted me the fact that it was obvious he wasn't feeling me.

Without hesitation, I left the studio immediately to find a Western Union. Lucky for me, there was one just up the street from the studio. I didn't want to be away from the studio for long. I wired my woman $200 and went right back to the studio. No one noticed I was gone. I went in to join Robert and acted as if I was cool and feeling his music. The only thing I was feeling good about was the fact I had taken care of my responsibility at home.

I felt bad about taking the money, no doubt. But at the same time, I felt I could hold my head up to my woman, I knew that I had lifted a burden from off of her, so I didn't care. I thought to myself, *"If Robert would have needed money; I would've sacrificed to help him."* That's how I thought we were for each other. But to think about it, Robert had always showed signs of being selfish. So I concluded right then, *"I have to do what I have to do!"* I was in survival mode and in my book, I did what I had to do.

Later that night in the studio, Robert said he was missing his wallet. I helped him look for it in the studio area. When he went into the lounge area, he found it, right where he had left it. As he went through it, he looked up, *"I know I had more money than this,"* he said. He made a big deal out of it. He was angry! *"Somebody took $700 out of my wallet like I'm stupid. I know somebody gone come up with my money,"* he said.

Word of the incident got to Jive Records executives, and the next day, Robert's money was replaced. I felt like he had gotten over on Jive Records. I knew I took $200 so either he was lying about someone taking $700 or somebody else came behind me and took money out of his wallet. Like I said, I didn't feel good about taking the money. However, I didn't feel good about being pushed in a corner either.

Demetrius Smith Sr.

A few days later, we went back to Chicago. Robert and I were cool. He didn't trip on me about the money. However, he did tell me that it had ran across his mind that I had taken the money. *"Man you had to feed me all while I was there"*, I told him.

On the way home, I was into my thoughts. Robert was grooving off the tracks he laid down for his first album. Once we got back to Chicago we waited for Lonneice, Robert's girlfriend, to pick us up from O'Hare Airport. While waiting, I had to, again, ask Robert for some money. I didn't have any to go home with. I did not feel good at all returning from New York with him and going home with empty pockets. He gave me $200, in which hefelt, he was giving me something.

When I got home, I was embarrassed. All I had to give to my women was $200; actually, $75.00 was all I could give to her. I had to give Tamekia, my other expecting child's mother, something too. I sat down with Lawanda and told her I was through working for Robert. I made up my mind I would not continue to work for him anymore. Lawanda told me to stick with him a little longer. She felt Robert was going to do the right thing. I couldn't see Robert changing. He had shown me signs that he really didn't care about anyone except for himself. My feelings for him were changing. He was changing, and I was starting to not like him as a person. To me, everything about him was fictitious.

R. Kelly, the name, was pussy to me. I was having thoughts of fucking him up. He was Robert Kelly, bigger than the image they were trying to make of him. Barry and Jive Records were portraying R. Kelly to be a kid who had come through some rough times being raised in the projects as a victim to the rough streets of Chicago. According to the story printed in *Vibe* magazine, he was robbed of his bicycle and shot. It's true, he was shot. The boy was shot with a BB gun, while outside playing with his brother Bruce; at least that's how his brother Bruce told it to me. Nonetheless, he was making me feel as if he was punking me and in all realness, I wanted to kick his ass.

Jive Records was building Robert Kelly to be this tough kid and Robert was sucking it up. His whole demeanor was changing. To be honest, I had never known of Robert to ever have a fight. The boy ain't never been tough a day in his life. Robert Kelly was a good kid.

I felt Jive Records as well as Barry Hankerson where allowing Robert to get away with things they knew were not right. But because Robert was producing music and money the way he was, he couldn't do no wrong in their sight. Therefore, I believe Robert there was nothing he couldn't t do. Robert was growing into his song (Because remember he writes what he lives) *"I believe I Can Fly."* The real story is Robert was pampered while he was growing up. His gift with music made people look out for him.

Robert was like a little brother to me and my family; I would even reach out to help his brothers, Bruce and Carey Kelly. Robert's brother Carey had awesome talent himself. He was just as talented as Robert. Carey, who we call Killa, could rap and put lyrics together just as Robert did when writing R & B songs. Carey had flow like Tupac when it came to rapping and writing.

You would have thought his brother, R. Kelly, would help him get a recording deal—but no! Instead he helped him to not get a deal. Robert shot him down, and every time someone wanted to work with Killa, Robert would intervene, causing those that were interested to back off. I don't know what it was with Robert that would not allow him to aid and assist the people close to him. He didn't seem to want any of his crew to come up. It was as if he thought he was going to have competition.

Since he realized he was our employer, now he wanted to control us. When we talked, he always had to be right about everything. He no longer allowed us to do our jobs on our own, and he wanted to be involved in every decision. Everything had to go his way, and then when things went wrong, he'd blame us.

I couldn't work for him any longer—especially for free. A decision had to be made. As a personal assistant/tour manager on the level we were on, others were paid $1,500 to $2,500 a week, plus a per diem of $50 to $75 per day. Robert was offering to pay me $400 to $600 a week on the road, with a $25 a day per diem. At home, he wanted to pay me $150 a week. He said I was at home and that I was getting paid for hanging out. He stopped seeing my value and he was losing sight of the reality of our relationship. I was making things happen, keeping things running smooth along with watching his back.

I don't think he had a clue. He was touching on my intellect. At this point I didn't know how long I could contain myself. I was having some wicked thoughts. This wasn't how it was supposed to be. Just a few months ago I was on the payroll. It was how it should have been.

At that time I felt ok about sacrificing and being patient to wait for the deal I was promised. I had hope that things could only get better. But now, coming home from New York, and back into the same condition of financial insecurity that I was in before I left, my vision of hope for brighter days were now filled with visions of selfishness and inconsideration. I was feeling misused and unappreciated. I didn't want to go down this road. I had been here before.

CHAPTER 13

Back on Board

ONE NIGHT ROBERT called me at home. I told Lawanda to tell him she didn't know where I was and as far as she knew I was with him. He kept calling. Two, maybe three weeks passed, and I hadn't returned any of Roberts calls. I ended up speaking to Earl, one of the PA members, and I explained what I was going through with Robert and how I could no longer work for minimal wages. Earl kept trying to convince me to go back but I declined. He promised me that our conversation would stay between us.

I hit the streets again. I was hustling, selling weed and rocks. The only hanging out I did was on the West Side to make money. I was stressed over the fact that I was once again on the streets. Although, I stayed drug free and they were accessible to me. I had grown. My weakness was now my strength. I remembered where I came from and what I went through with drugs in my past and that kept me focused and determined not to touch drugs again. I wanted to live to raise my children. I wanted to be a better dad. I wanted to be there for them. My sperm donor I never knew.

I sold drugs as I roamed throughout the city. During the daytime I was looking for a job. The thought of dedicating myself to an eight-hour job to support my family wasn't a bad idea. Anything was better than endangering my life on these streets, selling drugs, robbing people and sacrificing my life to be taken away from my family. The thought of not being there to give my children some direction in their life, working a 9 to 5 didn't sound bad to me at all. It would be a consistent pay check and with the right company I could build. More so than anything, I would be home, with my family. I enjoyed coming home.

One evening, when I got home, Lawanda told me Robert had come by the house looking for me. She said he asked her to come downstairs because he needed to talk to her. She said he seemed sincere and wanted me to give him a call. He said it was very important that I contact him. I wasn't interested. Lawanda stood behind me while I sat on the couch and started giving me a massage. I felt so much tension being released as she rubbed my neck and shoulder blades.

Lawanda started talking as she massaged me. *"Babe,"* she said, *"I know what you been through with Robert, but you're not doing what you like, babe. You were always excited and believed so much in what you were doing when y'all were together. I think you should give him another try,"* she said.

"I can't do it Wanda! With Robert I don't seem to ever come up, babe," I told her.

"Yeah, I know, babe," she said. *"But the way he sounded when I talked to him, he seemed like he was willing to sit down to try and work it out with you. That boy knows he needs you."* She said.

"That's Robert, babe, he knows what to say, when to say it, and how to say things to make you feel as if he's understanding. I know him, babe," I said to her.

"Yeah, but you can stay with him to hook up with somebody else," she said.

Hearing that made sense to me! Lawanda was persistent. I sensed that she really wanted me to go back to work for Robert. I couldn't understand her. One of the biggest problems we had in our relationship was her being insecure and jealous. For a long while I could not go anywhere without us arguing. Every time I went out of the house I was accused of cheating. If you let her tell it I was having sex with every woman I looked at. And I know she wasn't into R. Kelly as a fan. I could not figure it out why she was so adamant about me hooking back up with Robert. I sat there looking at her and honestly began to believe that she was sincerely concerned about me and my happiness.

"Yeah, I like the work. But it doesn't feel good at all coming back home with no money. I need to be paid and that's the bottom line babe. When I'm on the road, I need to be able to send money home to you. I have a responsibility to you and my children. She listened quietly for the moment as I continued.

"Babe, we going to need pampers and everything." I said as I rubbed on her big belly. But did she stop talking about it, heck no!

"Well Demetrius, I don't want you out hustling because sooner or later, you gone get caught. Working with that boy, (being Robert Kelly), better than you being in jail or dead," she said.

Her words sent a chill through my body as I listened to her go on. *"I want you to give Robert another try, Demetrius. I want you to be doing what you like."* She said as she moved closer to me and began kissing on me. This was the part of Lawanda I was crazy about. She was aggressive. It's something special when you know someone really cares. My grandmamma once told me, *"Boy, you better love who love you."* I thought about her words then looking at Lawanda. She made my day. I was overwhelmed with her so I sat there and thought about it. She was right; I was wasting myself hustling on the streets. I was taking unnecessary risk that would, in the long run, end up with me having regrets. *"So why do it?"* I thought. I just wanted to be able to provide a comfortable lifestyle to be with my family.

I knew the end road to a lifestyle of hustling the streets would lead to jail, or like she said, I could end up dead. I truly wanted better for us all. I didn't want to steal or sell drugs. I wanted to do what was right to make my life better.

I made a promise to Lawanda that day. I told her I would get a real job, that I would stop hustling the streets and selling myself short. She said she just wanted me to be safe and come home to her and our baby. That next day, I got up early that morning to go to find a job. I went all over the city submitting employment applications. I wasn't hired on the spot anywhere. It was kind of discouraging, but instead of going home empty-handed, I stopped on 71st and Jeffrey at the Jewel Food Store and hung around there offering people rides home with their groceries. Seven people allowed me to transport them home with their groceries and paid me $5 to $10 per delivery. I took home a little money that day.

It was really rough for me. I didn't know how I was going to support two families. I was living with Lawanda and visiting Tamekia too. I was finding work every day. I would even drive to the West Side working with Donnie and his family at V&W Liquors or I would work with them laying drywall or gutting out the walls in one of their apartment buildings. I was trying to do the right thing to make ends meet.

It wasn't easy. Lawanda and Tamekia were eating for two. I didn't have a job. It was hard for me to be around them and not have money. The more I worked with Donnie and his family on the Westside; attending to the liquors and doing drywall work on the apartments I didn't seem to be advancing in life. I could never make enough money.

I took another chance. I had begun burglarizing people's homes again. I figured I had done it for the drugs and got away with it. I could do it for the sake of my children. I didn't want to do it but I felt I had to because I couldn't find a job. When I got away with the first burglary I got excited, and after the second one I became fearless. I was seeing money and no longer was I smoking it all up in a pipe. It was all being saved—Robin Hood was back!

This one particular evening, Lawanda was waiting for me at the door. I hadn't gotten into the door good before she started telling me Robert came by the house looking for me.

She was in my ear before I had gotten into the house telling me, *"Demetrius, you need to go on and call that boy and y'all just need to sit down and talk. Long as you been with him, you shouldn't just walk away. I know I wouldn't with all the work you been doing for that boy. You the one be going around making stuff happen for that boy, and now you gone walk away. Shoot, it don't make sense to leave when the money gone start coming. Shoot, I'll just work it's still good money."* Wanda didn't stop talking.

She kept nagging in my ear as I walked into the house, following me everywhere I went. When I finally got to sit down on the couch, she was right there. *"I'd stick in there if I was you. All the time you out there doing things for him, I couldn't—!"*

"Wanda!" I finally cut in and said. *"Babe, please!"* I just wanted to stop hearing her talk. She wasn't letting me think.

She just went on and on. *"You know you wanna call that boy,"* she said, with an innocent baby kind of a look on her face; a sneaky look as if she knew she was bugging me but she didn't want to come off like she was and trying to be sexy with it too. She was getting on my nerves.

Wanda was like that. She was something else. When she started talking, you had to give in or run. I was too tired to run, and I couldn't make her stop talking. *"Wanda, give me the phone, girl!"* I said. *"Please!"* I said, putting my hands to my ears, letting her know I give in, I give in. Then she started to smile. I called him. When Robert answered the phone, it was as If I just woke him up from out of a deep sleep. *"Hey Rob, what's happening with you man?"* I asked, waiting on him to respond. The voice on the other end answered hoarsely.

I knew Robert. He always pretended to be so sleepy when he answered the phone. *"Hello, hello!"* He'd say hoarsely. That way when you called him you would have to get straight to the point of why you called. There was no chit-chatting unless you were somebody he wanted to talk to. I knew his game, so I just waited for him to wake up and respond. I knew he wasn't sleeping. It was only a few seconds before he came up out of his so-called deep sleep.

"Johnny, is that you?" he asked.

"Yeah, man, what's up, Rob?" I asked right back.

"awl, man, trying to put it together man. I need you here, man. What's happening with you, man? Where you been?" he asked.

I hesitated for a moment and then said, *"Out here trying to make a living to feed my family, Rob. What's happening with you?"* I asked.

I wanted to keep him answering questions. I was calling to see what he wanted with me. I wasn't excited about talking to him. I wanted to be in with him, but I wanted to be in right. *"Man, I moved, where you been, Johnny?"* he asked again.

"Oh yeah! Where did you move to?" I asked? Not that I really wanted to know, but I didn't call him to be answering his questions. What I wanted was to be paid the 5 percent he promised. I wanted to be given the opportunity and respect to do the job I had been doing for him for the past five years, and I wanted a written contract to do this job.

I didn't want to give in to Robert, but at the same time, I didn't want to put pressure on him to a point where he would say forget it. I knew I was valuable to him and I kept everything smooth when it came to the public. I got along with the intellects, the ladies, the bangers and everybody. I had away socializing with people. I liked and respected people. I was always considerate and passionate about what people wanted. That was how I was able to get along with people and make things happen for Robert.

I didn't want Robert to close the door on me. I wanted him to realize that I was valuable to the production and longevity of the R. Kelly production. Lawanda was right, my every day was in preparation to enhance R. Kelly's career. And now, we were at the door to success, and this dude did not want to play fair. I was obsessed with wanting to do whatever to help this kid make it. I was his biggest fan. He was a star in my book, while other people had to be convinced. I was giving my all when he didn't have anything and there was nothing promising to say that for sure he would be successful with his music. He had the will and I made the way. In my mind we were a team.

Robert went on to tell me where he lived, and he asked me if I could meet him at his new apartment, The Burnham Plaza Apartments, on 8th and State Street. He said it was important that we get together and talk. I decided to go, but my mind was made up that I would not work for him without being paid. It was going to be strictly business with us from now on. When I got to his apartment, I had to check in with the doorman who called Robert to announce my arrival. Robert Okayed him to let me up. He had a small one-bedroom apartment with a living room, small kitchen area and bathroom; nothing real fancy, but it was his.

I was there about business. I was not fascinated at all that Robert was living right in the heart of Downtown Chicago. Yeah, he had moved up, no doubt. But as I sat down, I could tell that he sensed I was not my usual self. Normally, I would have walked around, inspected the place, and been glad for him. I'd go in his refrigerator and make myself at home. This day was different. I did not feel that the closeness I thought we shared was mutual. This day I sat down as a guest, not as if I were at home like a friend would. I wanted to know what it was he wanted to meet with me about. I guess he sensed that I was not impressed with being in his luxury apartment and the fact that we were just up the street in downtown Chicago.

Robert's attitude changed. He pulled up a chair and sat down right in front of me. *"Johnny, this money thing, it ain't like you think man."* He said and shook his head like no, but at the same time began to say, *"Man I'm ma pay you. I already spoke to Barry. I told him I wanna make sure you get taken care of. Barry told me to call him when you got here. So, man, it's a lot getting ready to start happening and I want you right here with me, Johnny. We started this together and don't nobody know me like you do,"* he said.

Robert had a way with words. I liked what he was saying, but he wouldn't commit to anything. He kept saying to me that the three of us, (this included Barry), were going to sit down and get my contract together. I loved the sound of all he was saying, but at the same time, he was asking me to come back to work overseeing rehearsals and to continual being his personal assistant. Robert made me feel like we were on the same page when he began telling me he needed me with him in New York. It was his turn now.

Before, when we were in New York, Robert was writing songs to go on the albums of other artist that were signed with Jive Records. And being the awesome writer he was a few of the songs he had produced, he intended to use and put on his on his album. Now he was about to go to New York to record his day view album. This was what we had worked for and I wanted to be a part of it more than anything.

When Robert got finished talking, my first question to him was, *"how much am I going to be paid to start working now Robert?"*

"Hold on, he said!" He then dialed Barry Hankerson's phone number.

Robert spoke briefly to Barry before handing the phone to me. Barry was on the other end all jolly and joyful like as if we were all buddies together. *"How you doing Barry,* I plainly asked?

It wasn't shit jolly for me. I wanted to be taken serious and come out on top here.

"Johnny, what's happening man? You ready to get busy?" he asked.

"I'm being busy B, tell me what you got going on," I asked.

Barry confirmed the fact that Robert was about to go to New York and start his album. He also spoke about promotional tour engagements, phone interviews, personal appearances; radio station visits, music stores visits, photo shoots and video productions.

This was the beginning of the big time. Barry said as Robert's Personal Assistant, it would be my responsibility to make sure everything was scheduled and that Robert fulfilled his engagements. Barry made it sound exciting to be a front man for a major recording artist, but I didn't let the excitement of what was ahead distract me from the present. Before any of this could happen with me, I had to be paid. Not later, but now.

Being the master of manipulation and persuasion, Barry assured me that they would pay me all that I was owed from my years of hard work once Robert completed his album and making all of his appearances. He made it all sound so good, so I committed to being R. Kelly's personal assistant again. Before closing on our phone conversation, Barry offered to pay me a weekly salary of $150 to work with Robert and Public Announcement until we went to New York; and at that time, he said my salary would go back up to $400.00 a week. $150 wasn't a lot of money, but with everything that was about to happen, I excepted the job believing it couldn't help but get better. We were there, entering that door to the success we had worked so hard for.

When I got back home and told Lawanda how things went we talked about my being gone away on the road for periods of time. She told me she could handle it. I told her she was going to be a jealous fool. Together we shared a laughed. Overall, Lawanda seemed very happy for me that I had gotten back with Robert. For now, I was back on board. The first thing I did was schedule rehearsals. I was on the phone with Public Announcement, informing them of dates and times. I scheduled rehearsals between 4:30 p.m. and 7:00 p.m. daily at Robert's apartment complex. It had the same luxuries as the other one he lived in did. There was a dance studio, pool, cleaners and a doorman. So that's where we rehearsed.

Public Announcement was always on time for rehearsals. They were always eager to work. They wanted to succeed and to prove to R. Kelly that they had what it took to roll with him to the top in the entertainment field. They were like the Chicago Bulls and Michael Jordan, hungry for a championship. We had to work out a lot of things in the beginning because Robert was such a perfectionist and he wanted things his way. He was to be the star and did not want anyone to outshine him in any way. He didn't want Public Announcement to be recognized or looked at as pretty boys like MGM.

Robert had a problem with MGM because the girls would scream out for them during the performances. So, to keep everything focused on him, he would tell me to keep them in the dressing room after shows. Shaun, Vince and Mark were considered extremely handsome young men and Robert didn't want PA to have the same image. He made sure I had control of them and their actions from the beginning.

Rick, one of PA members, was the smooth one in the group. He was the ladies' man, sort of. He had a head full of hair so he kept it in a ponytail. Robert didn't like it, so he had me persuade Rick to cut his hair. After me and others in the group convinced Rick to cut his hair, we knew we had total control of PA's functions before and after shows. Robert wanted to be the one all the ladies wanted and he made sure that we knew that the only reason a woman wanted to be with us was because we were with him.

Robert was becoming a control freak. Rehearsals would go smoothly, but no matter how good things were, he would find something to complain about. The hardest part was keeping rehearsals closed to the young girls that used to come by. Later, after rehearsals they would end up in the apartment with Robert.

He stopped listening to me. He began to have parties after rehearsals. Lonneice, Robert's girlfriend, got wind of Robert and his little parties because the girls would leave items in his house and she'd find them. Later, they broke up. Oftentimes, when I would go to Robert's apartment to hang out, I would end up leaving because it was so uncomfortable being older and hanging around kids.

Finally, it was time to go back to New York. Again, the timing could not have been better. We needed get away. I needed this time with Robert to try and bring him back to reality from dealing with them young girls; things were beginning to get wild and reckless. Once we got there we checked into the hotel and immediately after putting our luggage into our rooms we were taken Jive Records Studios. Even though we had rooms at the Empire Hotel, we only showered there. We lived in the studio. I felt better being there this time. I was still getting $150 a week. Barry had also given me $25 per day for per diem. For now I was earning $290.00 each week. At least this time I was able to send money home to my two children's mothers.

On this trip to New York we stayed for three months. Robert was unbelievable to watch in the studio. He was coming up with new song ideas as we walked on the blocks in Manhattan. Robert went through outer body experiences creating his music. He once told me, *"Man I see myself in an audience looking up on the stage and I hear the ladies shouting and see them reaching out to me. When my vision begins to view the stage my mind goes blank and in the darkness I can only hear. I hear the song that they feel and it records in my mind. And the song plays in my head as I lay it down to track.*

Robert was deep like that. He kept a Dictaphone with him to help him record his ideas throughout the days. He would go out of character, pretending he was whoever he needed to be, whether it was Gladys Knight or Michael Jackson. He became that person. I would always tell myself, *"His gift was truly an anointing from God"*. I think that, that belief was the reason I was so devoted to this boy.

We made a few trips back and forth to and from New York. We didn't stay home in Chicago any longer than a week and a half at the most. In that short period of time I don't think we slept at all at home. Every chance I got I went to visit my children. I didn't get to spend a lot of time with them but the little time I did have for them I enjoyed it.

CHAPTER 14

Taking the Show on the Road

THE ALBUM BORN into the '90s was released and doing well on the charts. The single *"VIBE"* the people had caught it. Everywhere we went we would hear people singing it and see them dancing to it. We had worked hard in preparation for the video and now we were working even harder preparing for a promotional tour Jive Records had lined up. I was responsible for all those things Barry had spoken about months back.

On our first tour, my pay went up to $400 per week plus $25.00 a day per-diem. Still, I was under paid. Barry's excuse was that I did not have the experience of a tour manager to receive more money and I still had to prove myself. This, along with Robert always finding something to complain about frustrated me. And to add insult to injury, Robert invited a few of the young girls that had hung around at rehearsals to travel along with us for the ride.

We were scheduled to be on the road for eight days for this first tour. We were performing off tracks with the music and the background vocals that were recorded in the studio. Our crew consisted of R. Kelly, Public Announcement and R. Kelly's brother Bruce. Robert wanted me to use Bruce as my assistant. And then there were the girls. Not the dancers; they hadn't been hired as of yet. These were the young girls that hung out at rehearsals and at the studio. I'm talking about Tiffany Hawkins, who was called Tia, and then there was Javonte, Sha and Ronda. Now these young girls had talent. Tia had vocal range and a sound like Whitney Houston. Sha and Rhonda had her back nailing the background vocals.

They were young no doubt, and like kids, they were excited over R. Kelly, which made them gullible. I think they were being promised something, which is why they were at the studio on the regular. Barry Hankerson told me that because they were minors, they would need permission slips signed by their parents in order to go with us. He wasn't with the idea of allowing these young girls to travel on the road with us, but according to Robert, they were his next production. He told him that being with him on the tour would give them an idea of what to expect when it was their turn to venture out. There wasn't a whole lot of discussion about it. What Robert wanted Robert got. I typed a permission slip for them to take home to their parents. I guess it was their parents who signed the permission slips. We didn't give it a second thought. We just allowed them to travel along with us.

I had been on the road many times before, but this tour with R. Kelly was wild going and coming. It was a new experience for me. Dealing with my boys being alcoholics and partying with the ladies was one thing, but this tour was like taking kids out on a field trip to the museum, except they were old enough to travel without a legal guardian. I didn't like the idea of inviting the young girls along. I figured there would be a woman for us in every place we were traveling, but this is what Robert wanted.

Robert was just amazed with the newfound power he was learning he had with people. It was his free will to spend money that brought all the flies in. I don't think he looked at Tia or the other girls as being under aged girls. Hell, they hung out like young women when they came around the studio, and they didn't seem to have a curfew. There's no way my mom would have ever allowed my sisters to stay out late nights without calling all over looking for them, investigating their whereabouts and what they were doing. I often wondered who lets their sixteen-year-old go and stay out all night.

As the tour continued, the young ladies were the least of my worries. I was optimistic about this tour for the experience. Even though I had some prior experience, this was that next level. We were booked to be on shows with En Vogue, TLC, Jodeci, Bone Thugs and Harmony. It was all coming into reality.

The immaturity that was happening within our camp made me sit back to analyze my position at what was ahead. I knew the saying of Murphy's Law. *"Whatever can go wrong will go wrong"*. I wanted to do a good job, in spite of Mr. Almighty R. Kelly wanting to keep people off balance by exercising his power of authority. I had to have a mellow head to be able to handle it.

Robert Kelly was funny. He wanted to be smart. I think he thought because he could obtain wealth it was an indication of his intellectual capacity. His disposition was to control everybody. He wanted to run the whole show, production and all. I gotta give it to him. The boy wanted to learn, but he was just going about things the wrong way. What he should have been focused on and what he was doing were two different things. The boy should have just sang and let me do what it was he hired me to do. He hired me to watch his back, prepare things for him that were in his best interest, and make sure that everything and everybody else was doing what they were hired to do and at the same time keep people excited about him. But this cat wanted to do whatever he wanted to do, even if it inconvenienced somebody else.

I was seeing a monster being created, and it wasn't his music. The hardest part was to get Robert to respect his schedule when it came to interviews and being on time for the shows and after shows. He would get there when he got there. I was excited for Rob when it came to meeting and greeting people. I always believed a first impression is important.

I was representing R Kelly so whenever I met people, I wore the smile, I turned on the charm and I did my best to make him look good. I worked at making myself likeable to people by catering to their needs. To me everyone was a customer, and I wanted to make sure they were taken care of and left feeling good about their visit with R. Kelly.

In the beginning, no one knew who R. Kelly was. But to me, he was the *BADDEST* male singer alive. I didn't have a problem promoting him everywhere we went. It wasn't hard once we got rolling on the road. I came to learn that Robert was repetitious with what he wanted in every city. He liked to play ball and go to the mall. In the malls, R. Kelly and his crew would pass out notes to the young ladies they met and on the notes was information to the hotel where we were staying.

When we arrived at our destination, I would separate myself from him and the crew. I would position myself in the presence of a small crowd of people. When Robert would come toward me in the mall, I would ask, whoever was next to me, *"Wow, ain't that that dude, ah, ah, R. Kelly? He's the one just came out with that new song "Vibe"?* The people would look at him approaching and began to spread the word of R. Kelly being in the mall. Next thing you know, Robert was signing autographs and looking over the top of his glasses to his group of female body snatchers, indicating to them which girl he was interested in. There were so many women.

R. Kelly enjoyed the way I would draw a crowd to him and I met a number of nice beautiful women myself. Being the man behind the man had its perks. Robert loved the attention, so I was asked to do the promo game everywhere we went because Rob wasn't known yet. I didn't mind; I enjoyed promoting him. The flip side was the fact that I was always made to be the bad guy because I had to always make up excuses as to why he couldn't take pictures or at times sign autographs.

"Vibe" was the first single off of the album and we were on a promotional tour. It was upsetting to me that Robert didn't want to turn on his charm for the media or the fans. To me, this was the beginning of a lavish lifestyle. The people were the ones that were going to make R. Kelly rich and famous. I talked to Robert often about networking because Barry Hankerson already told me it was the key to being successful in this business. R. Kelly's music was hot, and he knew it. I admired R. Kelly a lot in respect to his vision of being a sought-after entertainer, but I didn't agree with the way he was going about doing it. The way he shunned his fans and the media away, I knew it would create a problem for me as his tour manager.

The first tour gave me an insight on what to prepare for on our next outing. I was glad to get back home after that first tour especially since I had gotten real frustrated with R. Kelly's disposition to control everyone. He really started to get on my nerves with having the young girls around and with how he was treating the media and fans.

All in all, I did enjoy myself. My life had made a 360-degree turn. When I got back home, I was busy as I wanted to be. I sat and wrote a progress report for Barry. I wanted to learn all I could about this business so I decided to speak to Barry about going to school. I wanted to take a course in public relations. I felt it would enhance my communication skills. I decided to talk to Barry about it because Mr. Hankerson always gave me good advice and I respected him for that. He surprised me when he volunteered to pay my tuition.

Nobody ever offered to give me anything, so I had mad love for Barry because he had my best interest at heart. He wanted me to do well. He wanted us all to do well in representing R. Kelly. If it wasn't for Barry, I would have had a hard time paying tuition with the salary I was getting. It was at that time I came to believe that Barry was the right man to manage R. Kelly. I felt since Mr. Hankerson was willing to invest in me, then everything was going to work out right. I was on board and again, I put my whole heart into R. Kelly's production and I enrolled in school at Columbia College in downtown Chicago. As R. Kelly's personal assistant and tour manager, I needed some additional knowledge about the business and the job I was doing. I had been working ever since I met him in 1984. Here it was 1992 and we were on our way to the top in the music industry.

I wanted to get all A's in school; I wanted to become another Barry Hankerson because he was the man to me. He knew all the ins and outs in the music business. One day, he told me, *"Demetrius, you're going to do well in this business as long you listen. You're personable, people like you, and that's a plus for you. Your enthusiastic desire to do well impresses me, and for that, I will teach you everything I know about this business so that you can have a good life when your run with Robert is over."* I felt like my daddy was talking to me. I wanted to be in his shoes.

Daily, during school and after school, I worked on the phone corresponding with Jomo Hankerson, Barry's son, who was the vice president of Black Ground Enterprises and Janet Kleinbaum, director of promotions for Jive Records. Things were about to take off. The album had been released and the people were buying it. The dates were coming in faster than we anticipated. We scheduled video shoots, personal appearances at clubs and at radio stations, as well as doing autograph signings at record stores.

My name was becoming known because I was R. Kelly's contact person. Everything that was scheduled for him to do came through me and I organized his schedule. I loved every minute of being important. I hadn't lost my desire to perform and I still had it in my mind that once Robert's *Born into the '90s* album had reached its peak, then I felt Robert would then put me in the studio and produce me as his first recording artist.

Besides me going to school, I had to now help R. Kelly put a band together to be added to the act. Robert didn't want to work with his brother Bruce, who played the bass guitar, or any of the other fellows that had worked with us in the past. He said they weren't on the professional level he needed them to be on. I could only do things the way he wanted them. Robert put me in touch with Keith Henderson, a guitar player who was working and doing a lot of studio work with other musicians.

After talking with Keith, it was decided that he would be the band director, and in doing so, it was left up to Keith to choose the other musicians. Keith handled that position well. He put together a four-piece band. Having Keith was kind of a relief for me. He handled everything for Robert when it came to the music.

The school semester was over and I ended the semester with a B average. I didn't have a life outside of working with Robert. After school, I would go work out of Derrel McDavid's office on 12th and State Street. Derrel had an accounting office where he handled R.Kelly's business. R. Kelly now had a company of his own, which he called Bass Productions. Now my checks were coming straight out of Robert's pockets. Derrel was hired as Robert's accountant to make sure that R. Kelly got to see firsthand what his money was being spent on.

While the band was rehearsing, R. Kelly was busy working with Public Announcement and I spent most of my time on the phone corresponding with Jive Records and the promoters that had booked us to perform at various clubs overseas in Europe. We were ahead of the game preparing to perform off tracks overseas and at the same time preparing to perform with the band once we returned from overseas. We were all busy; this was another level for us all and our first overseas appearance. I made sure that everyone going had their passport. We were ready!

When it was time to go we stayed awake for twenty-four hours in hopes that we could stay asleep during the long flight. We all wanted to wake up and be there. This was an eight hour flight; the longest flight any of us had ever taken. Rob had a phobia about flying, so it wasn't easy getting him to board the plane that night. But Bruce helped to convince him by keeping us laughing with his yo mama jokes.

This was the first time any of us traveled out of the country. It was just the guys on this trip. R. Kelly, Public Announcement, Torrey, Larry, and then there was me. We left Chicago's O'Hare International Airport at 5:00 p.m. and arrived in the city of Amsterdam at 9:00 a.m. Our tired and sleepy bodies were still back in Chicago. We were anticipating rest once we reached the hotel.

Amsterdam's skies were blue, but the air had the smell of a woman making the skies seem like they should have been pink. Robert immediately suggested finding a shopping mall. Amsterdam was nothing like the United States. I found a shopping area not far from our hotel. Boys II Men was in Europe doing a promo tour as well. We ran into them while out shopping. Then we came upon the red light district. There, we walked down the streets of Amsterdam to do a little window-shopping. We were amazed at the live mannequins that were in the windows. Never would we have imagined such a thing. We looked like little boys seeing naked women for the first time, going from window to window. Wow; and they were beautiful woman too!

I stood back and checked out the guys making small passes at the ladies, making them laugh without knowing their language. I wasn't feeling open enough to allow my buddies and co-workers to suspect in any way that I was anxious to spend my money on sex. I had never done it like that, just straight out give some money to some woman for her to get naked. This was game for me and I wanted to have fun, but not spend my money. The women in Amsterdam were awesomely beautiful, and we were all amazed at what was available to us for just a few bucks. But I still was not into it like that.

These women were some pretty ladies standing in the windows wearing sexy lingerie, advertising their loveliness, all shapes and sizes, selling their bodies. We spent the day flirting with the window models. And a few of the guys straight bought them some booty. As for myself, I was having fun with shooting my Mac game. I didn't want to just hit the cuchie, I wanted to have fun with it; I wanted to pull a girl with my conversation. Even though I could not speak their language, it was challenging and fun. When I would flirt, they understood. I was Max's Julian, Goldie! I felt I had the game that could convince a woman to be with me wherever I went. I was young and it was fun, so I played. As it turned out, I was very convincing when speaking a language of love with a foreigner.

Being that they understood my language, a couple of the girls I flirted with came to my hotel room after they got off work. I was still a bit jet lagged when I went to my door and saw these two beautiful women standing outside my room speaking in a language that was foreign to me,

"Hallo Demetri we zijn gekoman om tijd te besteden met je". Whatever it was they were saying, nonetheless, sounded so sexy and sweet to me. I was tickled inside! A new profound spark of energy overtook me as I invited them into my room. Leticia and MeLa were their names. It was hard communicating with them, but I managed to get through to them and convinced them to take me home with them to cook an American meal.

I went to freshen up while they relaxed listening to some of R. Kelly's music. I felt like a king when they came into the bathroom, with only their panties on while I was, like Bernie Mac would say, *"butt the fuck naked,"* giggling, talking in their sweet sexy language, touching me and spinning me around in the shower while they both washed my body down. I was in seventh heaven as they were drying me off at full attention. The girls wouldn't allow me to have sex with them even though I was getting my feel on and I wanted them. I was respectful and played along with them, enjoying them just being with me while playing with me while I was naked.

As they dressed me, I thought about what I wanted to teach them to cook. We didn't have anything on the schedule with the record company, so I was free to hang out with the ladies. They really wanted to learn how to cook American food. On the way to their house, the girls stopped to pick up some weed. We communicated with our hands in expressing what it was we were trying to convey to each other, which was fun. It was like playing charades. I thought we were going to someone's house to get the weed but we stopped in front of what looked like a Starbucks coffee shop. When we went inside, I couldn't believe it, it was a weed and hash smoke house.

We sat down at a table, and a menu was brought to us. Leticia and MeLa again in their sexy voices, *"Wat voor soort onkruid wil je"*, they were asking me what I wanted. I was just thrilled and happy. It was hard keeping my cool, but these ladies made me cool. I threw my hands up in the air to say, *"Whatever you ladies wanna get, I'm down with it,"* And I was. We smoked some of the best hash I had ever smoked in my life. And Leticia got a saucer full of weed. They were some real Columbian gold buds dude.

We stayed there for about an hour. When we left, I was blown, but cool at the same time. After we left the smoke bar, we went to Leticia's apartment, which right near the red light district and not far from the Hotel Metro Pole where I stayed. At her place, we cooked my favorite: fried chicken and rice with homemade gravy, salad and some dinner rolls. They were impressed with my cooking. It got me the dessert I wanted. I had big fun with Leticia and MeLa that night. It was about three thirty in the morning when I got back to the hotel. I had several messages on my phone from Robert. When I called him, he was upset with me. He didn't like the fact that I went off with my friends. He was really mad because they weren't interested in him joining us. Rob was like that. He felt everything had to revolve around him.

After the initial lashing I received from him, he wanted the extra plate of food I brought back from the girl's house. He took it down as if he hadn't eaten in days. The food in Amsterdam was not to our liking, so the way Rob dug into that plate was understandable. After we all finally fell out and got some real rest, it was time to go to work. The weekend of lounging around was over.

Our guide was a representative from Jive Records out of their London office. It was their first time meeting Robert. They were very nice and much about the business. Our schedule was mapped out in detail. We visited radio stations and performed on televised dance shows. It was just like back in the States. We had Soul Train and they had something else, which was just like Soul Train. At night we performed at nightclubs that were jam packed with mostly women. We were constantly moving from city to city, from Amsterdam to Rotterdam to Germany to Austria. We traveled all over the Netherlands and every night we ended up back at the hotel in Amsterdam.

The thing I liked the most about the shows we did was the fact that after every show, we were rushed off the stage and onto the bus. There was no meet and greet after shows because of the distance we had to travel every night to make it back to the hotel. The drivers there were not about to be held up waiting on the artist. They were strict on their work hours, and by law, they could only drive for a certain length of time. It was a shame because the women in the Netherlands were 10 to 1. It was ten women to every one man. I can't say it enough, the women were beautiful. I don't think I saw an out-of-shape fat girl or an ugly girl the entire time.

We did what we were there to do, promote the album. Our stay in the Netherlands was a very pleasant one. The night before we left, the hotel was swarming with girls. Leticia and MeLa visited me, but I didn't get any peace of mind being with them because the hotel security kept calling me asking me to control my people. They complained about the number of guest and that the music was too loud. I did what I could by speaking with everyone, but this was the last night. We were having too much fun. Leticia, MeLa and I ended up completing our shower together. My, my, my! We had a good time on our first trip to the Netherlands.

At sunrise we knew it was time to leave. It was a sad moment for a lot of us. As we were checking out of the hotel there were still a lot of girls roaming around. And at the Airport, we were greeted by a number of fans wishing us a farewell and a safe trip home. When it was time for us to check in and go through customs, we left several of the fans standing, waving at us crying. My two friends shaded tears as well. It was no doubt in our minds we would be looking forward to a return visit to the Netherlands. Robert even said himself; he wanted to return as soon as possible. It's was those kind of times that should have been the glue to our bonding. There we depended on each other and felt a closeness to share with one another. How could you not want the best for a loved one?

CHAPTER 15

The Motor City (Demon Lurking)

WHEN WE RETURNED to the States, Barry wasted no time informing me how well the song "Vibe" was rising on the pop charts. *"You may as well get you another suit case and pack it right back up. You've got two more tours ahead of you taking off in a month,"* Barry said as we were unloading the bus at the Best Western Hotel. In the meantime, before taking off again, Barry wanted me to make sure I had Robert in the studio ASAP. He wanted Robert to get started on the remix for Vibe and start production on the next single "Honey Love."

Robert chose CRC Studios as his home base for his music production. CRC was located right across the street from the Best Western Hotel where we had rooms reserved for our stay in Chicago for the month. I was digging that. We were at home and I had a roof over my head, at least for a month. Things were really looking up. Once I put my bags away I proceeded to update everyone on the schedule. After that I went to my sister De-Dee's house in Harvey, Illinois to spend time with my daughter Ashley. I missed my children. I was away from them and they were away from each other. We were all separated from one another and missing each other.

Demetrius Jr. and his mother Lawanda had moved to Savannah, Georgia, while I was out on the tour. That broke my heart. Now I knew I had to work with Robert and make it work in order to bring my family together. I wanted my son with me and I wanted Lawanda. She struggled with me and had been there for me when times were really hard. I wanted us to be together as a family. My heart's desire was for my children to grow up in the same household.

Lawanda convinced me to go back and work with Rob but all of a sudden she didn't agree with me being on the road. I wasn't home enough for her. She moved to Georgia and found another man. This was after we had discussed her and me raising the children together. She had made a 360 degree turn on me. It all started when she went to attend the "Freak Nik", in Atlanta, Georgia, an annual spring break gathering of college students, along with some of her friends.

When she got back from that event she began to change. She told me she had met someone in Atlanta. *"I found somebody else I want to be with Demetrius, and I'm moving down there to be with him."* She told me. I pleaded with her. Telling her how I could make things better for us and all the things I was willing to do. I was telling her all sorts of things. I was somewhat begging her to stay. But, like my boy R. Kelly said in one of his songs," When a woman's fed up, it ain't nothing you can do about it." Lawanda had it in her mind what she wanted to do and it was nothing I could do about it.

I went over to her place one night and I busted into the apartment, tearing the front door down, because she wouldn't listen to reasons anymore. I was angry as hell. I didn't want to except her leaving and taking my son away from me. I don't know if the man she fell for put his hand in her booty or what but, I felt like she didn't give our relationship a chance. I was devastatingly hurt. Here it was, right when I was about to start having a little something that could help us to build a relationship, I could have a normal life and come home to my loved ones, she belled out on me. She was the queen of my throne. She had my son. She held my daughter and called her, her own.

I sat up many nights hoping, wishing, and praying that my life would stop circulating into continuous storms. Often times, I thought life wasn't fair. It's like I'm climbing to the top of a mountain, and right when I'm about to reach the top to rest, stones start falling on me out of now here and I fall. I was so tired of starting over. Stevie Wonder said it better: *"A half a mile from heaven and you drop me back down to this cold, cold world."*

I was so tired but I kept working because I had an investment in the production I helped to build. Going through what I was going through was overwhelming and my mind was full. I was carrying a load. It was more than just feeding and clothing my children. I had an obligation to my family. I needed to be able to help them as well. I was trying to get to where I needed to be, the money was there, it just wasn't being given out to me. I had to wait a while longer, that's just the way it had to be.

I had often wondered if maybe Robert was going through some phase of dealing with his alter ego, struggling with himself to handle the power of having people be of service to him for a little of nothing. And with him being in control of the money, his head was outgrowing his big ears. Rob was acting like he was living in a movie and he was the only one to be seen in it. He was all the characters, Mr. Godfather. Then again, maybe this was something people went through who suddenly came into wealth after not ever having anything and then all of a sudden, they have almost everything. I don't know! I guess people do have to go through some kind of change in order to protect themselves from others.

I just couldn't see where it should stop someone from doing the right thing for the people there supposed to love. I was giving things a lot of thought. Like I said, my mind was full. I should be winning, but I was losing and I couldn't figure out why. I was feeling drained. I was doing the right things in my life, I thought, yet evil kept unveilings itself. My heart was being tested and I felt that God had to be against me. Evil was running through my brain and it hurt.

My mom lived in Palatine, Illinois, forty-five minutes northwest of Chicago. I went out to see her. She knew just from looking at me, that I was troubled. But I knew she would find a way to make me smile.

I knew at home with Momma, I was loved. She would say things and you would feel the words as she said them. *"It's all in God's time. Whatever you're going through with Rob,"* she would say, *"Thy will be done, babe. Its God's will and in his time. Whatever God got for you, Robert and nobody else can stop it. But it's in his time and don't forget that, baby,"* she'd say.

Momma would make me feel good listening to her. On my ride back to the studio, her words rang in my head, and I thought, *Yeah it's just a phase. We're going through a storm.* I would say to myself, there was no doubt it was going to work out.

Barry was hanging out in Chicago with us during this time while we were preparing for the next tour. Rob requested his presence; I heard him on the phone a lot of times telling him, *"B, I need you here with me."* They had become quite a pair. Often times I thought Robert was trying to take on Barry's personality."

One night, while we were in the lounge area of CRC Studios shooting some pool, Barry was talking about his niece, Aaliyah. Barry said he wanted us to drive to Detroit Michigan so we could meet her and her family. He told us how she was on Star Search. He wanted Robert to develop her skills and possibly produce her.

"I just need to know if she has what it takes to become a successful recording artist" is how Barry put it. He said every time he saw Aaliyah, she was singing.

"She really wants to be a singer, and if she's got what it takes and you can help her do a project in the studio, then I want to be behind her and give her whatever she needs. And if she's not ready, I think she'll know. She's a real smart girl, top of her class in school," Barry said proudly of his niece.

It was the fall in 1992, late evening, when Robert and I headed to Detroit, to meet up with Barry. He would then take us over to meet his niece, Aaliyah, and her family. Larry, Torrey, and DJ Mouse, another buddy of ours, were tailing along with us in a separate car.

We were given an address to Barry's home in Detroit and when we got there, we were received with a warm welcome. There was nothing we couldn't have in the house. Barry, being the busy man that he was, had a meeting and couldn't stay with us. He was trying to set something up for Robert to have a guitar player by the name of Michael Powell lay down some guitar licks on a few of his songs. Barry was making things happen. In his domain it was all about making us feel comfortable and at home.

Come to think of it, I don't remember any of us sharing a room. We didn't check or look around the house. I know I was tired. All I wanted to do was get some rest after that five-hour drive and being up since four in the morning. I settled in a room while Robert and the rest of the guys went to watch some of the videotapes Rob made with the new camcorder he recently bought.

The next morning, I spoke to Barry and he gave me the directions to Aaliyah's house. When we got there, it was another warm welcome. Everybody was polite. My first impression when meeting Aaliyah and her family was that of a close family. I felt a genuine goodness in meeting her mother, Ms. Diane Haughton, her father Mr. Michael Haughton and Aaliyah's older brother, Rashad Haughton.

Aaliyah had already heard R. Kelly's songs over the radio and she probably had a copy of his album. When they met Rob, he insisted they all call him Robert or Rob. He told them R. Kelly was just a show business name. Aaliyah was star-struck by his presence. As young as she was, it was only natural. In her girlish way, she was a giggly little sweetheart. Her magnetic smile had a glitter that showed she was mesmerized with R. Kelly the artist being there in her house. She was so adorable. And Robert's boyish ingenuousness had Aaliyah and her whole family charmed.

Aaliyah's mom, Diane, wouldn't stop offering things to us. She wanted to make sure that we knew that we were welcome. *"Just make yourselves at home y'all,"* she kept saying. She was also excited about our visit. She wanted to hear and see her baby girl entertain us. Aaliyah looked and carried herself like her mom—her hair was even styled just like her mom. It was like looking at Aaliyah as a child and then as a woman when you looked at the two of them together. The reality was mom was now watching the offspring of her beauty unfold. Diane was rejoicing along with and for her daughter. It was a happy time in the Haughton's house that day.

Mike Haughton, Aaliyah's dad, was laid back with his eye on his family's joy. Mike was cool! His goal was to learn the business. He wanted to know how to make good decisions. *"I mean, hey, for my baby girl, I need to know it all!"* he would say, keeping his composure so as to be taken serious. You could see the joy through his strength, which was covered by the seriousness of his facial expression. His only concern was for the safety and well-being of his baby girl Aaliyah. Mike and I didn't talk long, but when we did talk, it was truly an exchange of intellect.

The whole Haughton family was cool! As I looked at Barry, Aaliyah, and their family, they reminded me of *The Cosbys.* Diane was every bit like a Phylica Rashad.

Aaliyah's older brother, Rashad, was about fifteen or sixteen at the time. I never asked anybody's age. I know Rashad was a cool, laid back, young Grant Hill look-alike kind of kid. He carried his basketball around with him throughout the house. Rashad admired Robert too, but he was outspoken and pretty funny when Rob asked him if he could sing. He responded bashfully telling us, B-ball was his thing, and said he was working on his game. *"You'll have a problem with me though,"* he told Rob. Of course it brought laughter from us all, but Rashad was serious! He stood proud, knowing he had just initiated a challenge to R. Kelly to meet him on the basketball court. Accepting the challenge, Rob told me to find a gym, but Barry suggested I contact his son Jomo who was also in town. Jomo told me he'd come by to pick us up and that finding a gym would be no problem.

In the meantime, we were taken into the den and as soon as Rob saw the upright piano, he walked right over to it as if it were calling him. I smiled and watched because I knew what he was about to do. Rob had a way of using music to enchant people. Rob would have people under a spell as they listened to him play and sing at the piano. He was a true entertainer. He knew how to set the mood, and once he had his audience, he would go off into his emotions, touching the very soul of his listener. Rob was Donnie Hathaway when he sang "A Song for you," Luther Vandross when he sang, "A House Is Not a Home," and Marvin Gaye when he sang "Let's Get It On."

Robert Kelly was a young maestro with a gift of being able to express his heart in song. He would sing those songs, arrange them to fit his style, and then deliver the song from his soul directly to his audience. You could feel him! As he sat playing and singing for Aaliyah and her family, he would do one of his own original songs and while playing, he'd reach out for Aaliyah to join him. While into the melody of his music, he would give Aaliyah notes or parts to sing along with him, creating a new song in the eve of the moment. Robert was awesome; he could produce anybody. I couldn't wait for the time to come when he would summon me into the studio. I always saw Robert Kelly as being anointed with his gift in music. Barry, Diane, Mike, heck all of us were in awe at how relaxed and how freely Aaliyah's gifted vocals began to unfold. Robert brought the quality of her voice out of her in just one session.

It was magic! Aaliyah, with her girlish jitters, was hitting high notes on key and with a perfect enduring pitch. She sounded like the angel she was. I knew in the back of my mind as I watched and listened to R. Kelly coach Aaliyah, touching on the immaculate vocals she possessed, it was a done deal. Aaliyah was going to be R. Kelly's next production project. The first artist he would produce under Black Ground Enterprises. It was plain to see, at least for me it was, Aaliyah had a gift. There was uniqueness in her voice. The purity of her voice generated a blissfulness of enduring soft tones. It was easy to be captivated into Aaliyah's musical world.

Robert and Aaliyah worked out for a good thirty or forty minutes. Everybody was feeling good and knew something special had transpired. Barry, Mike, Robert and I wandered into the kitchen. Barry wanted Robert's honest opinion. *"So what do you think, Rob? Does she have it?"* Barry asked, with a serious look on his face that said he desired the truth. Rob looked at him as if he was surprised at the question. *"Are you serious, didn't you just hear her? Does she have it, that and more, Barry, that and more,"* Rob said, shaking his head, assuring Barry of his sincerity.

We hung out at Aaliyah's house until Jomo came over. He found a gym for us, not far from where we were. Our focus shifted straight to basketball. *"Yeah, I wanna see what you got now, buddy,"* Rob said to Rashad once we all grabbed our coats to leave. All of the guys, except for Barry and Aaliyah's dad, Mike, headed out in separate cars to a youth center Jomo had lined up. Jomo invited other ball players there to play a full court game. I started having flashes of my boxing days when I saw that one of our opponents was none other than the boxing legend, Mr. Thomas "the Hitman" Hearns.

Tommy Hearn's was my idol of the boxing world. I had mad love for him and Sugar Ray Leonard, and here I was on the basketball court with him. He was just a regular guy, but I was still amazed that I was actually playing ball with him. *"Pass the ball, Tommy man, damn dog, why you gotta be a hog?"* I would shout, kidding with him as we ran up and down the court. We played maybe four or five games, switching teams so that we got to play against each other.

Robert and Rashad didn't get to play against each other. Robert called himself pulling him under his wing so they played on the same team together. Robert was somewhat schooling Rashad throughout the afternoon. After the game we met Barry back at his house. After freshening up, Barry took us to a soul food restaurant. This place was a house that looked like a mansion and the food was out of sight. We feasted like we were rich. There was no limit to what we could order.

We were having a ball in Detroit with Barry, so we decided to spend another night. After we ate, we hung out at the mall for a few hours. I did our mall scheme; recognizing a celebrity shopping in the mall and bringing it to the attention of other shoppers. From that, Robert signed a few autographs and took a few phone numbers. One thing they didn't do is invite anyone over to Barry's house. Robert had much respect for Barry and he didn't want Barry to know any of his weaknesses. I think in Robert's eyes, Barry was his new daddy. Robert always gave the impression that he was a shy and naïve young kid, but he wasn't.

When the evening was over, it was back to work for me. I was consumed with putting together the travel plans for the tour. I had riders to prepare and memos to send out to the record company and to the promoters of the tour. I also had to schedule the phone interviews and ensure Robert did them. That in itself was a job. Most of the time, I would have to go wherever Rob was to make sure he made his calls because he wouldn't make them on his own. I would literally dial the numbers and connect with whomever, and at the moment of connection, I would hand Robert the phone. I used to hate doing that. I felt he should have been excited to talk to the people who were promoting his album and speaking to the fans who were buying his album. Nonetheless, we got the job done.

It was after midnight and I was in my room on the computer at Barry's house working on a rider. A rider is a list of equipment and food items an artist wants in the dressing room in every city. It also included a list of equipment needs for the band and anything else Robert wanted. I had to put it on paper and send it out to the promoters as part of the contract obligations. I was busy and lost in my work when Robert knocked on the door. *"Come on in,"* I told him as he stood on the outside knocking.

When he came into the room, he looked distressed. He had three maybe four VCR tapes in his hand. I didn't want to watch movies. What was wrong with him? I thought. But the more I looked at him, he wasn't flinching. He was struggling with something within himself. Concerned over his apparent distress, I asked in an urgent tone, *"What's wrong with you, Rob?"* I stood up to look over his physical appearance, to see if he was injured in any way, but he wasn't.

When Robert was troubled, it troubled me. Standing there looking at him with this disturbed look on his face, I thought somebody did something to him or something. Robert would come to me at times when something was bothering him. The way he confided in me was what separated me from everybody else. He knew I had his back. It was those kinds of moments that made me think Robert and I were close, and no matter what, we had each other's back.

It was my job to protect Robert. When he was going through some thing, I took on that burden as well. He began telling me he felt something had a hold on him. *"These tapes, Johnny man, I can't seem to control myself taping myself with my girls, man. And I know this ain't right and it's going to end up getting me in trouble, I know,"* he said, looking grievously vexed. I could not imagine what was so bad on those tapes, but for Robert to be hurting over them, I gave him my full attention.

Robert was crying over this something. I had no choice but to take him serious. This "something" as he called it, had him feeling he was addicted to recording the women he was sexing in his life. I didn't know how to handle this problem. I actually didn't see anything wrong with it. It was all in fun I thought. Then again there is a person's privacy. Robert had a lot of spiritual values implanted in him. After all, his music teacher was the Reverend Lena McLean. Robert was right. We had to confront this lurking demon. Something had my young brother feeling guilt, and I wanted to aid and assist him as best I could.

Robert knew the Bible and he felt as if he was being pulled in the direction of evil. He told me he was so active with the ladies and only for the reason to tape their actions. I believed him; and all I could come up with for us to do was to pray. So we prayed together, asking God to take away that which was making Robert feel controlled. We prayed to God, asking him to cover Robert from the evil which was lurking. However, during our prayer, we did not add any scriptures, which today I know would have allowed God to hear him.

This was all so weird and new to me. And for Robert to be as distressed as he was, I began to believe in demons myself. Robert was a spiritual young man. I wasn't sure of to what degree of spiritual knowledge he possessed—I just believed in him enough to know he was real about his apparent distress. We were young and it was early in our careers. I wasn't thinking about demons. We were supposed to be having fun. Thinking back, it was about this time when Robert started to disconnect from us, his friends. As time went on, he became heartless and selfish. Robert was in trouble and I didn't realize the seriousness of what he was telling me. I didn't know it to be a big thing.

We prayed over this demon, but we really didn't know anything about prayer; at least I didn't. I believed in God and I believed He loved me and would protect me, and that's all. I didn't really know how to communicate with him. I wish I had of known more about prayer and spirits because they do exist. This demon Robert was dealing with was just like the drug demon that entered my life to kill me back in the day. But, this was a demon with a different game. Recognizing this demon, Robert reached out for help, but there was no help for him in sight. He had a dark secret. He was obsessed with videotaping his private moments behind closed doors with his lady friends. The boy had a thing for pornography.

This was something Robert wouldn't share with Barry or anyone else. These kind of moments separated me from everyone else. Robert and I were like brothers. If only I knew what he was really dealing with at the time I could have been his better judgment. But, I didn't know any better myself. Robert was just a kid with a bunch of groupie friends that were willing to do whatever it took to be in his presence. We all reached out for help when we're in need, and for a lot of us, no one hears our cry. And because of our lack of understanding on how to deal with evil ways, that evil becomes a part of us, and it becomes easier and easier to dwell in that evil until we're lost and fully consumed. We all lack wisdom in making the best decisions. And when we make the wrong decisions, we find ourselves in need; sometime seemingly, there's no way out.

We pray because we want to believe things can go a better way. We hope, in our praying, for a solution and that things don't get any worse. It is because of my knowledge today that I will not throw a stone at Robert. James 2:14 asks, *"What does it profit, my brethren, if someone says he has faith but does not have works? Can faith save him?"* At the time, I thought my faith, along with us praying together, was enough to protect Robert from the demon lurking within him. James 2:15 says, *"If a brother or sister is naked and destitute of daily food, and one of you says to them, Depart in peace, be warmed and filled, but you do not give them the things which are needed for the body, what does it profit? Thus also faith by itself, if it does not have works, is dead."* _Nothing happened for Robert that night because I didn't give him that which he needed.

We believed in our prayer, at least I did; but it was faith without works, so it was nothing. The next morning, we headed back to Chicago. I asked Robert how he was doing with the problem he said he had. He told me he was cool. He did not really speak on it. So, I left it at that! I mean, you would think when you cry over something, one would have to add a little strength and say no to overcome something that was bringing him pain, if he wanted to truly beat it that is? I figured Robert would do what he needed to do to overcome his situation. I didn't ask again. I noticed that he never throw away his camera; he always kept that with him. I figured if he really felt that what he was doing was a danger to him that he would do the right thing. All he had to do was not record his intimate times with whoever he was spending those private moments with. How hard could that be? Little did I know however that, that would be proven eventually to be as hard as a drug addict denying themselves of a last hit?

Demetrius Smith Sr.

"MAN BEHIND THE MAN/ LOOKING FROM THE INSIDE OUT"! PHOTO'S

My Children, Deon with guitar, Ashley and D. Jay

My big sister (The Boss Lady) De-Dee holding my daughter Ashley

Cheryl James (Salt, Member Salt-n-Pepa group) holding my son, Demetrius Jr.

Cheryl Cobb with Demetrius Jr.

Me and Craig Hodges when he was with the Bull's

Demetrius Smith Sr.

Me and my children sharing good times

Deidre "Dee Dee" Roper, (Ms. DJ Spinderella of Salt-n-Pepa group, with son, Demetrius Jr.

Demetrius Smith

Larry Hood, Robert Kelly, Jim Pratt and Terrance Davis

After winning a talent competition our first group, M.G.M.—MGM—Mark, Shaun, Vince, R. Kelly and me

Demetrius at age 11

My children 2001 when I brought
them to LA.

My mother, (Ms. Betty)

R. Kelly & Aaliyah at her first
show in LA

R. Kelly & Craig Hodges

Me & R. Kelly 1991 at studio in
New York

Rob in the studio

R. Kelly, me & Barry Hankerson

Torrey Diggs, Larry Hood &
Robert Kelly 1989

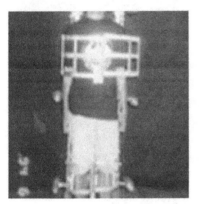

Stage prop, Ronald Powell

Scottie Pippin and me after a game
at the old Chicago Stadium

Doing time visited by my girl Sheila

Graduation picture 2001 me & my
children

Ma Ma & my sister Linda who
helped raise my twin son's

Ma Ma & sisters

Me with the band who I got to travel with back in 1983-84.
Bilalian Express. I am the one with the suite on and the
collar flipped out! The man over my left shoulder is
Donald Evans, the keyboard player. I consider him my brother and
my music teacher. An awesome keyboard player. Also there was
Paula and Larry Henderson on Sax, Lonnie Plaxico is back there over
my right shoulder. He was an awesome student of the Bass guitar then;
look him up even now! I believe Stanley Clark knows of Lonnie Plaxico.

CHAPTER 16

First Impressions

HE SONG "HONEY LOVE" was a hit. It was pushing the *Born into the '90s* album to the top of the charts and we were going to platinum status. R. Kelly turned us all into workaholics. From noon to 3:30 p.m., I was at rehearsals with Public Announcement, and from 6:30 p.m. to 9:00 p.m., we rehearsed with the band. During which time, R. Kelly would be on the phone with his personal studio engineer Peter Mokren. He wanted him to know exactly what he wanted added on the tracks. It would be after midnight when we would make it to the studio, after making stops at the clubs around the city.

By the time we got to the studio, it would be so late that most of us ended up making the studio our resting place for the night. Many nights I would drive, although tired, out to Matteson, Illinois, where my sister De-Dee lived. She was the one raising my daughter Ashley after Tamekia and I had went our separate ways. I wanted to spend every free moment I could get with my children. Even though it would be late when I got in, I'd be there when she woke up so I could have breakfast with her. I can't say that was enough, but only God knew how much I loved my mini MEs.

The schedule for the next few months was the same, and with each day the building of a dynasty was forming. R. Kelly wanted female dancers to back him up on the stage along with Public Announcement. When R. brought the request to me I organized a female dance audition. I got in touch with Dr. Love who was a host of the radio show for W.G.C.I. radio station. Dr. Love and I met at the Cotton Club. He too believed in R. Kelly and was supportive by giving us promotional time on his radio show. Every night at 11:00 p.m. he would inform the listeners of the date and times for the audition.

The director of A&R for Jive Records in Chicago,—Mr. get up and go get it done Wayne Williams, hooked it up for us to hold the audition at The Comfort Zone, a club on the West Side of Chicago. The word was out. On the day of the audition, the girls came out from all over the city with bags in their hands, portfolios and pictures. The ladies turned on their sex appeal to try to persuade the judges, which were Barry Hankerson, Derrel McDavid, Wayne Williams, R. Kelly, Dr. Love, and I. We were really impressed by the turnout. This was a serious audition.

The final outcome and decisions came from R. Kelly. He knew exactly what he wanted. The three dancers he chose were Asanta Beasley, who we called Sam; Vivian Chyna Edwards, who we called Chyna; and Andréa Lee, who we called Babe Girl (who later became R. Kelly's wife). These ladies were dynamic, and they did not quit until they accomplished exactly what Rob wanted to see. They were all workaholics, just like Rob and Public Announcement. They had the drive and expressed in their dancing exactly what R. Kelly felt in the production of his music. The three of them were the ingredients to *"Honey Love"*. They were every bit of dynamic, sensuous and electrifying together. I know I was enchanted and charmed by them.

They were smooth, beautiful and sexy. It was exotically appealing to watch them as they performed together, moving as one. Their deftness empowered them to inflict a sexual arousing from the men who sat mesmerized watching them. And the ladies, they got some wild thang in them and that is all I will say. These ladies were truly *"Bonita!"* Yes Sir, we had something for everyone to enjoy. Our plan was to make a lasting impression on the fans that were coming to get to know R. Kelly and Public Announcement.

We were there at the threshold of success in the music industry; lights, cameras and action! It took seven years to get him here from the first day he and I met at the Kenwood Academy High school talent show. Oh, how far we had come! It was like a Cinderfella night every night. There was even the possibility of Robert being nominated for a Grammy for Best New Artist of the Year.

We didn't have to pay to get into any of the clubs anymore. We would pull up in R. Kelly's Land Cruiser truck or his Benz, and like VIPs, the porter would valet park our car right in front of the joint. The doorman would open the doors, greeting us with the highest of admiration, and once through the door, the party was on. That respect and personal attention was something I didn't want to walk away from. I was a VIP everywhere I went. Once people knew I was R. Kelly's personal assistant, they offered their hospitality to me. I didn't take advantage of people. If I could accommodate them with an appearance from Robert I did. This business was where I belonged. It was all I knew and loved being a part of. You got to love the people!

There was plenty of drama along with some good times. We had some personal girlfriends we hung out with, and each one of them had another girlfriend that wanted to hang out with them. So there was always a party and hanging out with girlfriends. These two young, beautiful, women in particular, Mia and Jenna, I became very fond of. They were sisters. Mia liked her some Robert Kelly. But I have to think she was too much of a woman for Robert. Mia was for sure a beauty as well as a hot commodity. Robert took me over their house one day. Looking at Mia was like standing in a rose garden. She was so young and beautiful, with a welcoming happy spirit. She loved her some Robert Kelly though, at lease that is what I thought.

Mia and Jenna would keep me informed of when their friends were out of school so we all would get together on the weekends. We'd play all sorts of games with them. We'd play spades, petty pat, monopoly, spin the bottle and innocent kissing games. We even tried to create a board game we called 12 Play. We use to have some fun times. Rod Strickland who played for the New York Knicks at the time, use to hang out with us at Mia's sometimes. I felt these ladies kept us grounded. These were ladies with a high respect for themselves.

These young ladies were glamorous, beautiful and intellectual, and they were all in college. It was fun being around them. At times we would meet out at a club. There, they were the diva girls in the house, and it didn't matter which other entertainer was there, be it Aaron Hall, members of the Gap band, or even if Jimmy Jam and Terry Lewis were in the house, these ladies were friends and number one supporters of R. Kelly.

They let it be known by keeping our tables surrounded with beautiful women. They were the self-proclaimed street team. They didn't have a problem with keeping it real when Rob would appear to be on an ego trip. Jenna would ask at times for one of us to go and to get her a drink or get a waitress for her. This one time she asked Robert, He told her, *"Jenna come on now"* Seemingly as if he was too big to be serving her.

Jenna went off on him. *"Boy you better get your act right, what's wrong with you Robert? Don't you be acting like you can't do nothing for nobody. Boy you better go get me a drink. You still Robert, don't you forget that babe."* Jenna would say turning her nose up at him. We would all bust out laughing as Rob got up to go get Jenna a waitress. When the album came out, R. Kelly had their support.

Right before we were to depart on the tour with Gerald Levert, Mia told Rob to bring everyone over to their friend Lisa's house for a pajama party; that friend was Lisa Raye. I smiled at the thought because Lisa Raye was one very fine classy woman to me. The thought of being in her company was all about fun, she tickled me! Lisa Raye was just so much more mature and jazzy. I had the confidence of a real Mac, I kid you not. The way I saw things I was gone say the right thing to make an impression on her. She was a doll to me, but at the party she was always so dog-gone busy running around.

She always had something going on, seeing to the needs of everybody else. When I did have a chance to speak to her, it was only to say something to compliment her and she was off. "*Hold on, I'll be back. Let me go take care of this,*" she would go off leaving me waiting on her to return, knowing her mind was a thousand other places not worried about me. Back in the day, I never did get the chance to tell Lisa the charming things that I always wanted to tell her. Her personality was just as the character she portrays on her TV show "*All of Us.*" Lisa has always been very cool, down to earth, humble, and up front. She is one of the most driven women I have ever met.

The pajama party was like a Christening for us. We were entertained by the finest of young college students who were celebrating our successes with us but keeping us grounded with the reality that we are the same people from yesterday. "*Don't get shit twisted, thinking y'all all that and forgetting where you come from!*" Lisa would say.

After leaving Lisa's, we hit the club nightspots and from there we went to the studio. That very next morning, we were loading our things on the tour bus to head out. Although we were an opening act, we had plans to be recognized as a co-headlining talent. No disrespect to Baby Bear Gerald Levert, but we had plans to eat some of Baby Bear's porridge by making him work hard for the money.

We started the tour down south, in Memphis, Tennessee. This was my first time in Memphis; we visited the site where Dr. Martin Luther King, Jr. was assassinated. We also hit the malls and did the usual.

At our first show, we captivated the audience's attention with a loud explosion—**"BOOM!"** In the studio, R. Kelly worked earnestly along with his number one engineer, Peter Mokran, producing tracks for our show. R. Kelly figured a loud explosion would command the attention of the audience, silencing them and directing their full attention to the stage at, and from the sound of the blast.

Demetrius Smith Sr.

It worked! The audience was taken by surprise. They watched curiously to see who and what would be behind the cloud of smoke on stage. Starring in astonishment, they began to see the eight men dressed in black, rolling onto the stage a man strapped on a dolly wearing a Jason mask. At the same time, a loud vocal track was playing with the voice saying, *"secure all perimeters."* We rolled R. Kelly to the middle of the stage.

After he was placed at his marked spot, the men backed away, slowly and cautiously. They were moving as if there was a possibility that the man they had strapped was still able to harm them. They were giving the impression that this was a bad man that they were backing away from. Once they cleared the stage, R. Kelly stood strapped, alone, turning his head from side to side, staring at the crowd. As the smoke began to settle, the audience was frozen watching while Robert began to slowly reveal his movements.

There was a loud click of a button, releasing the restraints that held him. R. Kelly stepped off the dolly. He stood like a robot, looking around as if he was in a foreign place. The only thing moving was his head, looking around the auditorium. He began to move, one step at a time. Each step was accompanied by the sound effects of him making heavy footsteps like a gigantic monster coming towards you.

The thumping of his footsteps caused a vibrating tremor throughout the room. We had the audience's attention. R. Kelly stood motionless for a moment as the smoke got thicker. Red flashing lights came on and Public Announcement came running out on the stage to their marked spots. They were dressed in purple suites, like a Star Trek costume, yelling the lyrics to R. Kelly's first single: *"Vibe, vibe, you've got that vibe."* R. Kelly jumped right in step with them as they went into a professional choreographed dance routine. With the music bumping, the ladies in the audience started screaming. The party took off at the click of the drummers count: 1, 2, 3, 4. R. Kelly and Public Announcement were doing their thing and then a bright flash blinded the audience.

The lights quickly dimmed, settling into a sky blue clear light which flashed on a ramp which introduced the Honey Bees. R. Kelly's dancers came out dancing exotically, captivating an audience of their own. They were as sexy as sexy could be. It seemed all the men in the house were feverously keeping their eyes glued on R. Kelly's Honey Bees. These ladies were every bit of honey love. Truly everyone's eye's where glued on them. Yes, these ladies had their own fans, which were mesmerized by their every move. R. Kelly's female dancers demanded attention. They were every bit of sultry, each with their own from of beauty, shape and style, which shaped into one beautiful heart; because you did not want to take your eyes off of either one of them.

When we went into the song "Honey Love," their sexiness was, to say the least, exotically tantalizing. I know I loved watching them myself, But after the show, they had to march straight to the dressing room, change and go to sit on the bus until Mr. Kelly came and was ready to go. There was to be no personal interviews and no meeting with anyone for them. R. Kelly did not want any of us who traveled with him to talk to the girls. They were R. Kelly's girls so it was hands off.

We performed for forty-five minutes and held the audience's attention the entire time. Public Announcement did their thing too, stimulating the ladies with their sexy dance moves, grabbing their crouches and moving like male sex objects.

All the while, Baby Bear (Gerald Levert) and his crew watched from both sides of the stage along with the crowd, enjoying the show. I raised a power sign to Gerald. We were both laid back checking out the show. *"You better not be weak coming on to close the show behind our act,"* I thought to myself. R. Kelly and the crew worked hard on this show and they had the crowd totally into them. It was no denying that the ladies were warmed up and the men were on the prowl.

Gerald Levert went on to do his show. He began singing to the ladies smoothly, softly, but with authority. There was passion in every word as he called out his need for love to the ladies. He worked the stage and he worked the crowd. The ladies were screaming for him. I was totally impressed, but then again, how could I think anything less. Gerald was the son of Mr. Eddie Levert. In my book not only is Eddie one of the greatest and strongest vocalist I have ever heard, he also stands at the top of my list for being one of the most passionate singers. I watched Gerald Levert do his thing, massively charming the ladies and giving the men in the audience something to think about when he sang "Casanova."

I thought as I watched Gerald down on one knee, crooning, singing his heart out, and melting the woman whose hand he was holding, Baby Bear had held his own. There was nowhere at all in his show where he was weak. In fact, he was a complement to our show. Gerald was a true gentleman who displayed maturity for the respect of women at its finest. He had his daddy's chops no doubt. It was an awesome, awesome, good first night. We didn't mingle with Gerald and his crew that night, but all in all, I think we made a good first impression.

After watching Gerald that night, he was added to my list of mentors. He gave me something to think about. I wanted to implement some of the things he was doing into Public Announcement's representation of R. Kelly. Yep, we were going to have to drop down on one of our knees and reach out to the ladies like Gerald because to hear them scream for Gerald Levert was a different kind of a scream then what Robert would get. They were Loving and wanting Gerald; in that order. He was a women's man! It was what he wanted and they wanted to give it to him. Gerald Levert, he held down his throne.

I decided we were going to take some of Gerald's moves and add a touch of elegance of our own.

It was no doubt our show was dominating, but Gerald was the lover of the night, his rawness was passion. After listening to Gerald, I could only imagine a woman's thoughts: *"they would want to be loved."* And Gerald Levert, his songs touched a woman's heart. He was a crooner; truly his daddy's son. RIP, my brother. You are loved and your passion will be felt forever.

We were out on the tour with Gerald for six weeks and I learned a lot about the stage production, dealing with promoters, the press, the fans and the after show activities. All the shows went well. We had a few kinks to work out here and there but all in all, I had a strong will to organize things. The only thing that was hectic was getting Robert on the bus after our shows.

Our drivers would complain about R. Kelly taking all night to board the bus so we could leave and go to the next city. Our show would end at 10:45 p.m. and I would call the hotel at 11:30 p.m. to inform our driver that we were finished. An hour later, the driver would show up ready to drive eight to twelve hours to the next city. We would all be on the bus waiting for Rob to finish his personal autograph sessions. Four or five hours later R. Kelly would board the bus with us. This frustrated me and the drivers.

It would be five o'clock in the morning before we would pull out of the lot on our way to the next city. Many times we would drive straight to the arena after stopping at a Waffle House. Everyone would have to get dressed on the bus. The driver would drop us off, drive to the hotel, sleep four or five hours and then have to wake up to pick us up again and go through the same waiting period again.

I know the driver was making money, but he wasn't a robot. It was dangerous for all of us and the more I talked to Rob about it, the longer it seemed he took to get on the bus. He wanted me and everybody else for that matter to know that he was in charge. He was fighting against me and I did not know why? I was there with his best interest at heart. We were on the same team. Yet he did not seem to have an ear for anything in which I had to say or concern about our lives being in the hands of a sleep deprived person who was driving us across the country. His demeanor was to entertain the fans one by one as they lined up outside of his dressing room, who were willing to wait for hours for the chance to be with him.

I tried talking to R. Kelly's posse when I could get a chance to speak to them one on one. I was hopeful that they would understand the importance of us working together with me to protect R. Kelly for the longevity of his career. I was always on them about the girls they were choosing for him. They just always seemed to be real young and there were always beautiful mature women that wanted to get with Robert. However, my consistent hassling the posse led to them running to R. Kelly, complaining that I had a problem with them bringing girls to the hotels and to the shows. Robert and I talked about it, but he didn't debate with me about it either. He emphasized that he didn't like it and that he didn't want me getting into it with his boy's, but he knew I was right. But what he did do? He went undercover with him and his boys. He tried keeping things from me, on the down low.

Robert and the posse started avoiding me. They would see me coming one way, and they would go another way. Robert bought walkie-talkies, as a new way of communicating. Before shows, I would call them and security would tell me that they are on the way. *"We should be there shortly,"* was what they would tell me and I would be at the stage door waiting for them so I could rush R. Kelly to the stage. It wasn't funny though. I was being stressed out. Things were buck wild and the head of the team wanted to be Mr. Burger King and have it all his way. It was always a fight to keep things in order. When things should have been smooth, Robert was making everything a challenge. The posse had gotten on my nerves. I'm telling you, I was being stressed out.

As an attempt to limit the after show activities, I stopped giving backstage passes to R. Kelly's handpicked crew members. It didn't work. Tee, one of R. Kelly's boys told him that I wasn't giving out passes so Burger King, I mean R. Kelly started asking how many tickets he was getting per show. Things got frustrating after that; R. Kelly started dictating to me. I was the tour manager with no control of his artist. All I knew was that I had to find a way to get control of things. My first priority was to make sure that our drivers were taken care of. I stopped waking them up. Once

R. Kelly was done and had gotten on the bus, then we'd sit waiting for the drivers to show up. This method worked and helped the driver's uneasiness. I began organizing the rest of the troublesome things that I would have to figure out before the next tour, which was to be with the female rap group Salt-n-Pepa.

When we returned home after our tour with Gerald Levert, R. Kelly's fame had gone to a higher level in Chicago. Some of everybody was waiting for us when we pulled up at the *Best Western Hotel*. Radio people, fans, cousins and new friends who knew how to suck up to R. Kelly; and R. Kelly tried to accommodate them all, throwing most of the workload on me: *"Demetrius, do this, and do that. Take care of him, make sure they get that!"* I didn't mind, I was taking care of business.

CHAPTER 17

Shattered Pieces

AFTER A COUPLE days of roaming the club circuit, it was back to CRC Studios. Barry Hankerson negotiated a deal with Jive Records that allowed R.Kelly to produce an album for Aaliyah. Robert took writing songs for Aaliyah seriously. He asked me what I thought of a woman singing the song *"At Your Best"* by the Isley Brothers. *"It's a beautiful song"*, I told him. But little did I know how beautiful that song really was until R. Kelly began to lay down the tracks for Aaliyah.

It was time to meet up with Aaliyah again. R. Kelly and I drove to Detroit to meet with Aaliyah and her family. R. Kelly had laid down some tracks and wanted to go over some vocals with her. The hospitality was the same when we got to Aaliyah's house. Her mother, Diane, and her father, Mike, were the perfect hosts, accommodating our every need, which was only to have Aaliyah available for R. Kelly to work alone with her.

We arrived early that day. R. Kelly didn't feel we needed to stay the whole weekend. His intent was to synchronize her vocals to his tracks, but once we were there, we ended up staying over a few extra nights at Aaliyah's home with her parents. Robert and Aaliyah spent time together singing. R. Kelly was fascinated by Aaliyah's voice. I sat with them fascinated myself at how R. Kelly brought out the quality of this young girl's voice.

R. Kelly's sleeping habits were like that of a vampire. He would sleep all day and work all night. His day never began until night time. After sitting around all day watching television and playing basketball, it was around eleven o'clock at night when R. Kelly decided to go over some vocals with Aaliyah. Mike and Diane had already retired for the evening, and I decided to do the same, leaving R. Kelly and Aaliyah alone to work. That night, around two o'clock in the morning, R. Kelly finally came to the basement where we slept and woke me up. He said that he wanted to talk about the song that he had in mind for Aaliyah. *"Man she inspirers me,"* he said of Aaliyah! He was somewhat tender hearted (benevolent would be a better way to put it). Producing a platinum album for Aaliyah was a priority goal for him.

That night, Aaliyah and R. Kelly connected. As we were driving home that next morning, R. Kelly was on the cell phone with the sound engineer, Peter Mokren, giving him instructions on what to have ready for him, urging Peter to be there at the studio and to be ready when we got there. I knew Aaliyah was special, especially in Robert's eyes. For the next couple of months, we stayed in the studio. R. Kelly and Peter would work all night, and R. Kelly would sleep in the studio during the day.

The little, young, fast girls that had been hanging around R. Kelly at his apartment: Tia, Shea, and a few others were singing in the background for Robert on Aaliyah's tracks. Most people thought R. Kelly had something other than music going on with these kids, and I myself had wondered. I never saw him messing with those girls. He laughed and joked with them, but in a lot of ways Rob was a big kid himself. I mean, I did feel like he could have them sexually if he wanted to. But then again, in my eyesight, R. Kelly was a player. He had women. As far as the girls that hung around the studio with Robert were concerned I didn't know their age. I felt that they were of age. It was apparent their parents didn't have a problem with them being out in the late hours of the night. The girls came and went as they pleased. He always told me that they were talented and that he was going to produce them.

As I listened to Tia and Shea sing, I was totally surprised! Tia had a voice with quality and strength like Whitney Houston. R.Kelly saw things in people that others didn't. I never saw him messing withthose girls. He laughed and joked with them, but in a lot of ways Robert was a big kid himself. I mean, I did feel like he could have them sexually if he wanted to. But then again, in my eyesight, R. Kelly was a player. He didn't know what he was doing though; but at the same time I was admirable of the older women whom he kept company with, there was Somotta, Tina, Kim, and this is only a few names. These women had their own; they were independent woman and around the same age as Robert, if not older.

I'm just saying that to say Robert had choices. As far as the girls who hung around, it was apparent their parents didn't have a problem with them being out in the late hours of the night. The girls came and went as they pleased. I saw R. Kelly with his focus on producing a platinum album for Aaliyah, and whatever he needed to add to accommodate his goal, he added it. I tell you, this guy was a genius when it came to the God-given gift and talent with music he had. The young girls who were hanging around, they all had a purpose in Robert's music.

When it was time for Aaliyah to come to Chicago, R. Kelly wanted her and her family to be totally comfortable. He offered them his apartment in Lake Point Towers on thirty-sixth floor, overlooking Chicago's skyline. As a matter of fact, he insisted they stay at his place and he in turn would stay at the Best Western Hotel, But Aaliyah's mom, she was not with Robert putting himself out so they all stayed together at his place. I created an itinerary for Diane that informed her of the things R. Kelly lined up for Aaliyah. At ten o'clock in the morning, I would pick up Aaliyah to have lunch. After lunch, Aaliyah would go to the studio with R. Kelly, where he arranged for her to have vocal training (which Robert said it was only to strengthen her voice). After her vocal lessons, Aaliyah would return to R. Kelly's condo with her mom.

R. Kelly gave them the key to the city. I saw to it that wherever they wanted to go, whatever they wanted to do and whatever they needed was made available for them. It was always 10:00 p.m. when Aaliyah would be summoned to the studio, accompanied by her mother of course. It was all work in the studio with R. Kelly, Aaliyah, Tia, Shea, and Shauna. It was always amazing watching Robert work. He was cunning in so many ways to get what he needed in obtaining the best out of a person. He would stop in the middle of a song, if they weren't singing their notes correctly, or if someone seemed out of synch, he'd just jump up and tell Peter to shut it down for a few hours. *"Come on, everybody, I feel like ice cream and a movie. Johnny, go get the car for us,"* he'd tell me. Altogether, R. Kelly, Diane, Aaliyah, Tia, Sha, Shauna, and I, we would all end up at the movies. After the movie or ice cream, we'd be right at the studio continuing where we left off, but this time, whatever was not happening right came to order.

R. Kelly had a way of bringing the best out of a person. He was a young genius and Aaliyah was a happy spirit when she was in the studio with Robert. She use to sing in the dark. All of the lights in the booth had to be off. She got that from R. Kelly. She wanted to be as free as he was when it came to perfecting her art in music. The songs started flowing out of R. Kelly for Aaliyah to sing, and like the songbird she was, she sang with heartfelt feeling, bringing life to every song. It didn't take R. Kelly long at all to finish Aaliyah's debut album *"Age Ain't Nothing But a Number"*.

The next tour was the next level up. We were booked as a co-headliner act. People were paying big bucks to see us. One would wonder if I had a family or life of my own since all of my time was spent preparing for the next tour and assisting R. Kelly and Aaliyah. His status grew so much I was working 24/7 keeping busy with R. Kelly's career events. How I found the time to do all the things I got done, I do not know. But I was moving up and it wasn't easy.

While Lawanda nagged me about money and Tamekia fighting about everything other than anything that had to do with my daughter, how I found time to carry my work and manage my home life—was only by the grace of God. It was very difficult for me because more than anything, I wanted my children together and with the forces that were in my life it was a challenge to make that happen. Shit always all of a sudden changed directions on me in my life. Later I ended up getting custody of my daughter from Tamekia. Time was moving on. My life was so filled with so much to do. I wondered sometimes if I was overloading myself.

The only thing that kept me sane was the fact that I was so buried in my work, I did not have time to deal with all the things that were changing the course of my life. My daughter ended up living with my sister De-Dee in Harvey, Illinois and I stayed in the studio day and night working with Robert to make things happen. I needed this to work; my life was at stake. I had to be able to buy a home so I could get my family back.

With all the odds seemingly against me, there was still some good in it. Okay, R. Kelly, let's do this, let's try it your way, I thought. If you can't beat 'em, join 'em. I was going to turn a page and try again to put the pieces to my dream together. My life was going upward bound. I worked daily planning tours, monitoring the rehearsals with Public Announcement, staying with R. Kelly for the times he had to do phone interviews or have photo shoots and I was hanging out club hopping again.

I received and sent out all the information needed for the Salt-n-Pepa tour. I was looking forward to this tour, traveling with these lovely ladies. I loved me some Cheryl James, (Ms. Salt). She was the special one that caught my eye from the very first time I saw the group. Don't get me wrong, I loved Sandy Denton (Pepa), and Deidre "Dee Dee" Roper, (Ms. DJ Spinderella) too. This tour was special for me. It was scheduled to take off in Miami, Florida. In preparation for the tour, we built a whole new stage and R. Kelly had orchestrated a whole new show.

Time had moved on. The *Born into the '90s* album went platinum and began to peak. In what seemed like overnight, R. Kelly had finished his *12 Play* album and "Sex Me" was about to drop. Every night and all through the day, I would ride around with Rob, waiting in the car, getting mad at him on some occasions, for having me sit in the car for periods of time, while he entertained the beautiful women he had in his life. The boy had the makings of a true player, I kid you not.

It was strange when R. Kelly would pull me to the side at times and talk about how he was having second thoughts about releasing the single "Sex Me," which was also on the *12 Play* album. He was under a lot of stress about that song. Spiritually he felt that the song was too vulgar and he didn't think his mom would approve of the song at all. Can you believe it? R. Kelly felt as though the song was too sexual. The spiritual side of him was subconsciously hindered. He was very remorseful over the song, strange as it may sound; R. Kelly felt the song was sinful. During this time his mother was sick, so Rob was going through some things and maybe he was looking for an escape of some sort; I don't know.

There were two sides to Robert. There was Robert Kelly, who was caring, playful, and studious (when he would listen). Then there was R. Kelly. He was totally opposite. He cared about himself and he took selfishness to another level. At first I began to think his ways was because of youth and, I would say, his lack of education. He wanted to control everything and everybody and he was always right about everything. There was no listening. It was his way or no way at all. He had changed. He became egotistic and self-centered.

I spoke with Barry from time to time about Robert. I was searching for answers that would help assist me with him. Barry felt that Robert was going through a phase that most young artist go through in the beginning of their career. *"You're going have to be creative with arranging to have the things Robert wants, as perks, and the things Robert needs. Your job is not going to be an all-out easy job, but it's a good place to be,"* Barry said. I took his advice to heart. It was good solid advice. Robert and I weren't seeing eye to eye on a lot of things, and on the coming tour, I wanted to be ahead of the game with him. He knew the tour with Salt-n-Pepa was another level up the scale. We were now booked to perform in arenas in front of larger crowds of people.

All while we were preparing for the tour, R. Kelly was in the studio with Aaliyah. She and her mom, Diane, would fly back and forth to Chicago on the weekend because Aaliyah was still in school. It was always a joyful time when Ms. Lady Diane and Aaliyah were there. I called her that because that is how I remember Aaliyah's mom. She carried herself as if she were royalty. And I am saying that in a complimentary way; Ms. Diane was elegant. That's why Aaliyah was so, so special. One thing for sure, we hung out and stayed at the movies and ate popcorn a lot.

Aaliyah's album was R. Kelly's pet project and turning out a sound that was developing to be something really special. I worked along with Jomo Hankerson making preparations to shoot the video for Aaliyah's first single "Back and Forth" in Chicago. Jomo was the man that moved Roberts's career. He was Aaliyah's cousin and the man I communicated with once our tour negotiations were over. Jomo was the top man for Black Ground Enterprises. He was the one moving Aaliyah's career to rise.

Yeah, my future had promise! Teaming up with Jomo made me feel like I would be in an executive position myself one day. For this video shoot, I was on Aaliyah's payroll, making $800 for that entire day. I was also being highly considered to be her tour manager. Things were going to balance out. I was happy with the thought of working on the road as Aaliyah's tour manager too.

When it was time to shoot the video, Aaliyah's whole family came up with her. At the video shoot, which was on the top level of the parking lot next door to CRC Studio on Ohio Street, Aaliyah's dad, Mike, and I were talking while we were shooting the video. He confided in me on how uneasy he was with Aaliyah being out late in the studio all night. When he stated that to me, I was a bit uneasy myself because for one, I liked Mike, and two, I was feeling the same way.

Looking at Aaliyah as a minor and from a parent's perspective, I wanted him to know of my suspicions of R. Kelly, not being the gallant honorable man he was portraying himself to be. In the beginning Aaliyah's mom chaperoned her when she came to the studio, but because of the long hours in the studio she would get tired and because Robert was so cunning she trusted him with her daughter. It was when Aaliyah was out from under her mother, that is when her and Robert would take off and be alone together. A few times I dropped them off at his apartment. No I didn't say anything to anyone other than me asking Robert what he was doing. He would tell me he was tired and he and Aaliyah were going to chill for an hour or so before going back to work. *"I need to work with her (Aaliyah) on her vocals in a privet setting,"* he would tell me.

Much as I wanted too, I couldn't come right out and tell anyone of my suspicions What if I was wrong? I never saw what went on behind closed doors. R. Kelly was my boy, and there was no telling how Mike or Barry would react if he found out Robert was possibly sleeping with his teenage daughter. As I stood there talking to Mike, I tried to give him a hinting suggestion indicating that he should not allow Aaliyah to record late at night. I told him to tell R. Kelly and Barry that he wanted Aaliyah to record in the daytime and that he wasn't comfortable with her being out at night. I also told him R. Kelly would change his schedule around to accommodate Aaliyah.

Mike was not listening and did not heed to my push to get him to do the right thing for his daughter. He felt the hours were what brought the best out of R. Kelly and if he changed things, it would interfere with R. Kelly's creativity. I told Mike *"MAN, Robert is unbelievable with his music, he creates it all the time. It's who he is, it's what he does,"* I said that in hopes of Mike feeling comfortable in stepping in to pull Aaliyah out. But with Mike's confidence and trust in Robert, I felt I wasn't getting through, and I let it go at that. I didn't press on any further. I said all I could say.

I felt I was telling him in so many words to pull Aaliyah out and insist things run according to the way he wanted it to go. I even made a point of mentioning what I would do if it was my daughter. We were both saying one thing but really focusing on another. I was focused on staying in good to keep my job and money circulating, while Mike was watching his daughter fulfill a dream. Aaliyah was having fun shooting her first video. And I believe for her and for her family-sharing that moment with her friends and family was priceless.

Everybody's focus turned to Aaliyah and we were intrigued by the hype of the video and the next step in her career. R. Kelly spent a lot of time charming the family. I let it go because I hadn't seen anything other than something that didn't look right. To suspect and actually tell on someone just because something didn't look right didn't mean it wasn't right. And to set myself out and accuse someone on assumption, I wasn't ready to do that. I give out indications, and subliminal hints to my suspicions and that was all I could do. At this point I hadn't seen anything.

Nobody else seemed to see anything out of the ordinary and what I was thinking I saw, was as clear as daylight. Who am I? No one was listening to me. I wasn't important. So, I let it go! Besides, Aaliyah and her family were going back to Detroit after the shoot anyways. I had a family to feed and I needed to get my mind set on the upcoming Salt-n-Pepa tour. That was going to be an experience all by its self.

Demetrius Smith Sr.

CHAPTER 18

The New Crew

THIS WAS THE tour I wanted to be on. Oh my God! Salt-n-Pepa, I was in love with them and I didn't want the things that happened on the last tour to happen on this one. I told myself Robert and I were going to have to have a serious talk. I really wanted to make a lasting impression on this tour. This was to be a larger tour and I had permission to add some people. My focus was on putting together a crew while Robert worked on the *12 Play* album.

Robert wanted the *12 Play* album to have a true gospel feeling. He hired Mr. Lafayette Carthon to bring that about. Lafayette was an awesome gospel pianist. When Lafayette came to work for Robert on the album, he brought the gospel along with him. His spirit and the way he carried himself let us know he was not there for any foolishness. Lafayette felt like the *12 Play* album was all about sex and he did not feel comfortable with that because of his religious beliefs. But Barry must have made him an offer he couldn't refuse. With Lafayette aboard, the whole atmosphere in the studio changed. It was business, no more young girls visiting and no showing up late to the studio. I had to create an itinerary and R. Kelly kept to the schedule. Lafayette was a plus and I was so glad to have him aboard. R. Kelly had so much respect for him that I thought it would be ideal to have Lafayette travel on tour with us, but Lafayette was a gospel musician and had no desire to travel on the road with an R&B band. He was stable playing for *The Winnans* and playing for his church in Detroit.

R. Kelly asked me to pursue Lafayette as his musical director. "Yeahhh," I thought. Lafayette would truly be a great addition to our crew. I spent a lot of personal time getting to know him and sharing personal stories with him. I wasn't the only one working towards the goal of having him on our team; Barry, Robert and the rest of the crew did their share of convincing. Still Lafayette felt that the lifestyle on the road with an R&B group was totally against everything he believed in and lived for. Lafayette use to shake his head at the lyrics to *12 Play*; it seemed it truly disturbed him.

However, after a long period of pleading, Lafayette agreed to be the musical director but refused to travel. His job was to get the band ready to be on the road. Of course I don't give up when I am on a mission so I continued to pursue him. Lafayette worked day and night in the studio with R. Kelly, lived out of a hotel and rehearsed with the band so much that as time went on, he joined us on the road. Of course the $2500 a week contract he signed helped him decide to travel with us.

Lafayette stood strong in his beliefs; so he signed on to be the musical director on the road, but he did not sign on to play R. Kelly's music. Lafayette was no joke when it came to the way he negotiated his deal with R. I was impressed with the way he negotiated to get what he wanted. He slyly smiled and told me, *"A person don't get what they deserve, they get what they negotiate."* Watching how he did not allow anyone to manipulate him and how he stood on his convictions, made me start looking at my situation with R. Kelly in a whole new light. When Lafayette took the job of musical director, he brought in musicians he knew and put together a whole new band. R. Kelly's sound was solid and full. He had an awesome ear for music and did not tolerate excuses. There were some he had to fire for not executing—If they weren't putting out what he needed, he would tell them *"Thank you for your time today sir, but I won't be needing you any further. Please see Mr. Smith, he'll make sure you receive whatever it is you're owed."*

The dynamics and the timing of the music had to be perfect. He was a fearless leader, and everyone respected him. The band was impeccable and the background singers were symmetric. All of that along with the stoutly work R. Kelly and Public Announcement were putting in; we were ready to go on tour with Salt-n-Pepa. Things were better organized for this tour in many ways. My pay went up to $750.00 a week. R. Kelly was listening to me and allowing me to do my job without his input, things were looking up. I was really surprised when R. Kelly allowed me to hire an assistant.

While out on tour with Gerald Levert, I met a young lady who had a personality that was overwhelmingly charming. She had eyes that smiled at you. When she would look at you, you were captured by her gracefulness. In her I saw exactly what my mother use to say about me. *"She'd be likeable if she wasn't so lovable."* Her name was Cheryl Cobb. She worked as the hospitality coordinator for (Stage Right Productions), they were the promoters of the tour. Her job consisted of taking care of the artist's dressing rooms and making sure that the media and everyone that was allowed backstage after the show were taken care of. She was that somebody I needed to know who knew everything about being out there on the road.

Cheryl was perfect for this job. She knew what to say, how to say it and when to say it. She charmed people with her kindness and a smile. Cheryl had a mother's spirit, and the arena was her house. The way Cheryl and I communicated, I thought we could really be a good team together. I had just met her, but instantly I felt like I had known her all my life. She was grounded, level headed and in control of things. She was the sister I needed to have my back.

Cheryl had a way with making a person feel at ease. It was refreshing to meet a friend. She knew I was a rookie in the business and she was right there for me, like a sister, to help me out in any way she could. It was comforting to meet Cheryl. I could talk to her about anything. Talking with her was always a growing experience. She was every woman on this tour for me. I talked to her about the business, being out on the road and asked her a lot of questions about the ins and outs of the road. She would complete her own duties and then she would help me with mine. She knew I was carrying a heavy load being responsible for fourteen young adults.

She also knew and brought it to my attention that R. Kelly was a new young artist and that I was going to have my hands full with him and our crew, when it came to *"the ladies."* After that first tour, I asked Rob to hire Cheryl to work along with me as my assistant. I didn't believe it and I was overly excited when Rob said, *"Yeah, man, but keep it business."*

The small-headed man was telling me to keep it business. He would look at me and say, *"Johnny, Johnny man, I'm ma tell you, you can't be having no going-ons with Cheryl. You can't let that."* He reached down shyly between his legs, grabbing his pants at his crouch. *"Like, man, you know what I'm talking about Johnny. Man, girls a mess stuff up for you man, when you, you know."*

He started touching the top of his head. *"You gotta be up here, man,"* he said, touching his head with his finger. Rob was trying to tell me, in so many words, to not let my little head overrule my big head when it came to Cheryl. *"man, didn't we have this conversation at one time before?"* I asked him as he gave me a serious look and began to walk away smiling. *"Yeah"*, he remembered.

During the tour Cheryl got to R. Kelly too because he also found Cheryl to be like a sister. Cheryl was good people. She was Stage Right Production crew's baby sister. After she and Barry talked over her salary and duties the deal was done. Cheryl and I were on the phone right away, mapping out the tour for the next eight weeks. We were representing the hottest new and young singing sensation and his first album, "Born Into The 90's" had spread. I was hopeful that Cheryl's addition as my assistant would help me to build a stronger presence for the team which I saw to be a true value.

Things were falling into place: Our team was strong, reliable and trustworthy. There were still three more pieces I felt I had to put into place. I had to find R. Kelly a personal bus driver, a stylist and personal security. For the bus driver I had been talking to Alvin Lewis; who we called Big Al out on the road. He was one of the drivers I met on our first tour. I mentioned to him over the phone that I was very interested in him driving exclusively for R. Kelly. He was interested.

Al was a real cool and easy-going guy. He got behind the wheel of that bus and drove city to city in his shorts. This man would get off the bus in zero degree weather in shorts. He said he dealt with all kinds of situations dealing with artist and their egos. It wasn't hard to hire Al. All I had to do to get him was to hire the bus company, who employed him. So his company, Florida Custom Coach, was who we used.

I rented two buses. The one bus was for R. Kelly & Public Announcement, the Honey Bees and Robert's personal security. I rode on the other bus along with the band and crew members. Finding a security person to work for R. Kelly, who at the same time would report to me, wasn't easy. I had to find someone who I could truly relate with and would work with me to accommodate my dilemma; someone who would go against the grain after every show. More than anybody, I wanted Larry Hood.

Larry was R. Kelly's personal friend who started out with us. He was who I thought had earned the position and he would have been the help needed to take this to a Barbara Streisand, Rod Steward level in music. That is the talent of R. Kelly. But Larry wasn't ok with everything that went on *"Man Johnny, what's going on man with Robert and these girls? Man how old is them girls?"* he'd ask me. *I told him that I was not there to check ID's."*

Larry would look at *me* out of the top or from the side of his glasses and tell me, *"Man now you know I'm going to have to sit him down on this. Man because you know I can't get into nothing like that".* He was observing how things had grown since the last time he had traveled along with us.

Larry went with us on the first two tours, but like me, he was frustrated with the realization that he didn't have any control or say so with R. Kelly. He said Rob wouldn't listen to anyone anymore. *"Johnny man, we're supposed to be smoother than the way things are going,"* he used to tell me when I would constantly call on him to get R. Kelly out and onto the bus. In addition to the concern with the girls, he felt like there was a lack of control when it came to dealing with Rob so Larry decided he couldn't afford to go on this tour. He said he couldn't take off from his nine-to-five for the money R. Kelly was offering to pay him. *"Johnny, what's wrong with him, man?"* he would ask me. *"We were there for him when he was struggling to have a place to live and clothes on his back, and now he don't wanna give me enough to make up for the pay I make at my little job,"* he would say to me with anger and frustration in his voice. *"Why he wanna do us like this, Johnny?"*

I totally understood Larry's temperament. Rob only wanted to pay him $300 a week and no per diem. When I would submit a pay scale to Rob showing the estimated cost of the tour along with an estimated payroll summary, he and Barry would oppose the salaries because they felt no one in our camp was on the professional level to receive the pay as they said *"professionals received."* Unfortunately for me, not being able to get Larry aboard, the search was on for someone new.

I knew another brother, Tyree Jamison. We met him during our club hopping days and he had hung out with us as security for Robert on several occasions, whenever Larry wasn't available. Tyree was a smooth big young brother. He had a serious attentiveness about himself and he wanted to be a part of the crew. He and I collaborated on how to get Rob to and from the places he was supposed to be and trick him into scheduled phone interviews.

Tyree kept the schedule of interviews on a notepad and would call the interviewer at the scheduled time and no matter what R. Kelly was doing, Tyree would simply hand R. Kelly the phone forcing him to interview. R. Kelly would get mad at Tyree so he would tell him, *"Demetrius called and told me to give you the phone."* Over a period of time, R. Kelly even fought that system, by telling Tyree he worked for him and that his obligation was to him first; *"I'm the one paying your salary, not Demetrius."*

Nonetheless, Tyree *was* someone who would go against the grain. I got Rob to ok his coming aboard only because Tyree took less of a salary than what Larry turned down. He did it because he wanted to prove himself to R. Kelly.

To fill Torrey's spot as R. Kelly's stylist, I asked Lisa Raye if she would be available. She thought I was joking at first. We knew she was into modeling, but I also noticed that she had style. At her party, as well as when we would meet out on the club circuit, she would always talk about the different looks she thought would be attractive for R. Kelly on stage. Lisa didn't get high, she didn't drink and she was down to earth. I knew she would be an asset to the team and it was good to have someone you knew would be about their business. After a couple of days of pondering on the idea of going on the road, Lisa paid us a visit at CRC Studios. When she arrived at the studio, R. Kelly was in the booth laying down vocals to a song he wrote for Aaliyah. I was surprised she was there, but I'm sure R. Kelly knew she was coming.

No woman just showed up there without being invited or there would be no admittance and that pretty much went for anybody. *"Hey, Demetrius, did you guys find you a stylist to go out with y'all yet"* was the first thing she asked when she walked into the studio. *"Not yet, girl, we were still waiting on you,"* I replied. After chit-chatting for a few moments, Lisa told me she had given the idea some thought and said it would be good exposure for her. She would be able to network in hopes to expanding her modeling career.

We chit-chatted for about fifteen minutes before R. Kelly came out of the vocal room and joined us. *"What's up, girl?"* R. Kelly said, excitedly. He smoothly walked towards her, extending his arms out and they embraced, with a welcoming hug. After which, Lisa Raye went into her back to business mode, she got to running off at the mouth. *"Boy, okay, okay,"* she said, easing herself free of the hug and the kisses on the cheek. She modestly pushed herself away from R. Kelly's grip and went into being the same Lisa Raye you see on TV, having her way.

Lisa Raye couldn't play any other role other than being herself. Even in the flick she played as the cowgirl, along with Stacy Dash, (Gang of Roses), she was Lisa portraying herself. She can portray all characters because she is every woman in her walk.

After she got out of R. Kelly's hug, surprisingly she proceeded to confront Rob about the tour we were scheduled to leave out on in the next couple of days. *"Now, Rob, I know how y'all be acting crazy out there on that road, so how you gone act with me out there with you. I don't want to be involved in no wild parties, I am not into that,"* she made clear.

Rob looked over at me with an inquisitive look, like, what is she talking about? I jumped in to cut Lisa off. It seemed she wasn't going to give R. Kelly or me a chance to respond to her accusations. *"Lisa, you and I talked about you going, but you never confirmed your being able to go."*

At that point, R. Kelly playfully grabbed at Lisa, signaling to me not to worry. I was trying to find a resolution because Lisa was approaching the situation as if she had already been hired. *"Come on, girl, go with me. You and I got to have to talk about this; you talking about dressing me when you got on them old school Knickerbocker jeans."* R. Kelly and I burst out laughing. It was just a joke to break the ice. Lisa Raye always looked and dressed nice. R. Kelly was a jokester, real big on yo momma jokes.

When R. Kelly and Lisa came back into the studio mixing room, he told me Lisa was on board. For me, the stage was set. I had a whole new crew going out and I was looking forward to stepping up to the next level of management. I was responsible for more personnel but this time I had team members that I hand-picked myself.

CHAPTER 19

Trippin!

AS THE BUS pulled into Orlando, Florida, I was greeted by sunshine, beautiful women and Disneyworld. Stage Right Productions and its production crew rented a loft at Universal Studios for show rehearsals. Breaking down and setting up the stage was important. In arenas, the show had to be over and the set broken down at a certain time or the union would charge thousands of dollars for overtime.

Both acts performed and after each performance the set was broken down and reassembled the next morning. After rehearsals I would stay in my hotel room. There were still lots of loose ends I had to tie up before the tour actually took off. There were still hotels that needed to be booked so I had to map out the route we were traveling and get that information to our travel agent.

We did our first show in Orlando. R. Kelly and Public Announcement dazzled the crowd with their provocative sexy moves, while running across the stage during the song. R. Kelly crooned to the ladies telling them if they were eighteen and over they could come spend the night with him. Ladies were literally screaming, trying to make their way to the stage. It turned into a big party when R. Kelly sang "Slow Jam." We had another ramp built for the female dancers. We had video footage being shown during the show, and the light show was spectacular.

Salt-n-Pepa came on after us to close the show. They were truly a class act. I thought the show was a little off balance. We came on first stimulating the audience into a lover's mood and following us came a hyped rap act, but Salt-n-Pepa held their own. These ladies were not only beautiful, their exposition humbled me to recognize them as a force as I watched them captivate the crowd with intellectual sex appeal. They took the audience to school. Their whole show was to bring awareness to the deadly disease, AIDS. Salt-n-Pepa had the ladies shooting out at 'em when they performed "Push it."

Salt took time out to speak to the audience on the importance of safe sex. I found it impressive how they wanted to raise the awareness. Their show represented education. After the third show in the fourth city, Salt came to me asking if we would have a problem changing the order of the show. She suggested they go on first. That's how classy these ladies were. They were about the business of pleasing the fans.

Salt was right in her analyses of the show. *"I look at things from a fan's point of view when I can look out and see it,"* she said as we were standing on stage right together viewing R. Kelly's performance. It was a good show regardless of who went on first, but I agreed with Salt. We had to please the fans and sometimes that means changing things around.

We were working with a class act on tour with Salt-n-Pepa. We had seven more weeks to spend out on the road with these classy, sexy, and talented ladies whom I had the utmost respect for. As I stood next to Cheryl James (Salt), I could almost feel that she wanted to release energy within herself. I could tell that she had been shut down by the withdrawn personalities our crew portrayed acting unsociable.

I guess we kind of pissed them off when we arrived at the first rehearsal. We walked into the rehearsal facility having no regard of their presence. Nobody spoke to one another. I knew where the dressing rooms were so I lead the way as we walked straight through and to our dressing rooms. R. Kelly didn't want our performers or the crew for that matter to socialize with Salt-n-Pepa or their crew. Why, I don't know. A lot of things I did not know. The fact that he was paying everyone, seemed to make him think he could tell grown people when to come, go and who to speak to. Acting as if we were in competition instead of entertaining and having fun, R. Kelly and his way of doing things made everybody on the tour, including the production crew, feel uneasy. *"Why does he act like that?"* Cheryl James (Salt) asked as we stood watching the show.

I told her he wasn't really like that or a bad dude. *"He's young and just starting out, he tripping,"* I told her.

Salt stood with her arms folded. She liked R. Kelly, but she didn't know how to respond to the way he was acting. She was all lady; it was no doubt about that. She had a, (he'd better recognize) way about her posture. *"Too bad for him he don't have no social skills,"* she said.

As the tour rolled on across the country, we were once again pulling into arenas just in time, having to get dressed on the bus and running onto the stage. Regardless of R. Kelly's bus driver's susceptibility, R. Kelly's after show activities were wearing me down. I felt like a high school hall guard. After every show I had to monitor R. Kelly's long line of young girls. I found myself knocking on R. Kelly's dressing room door over and over so that I could keep the line moving to clear the area. He had to give every girl that came into his dressing room 30 to 40 damn minutes, for an autograph.

The weird thing about it was that the girls that stayed in with him the longest were the young girls and the ones who waited the longest were the older girls. Dude did not seem to have a concern about how things looked; and people were talking.

We were scheduled to stay in Miami Florida for a few days and I thought that allowed us to get some much-needed rest. It turned out to be just the opposite.

In preparation for R. Kelly's performance, I was busy talking to the lighting engineer, dome engineer, stage engineer and video projection, making sure the stage was set. I was ready for R. Kelly to rock the house. After checking on the Honey Bees, I made it to R. Kelly to let him know things were a go.

"Let's do this, boy," I told him, holding my right hand up for him to slap on me our usual love glove handshake, with a big smile! R. Kelly wasn't smiling this time.

He shook my hand and pulled me towards him. *"Johnny man, Aaliyah's in trouble, and I got to get her, Johnny. I need you to get us a flight to Chicago after this show",* He said.

I was disturbed at the thought that Aaliyah was in trouble. *"What do you mean Aaliyah's in trouble, Rob?"* I asked. *"She ran away from home,"* he said.

What was going on I thought to myself. He was still dressing while he was talking, putting the last of his clothes on. He was talking low and fast trying to give me instructions on what to do. It was time for him to go on stage. *"What, where is she at?"* I asked.

"She's still in Detroit, but I need for you to get her a plane ticket to Chicago and get her a room in a hotel. I've gotta call Derrel and let him know what's going on" he said.

"Do you want me to call Barry and see if he knows anything," I asked. I was truly concerned.

However, when I mentioned Barry, R. Kelly became disconcerted. *"No, we can't do that, Johnny. Don't call Barry!"* he said. *"You need to get us back to Chicago right after this show. She needs me man and I need to be there for her. It's a lot more to it than you know and I'll tell you, but right now don't call*

Barry. Get us to Chicago right after this show, Johnny man, I need for you to do that; alright man," He asked as he stepped onto the lift that was taking him up to the stage.

I knew that something wasn't right about this, but what was I to do? I had to follow the directions my boss gave me and make reservations for us to get to Chicago. All kind of things were going through my head. What kind of mess is going on and what am I getting myself into? With Aaliyah being Barry's niece, I couldn't understand why R. Kelly didn't want to contact Barry, especially since she ran away from home. I thought Rob and Barry were close. Calling Barry Hankerson should have been the first thing he should have wanted to do. I shouted out as R. Kelly was going up on the stage lift. *"Rob! Who else do you want to go?"*

"Me, you, and Tyree," he shouted back.

We were going to have to finish this conversation later. *"What the heck's going on?"* I thought to myself.

I was tired and mentally drained from doing a little of everything. With the tour just starting and with yet more unfinished things I needed to do I made sure I took care of Rob's personal needs. I was gonna have to be up for another four hours calculating the expenditures for the tour thus far, and now with R. Kelly's implemented drama, it looked as if it would be at the minimum twenty-four hours before I would be able to get any rest.

It's always something coming up out of nowhere with Rob. It was like he had to know just how much he could get into and get away with. As I dialed the numbers to the airport I thought this new found power he had made him feel invincible. The saying "no *rest for the weary*", was a reality in my life.

I had to arrange for Aaliyah to pick up a prepaid ticket in Detroit to go to Chicago on the red-eye flight with a return flight to Miami for the following night; getting us back in time for the scheduled show. It was going to be a long twenty-four hours for me. I was a guardian angel to this boy, but I was getting tired. A guru was not the position I wanted with this boy. He was in another world, a world that didn't consist with caring for the people who were in his life. Everything was coming to a boil and he was putting his hand in the water. I had a feeling that sooner or later he was going to see just how scorching hot the water was.

After the show I had a limo take us to the airport. On the flight, R. Kelly and I sat together. He talked to me a little, but for the most part he wanted to be left alone to clear his mind and think about things. I knew that he was not trying to hear anything I had to say that was against what he was going to Chicago to do. As I looked over at him sitting with his mind off in space, freely surrendering to his inner pain with tears dropping down his face; he reminded me of a lonely kid. I wanted to help. I wanted him to do the right thing.

I felt R. Kelly was alone in this matter. He came to me in the heat of battle and wanted me to jump right into the fire. I thought sometimes I was the only one who truly cared for R. Kelly. It seemed like everyone else working in R. Kelly's camp had a nonchalant disposition towards the complaints and rumors. *"Oh well, we're just going to have to deal with it and do what we can."* Even though I was starting to feel like an alienated hired hand, I continued to show Rob that I truly cared for him and his well-being. I wanted him to know I was there for him no matter what. R. Kelly wouldn't let me in on the heart of the matter. Ever since the money started coming in—it seemed like the more he made the further apart we were. It seemed like he distanced himself away from where we came from.

We were an hour into our flight when the flight attendant's came to serve the peanuts, coffee and sodas. Rob got his coffee, but continued with that same look on his face as if he had lost his best friend; a lot was on his mind.

As I poured the sugar into my coffee, I told him *"It's gone be alright Rob, we gone get it right."* *"I think she's pregnant"* he said, in a voice that sounded as if he wanted to bust out in tears. *"Oh man, Rob"* was all I could say at the time. Man! My mind was totally confused. I was somewhat angry and at the same time I wanted to protect R. Kelly. I just kept saying man over and over. He went on to tell me that Derrel McDavid arranged for a car to pick Aaliyah up at O'Hare airport and she had a hotel room available on arrival. This was crazy! How were we going to get through this without causing ill feelings with Barry, I thought? This was all disrespectful to Barry and Aaliyah's family.

Then I thought about how R. Kelly betrayed Craig Hodges' trust with actions that led us all to assume that he had been with his wife. I thought R. Kelly had a bit more sense and respect for Barry Hankerson and his family and would not violate their trust. I thought they were really closer than that. I felt R. Kelly could go to Barry with anything. Barry loved Robert and treated him like a son and I know Aaliyah's family, Mike and Diane trusted Rob. This was all bad. I wanted Rob to know that I was with him, but at the same time, I didn't want to be totally submissive so that he felt like I was condoning what was happening.

I wanted this to turn out right and I wanted Robert to do what was right. *"Rob, I think you should call Barry and talk to him about this man.*

Demetrius Smith Sr.

Barry loves you man, and he knows you love Aaliyah. What other way is there Robert?" I asked as the plane was making its descent into Chicago's O'Hara airport. *"I can't call Barry Johnny,"* he said sadly. *"Derrel said that he spoke to a lawyer who said that in order for me not to go to jail, I would have to marry Aaliyah man, so that's what I need to do,"* he said as if he had no vision at all to try seeing things rationally.

"How you gone marry Aaliyah Rob", I asked in bitter sadness? I wanted him to really think about what he was saying. Aaliyah was a baby. I was stunned and hurt that this had happened! I had asked Robert once before if he was messing with Aaliyah and he said no. I had hoped that he had told me the truth. Now, it was a fact, this grown ass man had been messing with Aaliyah all the time. This was crazy and I knew right away that it was going to cause separation throughout the whole camp. Just when things were looking like a brighter day was just ahead, here came another problem.

"Who's gone take care of her while we're out on the road Rob? Aaliyah still gotta go to school man," I told him! I was angry! I wanted him to step back to really look at what he was talking about doing.

Rob turned around towards me. His facial expression showed that he was offended with my statement. He became imprudent, in a soft tone as he snapped at me, *"Look, Johnny man, I don't need you in my head because I'm doing this. You're either with me or against me,"* he said. I took it as if he were giving me an ultimatum.

I knew what he was implying. *"You don't realize it, but man you don't know it all Johnny,"* he empathized in order to clear up the threat up he had just imposed on me. That idol threat he made drew a line for me. I was against it, but at the same time I had mouths to feed. I was nowhere near being financially secure enough to consider myself off the street. To stop right now would put me back on the streets. R. Kelly had lawyers. I didn't know what Derrel McDavid had going on but I was going to have to talk to him, I thought as I stood shaking my head, feeling dejected.

R. Kelly wanted an answer. *"Well, Johnny man, where you at with me?"* he asked.

I felt beaten and trapped into taking on a deep feeling of iniquity. I tucked my chin to my chest, *"man I'm with you man, I'm just saying though, Rob,"* in a final appeal looking at him with a look that said it was a stupid idea.

"I don't know, but we gone have to get it done," he answered with a confused look on his face. I thought Derrel and whoever was associating

with R. Kelly with had poisoned the boy's mind. Rob had changed into a whole other person. The humility he portrayed no longer glimmered of pride. R. Kelly had lost his respect. I began to look at him, question his morals and wonder if he had any. This was crazy and I knew it.

Here I was in the middle of some no brainier, dumb stuff. I did not want to do this. These situations kept arising changing the course in the direction I wanted my life to go. But at the same time I felt as if I had to hold onto my job. This was my dilemma; this was my stress, along with helping to raise Robert. I could not seem to bring balance to my life. Here I was holding on to something that in the end could leave me alone, struggling to pull myself up again and leaving me to have to start all over again to rebuild my life. I didn't want to be a part of this. This was crazy.

I wanted to stand on my own; be able to break away, but Rob kept a rope dangling that I kept holding onto. I couldn't let go of the rope now, I was not on level ground. Frustrated and thinking *"here I go again, straightening up his mess."* If he would only allow me to do my job, we would not be in this situation. But no, our administration had Mr. R. Kelly believing they had an answer for anything he might get himself into.

I strongly believed, whoever was filling Rob's head with the idea that marrying Aaliyah would make this right, wasn't someone that was truly in his corner and looking out with his best interest at heart. Nonetheless, it was a deep wound for many, and not one that was going to heal without leaving a scar. With this happening, I knew it would probably eliminate me from being Aaliyah's tour manager as well. And working for Aaliyah and R. Kelly would have made life a whole lot better for me. But now, my dreams were being shattered.

It was after midnight when we arrived in Chicago. We took a cab to the *Sheridan Hotel* a few miles from the airport where Aaliyah had a deluxe suite room 300-313; one of those extended rooms. When Aaliyah opened the door, she looked at me as if she was asking, *"Am I doing the right thing?"* I wanted so bad to tell her to go home, but R. Kelly was standing right in front of me. I felt I had done what I could. No one paid any attention to me. No one saw me. It was my business, but yet, not my business.

R. Kelly immediately took Aaliyah to the bedroom, while Tyree and I remained in the living room until he returned forty-five minutes later. I spoke to Derrel. We were to meet first thing the next morning at his office on Twelfth Street and Wabash. For that night I went to my sister De-Dee's home in Harvey, Illinois. It was another rare moment for me to spend some time with my daughter.

At seven-thirty the next morning I met Derrel at his office. Derrel McDavid was R. Kelly's personal business manager. He was handling all of Robert's money as well as all of his affairs now since Barry and was no longer in the picture. Derrel is a white guy who wants to be black. I wasn't in a good mood in his office. I let him know that I was not in agreement with R. Kelly marrying Aaliyah. *"Derrel man you know this ain't right. I've already told Rob how I felt, and I feel that you supposed to tell him too man. That's what's wrong with Rob man, nobody is letting him know when he's wrong. Everybody's looking over everything he does and he's getting reckless. He's thinking his money will get him out of everything; making him think his shit don't stink."* I was ferocious as I explained to Derrel how I felt.

I wanted him to take a stand with me to convince R. Kelly that marrying Aaliyah was not the right thing to do. Derrel felt that in R. Kelly's association with Aaliyah, he had committed a felony offense and he felt that the only way to protect R. Kelly was to help him do whatever needed to be done to get them married. He didn't agree with me involving Barry as part of the solution. He felt it would give Barry something to use against R. Kelly and in turn give him more control over R. Kelly's career and finances.

That whole thing was stupid to me, but Derrel didn't want to hear any reasoning. I had a feeling there was something else going on that I was not going to be let in on. It was crazy.

We drove to the hotel where Rob and Aaliyah were staying, picked them up and then we drove around City Hall in Maywood, Illinois to investigate what we would need in order to get a marriage license. They weren't asking for much at all. Basically, three pieces of ID and a state ID showing that Aaliyah was eighteen years old. When we left there, we went back to the hotel to put together a plan to make sure this marriage would happen. I was still wishing I could call Barry so he could help us fix this the right way. Maybe things would have been different had I walked away from this a long time ago. Maybe I should have continued with my efforts and desire to be an entertainer. I believed in an artist who didn't think anything of me.

Although I was opposed to everything that was going on, I still had to assist in this effort to make sure R. Kelly and Aaliyah were married. I knew a lady that worked at the Public Aid office; she was in charge of taking the photos for I. D.'s when people were approved to receive welfare so I went to see her and took Aaliyah with me. Aaliyah waited in the car while I went to talk to my friend to get her to do me a favor. I already told Derrel and Rob it might be possible to get my friend to give Aaliyah a state ID, but it might cost. They told me to make it happen and not worry about the cost. After negotiating a fee of $500, I took Aaliyah into the office where she took a photo ID stating her name, birth date, and a year that showed that she was eighteen. This was our first proof of identification and it was an official State of Illinois ID card.

R. Kelly also knew someone, who worked for FedEx, who would allow her to say that she worked for *FedEx*. So, we were able to get two IDs in Jew Town, and on top of that Aaliyah had a school ID card. With the three forms of IDs we were able to obtain a marriage license for Robert Sylvester Kelly and Aaliyah Haughton to be married. Once this was done, R. Kelly had another friend who knew a preacher who performed the ceremony. After they were married, we left Rob and Aaliyah alone for a few hours. Our time was limited because we had to board the plane in order to get to Miami in time for the show. I was angry at myself and disgusted at R. Kelly and Derrel.

Right before it was time for us to leave, R. Kelly called me back up to the room. Once up there he asked me if I thought he should let Aaliyah go to his condo over at the *Lake Point Towers*. I posed the question to him I had in Orlando, *"Who's going to look after her, Aaliyah still has to go to school,"* I told him. *"the best and safest thing to do is to send her back home. We still have six weeks left to be on the road. You can't expect for her to stay locked in the house all that time alone. What about when we get back and have to get ready to go overseas? Let Aaliyah go home Rob, she's your wife now, time will fix the rest of it."*

R. Kelly exhaled and shook his head from side to side. There was a look of sadness in his eyes. He looked exhausted. I imagined his thoughts were traveling a thousand miles a minute. Finally, he responded, *"You're right, Johnny, I've gotta send her home,"* as he began to cry. *"What did I do, man?"* was the question he asked himself as he sobbed like a broken man, deep in sorrow.

As I stood looking at him I wondered to myself, if R. Kelly talked with Barry, would Barry be able to forgive him? After all, Barry and Robert were always on the phone with each other and I felt they formed a special bond. *"You married her, Rob, and that was an honorable thing to do, a bit premature, but nonetheless, you're showing you mean well."* I *did*n't know what I was saying, but I felt sorry for him. I know I'd wanna kick his ass disrespecting me and my family but by me being Robert's right hand man I was trying to get Robert to feel we could somehow make some sense out of what he did and make it easy for him to make better decisions.

It seemed I had his attention and he was listening so I pressed a little more. *"I still think you should talk to Barry about this Rob."* Before I said another word, I had to take sudden notice to the fear he had is his eyes when I mentioned Barry. He began to wipe his falling tears from his face before he could speak.

I reiterated my statement to make sure he did not get mad *"but talking to Barry is totally up to you Rob, it doesn't matter, I'm going to be right here with you, all the way through, however if it comes out."* R. Kelly just sat, in total silence; he was numb to what was being said.

Looking into his eyes, he looked far away as if lost in another world. How was I going to help? I was just as confused as he was. I felt only God could fix this. I kept telling myself, God can fix this. R. Kelly and I struggled a long time together. We had been through a lot together and now I was his true partner in crime. I was hurt over this as well. I had so much admiration for Aaliyah and her family and I felt I had let them down too. I don't know, maybe I was just putting myself in it.

I ask myself the question, what would you do? I went back to my old way of doing things; when times got hard and things seemed real rough, I prayed. Praying always brings me peace. I wasn't feeling Derrel McDavid and all his big shot lawyer friends that I had never met. My young friend I brought up from Chicago was in deep worry and troubled, and his financial advisor was telling him he could buy his way out instead of calling a meeting amongst men.

Yeah, everyone had created a monster! They put all this money in this kid's hand and started kissing his ass; instead of schooling him and teaching him to care for others. They just sat around and watched as he lead himself into chaos; allowing him to pout, and have his way. Knowing all the time all they had to do was threaten to take something away and Robert, I believe, would have been molded to make better decisions. But in the sight of the people that were making the money, let the truth be told, the artist is just a product. Like Marvin Gaye said, *"Who really cares?"*

I remember one time, Tyree radioed to me saying that he was down the hall from Robert's suite looking at the police, and they were going into his room. I jumped up straight out of bed. *"Where is Robert?"* was the first thing I asked?

"Me and Big John got him out of the hotel already." he responded. I immediately went up to his room to find out what was going on.

Why were the police in R. Kelly's suite? Tyree was telling me that R. Kelly had invited a monster to his room. Those were the words he used in describing a girl they had been entertaining. I just shook my head. This boy was crazy. "*Man Johnny this girl was so ugly and nasty, Man; I don't know why dude even had her up there. Man if I would have bought a dick already hard to use on her, it would have went soft ugly as she was,*" Tyree said of the girl they had in the room. Come to find out after she had left the room she had gotten hold to one of our itinerary's and gave that to the police in hopes of identifying who was there in the room with her. She said she had been raped.

My main concern was Robert, where was he? Tyree said he had already put him on his bus. His reason for calling me was because Robert had sent him to get me and R. Kelly's bus driver. We began to walk and talk. With the police in the room I figured the safest thing to do now was to get R. Kelly on to the next city. I was walking with the driver going through the lobby of the hotel when I saw Clive Calder (CEO of Jive Records)and a few other Jive reps appear. Granted, we had just finished doing a show earlier, that evening. Clive and his guest were there to pay Robert a visit. Once Clive found out something was going on involving R. Kelly with the Hotel he went to investigate. Tyree and I went along with them to check things out too.

The girl had named everyone on the list as to the people she said were involved. She also pointed Tyree out as one of the persons involved. At that point of identification, Tyree went through a series of questions and because he was there and I guess, because he would not admit to anyone else being there Tyree was arrested for rape. He spent a week on Rikers Island, New York City's Department of Corrections. I later heard that Rock, another posse friend of Robert's, who was there that night. He had taken pictures of them all in the room with the girl. The pictures along with the attorney's R. Kelly had behind Tyree; he was able to walk out from under the ugly monster girls lies.

On the night of that incident I got a chance to once again talk with Mr. Clive Calder. He was very concerned about Robert. He too told me that I needed to stay with Robert. He felt it was a phase Robert was going through but he insisted that Robert needed to have good people like me around him to protect him. I agreed with him and I appreciated his compliment but at the same time I let him know that it was not Robert but that it was his posse who were bringing the girls around.

Everybody in the whole administration saw how Rob was living. I remember Clive Calder coming to me on a few occasions asking me if I could talk to Robert and stay close to him in hopes of helping him to see he needed to *"tone it down with the young ladies,"* as Clive would say. I even mentioned to Mr. Calder, *"Tell Robert what it is you want him to stop doing. Shoot man,"* I said, *"tell Robert you won't release his single if he continues the nonsense in messing with under aged girls."*

I let Mr. Calder know that it was not Robert but that it was his posse who was bringing the girls around. But he turned his head as well. It was about making sure Robert was happy so that he could produce good music and the rest, well, that's where the damage control department came in. In my opinion, Mr. Calder turned his head on Robert as well as everyone did. It was about making sure Robert was happy so that he could produce good music, they could make tons of money and the rest, well, that's where the damage control department came in at. I was pretty much the only one that half way stood up to Robert. And for me, I didn't want to be distant from my friend, Robert, so I was hesitant as well in expressing to him fully what I thought. R. Kelly was a young kid gone wild. Heck I don't know how I would have been had I been in his shoes. I didn't know the full story of his life and all that he had been through that made him who he was. All I know is no one stepped in to say, this can't happen. People pretended they didn't see and others they boosted him on. I just don't see where anything is one man's fault. In my opinion we are all a product of our environment. I believe we all can give a little more of caring and in being our brother's keeper.

By Nichiren Daishonin, *"The powerful may appear great, but in reality they are not. Greatest of all are the ordinary people. If those in power lead lives of idle luxury it is because the people are silent. We have to speak out with impassioned words; we need to resolutely attack abuses of power that can cause people suffering. This is fighting on the side of justice. It is wrong to remain silent when confronted with injustice. Doing so is a tantamount to supporting and condoning evil."*

CHAPTER 20

Moving On!

*W*E LIVE AND we learn; I was learning! This was a turning point in my life. It was one thing wanting to take on the responsibilities to be R. Kelly's representative with a devoted drive and with heart. To be his front man and keep the way clear for him; watching the crowd to make sure no one could get to him and cover his back. I was the man behind the man but I was tired of living as if he was the man behind me.

I was angry with this dude; he just was not cool! I didn't know what it was; I didn't know what was happening or what was going to happen. God was doing a lot of revealing! Robert was showing his true self. After all the drama I went through with him, I was right back in Chicago in the same boat. Robert was always finding ways to get himself caught up in something, and every time, it was because he was inconsiderate and selfish and every time, I was right there for him. Things were not going smooth at all. It was as if something evil coming from out of nowhere, would always find its way in the mix of things in my life and send my life into shambles. Sometimes I think I see someone is sitting back laughing at me.

The way things should have been and the way things were, were only pieces of a dream; I could not seem to put the pieces together. I wanted to wake up and be able to go home to my family. I asked myself, *"When were things going to start going right for me in my life?"* I was standing there on the thirty-sixth floor of Robert's apartment and found myself wiping tears from my own eyes.

I looked over at Robert; he was holding his head in his hands and I was thinking, if the possibility of serving time in jail was at the top of his list of worries, then he should have been really worried.

I walked over to Rob. I wanted to lift his spirits because we still had to go on. *"It's gone be a little hard in the beginning with this Rob, but we gone get through it man, and we gone get through it together."* I told him. I still thought that Rob's best solution was to talk to Barry. There was no getting around him with this. As far as I could see, Barry was still Robert's manager, and let's not forget, he was also Aaliyah's uncle.

Now they were related, may as well have the family feud, I thought. Barry Hankerson knew R. Kelly and Aaliyah had something special between the two of them. He watched how joyful and happy Rob and Aaliyah were when they were together; plus, Barry loved R. Kelly. I remember we were in LA and R. Kelly was performing at the Billboard Awards. Aaliyah and her mom Diane came up from Detroit. The three of them were inseparable.

Of course, I was with them, but I was always in the back of them. I was there to accommodate their needs. I was Mr. Kelly's personal assistant. I never looked or suspected that Robert was having an affair with Aaliyah; at least not for a long while. He was older than her and I took his word that their attraction for each other was their common love for music. But when reality set in and the truth was known I saw a different picture. What I saw with R. Kelly and Aaliyah, I can only say what I think. It wasn't that I didn't like it, it was just that I knew it wasn't going to turn out right, I knew the timing was all off for them two to be a couple. I don't think you can help who you love. In my opinion, I think Robert Kelly Loved Aaliyah and in my opinion again, I think Aaliyah loved him too!

Sure, she was young in age, but she was ahead of her age in so many ways Aaliyah in my opinion, processed a spirit of joy, fun and happiness that was all together and you could feel that when you were in her presence. She was a princess who wanted everybody to be happy. I wanted Robert to talk to Barry; it was the right thing to do. So I asked him, *"How you gone deal with Barry without dealing with him honestly, Rob? He is still your manager."* I was hoping he'd talk to me and be open to listen to me. But he wasn't, he was sold with the plan that Derrel and his lawyer friends had, that was the way he was going to follow.

Standing, looking out of the window on the thirty-sixth floor of Rob's condo, I could hear my momma's words like it was clear as daylight: *"You can cover something up, and it will be unseen for the moment, but as soon as you uncover it. Whatever was there will still be there. The truth don't change baby and because of that what's in the dark will come to the light,"* she would say with a sympathetic look on her face, shaking her head from side to side.

I smiled at the thought of my mother. It was almost time to leave; we had to make it back to Miami so Robert and I left his apartment and went back to Aaliyah's hotel room. When I told him how much time we had before we would have to leave, he spent the few minutes we had with Aaliyah.

It was time to go. *"Rob, come on, man. It's time to go,"* I yelled to him. Ten minutes later, he came out of the room again with tears falling down his face. On the way to the airport, he talked on the phone with Derrel, telling him to arrange for Aaliyah to get home. I was relieved, she was going home. Robert had told me Aaliyah wasn't going to say anything to her parents about the marriage, but I knew better than that. When we got back to Miami, we weren't missed, and no one knew we had been to Chicago and back.

A life-changing event had taken place in a twenty-four-hour period. We got back in time for the show. In spite of being tired, I went through the normal pass and checking of the stage props, making sure everyone was on point. That night, R. Kelly put on a super performance. I wondered where he had gotten the energy from. I was fatigued, and I looked forward to after the show so I could get some rest. I thought about Aaliyah. I wondered what she was doing and how she was holding herself up. After the show, I sought refuge in my hotel room bed. I did check in on Robert before retiring for the night. It seemed he didn't have any worries or at least he had found a way to hide what he was going through. Back at the hotel, Robert had a big party going on. I thought he should have been missing his new wife and worried about her but as it appeared to me, he was having a time of his life. Nonetheless, I let it be known, I was not going to be disturbed any more that night.

At check-out time the next morning, as everyone was boarding the bus, I went up to Robert's room to check in on him. Tyree was in there with him; when I walked in the door, Tyree shook his head in disgust as if R. Kelly was having a pity party with himself. *"What's up with it, Rob? You ready to get out of here?"* I asked in high spirits, wanting to pick his spirits up as well. *"Yeah, I'm ready! Is everybody else already on the bus?"* he asked. When I asked him how things were with Aaliyah, he wasn't too talkative. And for the next few days, it was like that. Robert stayed to himself. Any and everything about Aaliyah was now confidential.

Things were changing; Barry hadn't called me either, and normally he would have called to check on us. When I told Robert I had to call Barry about the video crew wanting additional money to transport the equipment to the next city; he told me to call Derrel. He said whatever I needed to talk to Derrel about it. Barry was still his manager, but he was dealing with Derrel McDavid now concerning the tour business. We continued our tour, and things hadn't changed in regard to R. Kelly and the group, when it came to them being snobbish in relation to Salt-n-Pepa.

Our last date with Salt-n-Pepa was Halloween in Buffalo, New York. Throughout the whole night, we celebrated the end of the tour during and after Salt-n-Pepa's performance. R. Kelly didn't join us. He entertained his guests in the dressing room. Public Announcement, the dancers, the band, Cheryl Cobb, Salt-n-Pepa, as well as Spinderella, their whole crew, and me were all having what James Brown called *"a funky goodtime."* This was really the first time we had all come together and socialized. We had a blast. I ate so many lobsters that night, my hands started clawing. That night was filled with fun.

When we got home, the drama over Aaliyah began. Rob was on the phone with me constantly. *"Where are you, Johnny? I need you with me man. Aaliyah told her family about the marriage,"* he said. I had already figured she would.

I knew Aaliyah couldn't hold back from her mother what she had done. She needed her mother. In my book, they needed each other. In the meantime, I looked at my career; this had hurt me too. I knew working with Aaliyah in anyway was out of the question. My chance to branch out and build a career was damaged.

Thirteen years now, I have been a personal assistant to Robert. He was sitting passively on six figures, and I was again wondering if I would have a job next week. Everything was coming through Derrel's office now that Robert had separated himself from dealing with Barry. Once again, I took on more responsibilities. After the family found out about the marriage, Rob told me they had the marriage annulled and Rob went into a depression. I didn't question Rob about him and Aaliyah anymore.

He didn't want to go home to his apartment in Lake Point Towers. All I knew is that he was hurt over the fact that he was not able to speak to or see Aaliyah. Daily he would call me to book him a room at the Nikko Hotel on Canal Street in Chicago. If and when I would have to go pick him up, I would notice he hadn't slept in his bed at all; Rob was sleeping in his closet. He said the darkness took him away from everything. For years I had been holding to this dream of success in the music business, and with Barry being gone, I felt Rob would now need me more, and maybe now an opportunity would present itself for Robert to pay me.

I wanted to buy a nice house maybe in North Carolina. In October of 1993, while we toured with Gerald Levert I met a very lovely lady in Charlotte, North Carolina. Robin was her name. She resembled Mariah

Carey with a body like Stacy Dash. She was beautiful. We talked for months over the telephone. Whatever city I was in, I would always spend my nights on the phone with her. We even made trips back and forth to visit each other. Robin was the type of woman who would put the first foot forward in support of what or who she believed in. he would put things in motion or want to converse to formulate the full idea of something. She could handle responsibility and she was the type of woman that would take care of business.

Robin became very special to me and I was fond of her over a short period of time. She invited me to spend Christmas with her and her daughter Fiona. She thought it would be a good way for us to get to know each other, and she insisted I bring my children. I needed to take a break from the stress of dealing with promotions, tours, photo shoots, video productions, and Rob's personal drama. I felt if I didn't get away, I was going to go crazy. I should have been able to fly where I wanted, see my children and spend time where I wanted to be.

Altering my mind-set, I started putting myself and my needs first. Anything Rob needed, I could have done over the telephone. I wasn't going to cling to him any longer. I packed bags for me and my children and I did what was in my heart. Three of my children and I drove for fourteen hours from Chicago, Illinois, to Charlotte, North Carolina. It was a totally mind-relaxing drive. Being with my children on the road was the best time ever. We were happy singing Christmas carols, looking at the mountains and enjoying sightseeing. We even pulled over in Tennessee where we saw a bear in the trees below the highway. This was all I wanted—to be with my family.

Let me introduce you to my children—you already know Demetrius Smith Jr. He wasn't able to go on this trip because he was living with his mom in Savannah, Georgia. I had custody of my other three children—my daughter Ashley and my twin sons, Deontae and DeAndre Smith. Tamekia gave birth to the twins March 3, 1992, exactly 1 year after my daughter Ashley was born. Yep, Tamekia and I went right back at it, this time producing twins.

The courts granted me custody of Ashley when Tamekia held her out of a third-floor window threatening to drop her if I didn't take my daughter with me to a birthday party. Ashley was just three months old at the time. Tamekia had a five year old daughter named Nikki and I was going to the party and decided to take Nikki with me. When it was time to leave, Tamekia became angry because I would only take Nikki and not Ashley.

Tamekia gave me a hard time about not taking both children, so I stormed out of the house without taking either one. In my mind, I was doing her a favor by taking her daughter with me. There was always a fight with Tamekia. She always wanted things to go her way. I was about to drive off when I noticed her holding my baby out the window. By this time, the police were driving by and witnessed it. Tamekia was immediately investigated and taken to a psychiatric hospital.

Tamekia was hospitalized for eight days and I was there visiting her every day. I felt bad for her. I really didn't think she was going to drop my daughter. She was just acting young and stupid. I don't know what it is about me and my devotion to women in my life, but I wanted this girl to know I loved her. In spite of the hurt I had caused her, she was family and was important to me, important to the growth and development of what I called "*my family.*" No matter what we had gone through, I wanted her to know, she was worth being there for. Tamekia was still angry with me for having a child, my oldest son Demetrius Jr., three months before Ashley was born.

I wasn't trying to have two kids at the same time by two different women. But because they both had my children, it was now my responsibility to assist with providing for them all. That meant Lawanda, Tamekia, Demetrius, Ashley, and Nikki. I refused to be a degenerate like the father I never knew. Whether Lawanda or Tamekia liked it or not, my dream was for my children to all be together and grow up together.

When Tamekia got out of the hospital, I made it my business to visit her at her mother's apartment, trying to keep her interested in being a part of the new life we had brought into the world. I stood by her side and supported her while she was dealing with the Department of Children and Family Services. While I spent time around Tamekia, our daughter Ashley was with my oldest sister Dee-Dee. Over a course of time, while traveling in and out of town, I would stop in to see Tamekia, and when the opportunity presented itself, I wouldn't deny myself the privileged moments that allowed for my twin sons Deontae and DeAndre to be conceived. They were born in Cook County Hospital.

I was in New York at the time, along with R. Kelly who was doing remixes of songs for the *12 Play* album. She called me in New York. That weekend, I flew home to go welcome my twin sons into the world. They were both premature and eleven minutes apart. They were so tiny as I held them in both of my hands. I felt like a giant. I thought about Demetrius Jr.

and Ashley. Here I was a father of four beautiful children. I felt so blessed and proud to be a dad.

As I held my sons, I realized that it was because of my children my life had become meaningful; they gave me purpose. When I got out of rehab and began working with Rob, it gave me a new start. I was out of the life involving drugs and being a part of the negative things. I felt I had a good head on my shoulder, and I'd have to find a better way. The stuff I was getting caught in was just stupid, dumb stuff. It was no wonder I couldn't produce children after many years of unprotected sex. My body and mind were polluted.

It was the time spent away in rehab that allowed my body and mind to be cleansed of all the poison I consumed in my past. As I stood in the hospital hallway holding my twin sons, I realized that when Demetrius Jr. was born, my whole focus on life had changed. All the prayers that I had prayed were being answered.

Holding my children, I knew it was only by the grace of God that I was here holding these two beautiful, little bity babies. I reflected on my life and realized that he led me to jail, to the rehab center and then back into music business to save me. It was all happening with my prayers were being answered day by day, I was being blessed with my four children; the Lord was giving me the desires of my heart, as He said He would. His Word was real.

When I reached Charlotte, North Carolina I felt free. There was so much pressure relieved from my mind just being away. Robin made me feel at home and I felt like I was where I was supposed to be. My time spent enjoying the holiday with my children, Robin and her daughter was interrupted. It was Rob on the phone. I knew he would call, but I was hoping he wouldn't because things were going so smoothly. The year before, I had spent Christmas with Rob, Barry, Aaliyah and Diane in LA. This Christmas, I could tell in his voice as he spoke over the phone that he was lonely. He wanted for me to ride with him to go shopping and buy gifts for Aaliyah and her family. He was hoping the spirit of Christmas could engender some compassion. I thought Rob must have thought that it was a small thing he had done.

When I told him I was in Charlotte, he asked me, "*You're in Charlotte! Where you at? What street is that on?*" he asked. "*I'm in Charlotte, North Carolina,*" I told him. "*I'm here spending the holidays with my family. I told you that,*" I reminded him. "*Yeah, but I didn't know it was out of town.*" He sounded disappointed yet somewhat sarcastic at the same time.

However, he didn't lose his focus, contrary to my being out of town. *"Well, I need to send Aaliyah and Diane something. There's a mall down there ain't it?"* he asked. He was talking to me in a tone where he was giving me a job assignment. *"Can you get to a mall there?"* he asked without giving me a chance to respond; remorsefully he said, *"You can pick them out some things for me, Johnny man. I know they hurt, but its Christmas. I just gotta reach out to let them know they're in my heart. I just gotta show them I love them. I just wish they understood, you know what I mean."* In his voice, I heard loneliness. The reality, however, was that this was his burden. He had brought this on himself. I couldn't feel sorry for him.

"I don't know Rob," I told him. *"You don't think you should just let some time heal the situation?"* I asked. He was persistent with sending them gifts, so I agreed to do his shopping for him. I had to go to the mall anyway to do my own Christmas shopping. When I talked to Robin about R. Kelly's idea to send Aaliyah and her family gifts, she didn't think I was serious until she heard me on the phone with my sister Dee-Dee and my brother-in-law Lenny., I was checking with them first to see if they wanted to spend their Christmas making a Christmas delivery and making some money.

R. Kelly wanted the gifts to arrive at Aaliyah's house on the morning of Christmas. I had three days to get this done. I hired my sister and her husband to drive the gifts from their home in Harvey, Illinois, once they received the package from FedEx, they were to head to Detroit and arrive at Aaliyah's house in the early morning hours. When I got off the phone after making the arrangements for R. Kelly's Christmas delivery, Robin said to me, *"You're serious aren't you? I can't believe R. Kelly could think a gift could ease the pain Aaliyah's mother is probably going through. I believe he's really got issues he needs to talk about,"* she said as she scooted down on the sofa, stretching out and laying her beautiful head on my shoulder.

Later that evening, Robin, the kids and I all went to the mall. It was fun being in North Carolina with Robin. I even daydreamed about staying there with her. It felt so tempting, but I had to dismiss that thought; things just weren't going right in the organization I was with. Walking, talking and holding hands with Robin—watching my children be happy . . . . NO, forget it, it just can't happen. Things weren't going good enough for me to put into this relationship what we needed to make it. I had to be able to provide for her and the children. I didn't have a plan in place to make that happen.

This relationship needed security and I didn't have that. I had to stay in the moment. Walking through the mall with Robin and the children, all felt so good and natural. The real fun part came when I got to use the company credit card. I spent a little freely when paying for the children's things. I dressed them all alike and then we took pictures.

Robin tried thinking of something special to get for Aaliyah and her family, but because we couldn't make sense of even buying gifts, she picked out a lot of teddy bears for Aaliyah and sweaters and scarves for her mom and dad. "*It's zero degrees in Detroit anyway,*" Robin said. We left the mall in a hurry. I had to rush from the mall to get to FedEx before they closed. Everything had to be shipped out that night in order for the shipment to arrive on time for Christmas.

We got to FedEx just in time. I knew that I was free for the remainder of the holidays and Robert knew I was not available. Once back at the house, I called my sister to let her know FedEx would deliver the package to her the next day. My sister said R. Kelly was "*a screwball*" for sending gifts. However, she was quick to take the job of making sure the gifts got there. *She was being paid* $800 to make a ten-hour drive. Dee-Dee and Lenny just had to hire a babysitter.

Besides, we provided the gas and a rental van. All they had to do was to get the gifts there and set them in front of the door. Later the next evening I spoke to my sister. She told me they delivered the gifts to the house, took everything out the truck, set everything in front of the house and then rang the doorbell! Aaliyah's dad answered and asked who the packages were from, but my sister said she just gave them a card and told him they were just making a delivery; they told him Merry Christmas and left. I later found out that Aaliyah's parents sent the gifts back to Chicago, to Derrel McDavid's office.

Christmas with Robin was beautiful. I just wished that things were better for Rob. I talked to Robin about how it was working with Robert, but I didn't tell her everything. I didn't tell her how underpaid I was or why I couldn't make plans with her. Yeah, I had thoughts of Robin being that special one in my life, but for now, we would be distant friends.

Saying goodbye to her and her daughter Fiona was sad for me. But I did it with a smile. I knew I was going to miss them. I knew I was going to be missing Robin for a while. We had such a great time. I knew I could only be happy for the moment. And that is exactly what being with her was, it was happiness for the moment. One day, though, I thought; one day! One day, I would be able to come home to a wife.

Demetrius Smith Sr.

CHAPTER 21

Nothing Seems to Change

$\mathscr{I}$ LEFT CHARLOTTE, NORTH Carolina, to go to Savannah, Georgia to pick up my son, Demetrius Jr. With him in mind, the drive to Savannah was another joyous moment for me and my children. We missed little Meechie. I made it my business to send for my son so he could be with us when time permitted. Every moment I could spend time with him was important to me. I wanted to see and be with my kids all the time and I wanted them to know that I was there for them.

Once we picked Meechie up, we drove back to Chicago. The first few days I rented a suite at the Best Western Hotel across from the studio. I still had to work, so being across the street from the studio was convenient for me. I could do what Rob needed and then spend my spare time taking my children to restaurants, museums and the movies. I loved my children dearly, and being with them was a joy, but I felt so alone. My life was so empty. I had no one to enjoy life with. I was a single father with four children. They needed a woman in their life as I needed one in mine. I missed Robin.

I was running around all over the city doing things for Rob. I was dealing with stylists, scheduling tours and rehearsals, working with merchandising vendors and running back and forth to the studio getting things signed.

Busy was an understatement! My children went with me when I was running the errands. They were having a great time hanging with daddy. This is where it hurt me the most—I had to take my children back. Splitting them up—one of my sisters took the twins, another sister took my daughter, and my son had to fly back to Georgia with his mom. The vacation was over. Monday morning I was back in the office and on the phone setting up our next tour, which meant being overseas for a month and then back to begin an eight-week tour along with LL Cool J. My workload was doubled, I didn't have a home to go to, my children were separated and I was living in the Best Western Hotel across from the studios for over a year.

We were so busy traveling doing video shoots, interviews and television shows. With everything that was going on I wasn't making that much money. Someone in my position should have been making $2,500 a week plus $75 a day per diem. In comparison, I was getting slave wages. I was a true rolling stone so to speak. Wherever I took my shoes off became home. Nonetheless, I loved what I did and I was in the circle of giants like LL Cool J.

This was in my dream. This was going to work out, and I was going to make it. I was in the office with Derrel every day, so I asked him to have a word with Robert about giving me a raise. Derrel and I had an understanding. He felt that I deserved to be paid, so I let Derrel know I was not going on the road for the little money I was making any longer.

No matter how much I disliked the fact that I was underpaid, this job was all I had going for me, along with hope. Derrel came back and told me Rob was willing to pay me $850.00 a week plus $35 a day per diem. I accepted, but only for this next tour. I told Derrel we were going to have to make things really right for me after we got back from Europe. He agreed. However, I had game to make up for the difference between what I was making and what I was supposed to make. I decided it wouldn't be bad to have a side hustle. I learned from previous tours how to pay myself.

Since I was the one setting up everything and hiring everybody, I negotiated income for myself with the different venders we used on our tours. The bus company, video production company, T-shirt company—all made money daily for their services on the road with us. In my dealings with each one of them, I negotiated a commission for myself. From the bus company alone I made an extra $1,400 a week. I negotiated the same deal with every other vender I hired to travel with us on the tour. I didn't feel bad about it either. I figured since Rob was not paying me what I deserved to be paid, I had to hustle for me and mines.

At the end of the day, I was still a single dad with four kids and no real place to call home. So now I was looking out for myself. I was tired of being loyal and getting treated like a slave. *"You don't get what you deserve, you get what you negotiate."* Thanks *Lafayette*—those words made a world of sense to me, and I applied them to my life.

In 1995, Madison Square Garden, Manhattan, New York, *LL Cool J* opened the show with a boom—he hyped the crowd the fuck up! LL was serious about rising emotions and he brought it on with authority. LL went out with his wife beater, baggy pants and a baseball cap. When he did what he did, he laid it down, giving it to his fans as they shouted along with

Demetrius Smith Sr.

his raps. *LL Cool J* tormented the stage with his cool, lover boy, gangster style.

The man was smooth. I was shouting along with the crowd as he performed "Mama Said Knock You Out" and then LL's music glided him into his next song, where he turned on his sex appeal making the ladies go wild. The ladies were screaming when he held his arms open and licked his lips. LL was Cool J. He took his shirt off, posed and smoothly told the ladies, *"I need love!"* The ladies went wild yelling and screaming as LL spit off the lyrics to his song.

LL COOL J was awesome on the stage. He was the same off the stage as well. The few times I met him, he was always polite. He had a sincere, caring charisma about himself. He was a man about his business. He went on the stage on time and got off the stage on time. He was there for the fans and he made it known that they were important to him. We had one incident with LL, and it happened on the third show of the tour.

As everyone signed a rider along with their contract, LL requested a fog machine, spot light, a back drop and lights, which was a simple request to fill for such a phenomenal entertainer. R. Kelly decided to test his power since he felt he held the headliners spot on the tour to close the concert out. Really, he was granted a co-headliner tour, meaning two stars on one show, but somebody had to go first. LL didn't mind because, like Salt-n-Pepa, the fans would rather get the party started and then wind things down with a little bump and grind. That's how it was marketed. I'm sure if he wanted to, LL could have negotiated closing the show, but he didn't trip. He was all about pleasing the fans and making money.

R. Kelly, on the other hand, was on an ego trip. Rob tried to take advantage of the technicality inside LL's rider. LL asked for truss lighting but did not stipulate backlights. R. Kelly told me to tell production to deny LL the backlights during the show and give him one spotlight. I stood ground with him and told him, *"R man, LL is a legend. We've got to give to him whatever he wants man. This is a co-headliner tour."*

"This is my tour Johnny. I'm headlining now. Those backlights are set for my show, and that's how that goes. He knows that he don't get everything if he ain't headlining. LL ain't just started doing this. He knows this better than me," I couldn't believe Rob was really believing in what he was saying. We were not using the back lights that were designed for his show. L.L. only wanted a spot light and the stage lights were electronically set there was no way L.L.'s light show could affect R. Kelly's light show. They were two totally different programs.

I felt it would be senseless to argue with him. *"All right man,"* I said. I decided I wasn't going to tell anyone to shut the lights off. This time I was going to give him something to be mad at me about. I knew that R. Kelly would be in his dressing room while LL was performing and wouldn't know what happened during the show unless somebody told him. I thought, *Who was paying attention to the lights anyway?* It wasn't until after LL's show that I realized R. Kelly's orders were carried out by someone else.

I was watching LL's show and saw him furiously leave the stage and head right over to R. Kelly's dressing room. I was following behind him, trying to hurry and catch up. I caught up with LL and told him *"My fault man. They misunderstood how I told them to work the lights."* LL said he knew I didn't do it. *"I know that punk-ass motherfucker you work for told you to do it."* LL started banging on the dressing room door. *"Bring your punk ass out,"* he said. *"Motherfucker, be a man!"* LL shouted. *"Tell me to my face I can't have my backlights. What the fuck is wrong with you?"*

When LL realized R. Kelly was not going to open the door, he went back to his own dressing room. He shouted as he walked away saying, *"That's all right, your punk ass gone have to come out sooner or later."* I knocked on R. Kelly's dressing room door. *"Rob, it's me."* He opened the door, looking like a scared chicken. Rob thought *LL* was crazy and wanted me to fix it. He wanted me to talk to him.

There was no doubt about it; R. Kelly did not want to tangle with LL. Rob knew I was always the one to handle confrontations head-on. Since I was not eager to help him, he humbled himself in asking me to take the blame. I did. I walked over to LL's dressing room and told him that it was my fault. *"L man, production misunderstood when I told him to lighten the amount of smoke for your show."* I was reaching out my hand in a jester of forgiveness'.

"Smithy"—that's what he called me—*"you didn't do that shit. You're a solid brother. We already talked and I gathered that about you. I ain't just get in this business. I know your boss had that shit done just like he got you to come down here."* I smiled as he was talking. L.L. was just that cool and real. He called it as he saw it. He confronted the situation and it balanced itself out.

I assured LL that nothing else would happen again and I apologized on behalf of R. Kelly. After R. Kelly finished doing his show he went to talk to LL., and LL let Rob know that he was on the tour for the fans and that if he had any more mishaps, he would leave the tour. *"I don't have time for the bullshit,"* he said as he sat sipping on a bottle of water.

R. Kelly apologized for his crew's mistake and told me to make sure LL got whatever he needed. I mean like he was running shit. I was laughing at Rob on the inside because he was just punked. No more incidents happened with LL the rest of the tour. Everything went along pretty smooth until we got to Madison Square Garden in New York City.

R. Kelly's brother Bruce went along with us on this tour. He was hanging out around the VIP entrance to backstage passing out passes and instructing security on which of his guest to let in. Walking in behind a couple of the ladies escorted pass security by Bruce was Suge Knight. Bruce told security that Suge was not with him or his guest and should not be let in.

Security let him in anyway because they knew who he was. Bruce continued to try and convince security that Suge should not be let in and pointed out the fact that he did not have a backstage pass. Suge took offense to Bruce's persistent attempt to keep him from entering backstage. By the time I showed up there was an altercation. *"Hold on, hold on, dog. What's going on?"* I asked when I entered the room.

Suge looked down at me. *"Who is you?"* he asked as his posse secured the door behind me. *"I'm Demetrius. I'm R. Kelly's tour manager. Is there a problem? What's going on?"* I asked, looking around the room into the eyes of the different faces surrounding me.

I was standing face-to-face with the huge Mr. Suge Knight as he stood flexing his muscles. *"Your boy here needs to learn a lesson in respect,"* Suge said, looking at Bruce up and down.

"Yeah? Your name is Suge right?" I asked him. *"They told me he didn't know who you were and so he had you stopped. So what now, you wanna have him beat down because he didn't know who you were?"* I asked with my arms open and my hands spread apart. *"I didn't know you either, until the guys told me who you were. Again, my name is Demetrius and now we know each other, it is a pleasure to meet you,"* I said sticking my hand out to him for a handshake.

He then looked at me up and down before shaking my hand. I didn't want to show any signs of being intimidated by him, so I said, *"Just a little mistake man. Now he knows who you are."* Shaking my hand, Suge said *"You aright man, you got some heart. You gone be in LA next week, Imma show you how it's done there."* I didn't know whether this was a threat or what. I just overlooked it and told Suge if he needed anything to let me know. I felt everything was cool.

The show went on without any further interruptions. On our way to LA, Rob decided that he wanted more security. He was a bit intimidated by

Suge Knight's comment and by the fact that he and Barry were not as close as they used to be. We hired the F.O.I. (The Fruit of Islam) for security, and I made arrangements for them to meet at the hotel when we arrived in LA.

We were in and out of LA, leaving right after R. Kelly's show. This was a good thing because our next stop was home. I was missing my children and I was ready to get back home. I was frustrated a lot with R. Kelly during this tour because he wasn't listening to anyone. Although everything was organized, nothing was ever good enough for him. He was doing everything he could to push me away.

I know I keep mentioning his after show activities and to be honest with you, dealing with Rob has been like dealing with a rich, spoiled kid. He is not a bad person. In my opinion, he is just an inconsiderate ass hole. His after show activities were always the same. Robert kept a piece of pussy in the dressing room or on the bus, in the hotel room or wherever he would be. He couldn't meet a girl and hang out and we all party and shit. He had to keep everybody waiting for him while he spent hours with each girl that waited around. I had to start asking the venue security to assist me with having people put out of the building or a hotel. That was selfish to me. His pride consistently put strife between us.

During our three-day ride back to Chicago, I would often lie in my bunk thinking about all I had been through with R. Kelly. I found myself becoming angry at the thought of him. Things were not getting better working with him. As I thought about our journey, I realized that R Kelly wasn't doing anything to help me come up; or anybody else for that matter. All of his actions were about him and him alone. This was his shit, as he once said. As if he created and put all of his success together all by himself.

Yeah, it was him who did the singing, him who did the writing and he created the choreography for the shows. But it was me who opened the doors for him to get in the game. It was me who opened the door to make sure people would listen to him. And it was me and people like me, Larry Hood, Torrey Diggs, Chuck, and Eric Payton that groomed him, supported him and made sure he was protected and safe. We made sure he had what he needed to get him to the next level and we made it possible for him to be where he was.

Robert had no sense of humility. He stepped over us like we were pieces of trash on the street and I was naive enough to believe that the good in a man would prevail. It wasn't until I read the book *The Battle for the Mind* by Bishop Noel Jones that I began to understand what I had been dealing with during my association with R. Kelly.

He didn't care about unity because he was never willing to offer himself to meet the needs of others. *"When people act as an individual in a collective environment, it creates problems, defeating teamwork and effective group participation"* (Bishop Noel Jones). That is exactly what happened with us. It was all about R. Kelly. *"This is my shit,"* he said.

With that attitude, it was long overdue for me pull away. He didn't care anything about me. I wasn't valuable to him at all. He never saw that I was sincere in my efforts and was looking out for his best interest. I was hurt over the fact that I loved R. Kelly like a brother, but I knew deep inside that I wasn't secure with him. With that in mind, I knew I had to begin thinking about my future without him because for now I was a slave in his camp. I wasn't able to make any moves without his permission. Everything, I mean everything, had to go through him. I was his puppet, and I didn't like myself for being so submissive.

I was a yes-man, doing things for him that I knew was not good for him or myself. A yes-man, turning my back on things I knew would hurt him in the long run. He knew I didn't approve of the rumors that were going around regarding his relationships with young girls. The relationship between me and Rob was forever changed but my duties remained the same.

My time in the studio was limited because Rob was working in the studio with Tiffany Hawkins and her young friends while I worked in Derrel's office. When I needed a signature from Robert, I would drive to the studio. I still didn't have a dependable car, so Derrel would let me drive his black 1994 Benz back and forth from the office to the studio, and occasionally, he would allow me to keep the car overnight. Once Rob saw me sporting the Benz he said something to Derrel. Next thing I knew, Derrel told me that Rob didn't approve of me having his car.

My credit had always been bad. It was one of the reasons why I didn't have a car. I could never really get together a good down payment. After learning that Robert was not comfortable with me driving Derrel's car, Derrel came through for me like a true friend and helped me to get a 1992 Black Honda Accord. Derrel—he was sympathetic to my needs and he wanted me to be there. He knew I was a hardworking, sincere and dedicated worker.

I was very upset at R. Kelly for the jealously he portrayed regarding me driving Derrel's car. I felt like when I made an appearance around people, it was a reflection of him, making him look good. He did not see it that way. He was on some other ego trip. He had to be the only one in our posse to shine. It was always about his selfish ambition or conceited attitude. He was never willing to consider the needs of others unless there was something in it for him.

Nonetheless, I continued working earnestly. I enjoyed the attention I received from the record company and all the other people that sought R. Kelly's services. I was the man to see or talk to in connection with R. Kelly. Even Barry was calling me to talk to me about upcoming events he wanted me to relay to R. Kelly. In spite of the Aaliyah incident, Barry was still R. Kelly's manager and he kept it business. I admire Barry, but then again, who would turn down millions over a sex scandal? Robert wasn't allowed to contact Aaliyah again after the marriage scandal. I think he went through guilt trips treating me the way he did. If I stayed away from him he would call and talk about how much he missed the old days. He would tell me how he wished he would have listened to me about Aaliyah.

I remember right after we came off the road, after the marriage, Robert bought a cell phone for Aaliyah and I sent it to her—it was their secret phone. Later, her family found out. For a long time, Robert wouldn't change his phone number in hopes that one day Aaliyah would call. I remember another time he cried telling me how much he missed her and her mom. For over a month, Rob stayed in the Chicago Nikko Hotel and he slept in the closet. He said it was the darkest place he could be. He said he wanted to fall out of the world.

I was actually worried about Robert. After two weeks he came out of the closet. He was passionate with his desire to get back into the studio. He buried himself into his music and laid down the tracks to the song "Trading My Life," which he wrote for Aaliyah. It was during his time of pain and suffering that I stood close by him. I would overlook his selfish ways and make sure he was ok. But right after the storm was over, he was back to being that fool, right back to having a faucet attitude.

Sure I wanted to be paid, but it was hard for me to sit back and watch him do things that would really hurt him in the long run. Everyone knew I had Rob's best interest at heart. No one knew him like I did and I was disoriented over how the closeness R. Kelly and I shared over the years was dwindling away. At times, when Rob was sitting at the piano in the studio, I would walk up to him and ask him to play a song entitled "Hard Times." This was one of the songs he used to sing in the subways. My reason for asking him to sing that song was because it always seemed to bring him back in touch with where we had come from. As he would play and sing I would join in and sing the background vocals, and together we would go back in time.

We would reminisce a little over how far we had come, and I'd tell him, *"Look how far you came Rob. I'm still trying to get there."* He didn't want to hear that, and it changed the mood. No longer did the reminiscing have any value to where we had been. Rob and I didn't hang out at all anymore. I didn't feel I was part of his plan any longer, and at the same time, I was trying to maintain my means to support my children. Dilemma after dilemma, I just could not seem to find my way through.

CHAPTER 22

More Drama!

I WAS DEALING WITH loneliness and distress? I was a wandering spirit who was lost with nowhere to hide and I had nowhere to go that I could call my own. Here I was a loyal humble servant working for a person who didn't seem to appreciate me. Even though I believed R. Kelly's talent was an anointing, He was constantly tearing me down. There were always problems occurring that could have been avoided had Robert not been so self-centered. He believed he had control of everything. If I only knew what I know now, I would have been able to project the personal characteristics of his actions in a way that could have made things different. Just as I had been possessed by a demon during my drug addiction in the '80s, here I was faced with another demon I didn't recognize or knowhow to deal with.

R. Kelly was dealing with a sex demon. This demon made his way into our camp and was working hard at being successful with his job to steal, kill and to destroy the good that could come out of the gift God had given. The devil's job was to push us away and to keep me struggling to survive while, at the same time create havoc in Robert's life. It began with Aaliyah. After that, we went through an interval which brought a chain reaction of negative publicity on R. Kelly and the team of people working with him. Then there came Tiffany "Tia" Hawkins. She was one of the young ladies that sung background vocals on Aaliyah's *Back and Forth* album. She was also one of the young ladies that hung out at Robert's apartment and in the studies with her girlfriends.

Tia was a very talented young lady I might add. I was working with Tia to help her get her career started and had her sign a contract with me as her manager. Robert was messing around with both Tia and Aaliyah at the same time. Tia became disturbed when she learned of R. Kelly and Aaliyah's relationship. This really messed things up because prior to finding this out, Tia was excited about going out on the upcoming tour with Aaliyah after the release of her album *Age Ain't Nothing but a Number*.

All plans were spoiled when R.Kelly and Aaliyah broke up because Aaliyah's family wanted nothing to do with anyone that had association with R. Kelly. Tia was so angry she sought out to hurt R. Kelly because, as she put it, *"He a low down ass dog and I hate him; among other things."* She would call the studio repeatedly screaming and yelling. R. Kelly got frustrated with her calls and would not take her calls anymore. Then she began to call me, leaving me messages to contact her. I didn't want to be in the middle of her and Robert's business so I ignored her calls.

I continued to ignore Tia until one night, she called and left a message on my phone, crying and saying she was about to kill herself. I contacted Robert immediately to let him hear the message. *"Call her,"* he said. I did and she told me she had a pistol and was going to kill herself, she said she wanted to make Robert hurt for the way he lied to her. She said she didn't feel like she had a future anymore. She said a career as a singer was all she wanted. Tia was hysterical, and she cried into the phone. I asked her to let me come over to talk to her so she agreed to meet with me. Robert agreed that I should go and meet with her, *"Go and see if she got a gun, he said."* I met with Tia at the corner of Ninety-eighth and University behind Chicago State University.

When I got out of the car, Tia stepped back. I noticed she had something in her hand. I couldn't see it clearly, but as I walked up on her, she put the object I was looking at to her Head. It was a small caliber pistol. Tia wasn't joking. She was crying, *"Y'all think I'm playing, don't you?"* she sobbed.

"Yawl, Come on, Tia, what are you doing? What's going on with you; come on Tia"? I said, pleading with her. It was what I felt I had to do when I saw this girl with that pistol. I wanted her to know, that I was compassionate to whatever she was going though. I was hoping she would feel that emotion. *"I came out here for you. You know I always been straight up with you just like I used to tell you at nights to go home. I always showed you concern like a little sister,"* I told her. *"Tia, don't do this. Come on now. Take that gun down, come on now, babe! Ain't nobody worth you hurting yourself for, baby girl,"* I said sympathetically.

Shocked at the sight of her holding a pistol to her head, I was cautious and concerned for my own life as well. She was not in her right state of mind, I thought. *"Tia, you don't have to do this,"* I pleaded.

My mind was going fast-forward. I was searching for the right words to say to calm her. I didn't want no freak accident happening.

"What about your son?" I asked.

"That's his baby and he knows it," she said. *"He don't want nobody else to know it,"* she continued with tears running down her face. *"He just lies to me and now look, Aaliyah can't even talk to me no more. I can't even go on the road with her because of him. I got nothing. He'll feel this I bet you,"* she said, rocking back and forth as if she was scared and nervous at the same time.

I thought it was over. I thought at that very moment she was going to pull the trigger. I felt so sorry for her.

"Tia," I shouted, *"you can make him pay you, make him pay for you and your son!"* I told her. *"You don't have to hurt yourself. You only gone be hurting your son and your family, Tia. Robert gone go on doing what they do when you gone, baby girl. We'll all be sad for a minute, but life gone goon, Tia. Please don't do this, put that gun down, Tia, please,"* I begged her.

I guess she saw the sincerity in my face as I plead. I felt as if I wanted to cry too. To be honest, I really felt sorry for her.

"I want him to pay, Johnny. I can't go on tour with Aaliyah now. Her family doesn't want anybody that socializes with him to talk to her. That's my friend, and he was doing her too. I want him to pay," she said sobbing while the tears ran down her face, like drips from a faucet.

"Tia, you can talk to a lawyer," I told her. *"Tia, please put the gun down, please,"* I begged her.

"But I want him to hurt, Johnny. I want him to hurt so bad," she said. You could see her pain as she stood their crying. I wanted to just hold her in my arms. She needed to feel love, and I wanted to give it to her, but I wasn't going to walk up on her with that pistol!

"Tia, he will hurt, he will hurt babe and you'll be able to move on with your life if you talk with a lawyer. Please, Tia," I plead with her to put the pistol down from her head.

She cried and looked at me. I saw in her eyes that she wanted to give in. I began to slowly walk toward her with my arm shielded out. *"Come here, Tia. Put that gun down,"* I said, reaching out to her. I stopped thinking about myself. I was concerned about her. She was in pain and felt all alone.

"Tia, I'll help you, just give me the gun," I said. *"You're just saying that,"* she said.

"No, Tia, I'm not. It's not right how he's treated you and that he messed with Aaliyah. When he did that he messed it up for all of us. I can't work with Aaliyah no more either." I was about to start naming off things that were now effected because we could no longer associate with Aaliyah when Tia

Demetrius Smith Sr.

interrupted. *"He doesn't care about nobody!"* She said with an expression that showed she was mad as hell.

"You'll be doing him a favor if you hurt yourself. You can come out on top if you get a lawyer. He'll respect you then, Tia," I said.

I guess she sensed I was sincere. She began slowly to lower the gun from her head. As I got closer to her I reached out for the gun and she gave it to me. I put my arms around her and hugged her, patting her like a little baby as she cried in my arms. *"Don't worry, Tia, it's gone be all right. We gone talk to Robert, and I'll help you. I mean it,"* I told her. And I did mean it, I felt a need to help her.

She laid her head on my shoulder as I put the gun on my waist. I pulled out my cell phone and called Robert. *"You tricked me,"* she said and snatched away from me. I held on to her with my free hand.

"No, I didn't, Tia, but we gotta deal with him," I told her. As I held the phone down, lowering my voice and showing her that I didn't want Robert to hear what I was saying to her. Robert's voice came onto the phone line. *"Hello,"* I spoke into the phone.

"Johnny, so what's happening with her?" He asked.

I was speaking real low as I told Robert she had the gun. *"Man, Tia's hurting,"* I said.

She was still trying to pull away from me but listened intently as I spoke to Robert.

"You need to talk to her, Rob. She really feels that you hurt and lied to her," I said. *"Where you at?"* he asked.

"Man, I just talked her out of taking a gun down from her head," I whispered into the phone. Because he acted like he didn't hear me the first time I had told him, He didn't seem concerned at all about that. This angered me. I don't know if he felt the vibe or what all of a sudden he responded.

"What? She got a gun? Let me talk to her," he said.

In a low tone, I explained to Robert Tia's state of mind and asked him to be kind to her. At first, she refused to take the phone, but it didn't take too much convincing. She wanted to talk to him. It was no doubt that she was weak for him. *"Tia, talk to Robert."* She shook her head no.

"It's gone be all right, Tia. Talk to him," I insisted, nodding my head to her to take the phone.

She then took it, and without hearing anything, she began to yell into the phone. *"You just keep lying to me. All you do is hurt people!"* she screamed in to the phone.

I sat back on my car as Robert talked to her. After about five minutes, she handed the phone back to me. *"Yeah, Johnny, bring her down here. I'll deal with her when y'all get here,"* he said and hung up without giving me a chance to say anything.

On the way back to see Robert, Tia told me that it didn't matter that I had her gun. She said the next time she won't call. She said she felt that I was only tricking and lying to her about helping her just like Robert. I talked to her about finding her an attorney. Tia then tried to talk me out of taking her to the studio. She no longer wanted to see Robert. She wanted to go home, but I continued telling her that she needs to face him so that she could clear her head and make up her mind about pursuing an attorney.

Once at the studio, I told Robert what had went down regarding the gun. He then took Tia into another part of the studio. I left, taking the 32 pistol with me. Later that night, Robert called me. He was somewhat angry with me for telling Tia to get an attorney. I let him know I felt I had to in order to convince her to give me the gun. He didn't believe she was really going to shoot herself, but I believed different and didn't want to take a chance on that happening. I didn't hear from Tia for a couple of weeks.

Then I received a call from her attorney, who wanted to meet with me to discuss Tia's allegations concerning Robert having sex with her as a minor. I went to meet with him to find out what I could so that I could warn Robert and he could prepare himself. I didn't think that the girl was really going to follow up on my suggestion to obtain legal counsel, but she did. It later turned out to be a real case against R. Kelly. Tia told the attorney of all the times she and her young friends had spent with R. Kelly at his Burnham Plaza apartment. She told of all the sexual things he had done with her and her friends at the apartment and at the studio. She even mentioned Aaliyah's name at some the "sleep over's". Several law suits were filed against R. Kelly by Tia and her friends. Tia offered me 10 percent of whatever she would get if I would sign an affidavit, but I declined, I am still trying to figure out myself, why?

After several attempts of trying to convince me to sign an affidavit, Tia and her attorney stopped calling me. Later, I learned that R. Kelly settled with them as well as Aaliyah and her family. R. Kelly wanted to go to trial with Tia but was advised to end the scandal before it got out of hand. We felt that Tia and her little friends collaborated together to come up with a story to damage R. Kelly and his career. Nonetheless, it stopped nothing.

Demetrius Smith Sr.

We continued working and moving ahead. Working with R. Kelly was my life. I was sure we could somehow recover from all the bad publicity that had been printed about R. Kelly. I felt and told Robert that the show and image had to be different, but he didn't listen. He continued on in his shows running across the stage, holding his private parts and grinding fans, instead of just singing and touching the people with his voice.

Meanwhile, I made another attempt to negotiate the 5% pay I was promised years ago. I had an attorney draw up a contract for me and then I presented it to Derrel, because Derrel had begun to take over a lot of the business matters when it came to Robert since he and Barry were not speaking. He read over it and felt it was fair for me to receive a percentage, as initially agreed. *"You've been the man behind him even before me, and I know I depend on you. It would be hell for me if you weren't here,"* he told me. Derrel told me that he submitted the contract to Robert and that after the tour we would sit down and work it out.

In the meantime, my salary was increased o $900 a week plus a $50 a day per diem. For the time being, I was content with that, or at least until we got back from the overseas tour. I couldn't see myself turning down this money when I needed it. Things would have to be put on hold again. Being overseas was again an exciting adventure for me. Everything went well. No one had to stress over Robert holding the bus up after a show here, overseas. In Europe, Robert performed and we were out of there.

After the shows, the bus came, and we had to board them or be left behind. They had different laws concerning the drivers; they could only drive for a certain amount of hours and if we weren't at our destination by the time their driving time was up, the drivers had the right to park the bus and go rest for eight hours. We would tell the ladies where we stayed and if they could drive to our next destination, we would be able to spend a limited amount of time with them. Two weeks went by fast.

When we got back to Chicago, it was as if we had never left to go overseas. Even the plane ride back was fast. I dreaded being home somewhat because I knew I was faced with the same problems, not having any security for myself. Being on the road, I had a place to come home to, be it a hotel room or the tour bus. There were times when I could go be by myself, close the door and feel a moment of peace. At home, I was a visitor everywhere I went. When we returned, I met with Derrel concerning my contract. Robert wasn't ready to deal with it, he said. He wanted to wait until he was finished with the tour we had scheduled in the States.

To compensate me, my pay went up to $950 a week; that was another notch up the scale for me, I thought, so I went along with it. $950 was cool, plus I was still on the payroll of the bus company and all the other companies I hired as vendors for the tour. I was engaged in setting up the Mr. Big Tour. Robert was busy working in the studio on the Isley Brothers album. Along with working on the show, Robert and I traveled back and forth to New York shooting videos for his next single as well as a video with the Isley Brothers.

We were set and ready for the Mr. Big Tour. Lisa Raye went along with us. This is the tour I think she made her connection that put her in the position where she is today. As far as how well the tour went, things were the same. You would think with all the negative publicity from Tia, her friends and Aaliyah, that he would have learned something or would have grown up at least a little. He didn't—that sex demon had a hold on R. Kelly and he was blind to the damage he was causing to his career and in the life's of the people that loved him.

He knew I would object to anything I thought was hindering his career. So instead of conversing with me, he tried to hide everything from me. He even had the security I hired for him keep me from entering his dressing room. *"Hold on, Demetrius, Mr. Kelly wants me to check with him before I allow anyone to go in to see him."* To say I was frustrated would be an understatement. I was fighting to protect someone who didn't have any idea what he was doing. I was mad as hell when he wouldn't allow me into Robert's dressing room, but I chilled. I allowed him to do his job.

When he came back to the door, he told me, *"Mr. Kelly said he would see you later."* *"What, man, I need to see Rob now, excuse me,"* I told him. When I attempted to get past him to enter Robert's dressing room, he put his hands on me to stop me. One word led to another to where I was about to hit him in the head with my walkie-talkie. Robert came out the dressing room just in the nick of time to stop me from getting in a lot of trouble because I was really mad and if I would've busted him in the head, I was going to jail.

I thought Kim was going to work with me as Tyree did. This is what we had talked about before I hired him. Robert came out the dressing room and stepped in the middle of us. *"Hold on, hold on, Johnny man, what's going on. I told him to not let anybody in here. He's doing what I told him,"* Robert said seeming angry at me for causing a confrontation.

"Robert, man, he don't stop me. I'm your main guy, I don't know what's going on in there"—pointing to his dressing room—*"shit, you could be in trouble or something, he don't keep me out without you telling me."*

I was angry and Rod heard it in my voice as well as he was looking at me as I was looking Kim up and down. *"I should be one of the only ones that can come in here and see you and be able to have full access to get to you with no problem, I don't know what's going on with this dude (pointing at Kim) telling me I can't go in."* I said to him with a smug look at Kim. Robert then told me to come into the dressing room where we went over the issue and talked about some promotional things he had to do but overall the situation with locking me out of his dressing room; he asked me to work with him on that.

After I left Robert's dressing room, I told Kim he would not be with us long. *"Yeah, whatever,"* he said. We did two more cities before Robert allowed me to fire Kim. Kim I felt was doing too much to get close to Robert. What he didn't know was that Robert and I were together regardless of how things appeared.

R. Kelly's brother, Carey "Killa" Kelly, was out on tour with us during this time. He was a rapper and was part of the show, so he stayed around R. Kelly since they started working together. Robert and Killa clashed a lot. They didn't see eye to eye when it came to Killa flowing on the tracks and gaining his identify as a rapper. Robert wanted to dictate how he should be rapping. He wanted to mold Killa to be how he wanted him to be and Killa had a style of his own. He was well liked and respected by other Rappers. Killa was complimented often for his skills in writing and how he flowed. The man had skills.

The way I saw it and felt about it, Robert had become a total control freak. I remember one night we were downtown Chicago, We had just come out of a restaurant. As we were walking Rod paid two of our crew members $100.00 each to walk a full block holding hands and switching down the street as if they were gay, just for a laugh. How controlling was that? So as he and Killa worked together, Killa had to suck it up and do things his big brothers way. I use to tell him as he walked around angry, *"don't worry about it Killa, we all waiting on bro to come back for us. He will,"* I'd tell him.

When we were in St. Louis, Missouri R. Kelly left his Rolex watch in the dressing room while he went to do his show and it came up missing. R.Kelly told me that it was my responsibility to secure his personal property. We argued because I never knew what he had or where he put his things, so I didn't feel like it was my responsibility. The argument got heated because he told me that he was docking my pay $150. I was heated, and on top of that, my computer was missing; someone stole it to.

As much as I felt that I would regret it, I felt it was time for me to move on. I knew inside that I couldn't contain my temper any longer, especially with Robert now fucking with my money. I went back into the area, and I told Derrel that I quit. He tried to convince me to be patient, telling me that he would talk to R. Kelly and work it out. I couldn't. I couldn't just wait any longer; this was the last straw. I couldn't afford to waste anymore of my life hoping my friend would help me come up.

My youngest brother, Joshua, was there at the concert. I got him out the crowd, and he took me home. I didn't talk to R. Kelly or Derrel after that for three weeks. I knew that the State to State tours R. Kelly was doing were over and they were on their way overseas to perform again. I had already done all the legwork; I sent the Rider, gathered all passport information and made the complete itinerary before I left. All the work was done for whoever would take my place. I was sincerely closing the door here!

CHAPTER 23

Unappreciated

$\mathcal{I}$ DECIDED TO TAKE this time to get a place to live I could call home and spend my time being a daddy to my children. Right away I sent to Georgia for my son Demetrius and we worked on music. They loved to dance and sing, so I spent my time working with them. I turned into Joe Jackson so to speak (minus the beatings)! They were babies, but they were so talented. I figured if I would put my time and experience into them, I could continue to be in the music business. The kids kept me grounded and were the very reason I did not lose my mind.

Inside I was hurting bad over my departure from R. Kelly. I wanted so much for things to work. I was heartbroken and I had malice in my heart. If it weren't for my children, I would have made good of the thoughts I was having about kicking R. Kelly's ass. I was angry at him. All the time and the loyal service I gave him, for him to treat me with no concern the way he had. Hatred for him was building up inside of me. I should have been taken care of a long time ago, I thought. Here I was again, having to start all over.

I was living off the money I had made off the Mr. Big Tour and the side deals I had made with the vendors. But the money was running short and fast. I had to find a job. Kirk Franklin had been pursuing me for employment as his tour manager when I met him and his manager while R. Kelly was doing some work with him in the studio. I sent my resume to him and a lot of other entertainers and record companies. Kirk's manager wanted to hire me to be his tour manager, but R. Kelly was working on a song with him, and when he inquired about me, he was told that I worked exclusively for R. Kelly. That was the same response I got from a lot of the people I sent my resume to in the industry. I didn't know this was going on, and when I called Derrel about it, he said he didn't know anything about it, and there was no way he would blackball me. It was Kirk's manager who told me Robert told her that. The fact that R. Kelly's camp had a reputation of being unprofessional and along with the allegations of R. Kelly having a thing for young girls, it all reflected on me, so my chances of working in the music industry were slim. *I'd be flat broke and homeless waiting for something to open up for me,* I thought.

I was ready to diminish my relationship and contacts with R. Kelly altogether until I received a call from Derrel asking me to reconsider my resignation and to go overseas with R. Kelly. He said that they were having lots of problems and he needed me over there. Finally, I thought of Lafayette's words: *"You don't get what you deserve, you get what you negotiate."* I was in a position to ask for more than $850 I was getting from the last tour. I thought about the $150 they had deducted from my pay the last time I was with him. I told Derrel I needed $1,500 a week, plus $50 a day per diem. Derrel, never rejected anything I asked for, he always felt I deserved it. He told me he'd talk to R. Kelly and get right back with me. It was within a couple of hours when he called me back. R.Kelly had agreed with giving me $1,100 a week and $40 per diem per day. I accepted it on the condition that once we got back from overseas, before I would go on another tour or do any other work for R. Kelly, we'd have to sit down and come to terms over the 5 percent I was promised from day 1and when I would get to Europe, R. Kelly would have to let me do my job and listen to me.

Derrel agreed. I was flown to London, England, that night. When I arrived, R. Kelly was in concert at the Wimbledon Arena. I was picked up at Heathrow Airport and taken straight there. When I got there R. Kelly's show had just ended. Everyone seemed to be happy to see me at least all the band members were. Backstage was crowded with people. It was like a circus there, people running around everywhere. Believe it or not, I was happy to be there too and happy people were glad to see me.

When I went to R. Kelly's dressing room, he was glad as well.

"Boy, what's up, I'm glad you made it man. Let me finish up in here. We'll talk on the bus," he said. I nodded in agreement as I left his dressing room.

On my way to the arena I was given an update on where we were. A Marshall Artist Aid told me we were running behind schedule and needed to leave. It wasn't like the other times I had come here. Before after our performance we were always rushed out onto the bus and immediately driven on to the next city. Robert had brought his whole act to the UK for real this time. Here and now, there bus drivers were waiting on him.

I met with Kirk Townsend, who was hired to take my place. He was so glad to see me when I walked up on him.

"*Demetrius, man,*" he said shaking his head left to right. *I envy you,*" he said. "*I wouldn't want your job for nothing, you can have it back. It is too buck wild out here for me.*" He said. "*Man, I get no cooperation out of Robert. How you do it, I don't know, but I am glad you're here,*" he said. Kirk told me he never would have thought Robert was so out of order, unprofessional, and unorganized.

Immediately, I took charge putting things together. His crew was running around like little mice. They were running around back and forth from the audience to R.'s dressing room, transporting young girls in and out of his dressing room. It seemed as if they were picking the youngest girls from the audience. I didn't fly across the waters to come back into the bullshit. I went back to R. Kelly's dressing room. I went to him and in a joyful way proceeded to do my job.

"*Alright Rob; let's get this rolling so we can leave. It's time to roll. We got a lot to go over,*" I said as I was picking up his bags to take them out. He got offended and told me that I was not about to come in and start giving him orders. I simply told him I did not fly across the world to get caught up in another country for some young girl bullshit. He looked at me surprised that I had said that. I didn't like it that Robert was not conscious of the danger he was putting himself in with the company he was keeping and I wanted to fight with him now. I wanted to take charge to be his true friend and if he wasn't going to listen to me, then I couldn't do this again.

It was no longer a question in my mind; underage girls had proven to be his weakness. He was obsessed, sickly addicted. One word led to another, and R. Kelly and I were arguing. A lot of hurtful things were said, it got heated. I told him I couldn't do it. I couldn't stay unless he allowed me to do my job. After stating that, I left the dressing room. I was hurt. I thought by Robert requesting me to be there, things would be different. I sighed to relieve the stress of my friend continuing to hurt himself. I thought to myself in lonely despair, asking him the question, "*Man, Robert, can't you see what you're doing to yourself?*" I just couldn't reach him or get through to him in any way.

As much as I regretted it, I wanted no part of supporting the evilness I saw forming. I just could not do the same things I had been doing with him. I couldn't turn my head and overlook the fact that his boy's weren't looking out for his best interest messing with possibly little girls. I had to let him know by making a stand against him.

As usual, it didn't work in my favor. That same night I quit again. Robert was not paying any attention to me as I told him my job was also protecting his image. As far as I could tell the girls R. Kelly would be entertaining, to be honest, looking at them I could not tell if they were of age. Robert didn't go for the girls I liked he went for who he liked. They weren't girls of whom I would ask to be my company because for me, they were too young. But for R. Kelly, I didn't know how old they were. I just hoped he wasn't having a problem with having to have to have an under aged girl.

The truth is, being a pedophile is a sickness and just like any other illness, it needs to be treated. It is no doubt that this is a condition that bears shame but at the same time, ain't nobody better than nobody else. Who is to say you wouldn't do what I have did, faced with the same situation or under similar circumstances? There is an old slavery song that comes to mind, *"Nobody knows the troubles I've been through."* I find that to be so true when it relates to my life. When it comes to people accepting one another for who they are and helping people to what they need, many of us fall short. We see people to be who we want them to be and that's not always who they are, we are all made better in God's plan.

Nobody knows what we go through that makes us who we are or makes us why we are the way we are. We are meant to be who we are and we go through things because it shapes us into the greatness God called us to be. When we help someone that is going through adversity and trials, or let me say when we help people period. I believe it allows us to bring out our best in each other and when we can bring out our best of each other, I believe it brings us closer to touching Greatness! I have been through some things and there are some things I might have done that you would think I should have known better, but I really didn't. We see each other go through things. Therefore, ask me about me. I just might not know what you think I should know. I believe we are here to help one another and by caring for one another we will grow into our gift to enjoy our gift of life. I don't think that anyone should ever assume anything of any one. Simply ask, and it will bring answers.

It is time to take the Band-Aids off and time to cut the poison out of the wound of the '80s. The way I see it, we have come a long way in life as people. We have all gone through some things and ain't none of us right, beyond sin and we are nowhere near perfect. The word said that we have all fallen short. Magic Johnson brought people into the awareness of AIDS. He stood up to fight and because of his integrity and his desire to help be a part in making someone else's life better, he saved lives. We need to help each other and we need to stand up to fight against any sickness or disease that is poison to our bloodstream and to our race as a people. I am not speaking Black & White, I am an American!

For my Mr. R. Kelly, I was willing to stand by him. And what he was going through was normal to me, to some extent that is, but we were at a point here where it was time to get control of things and balance ourselves. And if what he was going through with these girls was not viewed as a problem to him that was all on him. Robert was not a bad person, a bit selfish; ok a lot, but he was not a bad person. He was drunk with the joy of being who he wanted to be. And that was all cool too. But it was time to begin to have balance now. My overall objective was to run a smooth tour, make some money and have some fun. Robert, I don't even think he was seeing me; he was too busy with himself. The business part of the tour, he was giving me hell with running a smooth ship. Mr. R. Kelly was not seeing things, and I mean that literally; he was not looking. Robert was too busy having all the fun.

1st James 1:17 read, *"Every good gift is from God"*. And I have also read, *"What the devil means for evil, God will turn it to good"*. Romans 8:28 said, *"And we know that all things work together for the good to those who love God and to those who are called according to his purpose."* R. Kelly, to me, is a good gift and I would hope that he loves God. But as we all know—denial is blinding.

"Carry your ass back home if you can't do what I tell you!" R. Kelly said to me as I walked out of his dressing room, and that's what I did. The next morning, the promoter paid for me a first-class ticket back to Chicago.

As soon as I got back to Chicago and barely settled at home, I got a call from Barry. Yep, Barry was still Robert's manager. They had worked it out somehow. What I figured was that Barry was only in it for the money then. I had heard rumors that Robert had paid out about 3 million or more to compensate somewhat for the pain he had caused Aaliyah and her family. Barry and I talked about what had gone down in Europe. He told me that I had to learn to put personal issues aside when it came to business and to do what was necessary to continue to feed my family. I thought about his situation, and I was sure then he was there for the money and thought to myself how right he was.

"Sometimes, you have to look past or go around things to get where you need to be when it comes to making things work for you," he said. *"Look at what he did to me and my family. Was I supposed to walk away? No! Now what we have is unfinished business.* We laughed, for a moment and I got serious again.

"It has got to be hard for you," I suggested. *"It has been hard because I have feelings for Robert like a son, and he betrayed me. But business is business,"* he said. *"I have been talking to Robert, but strictly about business now, and I talked to him about you last night. I told him how he is not allowing you to do your job and I mentioned to him how loyal I thought you have been to him. We had a serious talk about you."* I could hear it in Barry's voice sincerity and I began to feel that emotion.

"Next week when he gets home, he's flying into New York to attend the Shaft *premiere. I told him I wanted you there so we could sit and talk. Get organized so he'll know exactly what your job is. Robert wants you there, he wants you to run his tours, and I want you there. You're supposed to be there running things. Will you come?"* he asked. I agreed to meet with them.

I had great admiration for Barry and thought if he was going to still be there, I was willing to at least sit down and talk. I was flown to New York the night of the *Shaft* movie premiere. I walked down the red carpet with R. Kelly and Barry, shaking hands with some of the actors that were there.

That night I got to hug Ms. Vanessa Williams, and she was looking good. She was not really dressed up she was home girl looking, as if she was at home, there at the theater. She had stepped away from doing choirs, kind of like I'm going back and chill as soon as this is over, kind of, looking good as she was. She made me smile hugging her and the beauty of Ms. Williams for me that night was watching her smiled. In so many ways I was amazed. I even shuck hands with Samuel L. Jackson. He was smooth and cool as he made his way through the crowd to exit after the show. It was a celebratory event, and as much as I would have liked to have had fun enjoying the festivities, my mind was on the meeting with R. Kelly and Barry.

As much as I enjoyed the lifestyle and the true feeling of exultation I just could not seem to understand how Robert dealt with being famous. I don't know why, but Robert never wanted to socialize with his peers. He felt being inaccessible made people more in awe of him. In my book, he was awful. The boy should have been an actor. The facade he was portraying was all an act.

After the Shaft premiere ended, R. Kelly, Barry and I got into the limousine and headed back to the hotel. On the way there, we discussed the issues and concerns I was having when on the road with R. Kelly. He did not deny holding everyone up for hours while he was having his autograph sessions in his dressing room, the fact that he deducted money from my check because he felt he could and how he made things difficult for me when everything was organized. He agreed to try to work with me and not against me.

When I brought up the 5 percent that I was promised, he said that he did not see that happening because it would equal up to him owing me money over all the years that we had been working together. He told me what he would do was pay me $1,100 a week and after six months he'd raise my pay to $1,500. Then if all continued to go well, he'd give me another raise. He agreed to replace the computer that was stolen off the bus from me and said he'd give me a bonus to help me out with my financial problems.

I was with that deal. It sounded good to me. And I thought at the same time I would have the leverage I needed to establish a better working relationship with Robert. I knew the 5 percent was a done deal. I wasn't going to get that. I accepted their offer to start over. The next day, R. Kelly and I boarded a plane back to Chicago. It was like old times for a few weeks once we got home. Wes stayed in the studio. Things were showing potential of working out.

My enthusiasm went to another level when Michael Jackson's camp called requesting R. Kelly to write a song for him. Robert and I had always talked about this. I remember telling him in his younger days that he would write for Michael as well as other famous entertainers. This was all becoming a reality. The vision was in clear view. R. Kelly would be in the studio acting like Michael to get in his writing mood to write the song for him. He came up with quite a few songs for Michael to choose from. "You Are Not Alone" was the song Michael chose. I was excited to be the one to set up all the arrangements for Michael Jackson to come to Chicago and record at CRC studios with R. Kelly, but right before Michael Jackson was to arrive, R. Kelly changed. He pushed me back and told me that I couldn't be there when he came. I was more than disappointed after making all the arrangements and then being shut out.

Again, I had to hide my anger and disappointment and keep things professional. There was no doubt I had plans to be as personable as I could to impress Michael Jackson. I wasn't going to kiss his ass, but I had planned on making an impression on Michael, but my plans were ruined. R.Kelly treated me as if I was his butler. After I got him everything he needed, he dismissed me and told me to take the week off. While Michael Jackson was there I stayed away as he requested.

My days away I spent with my children. It was always pleasant when my children and I were all together. All of the traveling around the world with R. Kelly and working long hours—I did it for my children. I didn't run the streets chasing women or live a fast life. I worked hard, sending money, providing for them as best as I could and as best as I knew how. The times we spent together were treasured. I just wanted to able to come to a home with my children, but it just seemed so hard to achieve. There was always unwarranted drama when God had provided a way to make things pleasant. We should have been happy. Especially since we struggled all our lives. There was plenty of money to go around so that everyone could live comfortably. All it took was for Robert to do the right thing by taking care of people properly, and not treat us like slaves or undocumented workers.

During this time, everybody was struggling to make ends meet. When I say everybody, I mean the crew, the guys we hung out with. Robert's brother Carey called me one evening and said, *"Man, I need you, because I'm tired of my brother treating me like shit,"* he said. He was upset. *"I'm gone do something about it too. I don't give a fuck, that nigga don't give a fuck about me or my brother,"* he said.

"Killa, what are you talking about?" I asked. I had no idea of what he was tripping on. I knew he and Robert didn't see eye to eye because Robert would not do anything to help him get his career off the ground as a rapper. But I did not have a clue about what he was talking about this time.

"I got those tapes I took from his ass, and I'm gone sell 'em," he said. *"And I want you to help me, Johnny,"*

"What tapes?" I asked.

"Man, Johnny, you know all the time he tapes himself fucking them hoes he be with. And I don't even give a fuck. I took a couple of his tapes out his bag. Fuck Rob, Johnny man. I'm tired of that muthafucka treating me as if I ain't his brother. He don't care shit about us. Robert just looks out for Robert; all he do is give them bitches, anything they want. He doesn't give us a second thought about shit. We don't fucking matter to him and I'm his brother."

Killa went on raving reasonless. He was running off at the mouth nonstop and totally irrational. He was angry and looking for a reason to feel good about what he was threatening to do to his brother. Yes, Robert did not care about any of our needs and that hurt the people that were really close to him, but I could not see myself helping Killa cross Rob the way he was talking about doing him. I had faith that his brother would come around once things got to a boiling point; and we were at that point. If I had anything to do with it, things were going to get better for us all. *"Killa you can't do shit like that to your brother!"* I told him.

"Man, he don't give a fuck about me or you either Johnny. You just be working your ass off and that motherfucker don't care about you." Killa was really upset and he wouldn't let me to say anything. He went on expressing his anger.

"Man, Johnny, you remember when that nigga got his Benz? You was cleaning it for him one day and he told me you was a good bitch to have around and if you was a woman, he'd marry yo ass. Now you tell me if that's a muthafucka that care anything about you? You know I'm telling the truth," he demanded.

Killa struck a nerve in me when he said that. Those words kept ringing in my head, *"good bitch to have around."* But now I am seeing something that is giving me some understanding that purposes a question? I remember back when we first started traveling back and forth to New York. Rob and I would be in a two bed-room suite, and often times he would walk to and from rooms, freely and in front of me, butt naked. He would laugh at times as if to take it for a joke; prancing through the room playfully. "What's wrong with you dude? Put some cloths on fool when you come through here." I would yell out in discuss. I wasn't into that, nor was I looking at Rob or thinking of him to have gay tenancies, but sitting here thinking back, if he said that to his brother, maybe it is a good man he misses having around? The nerve of that dude! I saw Robert as my brother, the brother I never grew up with and my loyalty to and for him was sincere. When Killa told me that, I felt like I had been stabbed in the heart. But at the same time, I had to keep my cool. I didn't want any part of helping Killa. I thought he was wrong. I mean, R. Kelly was his brother and I just didn't think it was right to sell out your brother, something Killa was threatening to do. Killa went on in his rage.

"Johnny, if you ain't gone help me, then fuck it man. I'll call somebody else, and you can tell him, I don't give a fuck," he said, and I could hear the frustration and seriousness in his tone.

"Where are you Killa?" I asked. He said that he was on the South Side of Chicago. I agreed to meet with him at his place. Carey "Killa" Kelly was a good kid. He had been going through some hard times himself and to be as young as he was, his heart was with his children. He had about eight of them, I think! Killa was only twenty-three years old. He could rap and write like R. Kelly did with R&B, but Killa didn't get the opportunity that his brother got. He was hopeful that through his brother he would get his big break.

We all thought that his opportunity was in his brother. We always thought Robert would record him and give him the same start he had been given, but Robert only looked out for Robert and the girls he kept around. Killa was upset over the whole thing and felt like all Robert needed to do was introduce him to his major connections. Killa felt like he could seal the deal for himself. As I saw him, Killa was an awesome talent. But now he was frustrated because he felt his brother should help him and since he wouldn't, Killa felt he wanted to make his brother feel the pain of not caring for a loved one. Killa wanted to hurt his brother back. *"Fuck my brother"* were Killa's words. And from the tone I heard over the phone, he meant every word of it.

When I got to Killa's house, he was home alone. He played the videotape for me. He said he had taken it out of R. Kelly's gym bag. The tape showed R. Kelly having sex with several girls and women; one of the scenes was with Robert's wife, "Baby Girl," before they were married. Another was with a white girl, he was eating her asshole out on top of his pool table at his house on George Street and the other scene was of him and a young girl. He was teaching her how to give him head. Killa showed me the tape because he thought I would be receptive to helping him obtain some money because of the way his brother was treating him. I wasn't feeling that even though I was insulted over what he had told me about me being a good bitch. But the thought of betraying Robert didn't develop at all in my mind because I knew that people and their lives would be devastated if this got out. I felt I had already been a part of too many ruins. I couldn't entertain the thought of helping him. Especially since the intent was not meant for good, but for nothing but more evil. I was just there to see what he had.

I always felt R. Kelly would come around and do the right thing by us all. It wasn't too hard to convinced Killa to allow me to talk to his brother. I don't believe Killa really wanted to hurt his Robert. It was just that he was hurting himself and he needed help.

"Johnny, before I go out here and stick a motherfucker up, I'll do this, cause Johnny I would not leave my brother out here hurting as I am. Man I can't even feed my kids," he would say! I was hoping I could get Robert to see the pain people around him were going through because he was not receptive to anyone's needs. These were the people who he was close to and who had also sacrificed in the early years, up until now.

I told Killa that blood was thicker than water and that it was not right for him to do what he wanted to do to his brother. While I was at Killa's house, I convinced him to allow me to call Derrel. I assured him that Derrel would not say anything until he heard from me. He allowed me to call and Derrel agreed to wait to hear from me before he mentioned anything to

Robert. He told me he was leaving it up to me to handle it. Derrel knew what Killa was going through because he had given Killa money on several occasions.

I spent about two hours talking with Killa, and he gave me the okay to allow Derrel to confront Robert about the tapes he had. Barry was in town at the time. When Derrel called me back, he told me he talked with them, and they were willing to assist Killa, but they wanted Killa to come to the studio where Robert and Barry were. Killa said he didn't trust them but said he trusted me and if I said it was okay, then he would go with me to the studio to try to resolve some of the things he was going through.

Killa gave me the tape and me with my stupid loyal self, took the tape right to the studio instead of going somewhere to make a copy for security purposes. But I wasn't like that and didn't feel I had to be like that with a person. I took the tape to the studio where Derrel, Barry and R. Kelly were waiting for me. Barry put the videotape into the recorder. He viewed just a portion of it; showing the scene where R. Kelly was in the sexual act with a white woman, eating her asshole out. Barry immediately took the VCR tape out of the tape deck and said he didn't want to see it. He then ripped the tape apart, destroying it.

After the tape was disposed of, Robert, Barry, and Derrel went into another room in the studio along with Killa. I don't know what happened in their meeting. But later that night, Robert accused me of putting Killa up to trying to extort him. I argued against the false accusation he made towards me, but it was fruitless. As the days went on, R. Kelly told Derrel to stop allowing me to hold on to Bass Productions' company checkbook. He said he no longer trusted me.

"It's nothing you can tell me to make me change my mind," R. Kelly told me when I confronted him about his distrust.

"If you distrust me, Rob, then I no longer need to be here. This is all bull shit you keep putting me through," I told him.

"Then you need to talk to Barry because I don't need you here if I can't trust you," he said. I didn't feel like going through any arguments with him because I was already five minutes away from taking off his head; the nerve of this snake after all I had been through with him.

I felt betrayed and disrespected, but I felt like David when he didn't understand why Saul wanted him dead. 1 Samuel 24:8. My feelings were the same. I didn't want to bring harm on Robert because I felt he was one of God's anointed. But I could not understand why he did not want for me to get ahead?

All that I did for him and all the money I saw him waste, if I wanted to take Robert for anything, I would have done it way before then. Robert was so selfish, I can remember when he first bought the house on George St. he was so excited that he had a 20 foot long fish tank built in the wall. I don't know how much the tank cost, but I do know that he bought 2 sharks that cost $30,000 apiece. There we were, all the people that worked for him were broke and he was spending that kind of money on fish. On top of that, the fish all died.

If I wanted to get at him, I could have arranged to be robbed when I carried $60,000 and $70,000 around in the trunk of the car for his disposal; I had his bank account number and all access, I could have cleaned out his bank account and took off; I picked all the cash up after every concert, I could have taken a large portion of the money for myself before turning it in. I'm just not that kind of person. I was out right loyal to this man.

But, here I was hurt and being driven away for something I did to protect him. It was the story of my life thus far. Just when things looked as if they were coming together, that old demon of destruction would come out of nowhere and bring havoc into my life.

When I spoke with Barry, he felt the relationship that R. Kelly and I had ran its course and advised me that for my best interest, I should put some space between us; at least for a while, he said. Barry asked me what I felt R. Kelly owed me, and of course I told him 5 percent.

"You need to get past that. That's not going to happen," he told me. *What I'm gonna do is tell Robert that you'd like to step away for a while because you're not getting along, I'm also going to ask him to give you a severance pay for all the years that you've worked with him. I'll be on your side in letting him know, giving you severance payment would be the right thing for him to do. Let's say about $50,000, would that be a good number for you to organize yourself?"* he asked.

Fifty grand, I thought, all at one time. What choice did I have? *"Yeah, that would be cool,"* I told him. *"I could get myself together with that,"* I agreed.

It was three days later when Barry got back with me. He told me R.Kelly would not agree to give me $50,000, but he did agree to $30,000. I met with Barry at the Knickerbocker Hotel, in downtown Chicago, to pick up the check. He had a couple of Muslim brothers meet me at the front desk to escort me to his room. I was excited to get that money. I was disappointed it was not 50,000, but I was in no position to turn anything down. I didn't know what I was going to do with the money, but what I did know is that I felt good about the fact that I was going to be home with my four children and be able to provide for them, at least for a while.

My plan was to get a job as soon as possible so that I wouldn't have to spend all my money fast. When I got the check from Barry, it was for$24,000. *"I thought it would be for $30,000?"* I said.

"Robert told Derrel to deduct the computer he just brought you, the watch that was stolen from him and also for my computer that was stolen." he said as he hunched his shoulders, giving me a smirk as if you know who you're dealing with. Here I was again, wanting to tear Robert's head off.

It was then I understood why Barry had security with him because if not for the Muslim brothers being there, I would have probably went off into a rage on him. I was boiling hot inside. Nothing was going right for me, yet again. I asked myself, *"Why were people taking my kindness for a weakness?"* As I drove home with the $24,000 check in my hand I told Barry right before I left, *"All right, Barry, but you know this is wrong. He gone end up fucking over you too."* I was warning him about Robert. *"Watch,"* I told him. *"Robert always crosses the ones closest to him. Watch what I tell you, Barry."* I shook his hand as I left. *"Take care, B.,"* I said and walked away.

CHAPTER 24

On My Own!

HE $24,000 WASN'T a lot of money at all for all the time and hard work I put in with Robert. All the years of service, I thought, as I drove home to my children, and this was the thanks I get. Oh well, I was determined to make the best of it. The first thing I had to do was to find a bigger and better place for me and my children to live in.

My mother had given me a number to call to see if I could qualify for low-income housing. I wasn't too proud to seek assistance for my children and me, plus they were already getting public aid because I never got insurance for them. At first, I used to be a bit embarrassed to go to the aid office, but I put that pride aside. My old days of doing wrong to make a buck were put behind me the day Demetrius Jr. was born. I wasn't going to do anything to jeopardize me being taken away from my children. For them, I was all they had, and for me, they were all I had. I needed them even more than they needed me; they were my life and my reason for living. Being with them, watching them grow and helping them develop was my very purpose.

Daily as I watched them grow, I saw in them the entertainer that was in me. There was nothing more important than for me to make a better way for them. When I made that phone call to the number my mother had given me, I got through to an operator who questioned me on my financial background. She determined that because I was raised in the projects and been on welfare all my life and now being a single parent, I qualified to receive section 8 housing. I thought it was truly a blessing because now I could afford to maintain housing for my children and myself without having being pushed into a corner to make ends meet.

Once I received the paperwork from Cook County Housing Authority, I found a three-bedroom house in Wheeling, Illinois. The rent was $1,200 a month; Section 8 would pay only $900 of the rent per month. But, the owner did not want to rent to me because I was not employed. He felt

I would have a problem paying him the $300 balance of the rent every month. That would have been a true assumption had it not been for the severance check I had received from Bass Productions. I made a deal with him, agreed to pay him $300 in advance for the whole year of the rental agreement if he would accept the Section 8. He agreed, and I gave him a check for $3,600. Everything was working and falling in place. Once the contract for the Section 8 was approved, I was able to move into my first house. Even though it was a rental, for the time being it was mine. I had a yard with grass, a two-car garage, wall-to-wall carpeting, and the best part of it all was that it was a safe environment for my children. It was out of the hood. Don't get me wrong, it's not that I was looking down on the hood and being raised in the projects. I learned some very valuable lessons coming up on the West Side of Chicago and the projects.

It was just that the street lessons my children would need to know I would teach them. I wanted them to have the best of everything I didn't have. The school system in Wheeling was better. They would not have to worry about being involved in gangs. I wanted them to be able to focus on school and getting their education. When it came time for us to move into our house, my children were so excited. Finally, we were all going to live together. Ashley was so excited because she would have her own room. *"This is my room Daddy,"* she would say joyfully. My three sons Demetrius "Meechie," Deontae "Lil Cool," and DeAndre "D. Jilla," were so glad they were going to be together. They had a thing for competing with each other. I was so blessed and not like other fathers who had baby mama drama, Lawanda had never had a problem with my son, Demetrius, being with me. She knew I wanted my children to be under the same roof and she supported that. She once told me, "you his daddy how else is he going to know how to be a man."

The house was totally empty when we first moved in. With the exception of the few clothes we had, I had never had furniture, dishes or anything, so I was going to have to go shopping. We went to Harlem Furniture Store and picked out furniture for every room. I brought a living room set, big-screen television with a surround sound stereo system, complete bedroom sets for my children's rooms, curtains, pots, pans, and, for myself, a king-sized bed, as well as televisions for each room. This was the happiest time of my life. I knew that finally I was going to be able to come home and be with my four children every day! I was going to be able to wake up every morning and have breakfast with my family. This was all I ever wanted to be able to do.

It was around August 1996 when my financial situation began to change. I got a job answering phones and taking catalog orders for J. C. Penny. It was a pretty good job. I was only earning $8.55 an hour. It was a means that I felt was better than nothing at all. During this time, I was dating "Sonia" Myles, a young lady I was attracted too. She was special. As a matter of fact, I used to rush home from work every evening to get home to that girl. With Sonia and all the children, everything was complete in my life. Her family, my family and our friends would come by for a visit and compliment us on how good and happy we looked together. I was very happy! On October 16, 1996, I asked her to marry me. I gave her a ring, I got on my knees, we cried together and she accepted. I was in love. For the first time in my life I felt that I was at home with Sonia; my family was complete.

The little money I was making working for JC Penney was not enough to feed and clothe a family of five. But I was willing to go to work as long as I could come home to my children and Max under one roof. Yes indeed, I was willing. Now I had a girlfriend and with both of us making a little money I felt together we could make ends meet. One good thing was I could at least feed the whole family because I was receiving food stamps. That little $24,000 had all been spent within a two month period. My babe, Sonia she didn't complain.

We were comfortable with each other. So that made things bearable. But with birthdays coming up, the children needing things for school and Christmas right around the corner, I began to stress about being broke all the time. Hell, I wanted to be able to take my woman out, and I wanted to be able to take my children out, to Chuck E. Cheese, Great America or just to the beach!

It had been years now since I was not able to go to the mall and just shop. We would go to the mall, walk around as an outing and watch others spend money. Being broke was getting to me. It was getting to all of us in some way or another. I had a partner named Rome who lived on 79th & Ashland. Rome and I had hung out together smoking for many nights. He had walked away from the pipe long before me and vowed he would never use again. I ran into him when I was out and about in the area of his house one day. I didn't know where he lived I just happened to run into him. We were friends and struggled together in our younger years. During that time, we became diehard friends. If there was some kind of dispute with somebody, I had his back and he had mine.

I decided to ride south to pay him a visit. I heard he came up in the dope game, and sure enough, when I met with him, he had come up. He was juggling keys of cocaine and pounds of weed. I sat and talked with him about my financial situation, and he was rather upset over what R. Kelly did to me when I was as loyal as I was to him. He told me *"Fuck that nigga Cool. You know it ain't nothing with me and you. Shit, you my brother. What you need? I can give you an ounce of this powder and a pound to get you started. Will that work for you?"* he asked.

I thought about it for a moment. I hadn't been around or seen any cocaine since 1985. The thought of having some of that in my possession, and an ounce at that, was making me have second thoughts. I decided against it.

"Hey, Rome, the weed I can handle, but I don't want no 'Cain," I told him.

"That's cool, Cool. You know you better than me," he said. *"I remember the times we went out on that shit. I put it in my mind not to ever fuck with it again, and I haven't, other than selling that shit. If you don't know for sure that you not gone fuck with that shit, then you doing the best thing for yourself to not want to handle the shit."*

I took the pound of weed that day and went home. Sonia and I bagged the weed up. We made it known to the few friends we had that we had weed for sale. But by us just starting off in the business and being in the suburbs away from everybody, we weren't making any money so Sonia and I ended up smoking the whole pound. We tried to sell it. She would even go and stay at her apartment complex because there were more people around her place that smoked and hung outside the building. But when I would allow her to go home, I would miss her at night, so having her out selling weed wasn't what I wanted her doing. I made enough money off the pound to pay Rome what it cost. He only wanted $400 back and then he gave me another pound. Sonia and I would smoke, smoke, smoke. We didn't make much profit at all.

Things started to change when I began going to my mother and borrowing money from her. One day Sonia, our children, and I were going on a trip to Milwaukee, Wisconsin to visit my sister Linda. We were at a gas station getting gas and I only had a couple of dollars. When I pulled out my wallet, I noticed that I still had R. Kelly's old American Express credit card with my name on it. I slid it through the gas machine and it still worked. I filled up my tank. I thought it would have been cancelled, but it worked. I went on a shopping spree on the way to Milwaukee.

We stopped and brought boots for the children. Then we went to the mall in Milwaukee and I brought gold chains, clothes, and when we got back home, we went to the mall again. I even took my mother furniture shopping at Harlem Furniture and brought her a living room set. I brought my sister Ce-Ce a computer, printer and all. Some of my family members who were hurting and sleeping on crates, I took them shopping and brought beds for brothers wife because he was incarcerated at the time. I also furnished Sonia's house with a living room set and a bedroom set for her son, Malcolm. It seemed that once she got that furniture then things began to go downhill. Sonia was still living by herself, and I was living in my house. More often she would spend days and sometimes weeks at my place, running back and forth from her house to mine, so I suggested she move in with me since she was always there and we wanted to be together.

For some odd reason, out of the blue, she decided that she wanted to spend time at her house. I would miss her on days when she didn't come over and stay with me, so we would spend time talking on the phone. Malcolm always wanted to be at my house, so I would keep him with me while she stayed home. One night my mom came by and it got too late for her to drive home so she thought about spending the night. That same night I talked to Sonia and before saying good night she kept reiterating how tired she was. *"I wish you were over here to give me a back rub babe,"* she said before we ended our conversation for the night. She did not know my mother was staying over when we were on the phone. When my ma said that she was staying for the night, I decided to go spend the night with Sonia at her apartment and give her that back rub that she had been wishing I was there for. I was going to surprise her with a bottle of Riuniti Lambrusco wine and kiss all over her body, all night. You had to be buzzed in to get into her building. However, when I arrived at the door, someone who knew me was going in so they let me in. When I got up to her apartment, I heard music and thought to myself, *"I thought she'd be sleep!"*

When I knocked on the door, she asked, *"Who is it?"*

"It's me babe," I responded. Instead of her opening the door, I heard whispering. A few moments later, she opened the door. *"What took you so long?"* I asked.

"I had just got out of the shower. I didn't have on any clothes," she said, looking a bit nervous.

"Well good," I said, looking at her with her robe on, stepping in and grabbing her at her waist and giving her a kiss. *"What are you doing here babe?"* she asked, closing the door behind me as I walked in. *"My mother came over while we were on the phone. She's there with the children and I thought I'd surprise you,"* I said as I reached at her to pull her near. The house smelled of some good weed and there were two cans of beer sitting

on her coffee table. I didn't say anything about it; I just felt something wasn't right. *"I'm going to the bathroom,"* I told her and walked in that direction. When I went into the bathroom, I closed the door, and a few seconds later, I opened and stepped back into the living room to see her trying to sneak a man out the front door.

"Babe! Who is that?" I asked

"This is Kim's friend," she said, referring to her sister Kim.

"So what the fuck is he doing coming out the kitchen?" I asked. *"And where is Kim?"*

"He was here waiting for Kim," she said.

"That's why you took so long opening the door, hiding him!" I said angrily.

The guy walked out, and when she closed the door behind him, I began to question her about the beer cans and why she was keeping him company with no clothes on under her robe; she was butt naked under her robe and speechless when I asked her about it.

"No wonder you want to stay home, the whore in your ass wanna roam, huh?" I said. I was hurt, and I couldn't believe she was cheating on me. I thought we were in love.

When I looked at her, she was no longer beautiful to me. I felt betrayed and disrespected. To be hurt by a woman was the story of my life with women thus far. Earlier that day I had made love to her, kissed all over her body, and now to think she was having sex with somebody else all the time. I went back into the bathroom to calm my nerves. As I was standing, looking in the mirror, I glanced down into the garbage and I saw two condom wrappers, and they weren't mine.

This triggered something in me. I stormed out of the bathroom. *"Whose are these?"* I asked, holding the condom wrappers, showing them to her. *"Kim was over here with him earlier,"* she said, lying through her teeth. She was disgusting to me. I was so hurt!

"You not supposed to just show up over here anyway," she said to me, trying to turn the blame around on me. *"I thought we had something real Sonia,"* I said with hurt in my voice, clearly showing my emotions.

"Demetrius, he don't mean nothing to me," she said like nothing she had done was wrong. *"So you admit it huh? He was here with you?"* I asked.

She just looked at me. I was so angry that I pushed her out of the way of the door, spit on her and left.

I was so hurt. All I have ever wanted in my life was one woman to love and build a family with. To be in one home with all my children, to come home from work and sit down in front of the TV with my family and loving on my wife. All I have ever wanted was someone that could withstand adversities with me.

Someone that was willing to go through the hard times as well as the good times. I loved every woman I have ever been with who had staying power. If they made a mistake, I was willing to forgive and use that mistake as a stepping stone. But it always seemed like I had to be perfect and not make mistakes. If I made a mistake, I could not be forgiven because I was supposed to be perfect. So I was often left to hurt as if my feelings never mattered.

I thought I was laying the pipe down and that no woman would cheat on me. Just the thought of me sleeping with her made me ill and it angered me even more.

What she didn't know was that I had keys to her house and while she was out with her new boyfriend, I went into her apartment. I searched through her things carefully so she wouldn't notice anyone had been there, and I found the title to her car that I bought her, as well as the engagement ring I gave her. I took them both and left quickly.

I knew she wouldn't know I took the title to her car. The ring yeah, but oh well, I thought. I felt somewhat vindicated, having the title and taking the ring back. *How you like me now?* I thought as I was driving back home. The next day, I had the title changed into my name. I approached her a few times while hanging out, trying to get her back into my life. I was lonely for her and hurt so much missing her. I felt like somebody close had died in my life. I was totally depressed.

She didn't care about my pain or the fact that she was a part of it. She called the police on me and had an order of protection put on me so I couldn't come near her. I looked forward to going to court. All that I wanted to do was see her paid back for the pain she caused me. Sonia resembled Robin Givens; and from her actions, she had some of her same characteristics.

When the judge told me that I had to stay away from her, I asked him if I could just have my car back that I was letting her drive. She was shocked at my request. She spoke up, telling the judge that the car she had was hers. All she knew was that the car was in her name. She had no idea that I had taken the title from her house. I told the judge I had let her use the car and that now I wanted it back. *"I have the title here, Your Honor,"* passing it to the court officer who took it to the judge to look at it.

I told Sonia as we left the courtroom that I had taken the ring too. *"What, you didn't believe me when I told you I used to be a burglar?"* I said sarcastically. I had heard she had accused her sister Kim of taking the ring. I felt good about paying her back and walked away with a smirk on my face. I did notice that she was wearing her boyfriend's name, Hosea, around her neck on the gold chain I gave her.

I was hurting so much over that girl. My brother Andre came from South Bend, Indiana, along with two women to comfort me, to help me get out of the depressed state of mind that I was in. I couldn't get into another woman. My heart was broken. And because I was ordered not go around Sonia it was hard living in Wheeling, Illinois not being able to see her, so I moved. I relocated me and my children to South Bend, Indiana. I decided to go live out there with my brother.

I found another house with the help of my brother and made the same financial agreement with my new landlord as I did in Wheeling, Illinois. I gave him a year's advance payment, and my section 8 was transferred. The house was even nicer and bigger than the one we had in Wheeling. I don't know what it was this woman had over me, but she had me going. I had to move 150 miles away from her. I had it bad. I think she put some voodoo on me or something in my food because I moped around like I had lost my best friend. Being away helped me to get over her and I soon began to get my life back in order.

South Bend, Indiana was not too much different from Wheeling other than the fact we were far away from the city. However, I found South Bend to be a very comforting place and my children loved it there. A park was right across the street, just outside the front door so we spent a lot of time there. My children and I also went to all the festivities that went on in South Bend.

My brother Andre and I didn't spend a lot of time around each other growing up because I was in prison. He went into the Navy when he was nineteen and we were out of contact with each other for over eleven years. It was a blessing for me to spend time and get to know my brother as well as him getting to know me. The last time I saw my brother, I was on tour in Virginia and he was stationed there in Norfolk on the USS Austin. We got to see each other during my time there. Other than that, we spoke over the phone on occasions. Now we were living in the same city.

I got a chance to know his wife, Tisha, and their children. On top of that my children got a chance to meet their cousins and other family members.

I lived in South Bend, Indiana for two years and began to get bored. I met a few women that were nice there, but things were too slow out there for me. I needed a woman in my life, but there I was stressed, cooking, cleaning, sleeping alone and raising four children by myself. The women I met in South Bend were all beautiful, but none of them wanted to be involved because of the children.

They all liked my children, but the attention in which they required none of them could love me and my children enough to give themselves to me. I thought that for them *"I had too much baggage."* I didn't have time to go out to meet women and take them on dates. I had to be home after work, pick up my children from school, cook for them, feed them, bathe them, get their clothes ready for the next day, help them with homework and get them ready for bed. After all of that I had free time for myself. I could not go out and leave my children in the house alone. The women I met wanted more attention than I could give them. It's like some men can't deal or get too involved in a relationship with a woman because she has several children. To sum it up, I was stressed and sleeping alone every night.

I needed to be around the hommies and friends I grew up with. I knew they would come by, cook, watch the games and play cards. These were my social buddies; Carlos, Landa, Tyrone, John, Denise, Maria, Sheila, Dee-Dee, and Cheryl—and my family, I needed to be, somewhere tha felt like home.

We'd leave on a Friday after the kids got out of school. I'd visit Carlos who at the time lived with his sister Maria. They were into church seeking the Word. Maria asked me to go to church with them and I accepted. I ended up with them every weekend driving up there going to different churches, being guided by the Word. We began having Bible study and I became really involved traveling to visit different churches. I didn't know what it was I was looking for. All I knew was my life was busy going to church, and I was finding joy in doing so. I was leading a lifestyle of becoming a Christian.

We found ourselves visiting the Greater First Baptist Church in East Chicago Indiana, with the presiding Bishop Travis L. Grant. There was something about the Word he delivered. For the first time in my life, I truly felt the spirit of the Lord within me. It was the first time I ever felt connected to the Word. It was at the Greater First Baptist Church where the spiritual power descended on me and a faith was born within me. I always had a faith and desire to know God and a need within me to be able to feel His presence. Immediately I was hooked, and like no drug I had ever experienced, I had a craving for the Word of the Lord.

Demetrius Smith Sr.

When Bishop Grant was preaching, it seemed as if he was talking directly to me. He told me that by the renewing of my mind, that God was now my material and spiritual source of life. I felt this. It was gratifying when I went to the altar and received prayer from the Bishop before leaving church. *"God's got his angels covering you. The devil can tempt you, and even if and when you fall, he can't kill you. GOD wants to use you,"* he said.

I needed to hear something like that. I needed to have a greater belief of purpose for my life and how God wanted to use me. I wanted to be a servant to Him. Other than my children, who had given me purpose, I needed to know that God had a purpose for me. I needed God, and I wanted to learn to be obedient to what God wanted me to do. I didn't know what it was he wanted me to do. All I know was I wanted to be in church to learn all I could to be closer to Him. Other than that I knew that my life was headed down a road to destruction. I needed the Lord in my life. I needed to be surrounded by good because the pain in me wanted to burst out. *"Lord help me,"* I cried out so many nights!

CHAPTER 25

The Voice Within!

EVERYTHING BEGAN TO balance in my life again, up until the day Derrel McDavid, R. Kelly's accountant, called to tell me he wanted to see me. Even though things did not exactly end on good terms, I was happy. I missed Rob and the way things were prior to all the conflicts we had. We were like family which makes it that much more difficult to just walk away without wishing things were different. On top of that I needed a job. I knew Rob wanted me to come back but I was not going to go back to work for him under the same conditions. I was not willing to give up the relationship or the security I had found with my faith in GOD and the joy of being able to come home to my children every day. Nonetheless, I accepted the invitation from Derrel to attend one of R. Kelly's concerts at the United Center in Chicago. I was given tickets and backstage passes for me and my children, but instead of going backstage, we went straight back to my home church in East Chicago, Indiana.

A couple of days later I received another call from Derrel wanting to know why I didn't see them after the show. I told him I was with my children and I shared my new found faith in GOD and how I no longer wanted to be a part of something that seemed to keep me falling backwards in life. I went on to explain that I missed the action of the business, but I was content with life without all of the melodrama. Derrel let me know that Rob missed me and he had somewhat changed. He made me think that my faith and walk with God as a Christian could have an effect on Rob.

In my heart I wanted that to be true. I knew R. Kelly was a spiritual person and that his changed personality was caused by some demonic spirit with a plan to destroy him. As I talked to Derrel, a scripture came to my mind, Romans 8:28—"And we know that all things work together for good to those who love God, to those who are called according to His purpose."

Derrel suggested I go see Rob so I drove up north to the studio over in my old neighborhood by the Cabrini Green Projects.

When I arrived I was met at the entrance by Generaall, one of R. Kelly's hang-out buddies. He was around when I was there and was still hanging out in the lounge area of the studio, hoping for the opportunity to be produced as a rapper by R. Kelly. For now, he was still being a flunky for Rob, hanging around and running errands—underpaid like most people that clung to him. He told me R. Kelly allowed him to rap and co-write the song *"Fiesta"* off the R. Kelly TP-2 album.

You would think that a person who co-wrote a song with the famous R. Kelly would be paid and happy; "Fiesta" was a hit! But Generaall told me he was very disappointed with the way things were going for him. I told him he had to take a stand for himself, that as long as he lay around under R. Kelly, being his flunky, he wasn't going to do anything for him. He agreed with me and asked me for my phone number. He said he had some things he wanted to talk to me about. After I gave him my number, I went up to the studio where Rob was.

When I walked in the studio, R. Kelly was sitting back on the sofa with a young lady in between his legs. She was giving him head. I was disturbed by what I saw so I told him I'd wait out in the hall while he got himself together. *"Hold on, hold on,"* he said, stopping the girl and giving her instructions to wait in another part of the studio. *"Man, what's up, boy,"* he asked, getting up from the couch to give me a hug.

"Nothing, just come to check you out man. I see you still busy with the ladies," I responded. *"Damn, dawg, you still look the same,"* he said. *"You too, except for that hair you tryna grow,"* I said, rubbing my cheek, indicating the smooth cut beard and goatee he had grown.

"Yeah man, so what you doing these days man? I miss you," he said.

"I miss you too Rob," I said, nodding my head in agreement.

"I'm staying at a church in East Chicago, Indiana. I got saved man. I'm trying to turn my life completely around," I told him.

"That's good man, that's really good," he said and then added, *"I've been doing some gospel writing myself. Hey, Peter, pull up 'You Saved Me,'"* he yelled to the engineer Peter Mokran over the intercom who was in another room.

It was a gospel song! *How ironic!* I thought as I listened to the lyrics. *GOD was truly moving to join us together again,* I thought. After listening, we began to talk about me coming back on board. I was persistent in making him understand that things had to be different. I told him how I was in his corner and had his best interest at heart. He then told me that I have to start over and work my way back up again so I told him I would think about it. In the meantime, he just wanted me to hang out with him.

I couldn't see myself just hanging out. I only wanted to be a part of the business this time. I wanted everything I did to have meaning and purpose. *If this was meant to be, then this would work,* I thought. How ironic it was that a few weeks before I met up with Rob, I met a white girl name Shannon that had a voice out this world. In this day and time I would have compared her to Christina Aguilera. I told Robert about her and the fact that I wanted to manage her. I asked him if he would produce her for me. The first thing he asked was how old she was. He said he couldn't work with any girls under the age of eighteen anymore, and said he didn't know who to trust. *"Demetrius, I feel like girls are being planted on me,"* he said. I assured him that Shannon was nineteen, so he agreed to meet with her.

The next day I returned to the studio with Shannon. She was overly excited to meet R. Kelly. On the way there, I made it clear that the only way we were going to get any production out of R. Kelly was for her to follow my lead in dealing with him. When she auditioned Rob saw that she had talent and was a cute white girl with a soulful voice, he agreed to work with her under my management. When it was time to leave, he wanted her to stay at the studio with him. He said he had some tracks he was going to let her sing. I told him we'd continue the next day, but Shannon interrupted me, agreeing to stay. Right then, I was pissed with her because I knew R. Kelly was going to lock her in one of the studio rooms and keep her hostage, promising her this and that. And that's exactly what he did.

A few weeks passed and nothing was becoming of Shannon's recording. He had her singing with some other girls, but the real deal was he was fucking her and she had stopped listening to me. She wasn't allowed to go anywhere unless it was with him so after about a month of the same old thing; she was ready to come back with me. During this time, Generaall, decided to leave R. Kelly. He called me and said that he took my advice to do things on his own. He told me that he spoke to Barry Hankerson. Although Barry hadn't heard of him before the call, he asked Generaall for my number and mentioned that he wanted to talk to me.

I didn't know why. I hadn't talked to Barry for over two years. All I knew was that he and R.Kelly were going through something and they were cutting their business ties. I found that out because Rob let me read a letter he had written up for Barry Hankerson. He said Cheryl Cobb wrote the letter for him. The letter was announcing Rob's request to terminate Barry as his manager. *"Johnny man, I need you with me, especially dealing with Barry,"* he said. *"Rob, you just gotta pay me man. Like you said, who you*

Demetrius Smith Sr.

gone share all that money you got with?" I said, looking him dead in the eyes and not a freckle of a smile on my face.

I was serious about wanting to work for Rob. I still believed the best of Robert was still yet to come. This kid needed somebody with him who loved him and was not afraid to tell him the truth. He needed a true right-hand man and not a yes-man. I wanted that position with him, but I also had partiality for Barry too. Personally, I always felt Robert should have apologized to Barry for disrespecting him and his family by being intimate with their little girl, Aaliyah. Nonetheless, that was their business. I didn't want any part of their feud. I just wanted a job. I was living in a eight bedroom home connected to the church I belonged too with my children and all I wanted to do was make a better life for them and keep the joyous feeling I had in praising the Lord. I thought if GOD wasn't going to have the glory for my association with R. Kelly, then working with him was not what I wanted to do.

Shannon ended up living in the studio. Literally living there! Daily, I would go to check on her and I'd end up hanging out with Rob. One particular day, Rob took me to a fitness gym called East Bank Club on Kinzie & Hubbard, in downtown Chicago. This experience was something totally weird and an experience I will never forget. I wanted to believe GOD was the reason for my continued association with Rob, but this experience had me confused with who was really the head in this journey I was on.

Rob met with a trainer there and worked out. After the work-out we went to meet with a couple of his female friends in the restaurant area of the facility. I sat at a separate table as if I was his security, sipping on a cranberry juice, while Rob sat at a table right across from me entertaining his lady friends. I kept noticing Rob staring at me as if I was doing something wrong. I was thinking to myself, *"What's wrong with this dude? I hope he don't think I'm flirting with them girls."* Even though one of them kept turning around smiling at me, I paid her no mind. I said to myself, *"If he starts tripping about these girls, I'm outta of here."* I just was not dealing with his egotistical, pompous attitude. I wanted to be able to share happiness and not be caught up in senseless drama.

After a few moments with him staring back and forth at me, he all of a sudden jumped up from his table and motioned for me to follow him. I did, I got up and walked behind him, wondering to myself what's on his mind. I followed him to the men's bathroom. This was where we were going to end things if he mentioned anything about me and them girls. I didn't know what was on his mind. There were no girls or mischief on my mind. My life was for God's glory.

When we got into the bathroom, I asked, *"What's up, Rob?"* He had a serious look on his face, as if something heavy was on his mind. Soon as the bathroom door closed, he turned to me. *"Johnny man, I feel the spirit of the Lord on me,"* he said with a crying remorseful voice.

"Praise the Lord," I said. I instantly thought that GOD had intervened into our lives and something miraculous was about to start happening. I was so happy that the spirit of the Lord came on my heart as well. I began praising GOD in the bathroom and then we both began to speak in tongues. I was surprised at this. R. Kelly was so fluent with his speaking. I was still a baby, just experiencing this newfound greatness I was feeling. As I was dancing and praising, Rob was doing the same, but he was slowly drifting and dancing his way into the stalls, still speaking in tongues.

Then all of a sudden, his voice changed and no longer sounded like his voice. He started sounding demonic, as if another voice had taken him over and began speaking through him. The stall door closed and I started hearing this voice. It was similar to a voice you would hear in a demonic movie where a spirit overtakes you. Like in the movie *Exorcist,* when the demon took over the girl's body and started speaking through her. I couldn't understand a word: "Be-Ici-zess-be lig, Shun-mo-co-das-ala-tame-shala." This voice continued for several minutes. I didn't know what the hell was going on.

I became fearful, to be honest with you. At that moment, I began to plead the blood of Jesus, asking the Lord to protect me, let no weapon formed against me prosper. The spiritual encounter we had in that men's bathroom went for forty to forty-five minutes, and even though we were in the only bathroom of a crowded facility, no one came in the bathroom.

When it was over, we came out and walked straight back to our seats as if nothing ever happened. I felt strange and wanted to understand, but Robert didn't want to talk about it. I didn't know what I was dealing with. This was on the top of my list of spiritual experiences. I didn't know if it was the Holy Spirit speaking through Rob or the devil. I was in a confused state of mind after witnessing what I had just gone through.

After we left the restaurant, he still did not want to talk about it. He felt like the Holy Spirit that was on him before going into the bathroom was just a moment that he felt he had to praise God. It was a deep moment for me though. I wouldn't let it go that easy. *"Rob man, I didn't know you spoke in tongues like that,"* I said to him. *"I know the Lord,"* Rob said. He

Demetrius Smith Sr.

turned the music up in the car to drown out our conversation. It puzzled me because now I was wondering if this was in any way connected with a demonic group I heard of, the Illuminati. He disregarded the situation, but it left me in wonder as well as slight fear, of the unrecognizable voice. Had this man indeed sold his soul to the devil for mere stardom?

That evening when I got home, I went to speak with my bishop, Bishop Travis L. Grant. He took me to 1 Corinthians, Chapter 14. He would not come straight out and tell me that I had come into contact with an evil spirit because he hadn't witnessed it himself, but from what I had explained to him, he said it was possible that I had come in contact with a strong demon. I believed him because that was the weirdest spiritual thing I ever witnessed. From that moment on, I knew that demons did exist. I looked at Robert in a whole new light.

After that day in the bathroom, things began to change for me with women. I began to have strong desires to have sex with every woman I saw. The women began to make sexual gestures and come on to me. I was leaving choir rehearsal and taking the members of my church to my house, which was adjacent to the church, to have sex with them. It was all so easy. It was like the women had the same spirit on them. They were seeking me out. My presence became a controversy within the church. The Bishop called me into his office one day and asked me what was going on with me and several members. I didn't lie. I told him that I was having sex with some of them.

Wherever I went, I was flirting or being flirted with. I began to believe that R. Kelly's sex demon had entered me in that bathroom. The oversexed attitude started the evening I left the restaurant. Things were changing. My spirituality was being tested, and I was losing the battle. I wanted to have sex with every woman I came in contact with. That wasn't me.

Generaall told me he gave Barry my number, but I wasn't expecting him to really call me, *"For what" w*as my thought?

"Demetrius, what's happening, man. I been tryna reach you, boy. How have you been?" Barry asked, sounding happy that he was able to reach me.

"I'm fine, B, what's happening with you?" I asked.

"You working?" he asked.

"Nawl man, I'm living in a church home, tryna get my life right," I responded.

*"Living in a churc*h?" he said. *"Why haven't you called me? If you were going through something, you can always call me, you know that,"* he said.

"Well I've just been tryna get my life right, Barry," I said.

"Well I got work for you. You don't have to live in a church, and how are the kids?" he asked.

Barry showed signs of true compassion towards my living situation. He informed me that Generaall gave him my number and he mentioned that Generaall told him that he had something he wanted him to see. Both Barry and I wanted to investigate whatever it was Generaall was talking about. *"But first, before you do anything, come down here to New York. Let me show you around the office, meet some people and let me get you started working for Black Ground. What I've got for you to do, you can do from home,"* he said. That information aroused my curiosity. That next day, I was on a plane to New York—round-trip ticket and with a room paid for by Barry Hankerson and Black Ground Enterprises.

Change was once again occurring in my life. The life I thought I had put behind me was resurfacing. When I got to New York, Barry put me at the Empire Hotel, a place and area I was familiar with from my travel back and forth to New York with R. Kelly. Barry had a car pick me up at the hotel, take me to his office at 155 Nineteenth Street. Barry was really happy to see me, and I was happy to see him also. He took me around to see everyone who worked for his record company.

The position he offered me was Director of Promotions. I was to be in charge of getting urban radio stations to play Black Ground Enterprises artists' songs. He gave me a list of every radio station's directory. My job was to call them and get them to play Aaliyah and Tank.

I was excited about this job. It was a real job and I could work it from home with the record company paying the phone bill. Barry offered me $40,000 a year and when I would have to travel to different cities, my expenses would be paid by the company. I accepted the job. It required me to talk and be persuasive, which was second nature to me. I stayed with Barry, visiting his office for two days. When I got back to Chicago, I had an $800 check with me. I had been paid for the first week in advance.

It had been a while since I had money. I was so excited that I went to work on the phone right away. Barry shipped cases of Tank's album to me so I began to call directors of radio stations in the South. After talking to several directors, I had to send them a copy of Tank's CD. I had a gift of gab already from way back when I was working with Clifford, so to be personable with people, to make them like me and to make them laugh was somewhat easy for me.

Within the first week I found myself making friends over the phone and being invited to attend different radio station functions from Georgia to

North Carolina. Barry began to get calls about me with people requesting that I attend their parties. I was definitely making an impression on the people I was in contact with. I was able to get a few of the stations to add Tank on their play list. I thought I was doing what Barry wanted me to do, but Barry told me to slow down. He wasn't ready for me to start flying here and there just yet. So basically, I mailed CDs out and gave the CDs a chance to reach its destination before making any follow-up calls.

As the weeks passed, Barry sent my checks to me by FedEx on time every Friday morning. During this time, R. Kelly was pursuing me also. I told him that I was considering working for Barry which really angered him. I asked him if he was ready to put me on the payroll. Once again he told me I'd have to hang around and work my way back up. *"I have to live Rob. I have to take care of my family,"* I told him. When I asked how much he was going to pay me to hang around, he told me he'd pay me $300 a week. *"But I can't have you with me if you're working for Barry,"* he said. I told him $300 wouldn't be enough for me, and that's when he mentioned Shannon.

"Yo girl, man I really won't be able to work with her. She really ain't got what it takes." I knew that was bullshit. Shannon apologized for not listening to me, but it was all good. I liked Shannon so I figured I would just introduce her to Barry. Since Shannon had been staying in one of the corner rooms of the studio, she had nowhere to stay so she went back home with me.

I was uncomfortable with her being there with me, and I was uneasy about what people in the church would think about me having a young white girl staying with me. So I kept her on the down low for a couple of days and then took her back to South Bend. Generaall was calling me a lot more now that I was with Barry. He wanted a record deal and was angry with R. Kelly. He asked me if I could keep a secret and when I told him I could, he told me he acquired some of Rob's personal tapes and he wanted to sell them.

It was a fact that R. Kelly's gym bag was recently stolen from him at a gym on the West Side. Inside the bag were supposed to be some personal tapes of R. Kelly and a diamond necklace worth 10K or more. Rob had a reward out for that bag and he asked me to keep an eye and ear open for information regarding it. Up until then, I hadn't heard or seen anything regarding the bag or the tapes.

The first person Generaall wanted to contact and show the tapes to was Barry. He asked me if I could set it up for him to meet with Barry. I told him I'd give Barry a call, and I did. Barry was not really interested in the tapes. He told me to keep my focus on the job and to beware of Generaall as well as R. Kelly. He told me he was trying to help me get my life straight and that I didn't need to involve myself in anybody else's drama.

A week passed and I hadn't heard from Barry. One night he called me after 10:30 p.m. telling me he had received a letter from Robert and his attorneys saying Rob no longer wanted him as his manager. Barry felt disrespected by R. Kelly. To Barry, R. Kelly was *"a piece of shit,"* he owed him a lot of money and was refusing to pay.

This betrayal peaked his interest in wanting to know what was on the tapes. Barry then asked me to meet with Generaall to view the tapes. When I called Generaall, he informed me that he was home in Philly so Barry flew me out there. Generaall met me at the hotel I stayed in. Of course he didn't come alone. He was accompanied by two other guys who stood while we viewed the tapes as if they were there as his security. Before letting me view the tapes he told me this was not a joke, the people behind him are playing for keeps so I better be looking out for myself. The tapes were of different sexual encounters that R. Kelly had with several girls. Please note—this was not the tape with R. Kelly urinating on that little girl he went to trial for.

Most of these girls seemed to be mature adults. However, Generaall didn't show me all the tapes he had. I asked Generaall what he wanted and he told me that he wanted a record deal and some cash. *"I also have some other tapes but I want to wait to show those to Barry if he decides to meet with me. If not, then I have some other people that are interested in putting these tapes out,"* he said. The tapes I saw were nonetheless incriminating and would indeed damage R. Kelly's reputation. Most of the woman on the tapes were of adult women. But there were two on there that did look like they were very young girls. This bothered me for some reason. I felt a bit of pain for R. Kelly and a need to help him.

I spoke to Barry once Generaall left my hotel room. I told him what was on the tapes, and after we talked, he said he'd give Generaall a call himself. I flew back home that night. I thought *if only Rob had me with him and had treated me right none of this would be happening. I protected him, I had his back. Now these other people he let in, they were snakes out to destroy him.* Once I arrived in Chicago and got into my car, I decided to drive over to the studio in hopes that Rob was there, and he was.

"What's happening Demetrius?" he asked. *"What brings you out?"* I didn't waste time with him, beating around the bush. *"Rob, somebody's out to hurt*

you," I told him. *"What are you talking about?"* he asked. *"I saw the tapes,"* I told him. *"Who's got 'em?"* he asked.

"I can't tell you that Rob, 'cause it would endanger me. All I know is we can get 'em. Even if you have to buy them back, you need to get them," I told him.

"You need to tell me who got them. Either you're with me or against me Demetrius. I need to get them and if you can't tell me, then you need to leave," he said. *"I'm not about to be extorted by nobody!"* he went on to say. *"Who got them?!"* he asked again.

"Rob, I can't tell you that. Every time in the past I have turned some information over to you, you'd set me up, leaving me to be the fall guy. I can't do it in this case, there are some very dangerous people in possession of your tapes man, and I'm not going to set myself up to be hurt."

Generaall gave me some names of some of notorious people that were also interested in the tapes. I didn't feel Rob would have my back, and because I would not expose who had the tapes, Rob told me he would look at me as his enemy along with Barry.

Finally, I left, and I felt good about what I did to warn Robert; it was all I could do. I wished he would have thought about how in the past I had always been upfront with him and how I always did what was needed to protect him. As I was driving, I thought to myself how Rob felt he and his money could get him out of anything. I left it at that. I was ready to get back to my life. I didn't want anything to do with the tapes or assisting Barry to get the tapes from Generaall any longer. I just wanted to work the job Barry gave me. I was somewhat disappointed though because although I had hopes of being back in association with Rob, I realized that it was not God's will.

It was clear to me as I was driving home who I was going to be working for. Rob was no longer someone I was going to concern myself with any longer. The job Barry had me doing was a new beginning for me. That job and that job only was good for me as far as I was concerned. Barry and whoever else wanted the tapes that were stolen from Rob were going to have to leave me out of that part of their business.

That night, when I got home, Generaall called. He had a young lady on the line with him. *"Demetrius, I got this girl on the line with us. I told her how you assisted Tia with getting an attorney, and she wants you to help her, and she's willing to pay you too,"* he said. I immediately told him I didn't want any part of it. I asked him why he was so stuck on bringing Rob down. He said he just thought I would be interested in making some real money. "*No, I don't want any part of any of it, the tape or nothing else,*" I said. "*As far as the tapes are concerned, we won't discuss that*", he said, seeming a bit nervous that I mentioned it with the girl being on the phone.

When I told them I had to get off the phone, the young lady spoke for the first time to ask me if I could refer her to an attorney. "*No young lady, I don't know of anybody.*" Generaall asked me if I knew the name of the attorney Tia used. I insisted at that time that I had to go. I wished the young lady good luck in her pursuit to find a lawyer and said my goodbyes. Generaall asked if he could call me back after he had finished with whoever the girl was he had on the line with us, said he had to speak to me about something personal.

It was an hour later when he called me. I was just about to fall asleep when the phone rang. "*Man, Barry Trippin',*" he said. He said that Barry wasn't interested in the tapes. He went on to mention that some of his own people had set up a meeting for him in LA with someone that was interested in the tapes. He asked me if I wanted to go along with him and offered me 10 percent of whatever he would get off the tapes. I asked him how much he was asking, and he told me $50,000 for each tape he had. I'm not going to lie. I thought about taking him up on his offer but I decided to pass. I turned over and looked at my daughter lying in the bed in a peaceful sleep; it confirmed that I was content working for Barry and receiving the $800 a week I was getting.

The next day, I spoke to Barry and told him about the girl Generaall had on the phone when he called me. Barry advised me to stay out of it as he himself said he didn't want anything to do with the tapes that Generaall was trying to sell him. After that Barry and I were on the phone with each other every day. I kind of felt he was a bit obsessed with Rob because he was all we talked about. We talked about the old days and what we thought could have been done to make things turn out better. Barry knew as I did that Rob was alone. The people that were around him in the beginning weren't there anymore, and he didn't really know the new people he had working for him. Barry and I both felt most of them were flunkies, and yes-men. We knew that R. Kelly's problems were just beginning.

Barry was sounding a lot like me, hoping that Robert would reach out, apologize and allow all of us to pick up where we left off-taking his musical career to the next level. It was just wishful thinking. Barry's love for Rob was mixed with the pain that was caused when he messed with Aaliyah. Rob would never admit that he was wrong concerning Aaliyah. He stood by the choices he made and the way he treated the people that cared about him most.

I took Barry's advice not to call Generaall anymore, but he still called me, giving me updates on the progress he was making with selling the videos. He also told me that the girl he had on the phone for a referral to a lawyer, found one in Chicago and they were coming to the Chi to meet with her. He asked me to talk to Barry to arrange an audition for him. Generaall still wanted a record deal.

CHAPTER 26

The Setup / L. A. Bound

ORKING AS A director of promotions was still bringing in a
weekly paycheck and I really wasn't doing a lot of work. I was
on the phone with Barry every day. As I said, he was obsessed
with Robert and I somewhat felt like I could get them together. I felt they
both needed to be face-to-face in the same room with one another. When
I would suggest it to either of them, they both had negative things to say
about each other. I saw through their façade and knew that they both had
a love for each other, but pride wouldn't allow either of them to humble
themselves to gain unity.

Once, while Barry and I were on the phone, the young lady from
Miami called. She was the one Generaall had asked to call me. She told me
she was in Chicago to meet with an attorney and she was at the Conrad
Hilton Hotel in downtown Chicago. I put her on hold and clicked over
to tell Barry that she invited me to the hotel to have dinner with her and
her aunt. I asked Barry what he thought and he told me to go see what
they were up to, but to be careful not to say anything to them that would
incriminate me as being part of any scheme.

Barry was like me when it came to R. Kelly. If we knew something
was going on that may cause him trouble, he wanted to be on top of it.
Barry always gave me the impression that in spite of what they were going
through, if Rob would just ask, Barry would, without hesitation, come to
his aide. I accepted the young lady's invitation and told them I'd be right
down. When I arrived to her room in the Conrad Hilton, which is an
expensive hotel, being that it was right in the heart of downtown Chicago,
I was uneasy and wondered how this young girl could afford to stay at this
hotel.

Nonetheless, when she came to the door, I was invited in and
introduced to her aunt who was lying on one of the double beds. Her
name didn't register because my mind was scoping out my surroundings.

Her aunt started to question me about what I wanted for helping her niece. *"I actually haven't done anything to help your niece and I don't want anything. This is all her doing."* I told her, pointing to her niece. *"I came down for the free meal and to meet this gorgeous aunt that she told me about,"* I responded in a flirtatious way.

Her aunt didn't move much from the position she was laying in when I walked in the room. Right when I was about to sit down, there was a knock on the door. I was somewhat startled, *"Just relax,"* the aunt said as she finally got up from the bed to answer the door. *"We ordered food just before you came,"* she said, opening the door. When she opened the door, a big bald-headed white guy came in, holding a badge out.

"Demetrius, just relax. My name is Jack Paladino, I'm a detective, and we've got you for trying to persuade this young lady to bring false charges against R. Kelly."

"What?" I asked. I was shocked and scared at the same time. I didn't feel like I did anything wrong and I wanted nothing to do with the law and being arrested. *"Just relax, Demetrius,"* Paladino said again as he began to sit across from me. *"We don't want you, Demetrius,"* he said, *"even though I can bring up several charges against you, with you looking at least doing five years in Statesville with your record. We want Barry Hankerson. "*At that point, I just sat back and listened, looking around calmly for the opportunity to escape.

I figured the way he came in, if he was a detective, I was set up, and I was waiting and looking for the backup police to come in. *"We know that Barry Hankerson is behind this by manipulating you to turn this girl against R. Kelly, and we know that you and him are in possession of some missing tapes. Mr. Kelly told me to tell you that if you work with us, we'll compensate you."*

In my mind, I thought, *Rob crossed me again.*

"Think about it for a minute Demetrius before you answer because as of right now, you're going down and you're looking at about five years." Paladino sat back trying to be cool as if he had gotten through to me.

I must admit, sitting there with the thought of going to jail and serving five years had me shaky, but when I didn't see any other Chicago police arriving, I began to think of a way to get out of that room.

"I need to talk to my pastor," I said. *"I ain't did nothing wrong,"* I said. I got from my seat and went to the telephone. *"I'm calling my pastor, he knows about all of this,"* I said and picked up the phone. I dialed a 1-800 number that gave me a direct line to call out so that the number that I had dialed would not register to the hotel room. I did not want them to know that I

called Barry. He was expecting my call because he told me to call him and let him know what was going on with this girl. He answered the phone.

"Bishop Grant," I said, pretending I was talking to my pastor, *"they got me in a room, saying I'm under arrest for trying to set R. Kelly up."*

"Are they right there with you?" Barry asked.

"Yes, sir," I said, and then I whispered into the phone letting Barry know that I was using a toll free 1-800 number so they can't trace the call. *"Yeah, well you need to get out of there. If there aren't any other police officers there, just leave. He can't stop you. He has no authority to put his hands on you. You haven't done anything wrong. Just don't talk to him about anything and call me when you get to a free line,"*

Barry said. *"All right,"* I said and hung up. I got off the phone and became belligerent, walking toward the door to leave. *"I'm not getting ready to sit here and allow you to threaten me, and I ain't done nothing wrong, y'all trying to set me up. I'm leaving! If you're a police officer, where is your back up?"* I asked him, hunching my shoulders to indicate to him I was ready to get physical! *"I don't know you and I ain't standing here and letting you intimidate me,"* I said.

I was hoping that this dude didn't reach out to grab at me as I made my way to the door; wondering to myself, *What the hell have I gotten myself into again, dammit,* I thought, *fucking with Robert Kelly!*

Paladino began to move at me toward the door as if he was about to try and stop me. *"You better not put your fucking hands on me man, 'cause I will be going to jail for fucking your ass up if you put your hands on me,"* I told him, and I was serious. My spirituality had been compromised. All I wanted to do was get out of that room and get back home. I walked out the door and Paladino followed close behind.

"You're not going to get away Demetrius. If I was you, I'd cooperate because I can have you arrested right now," he said. *"Well you ain't me motherfucker,"* I told him, and I left.

As I stepped into the hallway, I was looking for his back-up police officers, and there were none. Paladino was behind me and got on the elevator with me. I didn't say shit to him and wasn't hearing shit he was saying. My mind was thinking, *"When this elevator stops, if ain't no police in the lobby, dude would have to step up off following me."* When I got downstairs, there were still no police around. I turned to the dude, Paladino, that is, *"Man you need to get away from me. If you were going to arrest me, I'd be cuffed by now, so you need to get up off me man, and stop following me,"* I told him as I began walking toward the exit.

Demetrius Smith Sr.

Paladino looked the opposite direction, waving toward the main lobby of the hotel and yelling for house security. While he was looking for backup, I quickened my steps. As soon as I got out door and turned a corner, I broke and ran to my car. I was safe now. He wasn't going to catch me, not tonight that is. Lock me up? I didn't think so, at least not then. I was happy and nervous at the same time. When I got to my car, I felt the adrenalin rush from being a free man.

Just moments ago, my freedom had been threatened.

I had gone to Rob like a man, with his best interest at heart, warning him that someone was out to hurt him and this punk wanna put a private detective on me to try to set me up; some real Perry Mason punk-ass shit. Driving home, I thought about Generaall. I was trying to figure out how he was involved. This dude had tapes on Rob. But I wondered why would he put this girl on me like that. Maybe he didn't have more than one tape. Maybe he was using the one he showed me so he could pull me into Rob's web and set Barry up.

I thought about Barry's words, of how he felt like Rob was, "a low-down piece of shit." And I was saddened because I felt the same way. He tried to set me up instead of coming to me as a man, as a friend and as a brother. I always showed that type of love for him. This dude was out of pocket. He had sent a private investigator at me and threatened to take me away from my children. I was angry at Rob and at Generaall.

When I got back home to the convent, I parked my car a block away and walked to my house. I figured if the police or anyone came looking for me, I could get out of the house without them seeing me and get safely to my car. I wasn't going to jail, that was out of the question. I wondered why GOD brought these people back into my life to cause me trouble. My life was going well. I didn't have money, but I was building a life of promise by being in the church.

In the short period of time I had connected back with R. Kelly, I had come into contact with his sex demon, now I was a whoremonger and on top of that, I was about to become an outlaw; a possible fugitive on the run. The very thought of going to jail and leaving my children, made me ready to do a James Cagney on a motherfucker. Even though I hadn't done anything, I wasn't going down without a fight.

When I got into the house, I called Barry. *"B, what's happening man?"*

"You tell me. Where are you at?" he asked. *"I'm at home. I left that hotel as soon as I got off the phone with you."* I told him.

"So what happened? What was all that about?" he asked.

I told him what transpired throughout that short period of time. I told him that I felt Generaall and R. Kelly tried setting me up in an effort to get me to join sides with them by accusing him(Barry) of being the mastermind of any and all wrongful acts that were in R. Kelly's way.

"What?" Barry said, surprised. *"What are you talking about again?"* he asked, as if he didn't understand me.

"Yeah, B, that dude Paladino told me they knew you were behind R. Kelly's missing tapes and you were manipulating me to persuade the girl Generaall brought to me to file charges on R. Kelly."

"Demetrius you're kidding, right?" Barry asked.

"Naw B, Paladino told me I was looking at five years and that they were going to prosecute me."

"Well you need to get away from there for a few days. Come up here and let me get you an attorney to get them to look into this from a legal point to get them off you. What's wrong with Rob, man?" Barry asked me.

"I don't know, B. I just don't want any drama. I just want to work and be able to support my children B. I thought I had walked away from this drama and now they're pulling me right back in again," I said jokingly.

"Yeah, well you need to get on up here until we straighten this out. When can you get here?" he asked.

"Well, I've got to get my sister to come babysit, and I'm gone need some money to take care of her," I said.

"I'll get my secretary to call you with your flight information for tomorrow evening. What's your sister's name?" he asked. *"I'll wire her some money to keep the kids for you. Get in contact with me if you need anything before then. And call that boy Generaall and see what he has to say about this and I'll talk to you later,"* he said before he hung up.

I was fortunate to have Barry Hankerson on my side. Funny how GOD puts things in place—when we don't think there's a way out, he's already provided for us in advance. I wanted to do the right thing in God's eyes concerning the decisions I was making with going to LA and in dealing with R. Kelly. My true thoughts were to cut my ties with Rob. I just wanted to be able to be at home raising my children.

After I got off the phone I called Generaall. He was astounded when I told him of what I had gone through with the young lady he gave my number to.

"You bullshitting, that funky ass little bitch was planted on us man" were his words. I told him that I felt he was a part of the plot.

"If I was part of setting you up, then why would I have these tapes," he asked me. Generaall swore he wasn't part of any plot to bring Barry or myself down. He told me that he was going to be in LA the coming week to meet with some people that were supposed to purchase the tapes he had. Generaall offered to give me a little of the money he would make off the sale to assure me that he was not part of the incident with the girl and Jack Paladino. The idea to receive some cash sounded appealing to me. I wasn't going to turn down any free money. If he was just going to give, then for sure I would take it. Thank you!

In reality though? My plan for being in LA was to see if it was possible to establish a foundation and a relationship for me and with my children. If everybody around me was hustling and taking money from each other then that was their business. But for anyone to assume me to be guilty by association is not fare. I wanted to begin to separate myself from bonds which held me to the past. I did not want to continue to be in association with Robert, Barry and any and everything that was coming with them. For now I was going to go along and see if I could make my ride smooth. It had been too many years and it has just not been conducive for me. I was Leary of association. I was a victim in knowing there was no truth in these cats. Yeah, things would roll for a minute. But man, I was tired of holding onto a rope. With them, everything kept changing. It was like; Rob was a relative of Murphy's Law. With him, everything that could go wrong did go wrong. I wanted something solid for once in my life. Oh yeah, It would have been lovely, but that ride was over.

As I was sitting in the terminal waiting to board my plane, I read my Bible. I wanted to keep focused. I felt better than I had ever felt, being into church and a babe in Christ. I didn't want to go to LA and lose that feeling of joy that was a part of my life now. As I read I would flip open a page and the scripture which appeared in front of me would say something that seemed to always refer to what I was going through in my life or related to an answer I was in need of. Chronicles 20:15 says, *"Do not be afraid nor dismayed because of this great multitude, for the battle is not yours, but God's."*

When I would receive comforting words such as those, I felt my path was being guided by the Holy Spirit. Don't get me wrong, I wasn't a saint. I still had shortcomings that I was dealing with, but I was serious with the delight I was walking in and my efforts to live a righteous life. Somehow, I believed my travel was all a part of God's plan for me. I felt I was blessed. My belief was all I had, and it felt better than anything I had ever had or even been a part of.

There was no doubt in my mind, in my direction, as I read Psalms 37: 23-24: *"The steps of a good man are ordered by the Lord, as he delights in his way. Though he fall he shall not be utterly cast down for the Lord upholds him with his hand." I was being held.*

It was time to board the flight. As I stood in line, I recognized an old school mate. We had gone to Columbia together. Her name was Sandra, and we used to hang out between classes. She wasn't a girlfriend or anything like that. When I boarded the plane, she was already seated in the window seat on the right side of the plane. Once everyone was settled, I went to say hi to her. When she saw me, she remembered who I was. We talked briefly while I was standing in the aisle. The person who shared a seat with her asked me if I wanted to change seats. It was not just that he saw that we were old acquaintances, but favor had me by the hand. When I sat down with her, I noticed she had her Bible.

Immediately we had a common interest and our conversation went right into the Word. Once we started sharing in the joy of the Lord, the plane took off. We were so engrossed in our conversation of how GOD was moving in our lives that when we looked up to pay attention to the pilot's announcement, we were landing in LA. It was a four-hour flight, which for us seemed like only an hour. Barry had a car waiting for me when I arrived in LA. I offered Sandra a ride, not knowing at all where she lived. It was all so ironic because I was going to the Rose Garden Hotel in Hollywood, and she lived on Highland in Hollywood as well. What a coincidence, I thought.

We exchanged numbers before she got out of the car and I agreed to meet her that Wednesday to attend a Bible study with her. There was no doubt in my mind, GOD had a hand in the direction I was headed. Roman 8:28 says, *"And we know that all things work together for good to those who love GOD, to those who are called according to his purpose."*

The next day, I got in contact with Barry. He arranged for me to pick up a car. He was scheduled to leave to go to New York the following day. I was given directions to his office in Sherman Oaks where he left a check for me to pick up. There I was in Los Angeles, California cruising the streets in a 2000 convertible Camaro. I had been to LA several times but never wanted to be there for any length of time because of the fear I had of earthquakes. I was in LA in '94 during an earthquake and I always said I would never live there, but there I was.

I called Sandra and she and I hooked up and went to her friends church and then we went to church at Faithful Central in Inglewood. We did that for several weeks, going from church to church until we got to the City of Refuge where Bishop Noel Jones preached. When I heard him preach, I felt connected to his way of teaching. I knew right away his church was to be my church home while in LA. I attended his church every Wednesday, Thursday and Sunday.

When Barry returned, he asked me if I wanted to stay and he offered to help me get started. Next thing I knew, Derrel McDavid left a message for me at my hotel stating that he wanted to speak with me. *How in the fuck did he know where I was?* I wondered. I was freaked out.

When I talked to Barry about it, he sent me to meet with his attorney, Rickey Ivie, in downtown Los Angeles. He sat and listened as I explained what happened in Chicago with Jack Paladino. Subsequently, he sent a letter to R. Kelly's attorney demanding that he cease for harassing me. After two weeks in LA, it was clear for me to go home. But I chose to stay. I sent for my children and for the first few weeks we lived in a hotel in Hollywood. Once I found an apartment, I flew back to Chicago alone. I packed my furniture loaded it on a U-Haul truck and drove alone back to LA. My children and I moved into a condo in Inglewood. Once we moved in and got settled, I met a lady named Lena who worked at JC Penney at the Fox Hill mall. She became my children's babysitter while I attended school at the United Education Institute for Business Administration.

After graduating from the school, I was hired by the school as an Admissions Representative with a salary starting at $37,000 a year. I no longer had any desires to work in the music industry. It was gratifying for me to be able to go to work doing something I liked and come home to my children every day. We were a happy family. We missed home, but we went everywhere and were having fun going to Universal Studios, Great America, to the beaches and to church. We joined the City of Refuge Church.

CHAPTER 27

Cunning Ways

*L*IFE WAS GOING well, but then I got a call from Generaall. He was in L. A. He invited me to where he was staying. He was not far from the Crenshaw Mall. I hadn't seen dude in a while. He had been doing some networking with that video tape of Robert he had. Shit, I figured that Generaall should be a little bit moneyed up. He was staying in a nice little two bedroom condo. He looked relaxed and laid back. The first thing I questioned him on was the status on the video tape he had been circulating. He was anxious to show me the tape. He led me to a back room to view it. When it came on it was not the tape I had seen before.

This was a different tape. Actually, there were several tapes that had been put together. The one I was looking at was of R. Kelly pissing on a little girl. Once I recognized both of them, R. Kelly and the little girl, I chose not to watch the tape. I was sorry to see Robert making the adjustments to the camera he was recording himself on. And the girl, I forget her name but I remember standing and talking with her at the "I wish" remix video shoot. She had grown up,—filling out and looking like a woman that is. But, she was still a young girl.

That tape was made at his home on George street. I recognized the room in his basement and the room decorations on the tape. I was the one who picked that place out for him to live in when he was looking for property to buy. On top of that, I was with Robert for 13 years. Knowing that it was Robert Kelly on that tape I felt somewhat let down.

After viewing the tape, Generaall told me that the tapes were being sold all around the country. He opened a closet to show me boxes and boxes of tapes. There were copies packaged for distribution. He said that people were out on the streets throughout the country selling them. I was sad for Rob. I didn't feel he deserved that. But, he was the one that made the tape. I had a clear conscience that I had nothing to do with it. I actually tried to stop it. When Generaall initially informed me that he was in town, he said it was because he was there to record with Barry.

He wanted me to manage him, but I told him I was out of the business. I was happy working an eight-hour job and going home to my children every day. I left there without a tape in my hand. Generaall said that his money was due to arrive and he would get with me. I didn't trip on it. On occasion, Generaall would stop by my house in Inglewood, pursuing me to be his manager. He felt Barry would help his music career move if I was a part of it with him, but being in the music business was something I had no interest in at the time. Going out teaching my sons how to play basketball and baseball, taking them to vocal lessons and picking my daughter up from dance school was all more intriguing to me. Listening to them quote books and verses of the Bible and watching them grow was what I had passion for.

One day Barry stopped by the school where I worked and mentioned how impressed he was with the changes I made in my life for me and my children. Everything was going well for me in my life. I had not heard anything from R. Kelly, but Barry and I were staying in touch with each other, but it was just out of concern and friendship. Then one day Rob called me. I was so surprised to hear from him. My reaction was like that of a person awaiting a ransom call. You know, I got jumpy nervous but at the same time I had to be cool. When I answered the phone, I almost didn't recognize his voice.

"Hello," I said.

"Demetrius," the voice said, sounding as though they were crying.

"Rob, what's wrong man?" I asked with a tone of urgency. I was taken back to times I was there with him and ready to stand by his side. But I was 2,000 miles away and that reality set right in when I asked him, *"What you need Rob? What can I get you?"* I knew the porno tape of him and the young girl he urinated on while having sex with her had been circulating throughout the country.

"I'm an outlaw man. I need you to come up here," he said.

"Rob what can I do?" I asked. I truly wished it was something I could have done for him, but there wasn't.

He went on to say, *"Get with Derrel man, he'll take care of what you need to get here."*

I was living in Inglewood, and I wondered how he had gotten my phone number. *"Rob, I can't come up there. What is it? Talk to me, Rob,"* I asked.

I knew how R. Kelly was and how he acted. The strain he was trying to portray to me over the phone wasn't getting to me.

"Man I need you to get with Derrel," he said again, sounding as if he was crying. I shouted into the phone, hoping to get through to him to talk to me and stop whining. *"Rob! Rob man, talk to me! Rob!"*

I yelled into a dead phone. He had hung up. I felt Rob was trying to play on my emotions, hoping that I would react to the anguish he had portrayed over the phone, which would cause me to come to his aid. As I thought about it, there was nothing I could do other than tell him something that I know he wasn't going to do and that was to call Barry. Barry had ties to a lot of influential people and Barry would know what to do to help him. We talked about it in the past, and Barry said if Robert would call him, he wouldn't know what he would do. But I broke Barry down to recognizing that he loved Rob and after a short debate, he agreed.

R. Kelly needed to make amends to some wrongs he had done. He needed to fess up, come off the high horse he was on and pull the team back together. We all wanted it, all the old crew. Larry, Barry, Torrey, and Jomo, we all loved Robert, but he only thought of himself. After Rob hung up, I called Barry, but he did not answer his phone. He was en route to Atlanta, so I left a message. *"B, Rob called me. Can you believe it? Hit me when you get this."* He called me as soon as he touched down in Atlanta.

"Demetrius, did he call you for real?" he asked, without even saying hello first.

I felt that Barry had an obsession with R. Kelly. He was his artist, and Barry wanted to be there for him. It was R. Kelly who made everything difficult.

"You think he'll call me?" Barry asked, with a bit of hopeful excitement in his voice, I thought.

"I don't know, B. He was acting like he was crying, saying 'I'm an outlaw, I'm an outlaw, I need you!' And then, he hung up."

I told Barry that Rob asked me to come down there with him. Barry was inquisitive as I was. *"For what?"* he asked.

After we talked about R. Kelly's call for a few more moments, Barry advised me to stay away and that it could be a trick. He said R. Kelly was looking for a scapegoat. We both agreed my life was going fine without involving myself in something I have nothing to do with. Barry also assured me that whatever I decided to do, he'd stand behind me. With that said. I knew if Robert Kelly really wanted help this time, he would call me back. And if he would call I would try to persuade him to come to LA. I felt it would help if I could get R. and Barry to sit down and talk. At least, that is what I would have liked to have been able to make happen. Robert never called back, but Generaall did. This dude was in Chicago with R. Kelly.

"Demetrius I was with R. Kelly when he called you. I gave him your number. He called me in Philly, and as I was talking to him, I decided to come down and talk to him." Generaall had flipped the script. *Everybody looking for tapes and he got 'em.* I was shocked when he was telling me he was in Chicago with Rob.

"Man what are you talking about Generaall" was all I asked. I didn't want a part in any type of double-cross scene. I didn't want to talk to this dude. He was up to no good. *"What are you up to man?"* I asked him. *"Put Rob on the phone,"* I demanded of him. I was going to tell Rob of the snake he was keeping company with. I was going to tell him Generaall was the one responsible for the tapes being put out.

"Man I know how you feel about R. Kelly man, and you know like I do who put that tape out, and that wasn't right," he said.

"What are you talking about? You the one circulating those tapes, did you tell Robert that?" I asked him.

"I told him I knew about them, and I told him Barry sent someone who bought the tapes from the contacts I knew of and that you knew of Barry's involvement with the circulation of the tapes, in regards to who got 'em and put 'em out that is." Generaall whispered into the phone, *"Play along with me on this Demetrius. We gone get paid out of this."* This dude was crazy, I thought. *"Dude who you playing with? What is wrong with you, man?"* I asked.

"Why would you lie?" I asked him. *"Why would you tell him I knew of something I didn't? What are you trying to do?"* I asked him. I was again being put in the middle of someone else's game of trying to come up by using me as a tool to help them prosper, and at the same time, they would call themselves looking out for me by making me some petty ass bullshit monetary offer. So I listened to Generaall, and in my anger, I became heated. I shouted at him into the phone, *"Did you tell him who put the tapes out 'cause remember you brought me to a house where you had boxes of copies ready to be distributed? Did you tell him that?"* I asked.

Generaall was dirty as dirt could be, yet he was attempting to keep himself looking squeaky clean. I was enraged at this dude, the nerve of him trying to use me to throw blame at me for something he did. And then to try and set me up to be a part of his scheme, I had thoughts of setting a side my righteousness, get on the plane and go to Chicago to set him out. Generaall was as Barry said of Rob, *"a piece of shit."*

"Generaall, I don't know what you're up to, but I don't want no part of it, and I'd appreciate it if you'd lose my number because I bet you, you ain't told Rob. What he do, promise you your record deal or something?" I already knew that Barry wasn't interested in Generaall's music stating that he didn't feel he had what it took.

"Man they said they would compensate you. Won't you just fly down here and talk to the man?" he asked me as if he wasn't listening to anything I said and talked like he thought I was listening to what he was saying.

"Man listen," I said, *"if R. Kelly or Derrel want to talk to me about anything, they can come up here. You're perpetrating some crazy shit Generaall. I don't know why you would involve me with this. I'm out man, and I'm gone let Barry know you putting his name in some shit. You snaking man, and I ain't even trying' to know where you at."* I hung up the phone.

It was some strange shit going on. I called Barry!

"B," I said when he answered the phone laughing.

"Yeah, what's happening man?" he asked.

"Man you ain't gone believe this," I said. *"Generaall just called after I got off the phone with you. He's down in Chicago with R. Kelly,"* I told him.

"He's in Chicago with Rob, for what?" he asked.

"He called to try to get me to come there, saying they would compensate me."

"Compensate you for what?" he asked.

I explained everything that Generaall and I talked about. Barry was upset and told me he would have to call me back later. He wanted to contact his lawyers, said he was going to put an end to the bullshit that was being stirred up.

"Well, like I said Demetrius, if you feel that you've got something to offer them, then that's your choice if you want to go up there."

"No B, I have no intention at all of going up there." I cut Barry off in the middle of his sentence. I didn't want him to have any notion at all that I wanted to leave LA to go talk to Rob. I felt Barry was feeling I was going to betray him and go lie on him. But that was not in me to lie about something I didn't know anything about. If he did have something to do with putting the tape out, he did so without me having any idea of it. This was the last straw for me. I was going to cut ties with everyone from this day forward.

My whole life was being pulled in a direction I didn't want any parts of. There was evil in the midst of my association with Rob, and I wanted out for good. I was convinced no good was ever going to come about for me being involved with Robert Kelly. *"He's got them thinking you had something to do with the distribution of the sex tape that's out,"* I said.

"Well Demetrius that guy will pretty much try to do anything or say anything to get a record deal. It wouldn't surprise me, nor does it worry me. I know what I do every day. He can say whatever he wants, he don't know nothing about me," Barry said. *"Let me call you back later. We'll talk then."*

"All right then B. I was just letting you know, I told Generaall not to call me no more. I'll holler at you later man," I said.

"All right Demetrius, if you want to go up there to see if anything is in it for you, be careful," Barry said.

"I ain't going nowhere B, to see nobody. I'll talk to you later," I said, and we hung up.

CHAPTER 28

Tragedy Strikes

*B*ARRY AND I were growing to have a greater respect for one another as men throughout this R. Kelly saga/ordeal. Even though I didn't see him much at all while I was in LA, from our frequent phone conversations I was really getting to know him and I had grown to have a great deal of respect for Mr. Hankerson. He and I had gone through a few mishaps from time to time, but he never talked at me in respect to teaching me the ropes of the business. He showed me when and where I would go wrong. He would also compliment me when I completed a certain task.

In the earlier days I use to think Barry was somewhat of a snake in the grass. During this time I was getting to know the man and no longer saw him for who I thought he was. Getting to know Barry as a man helped me to understand the term, *"people don't believe what they see, they see what they believe."* I was getting to know Barry now as the good man that he was. He was no longer an image of a villain in my eyes. He was an inspiration of wisdom and a main factor for my reason for being in LA.

Things were going good for me during this time. With Barry helping me to get my life situated, I was making some real progress. My life was beginning to have some balance to it. The way my life was going with Barry in it, I could not help but think that this man had my best interest at heart. To come to think of it, Whenever Barry was around he wanted to see that I was coming up. He mentioned to me that he would be willing to match funds with me to help get a house for my children and I. Barry knew I was done working with or even wanting to work with Rob.

I was putting the pieces to my life back together, still! I had a condo, I had a good paying job working for U.E.I. and attending to my children. They were involved in acting and taking vocal lessons with Ms. Jody Sellers, an awesome vocal teacher (I must mention this lady because she offered her services out of admiration for the support I was giving to my children).

Twice a week, Jody would give my four children lessons. Also, I had the children working for a casting agency who kept me pretty busy employing them as extras in movies. My daughter Ashley and son Demetrius Jr. (Meechie) were both in Bow Wow's movie *Like Mike* and my youngest son (DJ) was on one of Bernie Mac's episodes of "The Bernie Mac Show.

It was August 25, 2001 and I had just returned from a vocal lesson with Meechie and Ashley. Finally, I thought, a chance to sit down to relax from a long busy day at the office. I turned on the television and a news broadcast came on announcing a plane crash that took the life of Aaliyah. My God, I can still feel the pain! I was heartbroken, as I know so many others who loved her were. *"No, no, no,"* I cried. *"Oh GOD, no,"* I cried. *I could not believe the report I was hearing of her fatal accident. But I didn't want to hear it. I did not want for it to be true.* In my pain, I thought about Barry, Aaliyah's parents, Mike and Diane, and her brother Rashad. *"Oh GOD"* was all I could think and say. The news of Aaliyah's death caused a pain in me that paused my breathing.

Just when things were beginning to balance I'm hit with another natural disaster. I could not begin to imagine the pain Barry had to have been experiencing. Let alone Aaliyah's parents and her brother. I even thought about Rob. I knew all of them as well as a lot of people in the world were grieving. I hurt as well. My pain was for Aaliyah's mother. I felt for her. I called Barry. When he answered I felt his pain. It was the first time I had ever heard him sound weak and hurt. *I'm sorry Barry,"* were the first words and the only words I could muster up to say out of my mouth. I didn't know what else I could say that could comfort him in this time. If I could have been a tear that could relieve him and his family from the pain they were suffering I would have taken their sorrow.

"Yeah thanks Johnny. Aaliyah's gone man." I could tell that it took a lot for Barry to say those words. He was holding himself up through this tragic moment. I am sure his family needed him to be strong. *"Lee le's gone and in God's hands now. He does what He do. I don't know man, but she's gone. My niece is gone Johnny,"* he said. Again I could hear it in his voice he was holding in his pain and not wanting to break down with me on the phone. He told me he had to keep himself together for the sake of his family. I didn't know what to say. I know his pain was deeper than mine. I sat holding my daughter as she cried in my arms.

"Barry I'm here if you need me for anything man," I told him.

"Yeah, I know, thanks. I'll talk to you later," he said and hung up.

After Aaliyah's funeral, Barry and I still talked, but not as much. We both wondered how things might have turned out had R. Kelly not violated the family's trust. He insinuated that I, more than likely, would have been Aaliyah's tour manager. And I truly believe, had I been with Aaliyah I would hope that things would have turned out better. God does what he does for his will through our purpose. We might not like it. In fact we never like chastisements, nor do we understand the debt of chastisement. We just know that it hurts and somehow we make it through day by day. Some of us are never able to let go of the pain.

My life continued with me working for the vocational college and making $45,000.00 a year, attending church regularly and being a single dad. Everything was going great. I joined the church choir and I had my children also active in the church. They formed a little group amongst themselves. They stirred up the "Joe Jackson" in me—I had them rehearsing, singing and dancing every day. Life was beginning to really be fun. On top of that I met a woman I was infatuated with; Veronica was her name.

There she was sitting under a tree in Ladera park with her daughter. They were a vision of loveliness, like a pretty picture. I couldn't get her off my heart let alone my mind. Though I had just met her, she was the lady I wanted to be mine. Veronica was someone I wanted to make everything of the past I had gone through with other women work with her. She was everything I desired in the beauty of a woman. When I approached her my words made her smile and laugh. Since she had her child with her I sought to take advantage of an opportunity. I excused myself and quickly drove home told my children to let's go to the park and we rushed back to the park. All the way back, which was only a ten minute drive, I was hoping the lady who had caught my eye was still there. And she was! She was surprised to see me back at the park and she thought it impressive of me to have gone to get my children. We sat enjoying each other's company, eating a hotdog and watching the children have fun.

My life was about to open like a rose in blooming season. Everything was coming together. I had a good job, I was working for U.E.I. The United Education Institute, I was being paid good money, I had my children with me, I had a condo, I was into church at the City of Refuge where I was involved with helping to teach kids in Sunday school and I had met a woman I thought was everything I wanted in a women. Life had a smile on my heart.

But as I stated before, I am "I am Murphy Law Jr." Anything that could go wrong for me, did! I had the luck of a black cat. Out of nowhere, another storm came into my life like a hurricane and tore my world apart. I'll call this storm Hurricane Furlow. Man, it is always some dumb and stupid stuff that can so easily snatch your life away from you.

On Labor Day, August 29, 2003, I was home relaxing with Veronica. This was the first day she had decided to come over to spend the weekend with me and it was our first time being with each other. We had only been kissing friends up until then. My sons Deon and DJ came into the house somewhat frightened, as they told me that Mr. Furlow's pit bull dog viciously attacked the basketball they were playing with in our back yard.

I got up from the bed to go have a talk with our neighbor, Kenneth Furlow. As I approached him on the patio area of our complex, with my sons following behind me, I picked up from his greeting he had been drinking. My approach to him was respectful. I mean, Furlow was 6'5" and 265 lbs. I wasn't looking for trouble. *"Ken how you doing man?"* I said to him as I walked up on him preparing to get his grill started up. *"A-man, what's happening,"* he said with a loud slurred voice. He had started his day off drinking early.

I was very respectful to Ken. *"Your dog got loose and my boys came in the house scared with the ball busted and ripped,"* showing him the ball as I made my petition to him. *"They shouldn't have their toys and things in the back area anyway"* he said. I thought he was way out of line and I didn't feel this was going to go the right way, so I stepped back from him. *"Ken Imma talk to you later. You're kind of tipsy right now,"* I told him and I turned to leave, asking him to please tie his dog down. I gathered my sons together, and we returned to the house. Ken was securing his dog as we were walking away.

I gave them another ball to play with hoping all would go well. We weren't bad neighbors; in fact, we got along pretty good. We even shared a drink, a smoke and a meal together from time to time. I knew it was the alcohol altering his thinking. It was less than fifteen minutes when my sons came running back into the house showing another busted ball. *"Daddy, daddy, Mr. Ken's dog keeps chasing us and he busted your ball too,"* my son Deon said, handing me the busted ball.

Veronica suggested that I call the police and have them get Ken to restrain his dog. But I was enraged. I jumped up out of bed with my beautiful Salvadorian woman to go back again and confront Ken about his dog. I wanted him to pay for the ball now. *"Baby, don't go out there. Call the police. Let them deal with that man and that dog,"* Veronica said as I was walking out the door.

When I got to the patio where Ken was, some of his family members were out there with him this time. There were a few older ladies, maybe his mom, his wife and a couple of guys. Seeing that there were ladies there made me calm down. I wasn't about to lose my cool and be disrespectful. I walked up with my sons behind me—I thought they were in the house, but they were right on my heels. I walked up slowly to Ken as he was standing at the table with the ladies talking. *"Aye Ken, can I talk to you for a moment?"*

I said respectfully and nodded, *"How are you?"* to the mothers who were at the table. Ken got loud. *"Now what do you want?"* His voice was slurping as saliva splattered from his mouth. *"Ken, you gotta get your dog man. He done bit up another one of my balls and chasing my children man. Come on man,"* humbly I appealed to him. *"I'm asking you Ken man, to please tie your dog down."* Everyone's eyes were on us. Ken irritated me. He was drunk and out of his mind. *"Man who the fuck you think you is? I ain't got to tie my dog down, shit,"* he said.

I just didn't dig his lack of respect for me and my children, but my thoughts were to remain respectful because of the women that were present. Again, I got my sons by the hand and turned to walk back home. *"Imma call the police. They'll be coming to see you about your dog. I ain't gone deal with it anymore,"* I told him. Ken walked behind me, yelling obscenities as he followed behind me.

"Motherfucker, you ain't gone do shit to my dog!"

When I went to my garage, I told my sons to go into the house.

"Ken you need to stop walking up on me," I told him as he continued to come towards me. My sons' scooter was in the way of me closing the garage door, so I reached down to move it, and Ken stepped up and hit me in the jaw. At this time, I had the scooter in my hand. I looked at him as though I was in a daze and about to fall down and asked him *"Why you hit me man?"* and at the same time, I saw one of his male friends or family members who had followed him down the stairs coming around the pole towards me. While Ken came towards me again ready to hit me, I instinctively busted him in the head with the scooter. He fell back as blood came pouring out of his head, covering his face.

I heard his wife scream at Ken telling him to stop, but as he tried to stand to come at me again, I slowly stepped back and into my garage, all along watching the man that was with Ken as he went to Ken's aide, to help him stand. I walked away and closed my garage, I was scared. I was hoping I hadn't hurt the man that badly, but he brought it on himself. I was definitely defending myself. In a quaking moment, all hell broke loose. Ken's sons were trying to get into my house by climbing over my patio. I chased them away with a bat, but at the same time, my door was being pounded on.

I went down to open it with an old antic revolutionary pistol I had in my hand. When I snatched the door open, it was the Inglewood police. They saw the gun and immediately withdrew theirs from their holster. I dropped mine. I felt I was lucky they didn't have their guns drawn already when they came to my door. After I explained what happened, I was arrested and charged with assault with a deadly weapon for hitting Ken with the scooter. They didn't do anything about the pistol I had. They knew it was outdated and it didn't work.

I stayed in LA County Jail for two days while Veronica and Lena, my children's babysitter, came up with $5,000 bail to get me out. My whole life changed after that day. When I went to court, the judge ordered me to not go back to my apartment. The restraining order that was placed on me said I could not be within 500 feet of Ken. The judge had no regard whatsoever for the fact that I was attacked or the fact that Ken followed me onto my property. He didn't care that I had nowhere else to go or that I was a single parent responsible for the lives of four young children.

The judge didn't want to hear anything I had to say. I was left without a choice. I had to move, and I had to move right away. The little money I saved had to be spent on a two-bedroom apartment that I found in Hawthorne. All of my expenses doubled and it was costing me an arm and a leg transporting the kids back and forth to school, me getting to work, food, moving expenses and the cost for storage. My life did a 360-degree turn over the course of a moment. I went back and forth to court, then I finally accepted a deal of probation; a $5,000 fine and a $5,000 restitution cost for Ken's hospital bill.

I stopped going to church. I was ashamed of myself for allowing the devil to pull me out of my comfort zone. I couldn't face the children or the members of the church that knew me and who looked up to me. Even though they probably didn't know what I did or had gone through, I just couldn't face them. Being in Hawthorne was too far for Veronica to travel to see me so she became distant. I was frustrated. My life was going downhill again.

I started smoking weed again. The next thing you know, I was trying to make ends meet hanging out and wasting my money at the Hollywood Park Casino, playing poker. I had to find a way to come up; everything was falling apart. A friend of mine, Frank Wilson Sr., knew somebody that got me a three-bedroom apartment in the Jungle. Even though Frank tried to discourage me from moving into the Jungle, He said it to rough in the jungle for young boys there. Frank felt that I was putting my sons life in danger living there. But in spite of what thought little did he know, I had grown up in this environment and now I was here with my children to raise them. We were going to have to weather the storm together I thought because the size of the apartment and the rent was compatible to my needs.

Believe it or not, I was comfortable living in the Jungle. It was almost like the West Side of Chicago. During the course of all the drama I was going through, Veronica and I broke up. As much as I thought we were a perfect pair, again, my heart was crushed. As I tried to put my life together, I was slowly pulling it apart, trying to do it all on my own. Barry and I were still talking, but my pride wouldn't allow me to continue asking him for money. He had helped me so much already since being in LA.

CHAPTER 29

I Surrender!

ONE DAY AFTER work, as I was getting into my car, I noticed a note under my windshield wiper, which read, *"Call me, and don't be scared."* I knew it was one of my students; they flirted with me all the time. After several days, one evening, I called the number. I was stressed out and lonely. I was missing Veronica.

"Hello," I said.

"Hi, who is this?" asked a female with a soft voice.

"This is Demetrius. Someone left a note on my car and just to show that I'm not scared, I'm calling," I said.

She laughed. Adrianna was her name; Ana was who we called her. A week had passed and after which, we hooked up. She was a student I had enrolled in school. Ana came into my life and helped me to get it back on track. She thought a lot of me, and I didn't want to let her down by being anything less than the man she was attracted to. As we began to spend time together, she got to know my children, and we got to know her son, Deon.

It was comfortable being with Ana, she lead me back to the church, and on several occasions she would attend services along with me.

Ana had been through some hard times herself, but she was a survivor with a heart like mine.

I was still trying to come up because all of my bills were backed up. I put aside my spirituality and became impatient. I couldn't pay my bills because I still had to attend anger management classes every week and pay $50 a session. Also, I had to pay Ken $180.00 a month for restitution.

Every time I take my mind off the joy of the Lord, my life takes a turn for the worse. Isaiah 54:17 says, *"No weapon formed against you shall prosper."* I had become a weapon against myself. GOD made a way out for me when there seemed to be no way, but this time, things worked against me. It started when I was gambling. I was losing more than I was winning, taking myself deeper into debt. I started shoplifting. Dressed like a business man, I would walk into Target department stores; empty display cases that were full of I-Pods put them in a basket and walk straight out of the door.

The first time I did it, I got away with it. That was easy as hell and I made so much money selling the IPod's for half price on the streets. I began traveling to different Targets and Wal-Mart's every day, repeating the act until I was finally caught. I was fortunate the first time to have made enough money to bail myself out of jail before word got out to all the other Targets I had ripped off. My picture was floating around.

Things just started going bad for me, and it was all because I was making bad decisions. I had been in LA for five years and should have been getting settled and ready to buy a house, but I jumped on a fast track back into the stupidity of my youth, and though I fooled myself into believing that I was invincible, GOD was covering me, even as I stole. I got real sick in the winter of 2004 with a viral infection in my throat and couldn't work for a month. This put me behind on my bills so deep that when I was able to go back to work, I was laid off. Living off unemployment, things got real rough. My children weren't happy in the schools they were in. Things were going downhill.

I decided to call my sisters Linda and Dee-Dee in Illinois. I told them I was having a hard time and asked if they would take my children. They had no problem at all taking them back. My sister Linda told me she was missing her boy's anyway. I was so thankful and blessed to have sisters that truly had love for me. I don't know what I would have done or where I would have been without my sisters. God puts people in our lives for a reason. I knew he knew what I was going through and how much I wanted to have my children with me, but I didn't know how to wait on him.

I was doing what I felt I had to do to make my situation better. God knows I didn't wanna hurt anybody, and I didn't want to be separated from my children. One thing was for sure: with what I was doing, I was taking a chance at getting in trouble. I didn't want to be locked up and my children stuck in LA under Children and Family Services, so I was going to do what I thought was best for them—take them back to my sisters. My mind was made up. I had to make some money. I was an angry man, living on the edge. I was tired of it, always starting over, never getting ahead. Like 50 Cent said, *"Get rich or die trying."* I was in that state of mind.

I was in the world and around people every day, but I was so alone. I had a feeling that things were going to go bad for me sooner or later, but at the same time I had a feeling of invincibility. Kind of like the time

I went to jail when I did the burglary with Bobby back in the day. I had that same helpless feeling where by the time the police pulled up on me, I was reaching out to anyone but no one was there. No one could hear me cry out and no one took time to look at my anguish. All I wanted were the basics in life: to be able to provide for my children, put a roof over our heads, and a job—and I would have been content. But it seemed so hard for me to be able to do that.

No one knew how deeply I was hurting inside. No one seemed to ever ask "*how are you, really?*" or "*are you going to be okay?*" Nobody asked, "*What are you going to do?*" No one looked into my eyes to see the pain and the burden I was carrying, living without my children, who I knew were going to miss and need me. My whole life seemed to be a merry-go-round of pain. I just could not seem to pull things together to save my life.

I was tired. I didn't want to steal. I didn't want to do wrong, but I wanted my own. The saying goes "God bless the child that's got his own." In my heart, I wanted to be right and do right in God's eyes. I never doubted God had a covering over me, but I did wonder why there was always disappointment for me when I was at the brink of accomplishing something. As much as people used to tell me I was blessed, I felt He was looking past me when I needed Him the most because I didn't feel blessed at all. In fact, I felt cursed.

I rented a room at the Courtyard by Marriott Hotel in Hammond, Indiana, for me and my children to stay in so we could spend some time together before I took three of them to my sisters and put my son Demetrius Jr. on a plane back to his mother in Georgia. The hotel was nice. It had an indoor pool, kitchenette inside the room, a weight room, and all of the comforts of a home. The only thing was that I was low on funds. After we left the pool, I told them to wait in the room while I went out to get pizza.

While going to get pizza, I saw a Target store in Calumet City not far from the hotel and decided to go inside and look it over, to see if it was indeed a Target for me to hit. The store was crowded, and it appeared to be ripe for the taking. I decided to take advantage of the opportunity and emptied the glassed case full of about eighty iPods into a plastic garbage can, walked right past the front register as if I had paid for the garbage, and went out the door. On my way to my car, pushing the cart, I looked behind me and saw the store security running out towards me. I turned to push the cart at them in hopes they would go after the merchandise, but they didn't. One went after the cart, and the other two came running hard towards me.

I ran in the opposite direction from where my car was. As I was running I thought about my children—they were in the hotel alone, with no adult supervision.

"*Oh my God,*" I thought. I had fucked up and fucked up bad. My mind was racing faster than my feet were running. With the security gaining on me, I pulled my cell phone from my pocket and called my brother Eric. He had been over to the hotel to visit earlier in the day, so he knew exactly where we were staying. It was crazy the way I went in my pocket for the phone. If those security guards had guns, they would have assumed I was pulling out a gun and would have had every reason in the world to shoot me. "*Please answer Eric,*" I cried out as I was running and pressing buttons on the phone. He answered!

"*What's up J,*" he said.

"*Eric, the police are after me. I don't know if I can get away. The kids are at the hotel. Man you gotta go get 'em,*" I cried out.

"*Ok J where you at?*" he asked. "*In Calumet City, Get the kids Eric. Please get em. They by their selves—Eric,*" I screamed into the phone.

By that time, the security guards were right up on me. I turned around and one was running at me so fast he couldn't stop once he got up on me. I ducked as he grabbed at me, lifted him up and threw him over my back. I began to run through the parked cars, hoping I could duck out of their sight, if only for a moment, so I could get to my car. As I got ready to cross over to the other side of the cars, city detective cars were pulling up. At that point, I had nowhere to go so I turned around.

One of the store security officers was coming up behind me. I pleaded with him as he got in hearing range. "*Man please let me get away. My kids man, are at the hotel. We didn't have no food man. Come on man, please.*" My plea was in vain as he grabbed me. I pleaded and fought him at the same time, hoping he would be compassionate and let me slip away. He wasn't hearing me, so I got desperate and punched him in the jaw, knocking him back. I got past him, but it was a useless struggle. It seemed a whole police force was there, and now all of them were grabbing at me, and when I went down to the ground, every one of them was punching and kicking me.

I was taken to Calumet City Police Department. My eye was swollen and my lip busted, but I wasn't feeling any pain—at least not in that sense. I shouted out in anger for them to allow me to make my one phone call. I told them my children were alone. All they wanted to know was where they were. I knew I couldn't tell them that. I was counting on my brother to pick them up. They threw me in a cell, and after ranting and raving about a phone call, one of the officers came to the cell and sprayed me with mace. That shit didn't bother me. It was worth it watching him get angry as I called him a bunch of bitches and hoes and he couldn't do nothing about it. I was angry at myself. Why couldn't I just hang out with my children? I was so disgusted with myself.

It was four hours later when I was allowed to make a phone call. I was relieved to know my brother had picked up my children. After getting that information, I let all my worries go. *Besides, what would worrying accomplish for me now?* I thought. I knew where I was going. After I was processed and taken to court the next morning, I was taken to the Cook County Jail; my bond was set at $75,000. I was caught up again! The county jail wasn't a joke either. It had been a while since I was there. The jail was full of younger men. I say that because every greeting I received from anyone was *"What's happening OG?"* They snapped me into the reality of knowing I was much older and I felt life was passing me by.

Whenever I was allowed to go into the dayroom where they played cards, dominos, and chess, I pretty much stayed to myself. I didn't know what was ahead for me, other than having a feeling that I was going to have to do some real time. Often I was disturbed by the character of my younger generation. Every word that came out of their months was *Nigger this and nigger that. What's up, nigger?"* This disturbed me as I laid in my cell listening to them shout out at one another as if it was just a common thing.

They had no idea of the pain that black people suffered being subjected to being called a nigger. The sacrifices and lives our people gave to free us of the racial bonds. They had no notion of what Martin Luther King Jr. or Malcolm X stood for. I was ill-humored by this and became belligerent when I heard a Latino in the cell beside mine yell out to a brother as he was talking, *"Fuck you talking 'bout nigger."*

I had heard all I could listen to and spoke out loud over the tier, *"You brothers need to stop using the n-word as if you don't know where that word comes from man."*

It got real quiet on the deck. I knew I woke up some of the thug spirits that were confined right along with me. So I went on to tell everybody how I was disturbed by the use of that word. And I made sure the Latino next to me knew I took offence to him saying it.

"Man, who the fuck is you OG," a youngster said. *"My name is Smithy man, that's who I am, and I got a problem with the use of that word. I don't mean anybody any disrespect, but I'm from that era, and if you got a problem with that, then we got a problem,"* I told him.

"Nigga, I'm gone say what the fuck I wanna say and how the fuck I wanna say it, Nigga. OG, I don't know who the fuck you think you talking to," the young, stupid motherfucker said.

"Nigga, I know if you call me that one more time, Imma let you know who you talking to, little, stupid motherfucker," I called him.

I didn't care. I was a bundle of guilt, seeking punishment. I was numb in the whole matter. I didn't feel anything. I probably needed to have my ass whooped anyway, for ending up as I was, locked up in a 6x8 feet steel celled cage. I didn't see myself going home. My decisions had shaped another passage for the direction my life was now heading. It wasn't about the thought of being taken out of my misery. It was about my misery taking off on this dude to relieve some pressure. I was in a whole different frame of mind. I wasn't new to this environment. This time though, my inner thoughts were somewhat welcoming the challenge of where I was.

This was where I had to be now. I heard my cousin, June Bugs voice, "When you in Rome cuz, you got to do what the Romans do." This place was a Rome to me. In this place, it was another country, where the laws were entirely different and the rules, they had all been broken. I was another man standing up, holding onto the bars and looking out at the wall with my forehead laid into the bars. I was indeed, an OG! I didn't have a pot to piss in. I was mad at world and wallowing in my own self-inflicted sorrow. I couldn't help but think about it over and over again the fact that it had been going on twenty years since I had been locked up or arrested for that matter. All I had now, was regret and I didn't see any way for me to get back at it. I wasn't going to be in denial or try to seek help. It was evident to me now that I really was a crazy man.

The lives I had abandoned and the people I had let down and not to mention the opportunities I had, had. Yeah, looking back on those and being where I was, I had to be a crazy person. Right? Something had to be wrong with me. I was a stupid man in my book. In my mind, in the direction my life was now heading, I was going to live my life conscious of how I had lived. I was now going to be, consciously crazy and fucking stupid.

There was comeliness for me as I thought of the present situation I was in. It was only because I believed I was standing up for something I felt was right, that made it easier for me to except the I didn't give a shit attitude I had about my life. There was one thing I did know as I thought about how I had just picked a fight. I knew that cultural disrespect, and using the "N" word as they were using it was cultural disrespect. I knew that, that kind of insolence would not be tolerated behind the wall. So, I felt good about feeling crazy because I was justified this time.

"*OG snapped on the young boy*". I was hearing people yelling in my head.

"*Yeah, but he was right,*" I would hear another voice say.

There was stillness to my thoughts. I needed to feel like I was alive.

"*OG, y'all needs to chill with that,*" one of the other inmates said.

"*I'll see you when the doors roll OG,*" the ignorant little youngster yelled out.

I knew I had gotten myself into a situation. I didn't have a problem with it. I wanted to feel something. Pain, I felt it was a part of me. This time, I was not going to beat up on myself anymore. I was going to be crazy. Shit, it was what I was. When the doors rolled, we got down. The fight didn't last long. We were in a little bitty cell, and as soon as I went into the cell and he came in, I went straight to work on him.

There was nothing to talk about. We were there to fight and settle a difference. It was all a matter of respect. I didn't give him a chance to get his vision as I hit him in his left eye with a jab and then an overhand right to that same eye. I kept on punching his ass till one of the older brothers pulled me off him. I let up off him and went to the dayroom to sit down as if nothing happened.

I was the talk of the tier. Because of what we were fighting about, I was allowed to go one on one with the boy. He was gang related and I was an OG. When the young gangster came out, his eye was fucked up! He didn't say anything to me, and I didn't say anything to him. A few brothers came up to me to compliment me for whipping the boy's ass. "*He had a big mouth any way,*" one of the guys said. After that little confrontation, the n-word was still used, but a member of the Vice Lords and one of the Disciple leaders both told their people to refrain from using the word. I still heard it, but they were conscious and apologetic when someone would say it. That was worth the fight to me. I gained respect, made a few friends and I made a few enemies.

I didn't give a care about the enemies. I was mad at the world. Sitting up in the county jail, I made up in my mind whenever I got out of there I was going for it. I was going to get money any way I could. I just didn't see a way around it. I couldn't get a job anywhere, and I wasn't going to continue to ask people for money. I was allowing my heart to turn cold. All my beliefs, my spirituality, the thoughts I had of feeling guilty for doing wrong, they were going to stay locked up inside of me.

This was a cold, cold world I was living in. Even though I knew I wasn't going to be getting out of jail any time soon, I was having thoughts in the direction of the type of person I was going to be once I was released. Hate consumed me. The thought of living a lifestyle of a gangster was overwhelmingly appealing to me. I was convinced that good guys finish last. I was through with allowing people to take me for granted. I did not want to be MR. Loyalty and nice anymore.

The notorious John Dillinger came to my mind. I wanted to be just like him. I was going to go hard at getting some money for myself and if I could help my children that would be even better. I wanted to be hard. It was the only way I could think for now. I really didn't care anymore. I figured I had been a good person all my life, and the only time life had anything to offer me was when I took it. If I was going to end up in jail, then that's where I was going to be. My anger led my mind to wanting to be a hardcore criminal.

I felt that I had lost everything that meant anything to me anyway. I made a fool out of myself by getting locked up and leaving my children in a hotel. I allowed myself to once again be taken out of my children's life. My world was crushed as far as I was concerned. It didn't matter to me whether I lived or died. All I knew was if I was to live, I was going to go hard *"in the paint,"* as my boy Tweet would say, to get my money. I didn't know what was going to happen to me and how I was going to get off from under this case.

I was alone again, and I couldn't call anybody in my family; everybody's damn phone was blocked. So I felt like nobody wanted to or needed to hear from me. The only people I was able to call was my son's grandmother, Dorothy, and my girlfriend Ana.

I would call Dorothy, and she would make calls for me to my family to let them know I was alright. After two weeks in the county jail I was sitting in my cell and got called for an unexpected visit. *"Who the heck is coming to visit?"* It was Derrel McDavid, R. Kelly's business manager. *"How did he know I was in jail? What the hell's going on?"* I thought. It looked like R. Kelly could not get out of my life. They had been following me. They went to California to get to me. What did I have that they wanted? I didn't have a clue. I guess with me being locked up, it was another opportunity for them to shoot another shot at me. *"What could I tell them that could get me out of here?"* were the thoughts I began to formulate in my mind.

During this time, R. Kelly had been indicted on distribution of child pornography charges so I figured they were searching for a way to get

Demetrius Smith Sr.

Robert off the chopping block. Nothing had changed with Rob. He sent Derrel to try to convince me to sign a statement stating Barry Hankerson was the one who put the videotapes out. During the visit, Derrel told me Robert was willing to get me out of jail, give me some money and have his attorneys represent me with the case I was on. The getting out part sounded good to my ears.

I didn't know what it was they wanted to hear from me, but I wasn't going to lie on a person. I actually didn't know anything about the distribution of the video. But if they thought I did, I was going to ride it out with them as far as I could go. My trial date was coming up and I knew if I had a good lawyer, it was possible I could get out from under this case. Derrel promised an attorney would be there on my trial date to represent me. I wasn't going to tell these cats to go away. I wanted out. My faith was willing to find a way.

The preliminary was important. If I could just get the lawyer to beat my case in the preliminary hearing, Rob and his lawyers could all kiss my ass. They already knew Generaall had taken the tapes, and that's the only part of it I knew. I didn't get into their business where I was allowed to profit anything. On my hearing date, a lawyer was there to represent me. Because I had not written anything other than what they already knew, they wanted me to sign some papers they put together. When I wouldn't, the attorney asked the judge for a continuance for the following day. At that hearing, they withdrew as my representative.

I hadn't talked to Barry for months. I could only call Dorothy and Ana collect from the jail. I had been locked up for three months when my mom told me Barry called inquiring about me. She told him where I was, and of course, he asked her why I hadn't called him if I was having a hard time. I guess he got to know my mother over the phone because she got him to get me out. When I called him to thank him, he told me he bailed me out because of my mother. I was somewhat ashamed of myself. I got lost for no reason at all and sacrificed the safety and security of my children for material gain.

When I got out of Cook County Jail, it was rough. My brothers Eric and Joshua picked me up. Josh was home for a leave from the Air Force, and Eric had just gotten out of the joint up in Wisconsin. Nobody had money. There I was stuck in Chicago, no money, my children were here and there; nobody could really take me in. What's a man to do? It was wintertime in Chicago and I didn't have a dime, so I called my friend Larry Hood.

Larry gave me money to help me get back to LA. I felt like the only one I could turn to was Ana, my beautiful Ms. Dark and Lovely. She had her own place since her nursing job came through. I thought about her and I being together. It was an uncomfortable of the two of us together, but still no money. I couldn't be under my woman like this. All I had was my Jeep Cherokee. The plates were expired, the repo-man was looking for it and it was hard getting gas money. Things were rough. How was I going to get back to Chicago for court? All kinds of things were on my mind.

I snapped and began to bring forth the reality of the thought I had planted in my mind during my incarceration. I didn't have a pistol and I was not really ready to step up to that level as of yet. But at the same time, if you didn't have a gun and weren't willing to shoot me, you weren't going to stop me from getting away. I wanted to do good but I was lost and I could not seem to find my way back to that road. I was caught up again between a rock and a hard place. Romans 7:19 *"For the good that I will to do, I do not do; but the evil I will not to do, that I practice. Now if I do what I will not to do, it is no longer I who do it, but sin that dwells in me."*

I went to a Target store for about forty or fifty iPods, the 8 Gigs that were worth $400 a piece. I'd sell them for $200. After I got away with that one, I went buck wild. I hit a store every day for about four months. The money was flowing, and things were picking up. When I went to steal, I was doing it out of anger. I didn't want this lifestyle, but it was all that kept me going. Once again I thought I was invincible and that I was covered and protected, but Target had my picture in all their stores. Romans 7:24—*"O wretched man that I am! Who will deliver me from this body of death?"*

Now I am in Solano State Prison, Vacaville, California. *"Looking from the inside out."* When I was in LA County Jail, I thought I would get a light sentence. After all, it had been over nineteen years since I was involved in crime. I did well for years; I just backslid a little. I was never a professional criminal. I worked and enjoyed being employed. I was charged with commercial burglary, which carried a sentence of sixteen months for the first offense, two years for a second offense, and three years maximum sentence for the crime. So I thought to even be sentenced to three years would be okay and I was willing and ready to accept my punishment. But I was wrong! When I was told that I was looking at a life sentence for stealing and they were serious, I almost lost my mind!

It was only when I was on my way to court one morning, sitting in the bull pen when this brother walked up to me and said, *"My brother, I'm being led by the spirit to tell you that GOD is with you."*

"*Thank you,*" I said to him, shaking my head up and down, receiving what he was telling me. I sat in sadness, wondering what fate had for me as I waited to be transported to court. The man paused in front of me, took a piece of paper, wrote the scripture down and handed it to me.

"*GOD wants you to read this scripture.*" He said.

I took the paper and put it in my pocket and thought to myself, "*God, I sure need you to be with me now.*" When I went to court on that day, the state's attorney offered me what he said was a deal—nineteen years at 80 percent. "*What? Are you crazy? I ain't killed nobody or robbed nobody. I just stole something,*" I said.

"*Yeah, but you have a strike for assault with a deadly weapon, and in 1980, you had an armed robbery charge in Illinois, that's two strikes Mr. Smith and along with the charges you have now, 22 counts of commercial burglary, you're looking at twenty-five years to life, Mr. Smith, if you don't take this deal,*" he said trying to sound sympathetically serious.

I threw my hands in the air. My life was over. To add insult to injury, he didn't stop there. He went on to tell me, "*If you end up going to trial and you are found guilty, you'll wish you would have taken these nineteen years.*"

"*You're out of your mind. Nineteen years is life to me dude,*" I replied.

"*Well, what do you want me to do, Mr. Smith?*" my public defender asked me.

"*I'm not taking no nineteen years,*" I told him.

"*Okay then we'll get a continuance and set a date for trial,*" he said.

When I left the court house that day, my heart was hardened. My whole being again was numb. I didn't want to be bothered with anyone. I felt my blood pressure getting high and I was lightheaded. I asked to have my blood pressure checked. I was taking medication already to keep my blood pressure down and I didn't want to pass out. I just wanted to have my pressure checked.

The officers paid me no attention as I yelled from my cell to be seen. When it was time to get my medication, I requested again to have my pressure checked. The medical technician told me to step away from the window and that he wasn't going to check me.

"*Why not?*" I feel sick man. I need you to check my blood pressure," I said rather loudly, only because I was hyperventilating. Three guards ran towards where I was at, and when they got to me, they were yelling and hitting me at the same time.

"*Get against the wall*" they yelled. Before turning around to do so, I tried to explain to them that I just needed my blood pressure checked. Without saying a word in response to my appeal they began to push me, knocking me down and then they began kicking me, hitting me, punching me and spraying me with mace. I was swollen up bad, but my blood pressure was what was scaring the hell out of me. It was 187/ 136. For that reason only, I was kept in the medical area for several hours and given medication to bring my pressure down. When it was okay for me to be transported back to my unit, I was taken to maximum security. I was locked up with the worst of the worse. Housed in a single man cell and every time I was taken somewhere, I was handcuffed and chained at the ankles.

I didn't do anything to deserve that. I had only asked to be seen by a medical professional to have my blood pressure checked. In a cell by myself, no longer having to be surrounded by people, I had my much-needed solitude. When I was placed in that cell and the guards left, I turned around and almost fell to my knees. There, drawn on the wall, was a life-sized figure of Jesus Christ carrying a cross. Whoever drew the image of Jesus on the wall was a true artist. The artist made Jesus look real, standing right in front of me. The cell was like a box, a little longer than my body, I'm 5'11", so the cell was maybe 6 x 9. There was only enough room for the toilet and the bed. So I couldn't turn anywhere in there without looking at the image of Jesus on the wall.

The artwork was very graphic, detailing Jesus' pain with the crown of thorns meshed into his head. After being in the cell forty-five minutes, a guard came to the cell to bring me the few personal items left in the other housing unit they had taken from me. Those items consisted of letters and my Bible; the only book I had. As I sat on the bunk, I opened my Bible and then remembered the piece of paper given to me by the man in the bull pin earlier that day; it was still in my pocket. I took it out and turned to the scripture he wrote on the paper.

Jeremiah 29:11-15: *"For I know the plans I have for you," declares the LORD, "plans to prosper you and not to harm you, plans to give you hope and a future. 12 Then you will call on me and come and pray to me, and I will listen to you. 13 You will seek me and find me when you seek me with all your heart. 14 I will be found by you," declares the LORD, "and will bring you back from captivity. I will gather you from all the nations and places where I have banished you, declares the LORD, "and will bring you back to the place from which I carried you into exile."*

As I sat in the cell after reading that scripture, I felt there was a reason I taken to that cell. I began to feel the burden of loneliness and depression lifted off me. I interpreted the scripture as saying to me that GOD led me

Demetrius Smith Sr.

there. From there I would pray to him with all my heart, and I would be heard and it was there I found him. I fell down on my knees as Jesus stood above me carrying the cross, and I prayed.

The days and weeks turned into months. Daily I began to write scriptures on the wall inside of the cross. Praying had become routine as well as me writing my life story. Daily I would write on paper I would borrow or write on the back of other papers. No longer was I worrying about my situation; I had found my peace in this little cell. I was all alone, but I felt I was in the presence of comfort and love. I had the joy of the Lord on me. Jesus and I talked one on one every day. I read my Bible through and through, being led to the scriptures. I continued to write the scriptures on the wall, and those written scriptures taught me how to talk to GOD. I would let him lead me to scriptures by closing and opening the Bible again. A new scripture would be a response or answer to my prayer. There was no doubt about it; I had truly learned how to communicate with a higher power.

Every time it was time for me to go to court, I took my Bible, my sword. As I sat in the bull pins, I would read and quote scriptures. I began to believe that I could ask for what I wanted and GOD would give it to me. When I went to court on September of 2006, my attorney, Ms. Warren, said, *"Mr. Smith, you need to make a decision. Because if you go to trial, you're going to die in prison,"* she said.

I looked at her with joy and said, *"I have made a decision Ms. Warren, you're fired. My family will get me an attorney. I don't know what it is you get out of sending a person to prison for years, but I know GOD doesn't like ugly. I only stole something and haven't been to prison or in trouble for over nineteen years. If nineteen years is the best you can do for me, then you do not have my best interest at heart. I can do bad by myself."* I told her.

She was speechless. I was shocked at myself for speaking so bold and clear to her.

"If that's what you want to do Mr. Smith, I'll tell the judge you're going to retain private counsel," she said. Then she stood up, looked at me with compassion and admiration and told me, *"Good luck to you, Mr. Smith. I hope you come out well in this."*

That day I was given another continuance. I called Ana when I got back to the jail and had her call my sister Ce-Ce for me. Ce-Ce knew I was locked up, and she also knew when I got in trouble I carried my own weight. Ana got Ce-Ce on the line. *"Hey Ce-Ce."* It felt good calling her name, knowing she was there. *"Boy I been waiting for you to call me. What the hell took you so long?"* There was happiness in her voice to hear from me; which gave me joy. She was her high-spirited self and not short with her words at all. I told her what I had been going through, and when I told her of the nineteen years and the life sentence threats, she went there for me. *"No the hell they won't give you no fucking nineteen years, bitch-ass jail system. You ain't did nothing but stole something. Imma get somebody down there to talk to you. Ana?"* she called. I let them talk over the phone and get acquainted. Ana knew what I needed. She had suggested I call Ce-Ce months ago.

When I went to court, representation was there for me. Ce-Ce was sitting in the court room too, waving and smiling. She had come through for me. She was truly a sight for sore eyes. After the attorney she hired reviewed my case, he negotiated a deal for me to serve five years and four months. It was a long way from nineteen years. My mind was relieved from the thought of nineteen years in prison, but to me five years was a long time away from my children and from the support of Ana. I knew I was going to miss her too.

I took the sixty-four-month deal the lawyer got for me. I saw my former public defender, Ms. Warner as I was leaving from the courtroom. I told her about the deal I took and she told me she was happy for me. After that careless comment she didn't mean, I decided to let her know exactly how I felt. I told her she was wrong to represent people the way she did. I told her if I had not been able to afford private counsel, I would have ended up serving the rest of my life in jail with her representation. I also told her she was evil to have no concern for a man's life and that people like her were the real criminals because they were selling people short, locking them up and giving them long sentences that did not fit the crime. I knew the state gets paid to lock us up and you got to have some money to stay out of jail.

"Well good luck Mr. Smith," the evil woman said walking away. It was two weeks later when I was transferred from LA County Jail to Solano State Prison. After being confined twenty-three hours a day, reading the Bible in solitude, I felt free and at peace. One would think I would have lost my mind, but I was filled with the joy of the Lord. On the way to prison my thoughts were of me becoming a servant of the Lord. Everything else for me had always failed me.

I knew I still had a lot of time remaining on my sentence. But as I had told the Lord, I would be ready to go when he felt I was ready. I didn't want to let him down, and I didn't want to ever lose or turn away from this feeling of joy I had. Not again, not ever again. I didn't know what to expect

Demetrius Smith Sr.

at the next place I was being taken to, but I did know I wanted to continue studying my Bible. I arrived at Solano State Prison and was placed on the 1 yard in building 2. It was a psycho building for people with disabilities and mental problems. I was placed on alert as being a nut case for going off in the county jail. And to be honest, I had lost my mind. The old me was dying, and I was okay with that.

What I wasn't okay with was the fact that I was placed in the cell with a guy that had life for beating his women and attempting to bury her alive. He actually turned out to be a good cell mate, and I would consider him a friend. It was after a month of my arrival that the prison went on a lockdown. It was strange to me because the only people who were locked down were the blacks. I found that to be racist. If one black got into any kind of confrontation with another race, all the blacks had to suffer for the incident. Slavery existed behind the walls of the California prison system. I had never experienced anything like it before in my life.

Because I was black, I was placed in a gang in which we were called "the Blacks." I found it insulting and humiliating to have to be subjected to being locked up in a cell for nine straight months for doing no wrong, just simply because I was black. In Illinois, we would have torn the prison down. You cannot imagine the injustice that goes on behind the walls in the California prisons. That's a whole other story. But trust me, the men and women were treated and housed as if they were cattle.

During the nine months I stayed locked down, my new friend filled me in on the way things were run at the prison. When we were allowed to come off the lockdown, I kept to myself. I tried playing cards, dominoes, and all kinds of games, but they were a waste of time. I was not even allowed to go to church while I was locked down but I still had the desire to seek that enriched feeling of joy that had overtaken me in the county jail. I didn't want to lose this feeling. I felt it was the reason I had to live. I felt whole and alive, and I didn't need anything.

I was happy reading and learning how to have a relationship with God. I knew inside myself that if I didn't continue seeking the Lord, I didn't have a reason to live anymore. I felt I didn't have any other purpose to live for unless I was dancing like David, for the joy of the Lord. The way the word unfolded to me when I was facing nineteen years and ended up getting five just by asking. John 14:14 says, *"If you ask anything in My name I will do it."* I was convinced by being shown that his Word was real and had true power. I knew if I didn't keep this joy, I had no purpose in life.

To just go to church and be able to sing again was something I was looking forward to doing. This richness I was feeling was not of worldly shallow things, but from OUR FATHER, as an irreplaceable fulfillment. I wanted my children to get to know me as a saved man. After a year on the 2 yard, I was transferred to the 4 yard because my points had been reduced and my security level went down. I was allowed to be housed in a dormitory unit. There I met a writer named John Jevial Smothers. Everybody in Solano knows him as Malachi. I mentioned to Malachi that I started writing while I was locked down in the county jail. Being locked down in a cell twenty-three hours a day, all I could do was release my thoughts on paper. Malachi became interested in my story and gave me direction on how to formulate a book. He encouraged me to continue writing down my thoughts and my past experiences. I started writing on a daily basis and at the end of the day I'd converse with Malachi while he began to edit my work.

The more I worked with him, the more I wrote, and the more I began to feel a testimony unfold. Malachi became busy with the prison obligations he had helping other inmates. He had a dedication to be a blessing to the brothers in the prison, so he taught classes and he was a speaker when groups were held to prevent gang violence. Because he was so busy, he told me I didn't need him. He felt I was on the right path. With the knowledge he had in writing, he helped guide me, but the more I wrote, the more I knew what I was doing. I was really into writing and I found it to be very therapeutic. I was reliving moments I missed and at times I found myself crying. I was feeling the pain from times in my past as if they were yesterday. Do I have regrets? Yes, I do! I regret I didn't let go of everything to raise my children because I felt they have suffered the most out of it all. As I lay here in this cell thinking of what I'm going to do when I get out of here, I'm scared.

I'm not the same person going out as I was coming in. I don't have the same mind to be self-destructive. I've learned to think as well as react with a more rational mind. As I look back on those days, I forgive myself for the bad decisions I made. I know I had a guardian angel looking over me, and even as I lay here today, I feel covered. All of my children have since grown up and gone their own ways without me. Demetrius Smith Jr. (Meechie) resides in Georgia with his mother and his toddler son, my grandson, Demetrius Ja'Mare Smith. Ashley Tierra has her daughter, my granddaughter Lauren; the twins Deontae and DeAndre both are in college in Milwaukee, Wisconsin, living with my sister Linda.

It would be a beautiful thing to go back out into the world and make a difference for the betterment of the lives of my children and the lives of the new people that will come into my life. I'm walking out of here for some reason and I am going to stay on the course of righteousness. I should have been dead a long time ago. You're right mama; apparently there is something He has for me to do. I pray I'm ready now. I have nothing but time it seems. As one of my friends, Vincent Parie, told me, *"You have fallen many times and from many places, but your life continues to prevail because you have not fallen from God's grace!" Thank you Lord!*

CHAPTER 30

Under The Influence

SO MANY YEARS have passed since I've talked with Robert Kelly, Derrel, and even Barry. After a long struggle, I was able to let go of that life, the era I stored in my memory under "R&B" (Robert and Barry). I was so infatuated with that lifestyle, the things it provided, the journeys it offered and the people it placed me with. I lost my way. I am clean and sober without regret in my history. I have made a lot of bad decisions, but I survived to tell my story. I followed the wrong people, places, and things and lost my life, my children and my integrity.

I was the man behind the man, which meant nothing to the world, but "everybody's fall guy." I was so busy making sure that everybody's life around me ran smoothly that I forgot to take care of my own. I didn't provide what my family needed most, which was for me to be the head of the family and to be there. It was my duty to love and provide for my family through the body of Christ; it was me that continuously invited the devil into our dwelling.

Most of all, I never invited God in with my heart. I meant well and my intentions were always for the good, but I always allowed the devil to occupy even the smallest space in my mind. He was always in my company, and it was not until now that I realize that He is someone who has been by my side for the past fifty-four years without me being aware of it. He accompanied and protected me through out my life. THE MAN BEHIND THE MAN is the guardian angel God assigned to watch over and protect me. That angel is real in my life.

I remember once I attempted to rob a guy at a used car lot with a fake pistol. When I pulled the pistol out and began to raise it on him, the guy was faster than me. He pulled a pistol on me and pulled the trigger. *Click, click* was what I heard, and I was standing still, stunned at the thought that I was dead, but I wasn't. The man stood shocked as well that his gun didn't fire. I turned and ran. Thinking of that moment, now I know I had to have had somebody looking over me throughout my life. Jeremiah 1:5 says, *"Before I formed you in the womb I knew you, And before you were born I consecrated you; I have appointed you a prophet to the nations."* God, you are amazing.

Thank you, God, for keeping me! Thank you God, for loving me enough to assign your archangel Uriel to me! *"For the Lord knows the way of the righteous, But the way of the wicked will perish"* (Psalms 1:6). I know it is only by your grace and mercy I live. I will trust in you! It is March 20, 2010—I am to be released in three days. It's been four years, and now I'm going back out into the world, and it feels like it was only yesterday. Except now I'm older. I won't have a car or money and I'm going back to the same cold world. Life is a bitch, and this I cosign. I have nothing but the clothes and shoes that I had before I was locked up. My intentions are not to have a pity party. I don't celebrate failure in any way. This is my release, my closure to the old life as I saw it. At this moment, I am letting it all go. I feel as if a burden has been lifted from my soul. And this time, when I start over, it will be my first chance at making a good life for myself and my family. My God is a jealous God, I am blessed. I feel like I have lived nine lives, like a lucky cat. But I have proven to be far from fortunate, so I know for sure I am blessed and highly favored, and this will be the beginning of the rest of my life.

My hope is in Jesus. Philippians 3:14 says, *"I press toward the goal for the prize of the upward call of God in Christ Jesus. I can do all things through Christ who strengthens me."*

This is my prayer:

Here me Lord! In Micah 7:19, it is said, *"You will have compassion on us, and will subdue our iniquities. You will cast all our sins into the depths of the sea."* Cleanse me of my sins, Father God, my sins of yesterday, today, and tomorrow. Strengthen me through my sin. Jeremiah 10:23-24 says, *"Oh Lord, I know the way of man is not in himself. It is not in man to direct his own steps. Oh Lord, correct me, but not with your anger, least you bring me to nothing."* As I walk out this gate, let you're anointing be upon me, and let me be in your favor. I ask You to guide my steps. *"Turn me back to you, oh Lord, and I will be restored; renew my days of old"* (Lamentations 5:21). I am a wondering spirit without you, lost. Lord, you know me better than I know myself. You are the creator of all things; and by your will they exist and were created. Blessings and honor and glory and power be to Him who sits on the throne and to the Lamb forever and ever. I know that nothing is too big for you Father God, so help me Lord! I confess to you I am a sinner. But my heart wants to do right. 1John 1:9 says, *"If we confess our sins you will be faithful and just to forgive us and cleanse us from all unrighteousness."* Jeremiah 17:14 says, *"Heal me, O Lord, and I shall be healed; save me, and I shall be saved, for You are my praise."* Thank you Father God, for the covering you placed over my life to make it out of this place. Thank you for Jesus Christ, your precious Lamb. Thank you for my family and for keeping them safe. Thank you for the people who are reading this. May they feel your presence and come to know Jesus. Oh Lord, I have learned that fear causes one to let go of the truth and the promise you have for us, so I will not fear what lies ahead for me. Chronicles 20:15 says, *"Do not be afraid or dismayed because of the great multitude, for the battle is not yours, but God's."* I give it all too you Lord, in Jesus name, Amen!

FINALE

"THOUGH IT IS hard to see how the next chapters of my life will turn out, I will rest assured knowing You, Lord God, are a God of happy endings—and new beginnings."

Exodus 34:9: *"If now I have found grace in your sight, O Lord, let My Lord, I pray, go among us, even though we are a stiff-necked people; and pardon our iniquity and our sin, and take us as your own inheritance."* Cause us to know the way in which we should walk, for we lift up our Soul to You. In Jesus Name, Amen!

The Beginning!

Last night I had a dream. I dreamed I was walking along the beach with the Lord. Across the sky flashed scenes from my life. For each scene, I noticed two sets of footprints in the sand: one belonged to me, the other to the Lord.

After the last scene of my life flashed before me, I looked back at the footprints in the sand. I noticed that at many times along the path of my life, especially at the very lowest and saddest times, there was only one set of footprints.

This really troubled me, so I asked the Lord about it. "Lord, you said once I decided to follow you, You'd walk with me all the way. But I noticed that during the saddest and most troublesome times of my life, there was only one set of footprints. I don't understand why, when I needed You the most, You would leave me."

The Lord replied, "My son, my precious child, I love you and I would never leave you. During your times of suffering, when you could see only one set of footprints, it was then that I carried you."

Mary Stevenson (Zangare).

Demetrius Smith Sr.

"Everyone has a story to tell and everyone's life has value. Our purpose, I believe, is for us all to be a blessing to one another's life. What you do today in your life affects the life of someone else. Your life, it's not all about you!"

Demetrius Smith, Author
The Man Behind The Man/
Looking From The Inside Out
October 2011

CPSIA information can be obtained
at www.ICGtesting.com
Printed in the USA
LVHW090207210120
644254LV00001B/3